A Jurisprudence of Movement

Law moves, whether we notice or not. Set amongst a spatial turn in the humanities, and jurisprudence more specifically, this book calls for a greater attention to legal movement, in both its technical and material forms. Despite various ways the spatial turn has been taken up in legal thought, questions of law, movement and its materialities are too often overlooked. This book addresses this oversight, and it does so through an attention to the materialities of legal movement. Paying attention to how law moves across different colonial and contemporary spaces, this book reveals there is a problem with common law's place.

Primarily set in the postcolonial context of Australia – although ranging beyond this nationalised topography, both spatially and temporally – this book argues movement is fundamental to the very terms of common law's existence. How, then, might we move well? Explored through examples of walking and burial, this book responds to the challenge of how to live with a contemporary form of colonial legal inheritance by arguing we must take seriously the challenge of living with law, and think more carefully about its spatial productions, and place-making activities. Unsettling place, this book returns the question of movement to jurisprudence.

Olivia Barr is based at the University of Technology, Sydney.

Space, Materiality and the Normative
Series Editors: Andreas Philippopoulos-Mihalopoulos and Christian Borch

Space, Materiality and the Normative presents new ways of thinking about the connections between space and materiality from a normative perspective. At the interface of law, social theory, politics, architecture, geography and urban studies, the series is concerned with addressing the use, regulation and experience of space and materiality, broadly understood, and in particular with exploring their links and the challenges they raise for law, politics and normativity.

Books in this series:

Spatial Justice: Body, Lawscape, Atmosphere
Andreas Philippopoulos-Mihalopoulos

Urban Commons: Rethinking the City
Christian Borch and Martin Kornberger

Animals, Biopolitics, Law: Lively Legalities
Irus Braverman

Forthcoming:

Placing International Law: Authority, Jurisdiction, Technique
Fleur Johns, Shaun McVeigh, Sundhya Pahuja, Thomas Skouteris and Robert Wai

Spacing Law and Politics: The Constitution and Representation of the Juridical
Leif Dahlberg

A Jurisprudence of Movement

Common Law, Walking, Unsettling Place

Olivia Barr

a GlassHouse Book

First published 2016
by Routledge
2 Park Square, Milton Park, Abingdon, Oxon OX14 4RN

and by Routledge
711 Third Avenue, New York, NY 10017

a GlassHouse book
Routledge is an imprint of the Taylor & Francis Group, an informa business

© 2016 Olivia Barr

The right of Olivia Barr to be identified as author of this work has been asserted by her in accordance with sections 77 and 78 of the Copyright, Designs and Patents Act 1988.

All rights reserved. No part of this book may be reprinted or reproduced or utilised in any form or by any electronic, mechanical, or other means, now known or hereafter invented, including photocopying and recording, or in any information storage or retrieval system, without permission in writing from the publishers.

Trademark notice: Product or corporate names may be trademarks or registered trademarks, and are used only for identification and explanation without intent to infringe.

British Library Cataloguing in Publication Data
A catalogue record for this book is available from the British Library

Library of Congress Cataloging-in-Publication Data
Barr, Olivia, author.
A jurisprudence of movement / Olivia Barr.
pages cm. -- (Space, materiality and the normative)
Includes bibliographical references and index.
ISBN 978-1-138-85039-2 (hbk) -- ISBN 978-1-315-72473-7 (ebk) 1. Jurisprudence--Philosophy. 2. Justice, Administration of--Philosophy. 3. Geographic perspectives. I. Title.
K235.B379 2016
340'.1--dc23
2015013568

ISBN: 978-1-138-85039-2 (hbk)
ISBN: 978-1-315-72473-7 (ebk)

Typeset in Baskerville by
Servis Filmsetting Ltd, Stockport, Cheshire

For Estrella, who shared her friendship with such generosity and care, and taught me how to camp at home.

Contents

Acknowledgements	viii
List of figures	xi
To the reader	xii
Introduction: walking with empire	1
Part I Moving jurisprudence	**31**
1 The responsible jurist	33
1.1 Lawful relations	37
1.2 Recollecting the office of jurist	48
1.3 A method of slowness	57
2 The importance of movement	65
2.1 Shaping movement	66
2.2 Jurisdictional movements	79
2.3 Placing burial	95
Part II Performing jurisprudence	**105**
3 A burial party walks	108
3.1 Movements into, movements within	110
3.2 Death in the woods beyond	116
3.3 Juridical walking	133
3.4 Camping with the dead	149
4 Jurisdiction of the dead	162
4.1 Movements in the polar South	165
4.2 A death at the south pole	187
4.3 Struggling to move	196
4.4 Instituting lawful relations	206
Part III Returning jurisprudence	**221**
5 Return	224
Index	237

Acknowledgements

I have lived with this book for a long time, often with a dose of exhilarated doubt dashed with the rhythmic joy of writing, before finally, slowly, trusting, while never quite knowing what lies around the corner. From Berlin to Bondi, Bremer Bay to Brunswick, this book carries the gloss of the swings and roundabouts not only of my life, but also the lives of many others. For this, I am overwhelmingly grateful to the many friends, family and colleagues who have shared this adventure and, while I do not name you all, trust me, you are with this book.

Long before I knew this was a book, others did. Shaun McVeigh, who is the one I can never truly thank, shared with me the gifts of generous conversation and the pleasure of thinking with another. He also started this. Some years ago, during one of many conversations with ideas overflowing well beyond the constraints of a PhD thesis, I distinctly remember Shaun telling me, somewhat wryly but with such calm certainty: 'That is for the book', a book I did not yet know I was writing. Later, the book I did not yet trust materialised in the joyful company of Andreas Philippopoulous-Mihalopoulos, when, mid-conversation, ideas snapped into place and, for this, I thank Andreas and Christian Borch, as well as Colin Perrin, Laura Muir and the editorial team at Routledge for welcoming me into their exuberant 'Space, Materiality and the Normative' series.

In writing this book, my thinking has been assisted and shaped through many encounters. For the relentless willingness to bounce ideas, and for continuing to offer such a creative and theoretically supportive home despite our current geographical choices, I especially thank Laura Griffin, Rebecca Goodbourn, James Parker, Luis Eslava, Nicholas Croggon and Angus Frith who kindly read and reread various chapters, as well as Edward Mussawir, Connal Parsley, Yoriko Otomo, Karen Crawley, Lia Kent, Rose Parfitt, Cait Storr, Tom Andrews, Eve Lester, Sara Dehm, Mark McMillan, Kirsty Gover, Darren Parker, Kevin Heller, Marc Trabsky, Maria Elander and Peter Chambers. Without the cross-hatching of our worlds, these words would not be. I am also grateful to those who have shared conversations that have resonated long after, especially Mick Dodson, Christine Black, Ross Gibson, Stephen Muecke, Chris Tomlins, Peter Goodrich, Margaret Davies, Oren Ben-Dor, Bianca Hester, Ian Duncanson, Rachel Hughes, Fleur Johns, Michael Jackson, Jim Aldridge, Peter Fitzpatrick, Jason Beckett, Alison

Young, Illan Wall, Anne Bottomley, William MacNeil, Marett Leiboff, Wendy Larcombe and Wesley Pue.

This book would not have been written without institutional support, and for this I am grateful to the Faculty of Law at the University of Technology, Sydney, for making this possible. I am especially indebted to Shaunnagh Dorsett and Charlotte Peevers for their unrelenting support, both of whom lived alongside the various shades of this book. This book began as a PhD thesis at Melbourne Law School, where it was generously funded by the University of Melbourne, and I would like to thank my PhD examiners, Karin van Marle and Desmond Manderson, for their encouragement. Melbourne Law School generally, and the Institute for International Law and the Humanities specifically, have long offered a scholarly community rich with ideas, provocations, lively conversations and shared friendships and for this I especially thank Anne Orford and Dianne Otto for their leadership, and for continuing to welcome me. I would also like to thank Ann Genovese, Lee Godden, Gerry Simpson and Sundhya Pahuja, who, in different times and ways, offered advice that made an indelible imprint on this book. Mostly, I thank my PhD supervisors, Shaun McVeigh, Maureen Tehan, Peter Rush and Jenny Beard for their lucidity, patience, enthusiasm and care, as well as their ongoing advice long beyond the PhD, all of which continues to craft my thinking.

This book relies heavily on a number of artworks, photographs and other images, as well as archival and restricted documents and, to this end, I am grateful to all who have assisted in allowing me access to these works. In particular, I wish to thank the Coronial Services of New Zealand for granting me access to their coronial files, and to the staff at the Archives Collection of New South Wales in Western Sydney, and the National Archives in Kew for their guidance. Thank you also to Richard Long, Francis Alÿs, Shaun Gladwell, Connie Samaras and Jenny Barr for granting permission to reproduce their artwork, as well as Viscopy in Australia and its British cousin, Design and Artists Copyright Society, David Zwirner, the Museum of Contemporary Art Australia and the Anna Schwartz Gallery for their generous assistance in navigating copyright permissions. Likewise, I also wish to thank Thomas A. Clark for his generous permission to reprint his poetry, as well as Alec Finlay, Laurie Clark, Cairn Gallery, Polygon and Birlin Books Ltd, whose assistance was immeasurable. For allowing me to reproduce their photography, I owe a sincere thanks to Pierre R. Schwob, as well as to Rachel Shephard and David Rootes of Antarctic Logistics & Expeditions (www.adventure-network.com) for providing photographs I could not otherwise obtain and, in this regard, a special thanks to Tamsyn Stephenson and Tom Hart for making these liquid introductions.

For invaluable editorial efforts, thanks also to Flordeliz Bonifacio and Mary Quinn as well as Mike Leach for compiling the index. Portions of this book are based on pieces originally published elsewhere. Parts of Chapter 3 were originally published as 'Walking with Empire' (2013) 38 *Australian Feminist Law Journal* 59. Sections of Chapters 1 and 2 originally appear as 'A Moving Theory: Remembering the Office of Scholar' (2010) 14(1) *Law Text Culture* 40.

To end, I thank my family and friends who have listened so patiently and always offered endless and unquestioning support for this project they have so generously walked alongside. Writing about movement, and increasingly sensitive to place, thank you to those who opened their homes to me and my wandering book, especially Benedict Anderson, James Parker, Alex Howard, Kate Francis, Rod Phillips, Jenny Zahara, Shaun McVeigh, Claire Sweeney, Tamsyn Stephenson, Penny Conor, Armanda Scorrano, Natalia, Alba and Luca D'Onofrio as well as Tancred D'Onofrio, Morna Sung, Meralyn and Des Pearce, and Tim and Agnes Sharp. For stepping inside the eye of a dragon, and sharing with me such joyful gentleness, I am grateful to Sid Sidlow for showing me the way home. To my family, Emma, Asha, Ruby, Stuart, Jenny, Maybelle, Jeremiah and Cassidy, and Robert: I thank you all and especially my parents Allison and Geoff, who shared this adventure, and let me come home to finish. My final and deepest thanks go to those who left before I could tell them I had finished. For sitting with me on the steps and helping me trust that I could write, I thank K-with-an-arl. For always letting me jump over the fence and believe anything was possible, I thank Harmsie. For sharing her life with such grace, I thank my lovely friend Joanna Braithwaite. For long conversations full of gentle understanding, I thank Tanya D'Onofrio. Finally, for showing me how to live with fragile boldness, I thank my grandmother, Betty May McLeod. Without all of you, I would not be here.

List of figures

Figure I.1	Richard Long, *A Line Made By Walking* (1967)	9
Figure I.2	Richard Long, *Dusty Boots Line, The Sahara* (1988)	11
Figure I.3	Richard Long, *Walking a Line in Peru* (1972)	11
Figure I.4	Richard Long, *Sea Level Waterline, Death Valley California* (1982)	12
Figure I.5	Francis Alÿs, *The Green Line* (walking past guard) (2004)	14
Figure I.6	Francis Alÿs, *The Green Line* (overlooking) (2004)	16
Figure PII.1	Shaun Gladwell, *Apologies 1–6* (2007–2009)	107
Figure 4.1	Connie Samaras, *Dome and Tunnels, V.A.L.I.S.* (2005–2007)	160
Figure 4.2	Connie Samaras, *Buried Fifties Station, V.A.L.I.S.* (2005–2007)	161
Figure 4.3	Pierre R. Schwob, 'Sign at the (Ever Moving) South Pole' (2006)	169
Figure 4.4	CIA, 'Map of the Political Antarctic Region' (2013–2014)	173
Figure 4.5	B&C Alexander, 'The Main Entrance to the Geodesic Dome' (2006)	181
Figure 4.6	'Aerial View of the Station' (1983)	182
Figure 4.7	Ben Cooper, 'The Ceremonial South Pole' (2007)	183
Figure 4.8	'Amundsen-Scott South Pole Station' (2007)	184
Figure 4.9	Devon McDiarmid, 'South Pole ceremony' (1 January 2015)	185
Figure PIII.1	Jenny Barr, *Untitled Ceremony* (2015)	223

To the reader

Reader, writing this book was my way of trying to think more carefully about how to live with a colonial form of law. Inheriting from the coloniser, genealogically and as a matter of legal training, I have dedicated my attention to thinking with the common law tradition as a way of taking responsibility for its material practices. With the political settlement of Australia as it is, the political question is the obvious one and so, for the jurist, it seems to me worthwhile taking a step back and looking at how Anglo-Australian common law comes into its relations, and how it comes to be in place. My motivation for writing in such a manner has been to try to find a way of taking responsibility for common law, even though this act of honouring law necessarily demands I confront my role as jurist in the continuing everyday practices of empire. An uncomfortable task, certainly. However, this is what I have done or at least what I have tried to do. Working with the resources of the office of jurist, in the writing of this book I have created a minor jurisprudence that seeks neither truth nor definitive answers but rather draws out certain strands of common law practice. Taking a step back from the political question, my choice of address for this minor jurisprudence has been an examination of how to take responsibility for the care of the dead. For a jurist such as me, living on Wurundjeri, Noongar and, most recently, Gadigal land, and living with a colonial form of law – sometimes in and sometimes out of place – thinking more carefully about how we might live this life well seems worthy of attention. Of course, Reader, this minor jurisprudence is not everything, but it is not nothing.

Introduction
Walking with empire

> Always, everywhere, people have walked,
> veining the earth with paths visible and invisible,
> symmetrical or meandering
>
> (Thomas A. Clark, 1988)[1]

> For as the law is the birthright of every subject,
> so wherever they go they carry their laws with them
>
> (William Blackstone, 1765)[2]

While the world hosts a variety of laws, one of the major types or forms of law that continues to dominate the practice of everyday life in many a locale is common law. Forged via the British Empire, sent and spread throughout the British colonies, English common law drifted into previously unknown places, including the colonies that translated into Australia. In Australia, today, common law continues in its cross-inheritance as Anglo-Australian common law, still bearing the markers of England, but also the abrasions of inhabiting a different land; a different ground.

Primarily set in Australia, although ranging beyond this nationalised topography both spatially and temporally, this book focuses on Anglo-Australian common law, and how to live with this law, as one way of addressing a contemporary form of colonial legal inheritance. However, as in other parts of the postcolonial world, in Australia, the challenge of how to live with a colonial form of law continues to be especially stark. That Empire continues today through the ongoing practice of colonial forms of law and that these practices continue to occur on unceded Aboriginal land is obvious. So too is the political question of sovereignty, statehood and Aboriginal dispossession also the obvious one, with the political settlement of

---

1 Thomas Clark, 'In Praise of Walking', in Thomas A. Clark and Olwen Shone (eds.), *Distance and Proximity* (Edinburgh Pocketbooks, 2000) 21.
2 William Blackstone, 'Of the Countries Subject to the Laws of England', in William Blackstone, *Commentaries on the Laws of England* (Clarendon Press, first published 1765) Book 1, Chapter 4, 106.

Australia as it is. Despite the false promise of reconciliation, it is the tenacious intensity of an unresolved colonial inheritance that continues to structure the everyday lived experience of the legal subject, both coloniser and colonised. While details may differ, in Australia at least, the problem is, quite simply, that laws do not meet well. Placing the blame squarely with Anglo-Australian common law, as I do, in this book the landscape shifts and we are reminded that those who represent common law in matters of reconciliation must take responsibility for the basic forms of law through which they conduct their lawful lives.

The challenge posed, then, is to rethink the meeting of laws, and hence, questions of sovereignty and territory, in a colonial context. To do so, we need to break out of current habits, and look at the issue differently. For instance, does the way common law work and its ways of doing things, including how it relates with not only other laws, but also other bodies and lands have anything to do with the static power imbalances that continue to be lived in setter colonial societies? If so, what is the role of common law in the continued maintenance of modern understandings of the interlacing concepts of sovereignty, territory and the state – such dominating legal stories – that overwhelm other forms of law? When it comes to the problem of laws not meeting well, we need to approach the issue again, and notice how, from where, and with what it is that we approach. For we do not all approach in the same manner or carry the same laws; and the common law approach is quite particular. As a way of thinking more carefully about how and why legal relations so often fail to be conducted well, especially in a colonial context, this book wagers it is worthwhile taking a step back from the political question to look at questions of how common law actually works.

The objective of this book, therefore, is to take seriously the challenge of living with law, and to think more carefully about ways of living with a colonial form of law, and living that life well. To do so requires deepening an account of how common law actually works, and attending to ways in which these workings or mechanics relate to the conduct of lives lived with common law. As the discipline responsible for the *prudentia* of law (i.e. its practical wisdom or good conduct), this is a task that falls within the realm of jurisprudence. Directed especially, albeit not exclusively, towards the jurist, as one of the primary offices responsible for jurisprudence and the continued practice and ongoing workings of common law, a jurisprudential attention to what might be considered common law's 'mechanics' or 'internal workings', which focuses in particular on the material and technical practices of common law, offers one way this might be done. By stepping back from the seemingly irresolvable and constantly looping stories of sovereignty, territory and the concomitant unimpeachable supremacy of the state as the major tales of how laws meet (or why these legal meetings are so well hidden) and paying attention to how common law works in practice, what is noticed is rather surprising. To begin, common law is a rather low-level technology that repeats its patterns, again and again. Relatedly, the continued performance of colonial power in the conduct of lawful relations, coupled with the repetition of a static external life of sovereign power plays are both dependent on these repeated common law practices. Unexpectedly, and more significantly, supporting these conceits are the habitual ways in which relatively mundane material practices of common law, such as walking, contribute to the constitution of common law's relations, as well as locating its place.

It is therefore impossible to understand the nature of common law's relations, and why laws often do not meet well, without understanding the inextricable nature of common law's place. If we hope to contribute to, participate in or simply live a postcolonial life, it becomes necessary to better understand the workings and placement of common law in its local context. To do so requires attending to how common law comes into its relations with various bodies, lands and laws and think more carefully about where these relations occur. This is the task taken up in this book, that is, to think more carefully about the place of common law and where common law actually is. This requires, strange as it may initially seem, an attention to movement.

Why movement? Because, to put it bluntly, there is no law without movement. Without movement, common law simply would not be. The central argument of the book, therefore, is that *common law moves* and that it moves in very particular ways through patterns of technical and material practice. The technical is neither sovereignty nor territory, but rather, the technical is jurisdiction, that is, technologies of jurisdiction.[3] The material are many, but two significant material practices of movement foregrounded in this book are the juridical practices of walking and burial. Equally important, although each example carries distinct jurisprudential aspects, I argue that both burial practices and walking practices are significant material movements that carry legal meaning. This is in the sense that walking and burial are not only spatial productions, but also place-making activities of common law.[4] The book concludes that it is through material practices of movement, such as walking and burial, that common law not only comes into its relations, but also comes to be in place, which is a place that is more temporary, and not as everywhere, as it might sometimes seem. Unsettling place, this book reminds the jurist, as well as others who live with common law, that to move and to walk, for instance, is to materially practise common law and participate in the creation and conduct of lawful relations, as well as the moving maintenance of an unsettling place.

As the place of common law is unsettled by movement, so, too, are the examples used in this book. Concertinaed throughout, the material examples of walking and burial carry the conceptual burdens of space, movement and place unevenly, with walking relating more heavily to questions of space and movement, and burial more directly to questions of place and place-making. For that reason, this introduction shortly sharpens its focus to the example of walking as a way of entering

---

3 Shaunnagh Dorsett and Shaun McVeigh, *Jurisdiction* (Routledge, 2012). On technologies of jurisdiction, see, especially, Chapter 4.
4 Henri Lefebvre, *The Production of Space* (Donald Nicholson-Smith trans, Blackwell Publishing, 1991) [trans. of *La Production de L'espace* (first published 1974)].

ideas of the materiality of movement and how this materiality may link to questions of law. As the book progresses, however, and the outcome of movement, that is, the relationship between movement and place becomes more prescient, the example of burial comes to the fore, and in a counter to this introduction, features prominently in the conclusion. For now, before turning to walking, a short note on the jurisprudential practice of burial and why it is such a central feature of this book.

Although for some common law may emerge as social fact, in this book, common law is understood as a tradition.[5] In a book concerned with how to live with the traditions of common law, and, hence, matters of inheritance, it would be an unusual oversight not to address the dead. More specifically, burial is the practice that relates, most materially, to the care of the dead and, in this regard, is not an unknown jurisprudential topic.[6] Whether ceremonial burial or the covering in memory, it is through the institution of burial that we live in relation to the dead, and we inherit from the ones that came before.[7] Yet more than biological, genealogical or familial inheritance, this is the dead ordering the relation between time and space; an institutional inheritance of the ways we order and conduct our lawful lives.

Burial is also the practice that relates, most distinctly, to the place-making activities of common law. As Italian humanist philologer Giambattista Vico proposed, it is through the institution of burial that the dead humanise the earth.[8] If we accept this proposition, as this book does, the jurisprudential question raised is whether the dead not only humanise but also contribute to a juridification of the earth? While a full answer to the question of the juridical earth is beyond the scope of this book, one important strand is offered, which is that part of the answer relates to common law's ongoing movements in relation to the dead through practices of burial. For these reasons, while certainly not the only form of jurisprudential movement that could be investigated, common law's movements in relation to the dead are quite distinct, and form the focus of this book because of what they reveal about how common law moves into place or at least *seems* to move in place.

Consider another form of movement that is also a material inheritance: the example of walking. William Blackstone's well-known aphorism, quoted in the opening to this introduction, hints at one of the ways in which the jurisprudential

---

5 See, generally, Frederick Pollock and F.W. Maitland, *The History of English Law Before the Time of Edward I* (Cambridge University Press, 1905); J.G.A. Pocock, *The Ancient Constitution and the Feudal Law: A Study of English Historical Thought in the Seventeenth Century, A Reissue with Retrospect* (Cambridge University Press, 1987). See also Piyel Haldar, *Law, Orientalism and Postcolonialism: The Jurisdiction of the Lotus Eaters* (Routledge-Cavendish, 2007); Peter Goodrich, *Languages of Law: From Logics of Memory to Nomadic Masks* (Weidenfeld & Nicolson, 1990).
6 See, e.g., Desmond Manderson (ed.), *Courting Death: The Law of Mortality* (Pluto Press, 1999).
7 See, e.g., Peter Metcalfe and Richard Huntington, *Celebrations of Death: The Anthropology of Mortuary Ritual* (Cambridge University Press, 2nd edn, 1991).
8 Giambattista Vico, *The New Science of Giambattista Vico* (Thomas Goddard Bergin and Max Harold Fisch trans., Cornell University Press, 1967) [trans. of *Principi di una Scienza Nuova* (first published 1725)]. See also Robert Pogue Harrison, *The Dominion of the Dead* (University of Chicago Press, 2003).

links between common law and movement are teased out in this book. According to an ancient common law doctrine quipped so neatly by Blackstone, one of England's most established jurists, if an English subject goes wandering in a place categorised as uninhabited land, it is deemed 'they carry their laws with them', that is, English common law.[9] To state the obvious, in Australia, as elsewhere, people continue to walk. Yet, what is important is not just the banal observation that people walk, but paying attention to how we walk, and how that might relate to ongoing legal practices, and more specifically, ongoing practices of common law that are not only technical, but also material. For if we do so, if we attend to the materiality of how we walk, what we notice is that for those that are subject, when we walk, we also carry law. To walk, therefore, is *to walk with common law* and carries not only physical meaning, but also legal meaning; and the meaning it carries relates to matters of movement: common law's movements.

On a broader scale, what this means is that in *Terra Australis Incognita*, a land originally 'discovered' as the Colony of New South Wales, English subjects went wandering, 'veining the earth with paths visible and invisible' as Thomas A. Clark poetically notes in his 'In Praise of Walking', but in doing so, they veined the earth with English common law by carrying their laws as they went.[10] This practice has not yet past, but, in fact, continues with every footstep, tracing invisible veins of common law. Walking across a land only subsequently perceived and then later legally reimagined as *terra nullius*, despite its obvious inhabitation by indigenous peoples and their indigenous laws, the movement and presence of common law is the controversial legal fiction the nation-state of Australia still fumbles to explain.[11] Whether by walking or by other forms of material movement, the awkward placement of common law in a legally inhabited land continues to operate as a structuring device in the practice and conduct of legal relations between Aboriginal and non-Aboriginal people, and Aboriginal and non-Aboriginal laws. Part of the problem, it seems, is that there is little comprehension of the significant fact *that* common law moves, let alone the requisite practical and technical knowledge of *how* common law moves.

By paying attention to movement as its primary task, *A Jurisprudence of Movement: Common Law, Walking, Unsettling Place* reveals there is a problem with common law's place. Despite the conceits of sovereignty and territory suggesting otherwise, common law is not as everywhere as it seems to be. This has ramifications. With common law not everywhere, the place of common law bursts open, raising questions about the ways and wheres of common law, including how it comes into place, and in doing so, how it relates to other forms of law also inhabiting that same place. As a result, if we better understand how common law operates, it becomes possible to rethink questions of sovereignty and territory not as a static form of colonisation but as the result of ongoing movement.

---

9 Above, n 2.
10 Above, n 1 and n 2.
11 This is explained in more detail in Chapter 1.

This book, therefore, returns the question of movement to jurisprudence and it does so across three parts. The first part is conceptual and explains why the question of movement is important to jurisprudential thought, offering new ways of understanding the material forms common law has taken in Australia. The jurisprudential account of common law developed in the first part is then put into practice in the second and third parts of the book. The second part is performative and illustrates the importance of movement through a method of jurisprudential narration, description and redescription. Through a close reading of two sets of legal materials, one historic and one contemporary, two case studies are developed. The first case study is a burial party that walked in colonial New South Wales; the second is the struggle to bury the dead at the south pole in Antarctica. Each case study reveals the material dynamic of movement and its relation to the practice of the care of the dead as integral to the common law form. The short third and final part of the book is allegorical and returns the question of movement to jurisprudence through the double repatriation of the dead and a jurisprudential tradition of conduct.

Across three cumulative parts, therefore, this book develops the argument that common law moves through technologies of jurisdiction and raises the legal, ethical and political challenge of how to move well. This challenge can be seen most clearly if we consider the example of walking, and temporarily take William Blackstone's aphorism seriously, as well as quite literally, namely: 'So wherever they go they carry their laws with them'.[12] In other words, if we walk with Empire, as this introduction asks, 'veining the earth with paths visible and invisible', the challenge we are faced with is: How, then, might we walk *well*?

An invitation to walk

Walking is a basic technology of humankind.[13] As I argue in this book, which contemplates the relationship between movement, common law and its material practices, walking is also a basic technology of common law and its movements. Yet, despite its basicity and baseness, there are many ways and many modes of walking. There are also many genres of thinking about walking, and habits of associating walking: walking and thinking; walking and being; walking and political action; walking and religious transcendence; walking arts and the art of walking; as well as the relatively lesser explored relationship between walking and law. When coupled with philosophy, geography, politics, history, art, law etc., walking is surprisingly complex; somewhat bewilderingly so: 'At once bewildering mists around him close.'[14] Yet, losing one's way with walking, not

---

12 Above, n 2.
13 David Wills, *Dorsality: Thinking Back through Technology and Politics* (University of Minnesota Press, 2008).
14 William Wordsworth, *Descriptive Sketches: Taken During a Pedestrian Tour in the Italian, Grison, Swiss, and Savoyard Alps* (Joseph Johnson, St Paul's Church-Yard, 1793).

Romantically, but literally and physically, is precisely what needs to be done: to just walk.

I would like to invite you to walk.[15] Albeit an unusual invitation, this is offered as a way of introducing and bringing into relation the problematic this book inspects, that is, the question of how common law moves. As we shall see, it is surprisingly hard to *just* walk, as we strut, stroll, swagger and sway our distinctive ways in the world. It is hard to walk without purpose, intention, direction: perambulate, peregrinate, parade, promenade. To walk without a path, a road or a way: ramble, range, roam. To walk without meandering into reverie, or abandoning the materiality of walking for something other, something elsewhere: tread, tramp, trudge, traipse, traverse. Yet, to begin, the task here is just to walk. To notice the action of walking: lurching, lumbering, limping, locomotion. To notice its materiality: step, stretch, stride. To notice its techniques: balance, bipedal, base. To notice its activity: motion, movement, messy. Balancing imbalance, precise imprecision, moderating the immoderate: walking.

For these reasons, while I could quite contentedly begin this book by walking alongside the ancient Greek Peripatetics,[16] travelling with Roman scholars,[17] rambling with Jean-Jacques Rousseau,[18] taking a pedestrian tour with William Wordsworth,[19] strolling with Charles Baudelaire's and Walter Benjamin's *flâneur*,[20]

---

15 Although walking is one of the two examples addressed in this book, it is more difficult, and perhaps somewhat awkward, to invite you to bury.
16 With Aristotle and the Peripatetics, the bipedal form of physical movement is intrinsically linked with a form of thinking and a form of conduct linked to a particular office: the office of philosopher.
17 Like the Peripatetics, another officeholder who links walking and thinking is the medieval Roman scholar. In the Roman Empire, it was not only the Roman legions that walked or marched, but also the Roman scholar. See, e.g., Olivia Barr, 'A Moving Theory: Remembering the Office of Scholar' (2010) 14(1) *Law Text Culture* 40; Costas Douzinas, *Human Rights and Empire: The Political Philosophy of Cosmopolitanism* (Taylor & Francis, 2007) prologue.
18 Jean-Jacques Rousseau, *Reveries of the Solitary Walker* (Peter France trans., Penguin Books, 1979) [trans. of *Les Rêveries du Promeneur Solitaire* (first published 1782)]. Rebecca Solnit suggests walking such as Rousseau's as the beginning of a 'history of walking as a conscious cultural act rather than a means to an end', Rebecca Solnit, *Wanderlust: A History of Walking* (Verso, 2001).
19 Wordsworth, *Descriptive Sketches*, above, n 14. For the Romantics, walking was more than a form of transport but a cultural act, and the internal contemplations were individual and although not un-bound from public life, not held to office in the same manner as some of the ancient walkers. See also Johann Wolfgang von Goethe, *The Sorrows of Young Werther* (Burton Pike trans., Modern Library, 2004) [trans. of *Leiden des Jungen Werther* (first published 1774)]. See generally Robin Jarvis, *Romantic Writing and Pedestrian Travel* (Macmillan Press, 1997).
20 For Baudelaire, the 'gentleman stroller of city streets', that is the *flâneur* is both an active participant in the city but also a detached observer whereas for Benjamin, Baudelaire's *flâneur* was transformed from a more aesthetic walker into a product of modernity; Charles Baudelaire, *The Painter of Modern Life and Other Essays* (Jonathon Mayne trans., Phaidon, 1964) [trans. of *Le Peintre de la vie Moderne* (first published 1863)]; Walter Benjamin, *The Writer of Modern Life: Essays on Charles Baudelaire* (Howard Eiland trans., Belknap Press, 2006); Walter Benjamin, *The Arcades Project* (Howard Eiland and Kevin McLaughlin trans., Belknap Press, 1999) [trans. of *Passagenwerk* (written 1927–1940)].

surveilling with Michel de Certeau,²¹ navigating a sidewalk with Nicholas Blomley's pedestrian,²² falling with Brian Massumi,²³ walking and talking with Christine Black on country,²⁴ or roaming with Robert MacFarlane and his poetic literary histories,²⁵ among others, for instance, I choose not to.²⁶ Rather, it is important just to walk, and to this end, I begin this book with a series of excursive walks in rural England, Jerusalem and Berlin. For, as these walks remind us, there is a materiality to walking; there is *movement*: an action and activity, a conduct, a responsibility as well as an ethics, perhaps, to walking well. By casting attention towards the materiality of walking, a connection with law too long overlooked is also introduced, hinting at a more significant relation between law and movement developed in this book. So, as with any walk, there must be something that resembles a beginning, even though when it comes to walking, the beginning rarely is.²⁷ The beginning here is with the materiality of walking.

A line made by walking (Excursion I)

In 1967, Richard Long created the artwork, *A Line Made By Walking* (see Figure I.1).²⁸ A prominent English artist, Long is a sculptor who works with different mediums, mostly earthly products of stone, mud and wood, creating site-specific installations both inside galleries and in the landscape beyond.²⁹ Known

---

21 Michel de Certeau, *The Practice of Everyday Life* (Steven Rendall trans., University of California Press, 1994) Ch 7 [trans. of *L'invention du Quotidien, Vol I, Arts de Faire* (first published 1980)]. Contrasting the position of surveillance from the top of a skyscraper with the movements of a walker in the city, de Certeau's walker is dynamic and subversive, playing with the rules and boundaries that from above seemingly capture the walker, and moving in ways never quite captured by the vision of a unified city.
22 Nicholas Blomley, *Rights of Passage: Sidewalks and the Regulation of Public Flow* (Routledge, 2011). In a move away from de Certeau, for Blomley, 'pedestrianism' attends to the material and legal movements of the public space of the sidewalk in contrast to a 'civic humanism' interpretation of the sidewalk as a 'space of people'. This is addressed below, n 62.
23 On Brian Massumi commenting on the notion of 'walking as controlled falling', see Mary Zournazi, 'Navigating Movements: A Conversation with Brian Massumi' in *Hope: New Philosophies for Change* (Routledge, 2002) Ch 10.
24 C.F. Black, *The Land is the Source of the Law: A Dialogic Encounter with Indigenous Jurisprudence* (Routledge, 2011). Starting at her camp, in this book, Black shares her law stories, as well as those of senior lawmen, and opens with a powerful retelling of a cosmological story of dogs; 4–6.
25 Robert MacFarlane, *The Old Ways: A Journey on Foot* (Hamish Hamilton, 2012).
26 See, e.g., Joseph A. Amato, *On Foot: A History of Walking* (New York University Press, 2004); Solnit, *Wanderlust*, above, n 18.
27 Cf: 'Let us not begin at the beginning, nor even at the archive', which is the opening line in Jacques Derrida, 'Archive Fever: A Freudian Impression' (1995) 25(2) *Diacritics* 9, 9.
28 Richard Long, *A Line Made By Walking* (1967, England, photography and pencil on board, 375 × 324 mm). See figure I.1.
29 See, generally, www.richardlong.org. See, e.g., Richard Long, *Mirage* (Phaidon Press, 1998); Richard Long, *Walking in Circles* (G. Braziller, 1991); Richard Long, *Walking the Line* (Thames & Hudson, 2002). See also Richard Long, *White Water Line* (Tate Gallery, London, 1990), which received the Turner Prize in 1990.

Figure I.1 Richard Long, *A Line Made By Walking* (1967) © Richard Long. All Rights Reserved, Viscopy, 2015

for linking walking to art and art to walking with a noticeably distinct style, this early work by Richard Long is now well recognized as constituting one of the key works in the 'land art' movement that played out across the United States and the United Kingdom in the 1960s and 1970s.[30] Made in 1967 while he was still a student, this work continues to resonate. Created by walking across a field in the English county of Wiltshire, backwards and forwards, to and fro, again and again, until the markings of the repetitions were visible, captured by the sunlight, this is a line made by walking. A straight line in a grass field not really going anywhere, this is a material line, visibly marking the earth, compressing the line; a line made by the human technology of walking. Yet, while this line made by walking is both material and technical, what is most striking about this artwork is not only its intense linearity, but also its fragility; all that remains is the image.

One of the reminders of Long's work, which is both present in this early piece and his art more generally, is a reminder there is a materiality to walking, and a transient quality to the materiality of walking. In his art practice, the presence of Long as artist rests quietly, carefully underplayed. What also emerges is his careful attention to place, and to its production. Walking in different locations, directions and ways, whether walking in a straight line, a certain distance or in accordance with a lunar cycle, Long crafts the landscape into images, and creates artworks in place. With minimal intervention, this is art that is attentive to the mode and manner of being in place; of coming into and out of place; noticing the texture of place.

Yet, at the same time, there is an imperial inattention to place, captured in the gesture of repeatedly bold lines (see Figures I.2 –I.4). Sculpted in unknown locations where all that remains is the photograph, there is a tension between the colonial force of the ubiquitous line,[31] and the particularity to *this* place, with its open plains, hilltop ranges or lakes ashore in the background, which notices the distinctly complicit practice of walking in place.[32] Despite the repetition of the line, the artworks shown in Figures I.2, I.3 and I.4 are not the same places or

30 See Dieter Roelstraete, *Richard Long: A Line Made by Walking* (Afterall Books, MIT Press, 2010). More generally, land art is a movement that began in the United States in the late 1960s, and known for earthworks such as Robert Smithson's, 'The Spiral Jetty' as well as other, more minimalist, interventions in the landscape. For a good overview of the development of land art, which places Richard Long in this context, see Ben Tufnell, *Land Art* (Tate, 2006). Of course, Richard Long is also often placed in other categories of contemporary art, most commonly associated with other walking artists, such as Hamish Fulton, see, e.g., David Evans, the catalogue essay of Cynthia Morrison-Bell and Mike Collier (eds.), *Walk On: From Richard Long to Janet Cardiff: 40 Years of Art Walking* (University of Sunderland, 2013). See, especially, David Evans (ed.), *The Art of Walking: A Field Guide* (Black Dog Publishing, 2012). However, as always, for the best introduction to Long's work, see his work directly, ibid.
31 See Paul Carter, *Dark Writing: Geography, Performance, Design* (University of Hawai'i Press, 2009); Tim Ingold, *Lines: A Brief History* (Routledge, 2007).
32 Richard Long, *A Line Made By Walking* (1967, England, photography and pencil on board, 375 × 324 mm) (See Figure I.1); Richard Long, *Dusty Boots Line*, The Sahara (1988) (See Figure I.1); Richard Long, *Walking the Line in Peru* (1972) (See Figure I.3); Richard Long, *Sea-level Water Line*, Death Valley California (1982) (See Figure I.4).

Introduction: walking with empire 11

Figure I.2 Richard Long, *Dusty Boots Line, The Sahara* (1988) © Richard Long. All Rights Reserved, Viscopy, 2015

Figure I.3 Richard Long, *Walking a Line in Peru* (1972) © Richard Long. All Rights Reserved, Viscopy, 2015

12 A jurisprudence of movement

Figure I.4 Richard Long, *Sea Level Waterline, Death Valley California* (1982) © Richard Long. All Rights Reserved, Viscopy, 2015

the same walks as his earlier work, *A Line Made By Walking* (Figure 1.1). These are not fields in Wiltshire. Noticing these differences, there is a texture to Long's art that attends to the transient materiality of the practice of walking in place, producing space, and being in place. For to walk is a productive activity, a technical and material practice that occurs in place, an impermanent visceral place, where often all that remains is the image, photographic or otherwise.

Following Long, this book pays attention to the movement of walking as a technical and material practice; a productive activity that moves in place. While Long's art is not overtly attentive to questions of law, read jurisprudentially, his art offers a way of beginning to think about the relation between law, movement, materiality and conduct amongst different textures of place: unsettling place. More specifically, it is this doubling, this complicit duplicity between the placeable site and the always-from-elsewhere-line that intrigues; opening up questions of law and how common law might come to be in place. One answer offered to such questions in this book is that movements of common law from England to Australia are more than simply linear historical empirical movements drawn from the metropole to colony in both time and space, but also include everyday, continuing, multiple, fractured movements within Australia, carried by the subject walking; legal practices in place. Akin to Thomas A. Clark, whose poetic walkers vein the earth with paths visible and invisible, as Long illustrates, the line that follows our walk, no matter how unfathomable, is always somewhere.[33] The question

33 Above, n 1. On taking a line for a walk, see Paul Klee, *Pedagogical Sketchbook* (faber & faber, 1953) and in response, Chloe Regan, 'Untitled (After Paul Klee)' in David Evans (ed.), *The Art of Walking: A Field Guide* (Black Dog Publishing, 2012).

Introduction: walking with empire   13

raised, then, is how might the practice of walking, as well as the line that follows, be connected to law?

Walking the Green Line (Excursion 2)

We live in a world of excessive linearity, and our understanding of the dynamic place of law suffers as a result. Lines, however, are not so straightforward.[34] Lines have linings; they have outlines and inlines, texture and detail, they break and cross paths, moving and wandering as they occasionally fail to meet. Set parallel and directed to the horizon, straight lines curve towards meeting, touching in a gentle kiss of blurred understanding. Directed towards each other, these same straight lines boldly clash, merging in a point of indistinction where one line becomes the other, disappearing into a point. Lines, it seems, are more complex and deceptive than a mere projection of straightness.

In June 2004, Francis Alÿs walked the Green Line (see Figures I.5 and I.6). Established in the Armistice Agreements of 1949, the Green Line is, of course, the demarcation of the pre-1967 border between Israel and its neighbours, and is a line that continues to feature in varying ways in politics, memory, as well as the intifada and Palestinian and international calls for justice.[35] Created on 30 November 1948, the first Green Line was drawn on a map. As political scientist and former Deputy Mayor of Jerusalem (1971–1978) Meron Benvenisti observed:

> Moshe Dayan drew the Israeli line with a green grease pencil, while Abdullah al-Tal marked his front line with a red one. The grease pencils made lines 3 to 4 millimetres wide. Sketched on a map whose scale was 1:20,000, such lines

---

34 See Ingold, *Lines*, above, n 31. See also Felix Klee (ed.), *The Diaries of Paul Klee, 1891–1918* (University of California Press, 1964) 228, where Paul Klee writes:

> The line! My lines of 1906/07 were my most personal possession. And yet I had to interrupt them, they are threatened by some kind of cramp, perhaps even by finally becoming ornamental. In short, I was frightened and stopped, although they were deeply embedded in my emotions. The trouble was that I just couldn't make them out. And I could not see them around me, the accord between inside and outside was so hard to achieve. The changeover was complete; in the summer of 1907 I devoted myself entirely to the appearance of nature and upon these studies built my black-and-white landscapes on glass, 1907/08. No sooner have I mastered that stage than nature again bores me. Perspective makes me yawn. Should I now distort it (I have already tried distortions in a mechanical way)? How shall I most freely cast a bridge between inside and outside?

In response to this diary entry, Paul Carter asks, 'How, to invert Klee's problem, does the outside line acquire an inside, a lining that adheres to it, and underwrites it?'; Carter, *Dark Writing*, above, n 31, 266.

35 While literature on the Green Line is vast, for an insight into an international law perspective, see how the ICJ addresses the Green Line in *Legal Consequences of the Construction of a Wall in the Occupied Palestinian Territory, including in and around East Jerusalem* (Advisory Opinion), International Court of Justice, 9 July 2004, GA RES ES–10/15, UNGAOR, 10th special sess, 27thPlen Mtg, UN Doc A/RES/ES–10/15 (2004).

14 A jurisprudence of movement

Figure I.5 Francis Alÿs, *The Green Line* (walking past guard) (2004)
In collaboration with Julien Devaux; video documentation of an action
Courtesy David Zwirner, New York/London

in reality represented strips of land 60 to 80 metres width. Who owned the 'width of the line'?[36]

Nearly 60 years after this first Green Line was drawn on a 1:20,000 scale, Belgian artist Francis Alÿs redrew the Green Line on a 1:1 scale.[37]

Walking for two days across 24km constituting the then current boundaries of the municipality of Jerusalem, Alÿs not only walked, but also traced a portion of the Green Line. Walking with a leaking can of paint, constantly dripping, Alÿs writes the Green Line on the surface of the land with droplets of bright green paint. Videotaped, the substantially silent performance aches. As Alÿs walks across hills, under and along roads, across railway tracks, footpaths and through busy intersections, he occasionally meets others. At one point, as he scrambles up a dusty hill, the dripping paint seems to fade as it hits the loose and lightly textured dusty surface of the earth. At another point, an Israeli checkpoint guard, armed with a large automatic gun slung over his right shoulder, hands casually placed in his pockets, stands and watches as Alÿs walks past him down the middle of the road, seeming not to notice the trail of green paint that follows (see Figure I.5).

Both the mundanity as well as the material and topographical awkwardness of assigning legal distinction through the drawing of lines is starkly illustrated in Francis Alÿs' artwork, *The Green Line: Sometimes Doing Something Poetic Can Become Political and Sometimes Doing Something Political Can Become Poetic*.[38] Inviting a selection of commentators to respond to his art, including an historian, anthropologist, architect, filmmaker, journalist and activist (although interestingly no jurists), Israeli architect Eyal Weizmann commented:

> Walking being a form of design, *there is no neutral walk*, and especially when you walk with the paint, you are designing, you are making a gesture, you are drawing a line and implying, for me at least, that you request two kinds of spaces on two sides – you request a difference between the right and left side of the line; you project a difference. And if it's a legal difference (economic/ethnic), you are creating a kind of barrier that requires that the two sides are no longer part of a kind of smooth continuity.[39]

---

36 Meron Benvenisti, *City of Stone: The Hidden History of Jerusalem* (University of California Press, 1988) 57. Serving as context, this quote is slowly scrolled in the opening frames of Francis Alÿs, *The Green Line: Sometimes Doing Something Poetic Can Become Political and Sometimes Doing Something Political Can Become Poetic* (Created by Francis Alÿs, Jerusalem, 2005) 00:01:14–00:01:50.
37 Alÿs, *The Green Line*, ibid. The original video is 17 minutes and 34 seconds and can be viewed at http://francisalys.com/greenline/original.html. For the catalogue essay, see Francis Alÿs, *Francis Alÿs: Sometimes Doing Something Poetic Can Become Political and Sometimes Doing Something Political Can Become Poetic* (David Zwirner, 2007). For still images of this work, see Figures I.5 – I.6.
38 Ibid.
39 See http://francisalys.com/greenline/weizman.html. See generally Eyal Weizman, *Hollow Land: Israel's Architecture of Occupation* (Verso, 2007). Comments by others interviewed can be viewed at http://francisalys.com/greenline/.

16 A jurisprudence of movement

Figure 1.6 Francis Alÿs, *The Green Line* (overlooking) (2004)
In collaboration with Julien Devaux; video documentation of an action Image: Julien Devaux; Courtesy David Zwirner, New York/London

We do not walk without impact. As a material practice and a form of design, walking is never neutral. In this context, Weizman critiques Alÿs' non-neutral actions as implying a barrier, a space separator, that denies a smooth continuity between by emphasising legal difference, which is a critique often directed towards overtly legal lines, whether borders, armistice lines or walls.

While I agree to an extent, I would add that lines do more than separate, they also draw together, even if that drawing together is violent, uncomfortable, or more commonly, actively ignored. In other words, lines are relational: they not only divide but also connect. Legal lines, such as the Green Line, on one register operate as the site between, marking a pause in the distinct transition from the place of one law to the place of another: not quite either; holding them both at bay. Yet on a different register, these lines are the site of meetings between different forms of law, in this case, Israeli and Palestinian laws. Drawn with another law – the law of the international or the law of treated agreement – the Green Line absolutely separates, that is not denied. But this is a line that is more complex than the violence of separation, as seen in Moshe Dayan's provocative evocation of the property and provenance of its material width. The Green Line is also more complex in the sense that such legal lines not only separate those on either side of its width, but also through the activity of the line, bring together, connecting multiple forms of law. This is the obverse of lines as separator; this is the line as a meeting place, and a meeting place of laws.[40] Both jurisprudentially and materially, lines are more than a straight line that divides.

In Jerusalem, the quality of the Green Line Alÿs rematerialises is complex and far from straight (see Figure I.6). Mimicking the rolling sway of the step-by-step of human perambulation, green paint splatters in irregularly repetitive patterns as it meanders, splotches, loops and separates, as the topography guides the steps of Alÿs. Weaving, crossing, exploding over hilltops, the imagined legal line that is drawn on the surface tracks neither topography nor urban borders, but an idealised legal line that does not translate to the landscape. Weizman is correct when he says: 'The Green Line is not always a line.'[41] For as Alÿs' *Green Line* illustrates, the strict linearity of lines is actually quite difficult to maintain. Yet this is precisely what many try to do; this is precisely the conceit of modern law; and this is precisely what an attention to the materiality of walking reveals: the wobbliness and instability of lines; the wobbliness and instability of the place of law.

A half-broken brick (Excursion 3)

Layered in clothes, hands exposed, I walk in a Berlin winter. The snow is melting with the rain and only those from elsewhere, like me, seek the cover of an umbrella. Approaching the Mauerpark Flea Market in Prenzlauer Berg, the umbrellas multiply despite the market offering only a diminished version of its summer stalls. Stepping across puddles that form in the indents of the narrow paths running between, hoards of lamps, scarves, toys and shoes display themselves erratically in temporarily dry spaces under a mixture of tarpaulins and stall covers. The crowd weaves through long corridors as food smells and the experience of damp socks start to dominate, persisting as the outline of my thoughts. Leaving Mauerpark, I cross Bernauer Straße. Umbrella poised, and glad to be wandering again, I do not even register this unremarkable road crossing.

Yet, I just walked across the Berlin Wall. Crossing Bernauer Straße, I walked across what used to be the Berlin Wall, moving from the former West to the former East. If my German were better than non-existent, I might have realised that '*Mauer*' means 'wall', but this linguistic megalith was lost on my despairingly persistent Australian monolingualism. Continuing, walking south along the footpath of Bernauer Straße, my footsteps now more knowingly trace the former Wall. I keep glancing from one side of the street to the other, trying to work out how it was here – *here* – the Wall was. One side West, the other side East. One side locked in, the other waiting, or maybe that is just one perception of lives lived with the Wall. At first glance, before starting to notice, the material signs do not penetrate deeply. A sauna on one side, a new apartment block on the other; buildings

---

40 Paul Carter, *Meeting Place: The Human Encounter and the Challenge of Coexistence* (University of Minnesota Press, 2013).
41 Weizman, *Hollow Land*, above, n 39.

and more buildings, repeated on one side of the street, and then the other. Of course, as with any physical object, a wall has to be somewhere, and this one was here, in the instant between two strides.[42] I slowly start to see. The vacant lots on the eastern side of the street hint at the previously hyper-regulated spaces existing between the double walls of the Wall that still carries its misguided naming of the singular.[43] An opening to the local U-bahn station, Bernauer Straße, barely hints of its history of closure as a *Geisterbahnhof* or a 'ghost' station through its location within the path of the formerly in-between. Yet, the double row of cobblestone markers, two stones wide, cutting across an otherwise tarmacked road concretely declare: this was the Wall.

At the next street corner, it finally becomes clear: a memorial has risen; rusted industrial red steel poles erected roughly 12 feet high, mimicking the height of the final version of the Wall; so boldly marking the line.[44] With this steely rewriting of the Wall, a constructed memorial begins; encouraging with its paths and objects of interest a walking practice of memorialisation. To begin, iconic images on the white outer walls of buildings overlook the mainly open space, including photographs of people peering through holes in the brick wall as it is constructed; a woman falling from the window of an apartment; and Peter Leibing's famous image of East German border guard Konrad Schumann jumping over barbed wire to West Berlin.[45] The largeness of black and white images and the preciseness of the rusty poles collaborate to govern this public space. On closer inspection, the metal poles of this new Wall; this post-Wall; this Wall-in-memory; are inconsistently spaced, allowing for bodily passage and a radical movement of cross-hatched walking between what used to be impenetrably solid. In the centre of the open space, a path weaves between silver nodal stations containing snippets and snapshots of information, beginning with a large metal model that maps some of the buildings as well as the divisions this piece of land used to contain. The memorial goes on.

---

42 'The history of mankind is the instant between two strides taken by the traveler', in Franz Kafka, 'The Blue Octavo Notebooks', in *Dearest Father; Stories and Other Writings* (Ernst Kaiser and Eithne Wilkins trans., Schocken Books Inc., 1954) from the diary entry on 20 October 1917. This is a refrain Paul Carter often returns, too, see especially Carter, *Dark Writing*, above, n 31; Carter, *Meeting Place*, above, n 40.

43 Cf: Marc Augé, *Non-Places: Introduction to an Anthropology of Supermodernity* (Verso, 2008).

44 Designed by Stuttgart architects Kohlhoff and Kohlhoff, and overseen by Günter Schlusche, an architect and urban planner for the Berlin Wall Foundation (also head planner for Peter Eisenman's Memorial to the Murdered Jews of Europe) the Berlin Wall Memorial includes a line of rusted red steel poles, roughly 12 feet high, which mark the line and mimic the height of the Wall. See Günter Schlusche, 'Remapping the Wall: The Wall Memorial in Bernauer Strasse – From an Unloved Cold War Monument to a New Type of Memorial Site', in Nick Hodgin and Caroline Pearce (eds.), *The GDR Remembered: Representations of the East German State Since 1989* (Camden House, 2011) 112.

45 Peter Leibing, *Konrad Schumann Jumping a Barbed Wire Fence During Construction of the Berlin Wall* (August 15, 1961), https://iconicphotos.wordpress.com/2009/05/11/conrad-schumann-defects/.

There are different ways of walking with history, and of living with difficult inheritances. In Berlin, walking the accentually fading sites of the wall, there is an intoxicating amalgamation of erasure and crafted memorialisation; a memorial of overt touristic education and slightly more subtle formations of statehood, but there is also something else. Captured in the remnants of the Wall I can now walk through, I also notice this something, for instance, in the minor details of a DDR architectural aesthetic. There is, it seems, a 'something else' to the continuing life of the material inheritance of Berlin's complex history, and more specifically to the ways in which life is both lived with and among this inheritance that is the source of this intoxication, this enchanted entrancement, at least for me. Yet it is only when I walk Berlin's modern hill of *Teufelsberg*, and notice partially unearthed and half-broken red bricks, that I realise the colloidal overlay connecting these Berlin walks with the task I set myself in this book.

The highest point in an otherwise topographically flat and low-lying Berlin, *Teufelsberg* is an artificial woman-made hill on the outskirts of Berlin's suburbs.[46] Built by the hands of the *Trümmerfrauen*, or Berlin's much adored rubble women, *Teufelsberg* is constructed from the rubble of destructed buildings following the bombing of Berlin towards the end of World War II.[47] Constructed over several decades, as rubble was moved from the city to the hill-in-making, the ground has now settled. In the winter of 2014, I went walking – or more accurately I moved in an indelicate mixture of slipping, plodding, lurching, grasping and sliding – along single-track goat trails of icy snow set beneath the sublimely graffitied echoes of a former American listening station, where the tall trees, low shrubs and woodland grounds, coupled with the sound of birds, recent markings of wild boars and vistas of vast forest openness projected a natural wilderness and longevity that belied *Teufelsberg*'s architecture. Walking down this woman-made hill, with its archaeology so often, so readily and so understandably overlooked as it is walked over, buried, and only occasionally subject to the diggings of a curious dog, a half-broken red brick interrupted my stride, and hinted at the larger resonances of a challenge I had previously thought of as distinctly Australian, or at least particularised to the colonial, and to lives lived in a former colony.

Walking in Berlin, the question of this half-brick – also the question of the Wall we can now walk through, across and between – was one of how to live with the material aftermath, and the material and legal inheritance of Empire? This resonated with a question I have long been asking on another side of the world, which is also a question of inheritance, as well as one of conduct. For me, the driving question has long been one of how to live with colonial law on unceded Aboriginal

---

46 See, especially, Benedict Anderson, *Buried City, Unearthing Teufelsberg: Berlin and its Geography of Forgetting* (Ashgate, 2016, forthcoming). See also Benedict Anderson, 'Self-Ruining and Situated Vagrancy: The Geography of Performance', in Lynn Churchill and Dianne Smith (eds.), *Occupation: Ruin, Repudiation and Revolution* (Ashgate, 2015); Benedict Anderson, 'The Architectural Flaw', in Leon van Schaik and Sue Anne Ware, *The Practice of Spatial Thinking* (Onepointsixone, Melbourne, 2014, 41).
47 Ibid.

land, and how, in such an unresolved political and legal context, we might live this life well? While this question relates to others, such as Albert Memmi's questioning of relations between the coloniser and the colonised,[48] and continued postcolonial interrogations as to how these colonial structures manifest in the contemporary world, to ask the jurisprudential question of how to live *with* law, and how to live with Australian law (or Anglo-Australian common law), is quite distinct.

Yet in Berlin, as I walked, the jurisprudential question I had localised as a specifically Australian question, or at least a colonial question, one of how to live with law, and how to live with a difficult legal inheritance, was reframed outside the former British Empire, and connected to other difficult inheritances, whether practices of war, Empire, colonial or postcolonial; and other material practices; other ways of walking. Captured in one broken *Teufelsberg* brick, in its distinctively textured colloquial redness, resting alongside autumnal debris paused in its winter freeze, was a small but significant reminder of the materiality of inheritance; a reminder of myriad ways we live with history; the place of law in those histories of destruction and reconstruction, and how we walk both amongst and with these remnants, patterning our stride.

Terrain

While Richard Long and Francis Alÿs, through their art practices, along with a Berlin walk, have together offered a reminder of the materiality of walking, and hinted at the dynamic relation between movement and law, to extend this invitation to walk, it is both helpful and polite to offer a description of the terrain; an orientation, and a location of both the walker, and the ground for this book. While a number of walkers are noticed in this book, what is required is noticing who has responsibility for noticing law, and its moving juridical forms. For this reason, this book is directed towards those charged with particular responsibilities in relation to common law, especially and most notably the jurist.[49] To this end, this section considers how and where the jurist walks, and answers: the jurist walks certain material and intellectual terrains and does so with office.

The physical ground is, of course, primarily Australian, and in Australia, the question remains one of Empire, of how we walk with a colonial form of law (an example of a difficult history), which is embedded in a question of location. Consider the location of legal meetings, as well as meetings more generally. Whenever or wherever we walk, we also meet; whether it is the ground, or meetings with others. As there are different ways of walking, moving through locations, striding topographies, so too are there different ways of meeting. Whether we sidle past a stranger as we negotiate urban crowds or greet a friend with a smile, the management of meetings, and the institution of meeting places is a vastly

---

48 Albert Memmi, *The Colonizer and the Colonized* (Howard Greenfield trans., Earthscan, 1990) [trans. of *Portrait du Colonise Precede du Portrait du Colonisateur* (first published 1957)].
49 See Chapter 1.

animated complex. Writer, historian, philosopher and artist Paul Carter, known especially for his spatial histories, in his recent book called *Meeting Place* 'stages an encounter between northern and southern modes of meeting'.[50] In doing so, Carter comes to an unexpected conclusion: 'There is no meeting place. A meeting place would simply cancel out the meaning of the journey.'[51]

Following Carter, this book argues it is the journey that matters. It is the manner of approach, the conduct of preparation, movement and entry that is significant, not the meeting itself. Whether understood as means rather than ends, although this is too simplistic, what is required is an attention to practices: for the meeting is only ever a set of practices. In Australia, the proposition that meaning carried by actions and activities *before* the meeting, therefore, demands attention, and more specifically demands legal attention: the attention of the jurist. For, of course, in Australia, the meeting place that is not, or the one that always disappoints, structuring inequalities, hastening divides, is the legal meeting place: the meeting of Australian and indigenous laws. Whether this is a non-meeting, as often articulated within Australian legal discourse, or a meeting of questionable quality, it is worth stepping back from the meeting itself, or set ideas of the meeting, as Paul Carter suggests, and think more carefully about how we approach; how law approaches; how Anglo-Australian common law approaches, that is, attend to common law practice.

For this reason, although it is the driving normative impulse, except for a brief introduction as context in Chapter 1, this book elects not to address the meeting between Aboriginal and common laws, at least not directly. While others have engaged, and will continue to engage with legal meetings, whether through the lens of colonialism, postcolonialism or legal pluralism, this book does not.[52] Rather than attempting to somehow locate omnipotently between the meetings of laws, translating between, a different approach is taken. Focusing on Anglo-Australian common law, the mode of law that dominates contemporary meetings in Australia, this is an approach wed to jurisprudence, an approach to law cognisant of and attentive to matters of role, responsibility and conduct, which are captured in this book most predominantly through the language of office, explained in depth in Chapter 1. Attending to the prudence of common law – its practical wisdom – through an attention to its technical and material practices, this is an internal investigation into how common law comes to the meeting place.

---

50 Carter, *Meeting Place*, above, n 40, 1. For examples of spatial histories in his earlier works, see Paul Carter, *The Road to Botany Bay: An Essay in Spatial History* (faber & faber, 1987); Paul Carter, *The Lie of the Land* (faber & faber, 1996); Paul Carter, *Living in a New Country: History, Travelling and Language* (faber, 1992).
51 Carter, *Meeting Place*, above, n 40, 171.
52 For an explanation why, see Chapter 1. On legal pluralism, see, e.g., Sally Engle Merry, 'Legal Pluralism' (1988) 22 *Law and Society Review* 869; Brian Tamanaha, 'Understanding Legal Pluralism: Past to Present, Local to Global' (2008) 30 *Sydney Law Review* 375; Martha-Marie Kleinhans and Roderick MacDonald, 'What is a *Critical* Legal Pluralism?' (1997) 12(2) *Canadian Journal of Law and Society* 25.

The answer offered, perhaps at this stage no longer surprisingly, is that common law approaches through practices of movement.

Weaving through movement, motion, space, materiality and place, therefore, are questions of the technical means by which law manifests in the world: its material practices. This is where jurisprudence comes to the fore. Rather than placing law to the side, or rendering it mere social fact, this book makes a case for jurisprudence, and for thinking jurisprudentially, that is, for a considered engagement with the practical knowledge of law. As suggested by the opening walks, this book focuses on ways in which law manifests in the material world. How is law materialised, practised, moved and revealed in the everyday footsteps along a coastline, a corridor, or among the heavily sacralised spaces of a courtroom? How can we learn to notice law in the footpaths and letterboxes, light poles and garbage bins, or in the transitional spaces of a building site? What might be revealed if we attend to law in its material practices? These are questions of jurisprudence; questions of the technical practice and conduct of law, and of how we live our lives with law. Through jurisprudence, therefore, the project of this book is to think *with* law: Anglo-Australian common law. Taking such an approach, what is revealed is that common law operates in certain ways, and that some of those ways – especially for those located in certain offices – carry additional responsibilities that need to be attended to and accounted for.

Where, then, does the jurist walk? Although clearly set geographically in Australia and its surrounds, this book also wanders to Antarctica, New Zealand and briefly into Iraq, Bosnia and Kuwait. Yet it is not the physical terrain that is of concern at this point in the introduction, but rather, the intellectual setting of this book. While primarily jurisprudential, the work in this book is also interdisciplinary in the sense that it contributes to scholarship in the broad field of 'law and the humanities'.[53] Navigating its way through geography, history, anthropology, art history and philosophy, this book is set among a spatial turn in the humanities, and jurisprudence more specifically. In this regard, it is helpful to locate this jurisprudential work in its two major literary contexts. The first is the ongoing spatial turn in the humanities more generally, and law more specifically and the second is the conceptual development of jurisdiction as a central concern of jurisprudence.

Among a series of 'turns' that have rotated their way through contemporary scholarship in recent decades,[54] the spatial turn in the humanities has been picked up with enthusiasm in legal scholarship.[55] Influenced by the work of Henri Lefebvre, who classically emphasised the distinction between abstract and social

---

53 In an Australian context, consider the activities of the Law, Literature and Humanities Association of Australasia http://lawlithum.org/. For an example of relevant work resulting from the 2013 conference, see the special issue of *Law and Literature* (2015, 27:2 *Law and Literature*).
54 For a critique of the turning of 'turns', see Wills, *Dorsality*, above, n 13, ch 1.
55 For a recent example, see the edited collection by Irus Braverman, Nicholas Blomley, David Delaney and Alexandre Kedar (eds.), *The Expanding Spaces of Law: A Timely Legal Geography* (Stanford University Press, 2014).

space by arguing for an attendance to space as a mode of production,[56] and whose work was introduced to the English-speaking academy in human geography through the work of David Harvey,[57] the spatial turn in the humanities translated into the legal academy through critical legal geography. While not the first to walk across this particular disciplinary divide,[58] this formerly emergent – although now fully emerged – field of critical scholarship was established by Nicholas Blomley's book, *Law, Space and the Geographies of Power*.[59] The shape of research in critical legal geography was further framed by several influential edited collections in the early years of the new millennium, with the emphasis primarily on the interdisciplinary project of thinking law with space, and vice versa.[60]

Despite the presence of movement in the dynamic activity of the production of space, that is, in Lefebvrian social space, in the coming together of law and geography, while not entirely absent, questions of movement have certainly not been afforded central stage.[61] An exception, however, is Nicholas Blomley, *Rights of Passage: Sidewalks and the Regulation of Public Flow*, which is a work of critical legal geography that attends to the materiality of legal movement in certain spaces of the city, that is, the sidewalk or the footpath.[62] However, while Blomley notices movement, and explores technical details of municipal regulation in British Columbia, Canada, and their spatial manifestations on the lived experience of the public usage of footpaths, what Blomley fails to register, strange as it may seem to say, is the form or forms of law. For Blomley, law is most often rendered as mere technical detail or social fact, which overlooks the dynamic activity of material practices of law and, as a result, overlooks jurisprudential questions, such as

---

56 Lefebvre, *The Production of Space*, above, n 4.
57 Henri Lefebvre's influence on Marxist and critical geography and the 'spatial turn' can be substantially traced through the work of David Harvey. See, e.g., David Harvey, *Social Justice and the City* (Edward Arnold, 1973).
58 See, e.g., Keith Harries and Stanley Brunn, *The Geography of Laws and Justice: Spatial Perspectives on the Criminal Justice* (Praeger Publishers, 1978); Gordon Clark, *Judges and the Cities: Interpreting Local Autonomy* (University of Chicago Press, 1985).
59 Nicholas Blomley, *Law, Space and the Geographies of Power* (Guilford Press, 1994).
60 Nicholas Blomley, David Delaney and Richard T. Ford (eds.), *The Legal Geographies Reader: Law, Power and Space* (Blackwell Publishers, 2001); Jane Holder and Carolyn Harrison (eds.), *Law and Geography: Current Legal Issues* (Oxford University Press, 2003); William Taylor (ed.), *The Geography of Law: Landscape, Identity and Regulation* (Hart Publishing, 2006); Desmond Manderson, 'Interstices: New Work on Legal Spaces' (2005) 9 *Law Text Culture* 1, which introduces a special edition of *Law Text Culture* dedicated to law and geography; Jane Holder and Tatiana Flessas, 'Emerging Commons' (2008) 17(3) *Social and Legal Studies* 299, which introduces an edition of *Social and Legal Studies* dedicated to the idea of the commons and substantially engages with law and geography. See also the edition of (2010) 6(3) *International Journal of Law in Context* and (2011) 7(2) *Law, Culture and the Humanities*. For a recent and comprehensive treatment of the spatial turn, see Braverman et al., above, n 55.
61 For a notable exception where the relation between law, territory and movement is addressed, see Andrea Brighenti, *Lines, Barred Lines: Movement, Territory and the Law* (2010) 6(3) *International Journal of Law in Context* 217.
62 Blomley, *Rights of Passage*, above, n 22.

questions of lawful conduct or lawful place. This overlooking of law, and of lawful conduct in particular, is a problem accentuated in Blomley's recent book, but is a deficiency that can be found in the substratum of much, if not most, research falling under the banner of critical legal geography.[63]

Put most boldly, while time and space have become central concepts for socio-legal scholars, including through the legal inheritance of the spatial turn, the question of law too often gets lost. Although critical legal geography has done much to return questions of space to law, the failure to hold onto the law question is a significant deficiency, and has been noted in recent work, such as David Delaney, *The Spatial, the Legal and the Pragmatics of World-Making: Nomospheric Investigations*.[64] However, while Delaney notices the problem of the loss of law in critical legal geography, his response is quite different from the response taken here. While Delaney responds by returning to the *nomos*, and in a traditional critical move, seeking to escape from and transcend law, this book is a work of jurisprudence and necessarily takes a different approach where the task is not one of transcending law, but rather thinking with law as a way of living with law.[65] A further response to this problem, and one much more akin to the approach of this book, is offered by the work of Andreas Philippopoulos-Mihalopoulos, including, most comprehensively, his most recent book, *Spatial Justice: Body, Lawscape, Atmosphere*.[66] While addressing the distinct concept of spatial justice and not movement *per se*, through an attention to materiality Philippopoulos-Mihalopoulos offers a distinct but conceptually companionable approach to the limitations of current research in law and geography, especially in his acceptance that 'there is no outside' and, as he writes: 'Since I cannot "forget" that there is no outside, I dwell fully in the inside.'[67]

Therefore, despite the various ways in which the spatial turn has been taken up in legal thought, questions of law, movement and its materialities are too often overlooked. By calling for a greater attention to legal movement, in both its technical and material forms, this book addresses this oversight, and it does so through an attention to material movements, and the materialities of legal movement. The difficulty, however, is that common law's movements too often slide by unnoticed. The task then becomes how we might begin to pay attention to legal movement. This is done in this book through jurisprudence, and more specifically, by attending to and accounting for technologies of jurisdiction. In what is a small but fast growing field of critical and jurisprudential research on jurisdiction, this is the first book that conceptually links jurisdiction to movement. In this regard, a brief introduction to a second literary context: jurisdiction.

63 For more detail, see Chapter 2, 2.2.
64 David Delaney, *The Spatial, the Legal and the Pragmatics of World-Making: Nomospheric Investigations* (Taylor & Francis, 2010).
65 For more detail on a minor jurisprudence, see Chapter 1, part 3.
66 Andreas Philippopoulos-Mihalopoulos, *Spatial Justice: Body, Lawscape, Atmosphere* (Routledge, 2014).
67 Ibid, 1.

As a matter of jurisprudence, the question of jurisdiction is and must always be the first question of law.[68] This is most obviously so in its etymological heritage of the Latin noun *ius* (law) and verb *dicere* (to speak), which roughly translates as the saying or the speaking of law.[69] As Peter Rush explains, jurisdiction 'refers us first and foremost to the power and authority to speak in the name of the law and only subsequently to the fact that law is stated – and stated to be someone or something'.[70] This is jurisdiction as idiom, as a way of speaking and practicing law. In this regard, it is the first question of law in the idiomatic sense that without jurisdiction law cannot be spoken, yet it is also the first question in the sense that jurisdiction is a mode of authorising law, asking whether something belongs to law – a question of what is lawful – and only subsequently turning to the question of what that law is.[71] Problematically, as both authority and authorisation, the question of jurisdiction is often tied to and obscured by questions of sovereignty, territory and the state. Yet jurisdiction is not the same as sovereignty, and neither is it the same as territory. As will be explained in more detail in Chapter 2, jurisdiction is much more than simply boundary-making processes, marking that which is within or without. Rather, jurisdiction is how things can be done with law (i.e. jurisdiction is technical), and it is also productive in the sense that it produces and crafts law (i.e. jurisdiction is practical). Always technical and never less than practical,[72] jurisdiction is the legal technology that gives form and shape to common law, including its movements. Most simply, yet significant in its simplicity, this is the contention that it is through the technology of jurisdiction that common law moves.

Drawing on recent scholarship reinvesting jurisdiction as a central concern of jurisprudence, this book contributes to this literature by linking jurisdiction with movement as a matter of jurisprudence. Largely initiating this renewed interest in jurisdiction, which is now a rapidly growing field of contemporary critical jurisprudence, Shaun McVeigh's edited collection, *Jurisprudence of Jurisdiction* convincingly called for the return of questions of jurisdiction to jurisprudence.[73] This call has been taken up in a number of different ways, some more direct than others and has also led to a reimagining of already established jurisdictional

---

68 Dorsett and McVeigh, *Jurisdiction*, above, n 3, ch 1. See also Peter Rush, 'An Altered Jurisdiction: Corporeal Traces of Law' (1997) 6 *Griffith Law Review* 144.
69 Dorsett and McVeigh, *Jurisdiction*, above, n 3, ch 1; Shaun McVeigh (ed.), *Jurisprudence of Jurisdiction* (Routledge-Cavendish, 2007) ch 1; Shaunnagh Dorsett and Shaun McVeigh, 'Questions of Jurisdiction', in Shaun McVeigh (ed.), *Jurisprudence of Jurisdiction* (Routledge-Cavendish, 2007). See also Rush, 'An Altered Jurisdiction', above, n 68; Peter Goodrich, 'Visive Powers: Colours, Trees and Genres of Jurisdiction' (2008) 2(2) *Law and Humanities* 217; Bradin Cormack, *A Power to Do Justice: Jurisdiction, English Literature, and the Rise of Common Law 1509–1625* (Chicago University Press, 2007) 5; Emile Benveniste, *Indo-European Language and Society* (faber & faber, 1973) 392.
70 Rush, 'An Altered Jurisdiction', above, n 68, 150.
71 Ibid.
72 Ibid, ch 1.
73 McVeigh (ed.), *Jurisprudence of Jurisdiction*, above, n 69.

literature as carrying the potential for jurisprudential meaning. The most recent and also the most significant book currently in this field is Shaunnagh Dorsett and Shaun McVeigh's, *Jurisdiction*.[74] This book provides a clear statement of ways in which this emerging field of research is unfolding and in particular makes a strong argument for an attention to technologies of jurisdiction, which is an argument taken up here in the context of movement.[75] In addition to Dorsett and McVeigh's, *Jurisdiction*, notable works overtly contributing to the jurisprudential work of 'jurisdictional thinking'[76] include Edward Mussawir, *Jurisdiction in Deleuze: The Expression and Representation of Law*, Piyel Haldar, *Law, Orientalism and Postcolonialism: The Jurisdiction of the Lotus-Eaters* and Bradin Cormack, *A Power to Do Justice: Jurisdiction, English Literature and the Rise of Common Law 1590–1625*.[77] In a slightly different register, Peter Goodrich, *Law in the Courts of Law: Literature and Other Minor Jurisprudences* and Martha Minow, Michael Ryan and Austin Sarat (eds.), *Narrative, Violence and the Law: The Essays of Robert Cover* remain influential in this emerging jurisprudential research in jurisdiction.[78]

Finally, located at the interstices between the major two working sites of this book, that is, questions of jurisdiction and space, is Mariana Valverde's current research culminating in her recent book on chronotopes of law.[79] Working in a similar frame of jurisdiction and space, in a similar move to that of Delaney, Valverde also seeks to steer the conversation away from space, but unlike Delaney, Valverde does so through a return to temporality and geographical concepts of scale.[80] While this book is not oblivious to questions of time or scale, unlike Valverde, who works within socio-legal studies and traditions of critique, this book is jurisprudential. As such, it moves away from more traditional modes of critique, which as explained in more detail in Chapter 1, too often abandons questions of law for a false sense of escape. While remaining critical, instead of embracing the more familiar approach of critique, this book turns to jurisprudence in order to hold onto law and think more carefully how we might live with law.

For these reasons, most notably through its attention to movement, and its return to questions of law through an embrace of jurisprudence as a response to the limitations of critical legal geography, this book offers a unique contribution to current research in both critical legal geography and jurisprudence. Set among a spatial turn in the humanities, and jurisprudence more specifically, this book

---

74 Dorsett and McVeigh, *Jurisdiction*, above, n 3.
75 On technologies of jurisdiction, see ibid, ch 4.
76 Dorsett and McVeigh, *Jurisdiction*, above, n 3, 1.
77 Edward Mussawir, *Jurisdiction in Deleuze: The Expression and Representation of Law* (Routledge, 2011); Haldar, *Law, Orientalism and Postcolonialism*, above, n 5; and Cormack, *A Power to do Justice*, above, n 69.
78 Peter Goodrich, *Law in the Courts of Law: Literature and Other Minor Jurisprudences* (Routledge, 1996) and Martha Minow, Michael Ryan and Austin Sarat (eds.), *Narrative, Violence and the Law: The Essays of Robert Cover* (University of Michigan Press, 1992).
79 See Mariana Valverde, *Chronotopes of Law: Jurisdiction, Scale and Governance* (Routledge, 2015).
80 Ibid.

calls for a greater attention to legal movement, in both its technical and material forms. Significantly, this book is the first to conceptually link jurisdiction to movement, which it does by creating what is described as 'a minor jurisprudence of movement'. As explained in more detail in Chapter 1, the jurisprudence created is 'minor' in the sense that a position is taken accepting the institution of common law.[81] That is, rather than revolution, the book asks questions such as how to live with common law, and, how, perhaps, to live that life well. To be clear, this is not to dismiss the task or desire for revolution or radical change, but it is a considered stance to accept, place with and work from within current legal structures, maintaining hopes and creating opportunities for internal critical disruptions. Topographically, this is the material, jurisprudential and normative terrain walked in this book.

Itinerary

Before embarking, it is helpful to explain how *A Jurisprudence of Movement: Common Law, Walking, Unsettling Place* unfolds. An itinerary can be the sketch of a proposed route, the route itself or the account of a journey in the form of a record or journal of travel.[82] The itinerary proposed here is in the form of a sketch of a proposed route. To account for a journey not yet taken is to anticipate a line or course of travel: an outline. But, as already suggested, and as will be developed in the accounting of this book, we should be cautious of lines.[83] Lines conceal other lines; they conceal other possibilities. The hesitation embraced in this book is a cautionary and, it is suggested, a healthy suspicion of the ease of following lines. Travelling carefully, in its creation of a minor jurisprudence of movement, the question of method is approached as a question of how to move well. This is a jurisprudence that pays attention to material movements that may or may not be linear: to linear movements that carry linings and to non-linear movements that are more than simply movements in opposition to the line.

So, how does common law move? This is the central question asked in this book, and the response developed is that *common law moves with a tendency to slide by, unnoticed, but through jurisdiction*. Noticing, the book pays attention to some of the ways in which Anglo-Australian common law moves, especially through walking and practices of burial. Across five chapters, separated into three parts, which in turn work to move, perform then return jurisprudence, this book seeks to better understand the place of movement in the technical and material forms of common law practice. This is how it is done.

After this introduction, Part I begins with Chapter 1, which asks how to account for and take responsibility for forms of common law practice. Addressing the

---

81 Cf: Goodrich, *Law in the Courts of Love*, above, n 78. See Chapter 1 for more detail.
82 Charles Talbut Onions (ed.), *The Oxford English Dictionary of English Etymology* (Clarendon Press, 1966).
83 Carter, *Dark Writing*, above, n 31, 266. See also Ingold, *Lines*, above, n 31.

jurist, the chapter is concerned with the office of jurist and its relation to common law: a relation of responsibility. Noticing that common law is not without its problems in the conduct of lawful relations in Australia, including its relations with indigenous laws, and its relations with the dead, it is argued that the jurist must take responsibility for common law, and its problems. The chapter considers ways this might be done. Examining the tasks of office, the jurist is offered a way of thinking with common law that attends to the technical and material forms of common law practice, including how it comes into its relations and into place. This is through the creation of a minor jurisprudence, which in this book takes the particular shape of a minor jurisprudence of movement. The chapter concludes with an explanation of method and how this is done.

Chapter 2 considers the importance of movement for the jurist in office and in doing so, raises some issues with the technical forms and material practices of Anglo-Australian common law. This is the contention that common law moves and that these movements are not meaningless. Asking the central question of the book 'how does common law move?', the chapter explains that it is for the jurist to pay attention to movement as a way of accounting for common law practice as a matter of office. To assist the jurist in this task, the chapter sets out a number of key ideas about the importance of movement. This includes registering different forms of movement, placing the technology of jurisdiction as a technology of movement, an explanation of the problem with common law's place, the relation between movement, space and place, and introducing the institution of burial as one of the ways in which common law moves in relation to the dead; resting in place. The chapter concludes by proposing that common law's movements in relation to the dead through the institution of burial contribute to the making of place and the humanisation of both land and law; a proposition attended to in Part II of the book.

Part II of the book shifts registers from one of advice giving to one of performance. In Part I, the jurist was advised as to how they might go about accounting for movement as part of their tasks of office, and it was suggested that the creation of a minor jurisprudence of movement was worthy of attention. To assist the jurist, Part II takes up the task of this minor jurisprudence, describing and redescribing some of the technical and material forms of common law practice as a way of accounting for movement and revealing its jurisprudential significance. In this regard, Part II illustrates how common law moves by putting into practice some of the ideas considered in Part I. Each chapter does this through a close engagement with a case study, as exemplar, which takes up aspects of movement within common law practice. Fundamentally asking the same question: 'How does common law move?', together, and in response to this question, the chapters in Part II reveal movement and illustrate the work of a minor jurisprudence of movement.

Chapter 3 asks how common law moved into, in and within the Colony of New South Wales. Less concerned with more obvious empirical movements between metropole and colony, this question is investigated through the case study of a burial party that walked into the woods beyond an emerging frontier settlement in 1799.⁸⁴ Illustrating some of the ways in which common law moves, significantly it shows that common law moves through the technology of jurisdiction. This is most noticeably so through the jurisdictional status of the person, which includes movements through walking. The chapter also shows how common law moves in relation to the dead in what is described as 'camping', which captures something quite particular in the lawful form of common law's relations with the dead.⁸⁵ This is a relation of responsibility to care for the dead and it is through this relation of care that the burial party, and hence common law moved, and moved beyond. This is the argument that camping is a jurisdictional technology of movement, exercised through the institution and conduct of lawful relations with the dead. Through both walking and camping, therefore, the chapter illustrates some of the ways in which common law moves. What the chapter also does is link movement to place. In doing so, it draws out the sense in which movement puts common law in its place, and reveals that place as temporary. The chapter concludes by noting the absence of proper burial, which is a matter picked up in the next chapter.

Chapter 4 considers how common law moves in a more recent southerly situation. What happens when a person dies and is buried in Antarctica? Who has jurisdiction of the dead? How are lawful relations instituted and conducted in the polar South? And what might this have to do with movement and the place of common law? These are questions raised in the chapter through the consideration of a New Zealand coronial investigation into the death of an Australian scientist at a US-run research station located at the south pole in 2000. Again noting jurisdiction as a common law technology of movement, this case study also illustrates some of the ways in which common law moves. This includes incomplete and largely ineffective movements of Anglo-Australian common law through jurisdictional technologies of mapping. Ultimately, a redescription of Anglo-Australian common law's movements reveals this as an unsuccessful attempt to move and come into relation that amounts to an inability to care for the dead in the polar South. The chapter also shows how a New Zealand coronial jurisdiction more successfully moves in relation to the dead. Concentrating on the office of the coroner and its medieval inheritance of a jurisdictional relation of responsibility to care for the dead, this example shows how a coroner institutes and conducts lawful relations with the dead through jurisdictional movements along anticipated flight lines. To this end, the chapter illustrates some of the technical and material forms of common law practice, including jurisdiction, walking and camping raised in the previous chapter, as well as introducing the office of coroner, flight lines and repetition as additional aspects of

---

84 An article based on this chapter has been published as Olivia Barr, 'Walking with Empire' (2013) 38 *Australian Feminist Law Journal* 59.
85 Gilles Deleuze and Felix Guattari, *What is Philosophy?* (Hugh Tomlinson and Graham Burchell trans., Columbia University Press, 1994) ch 4 [trans. of *Qu'est-ce que la Philosophie?* (first published 1991)].

movement. Having previously linked movement to place, what the chapter also does is examine the proposition offered in Chapter 2 concerning the importance of burial for the movement and place of common law. In doing so, the institution of burial is attended to both in relation to the humanisation of the earth and the humanisation of law.

While Part I was explanatory and Part II performative, the conclusion in Part III is allegorical and completes the task of returning the question of movement to jurisprudence. This is done in this final part by rejoining contemporary jurisprudence with philosophical and ethical traditions of conduct. More precisely, Chapter 5 shifts attention from the technical and material forms of common law practice, the primary subject of previous chapters in Part I and Part II, to matters of conduct by asking: 'How to move well?' Addressed to the jurist, a final example is offered that places repatriation, in this instance a military repatriation of the wrong dead, as both a return to land and a return to law. This serves as a reminder to the jurist of the practical relation between common law and the care of the dead, the technical movements of jurisdiction shaping common law's form and the responsibilities of taking up and holding office. Thinking with common law, in this final chapter, the question of movement is returned to jurisprudence.

Part I
Moving jurisprudence

Chapter 1

The responsible jurist

With multiple forms of law in Australia, including Anglo-Australian common law, indigenous laws and religious laws, it is not surprising that these laws meet in various material and immaterial ways. Yet one quite major problem with the practice of common law is its role in what I suggest is the continued failure of laws to meet well: one of many common law failures in the conduct of lawful relations. Although there may well be other factors contributing to these failures, in this chapter, I argue there is something quite particular to common law and to the way it conducts its practices that contributes – and contributes necessarily – to these destructive legal patterns. Providing a context for the remainder of the book, this chapter introduces some key moments in the Australian legal and political landscape as a way of explaining what it means to 'meet', why I argue laws do not meet well in Australia and why I reframe these meetings into a broader habitual problem with the practice of common law. For common law, as we shall see, not only struggles to meet with other laws, but also struggles in its lawful relations with bodies, both living and the dead, as well as its relations with old and new lands. This is a problem with common law and as such, it is problem for the common law jurist.

What, then, is common law? Despite the legally trained instinct that its meaning is palpable, unmistakeable even, the term 'common law' is not self-explanatory, but rather garners meaning from its context.[1] As medieval legal historian Raoul van Caenegem explains:

> Its basic meaning of 'a law common to various people or provinces or countries' does not by itself mean much: it all depends to what people or countries the law is common. The English common law was historically so called because it was common to the free people of England, who all fell under

[1] See Raoul van Caenegem, 'The Common Law is Different: Ten Illustrations' in *Judges, Legislators and Professors: Chapters in European Legal History* (Cambridge University Press, 1987) 43–4. See also Raoul van Caenegem, *The Birth of the English Common Law* (Cambridge University Press, 1988). See also Tim Murphy, *The Oldest Social Science?: Configurations of Law and Modernity* (Oxford University Press, 1997); Tim Murphy, 'The Oldest Social Science? Configurations of Law and Modernity' (1998) 61(6) *Modern Law Review* 920.

the direct jurisdiction of the central royal courts. This meaning marked the contrast between the common law and various local customs; in a later phase common law was contrasted with statute law, the one being judge-made and the other made by the legislature – this is the current, modern meaning.[2]

As van Caenegem correctly observes, the contemporary understanding of common law is most often one associated with legal cases, judges and courtroom judgments set in dichotomous opposition to another major source of law emanating from legislation, politicians and parliament, that is, statute or statutory law. Yet common law in this sense, as a source of law in a particular legal system made by the judiciary, rather than the legislature, is only one of the ways the phrase is regularly used.

Operating on distinct scales, common law is routinely contextualised in three overly familiar binary couplings: common law and civil law, common law and equity and, of course, common law and statute law (i.e. cases and legislation). In this book, I am less interested in the jurisdictional fusion of law and equity, and while I certainly notice the mannerisms apparent when working with cases as a distinctive legal source, it is a much older concern, one that van Caenegem phrases as 'the contrast between the common law and various local customs',[3] that remains my primary interest. Leaving equity aside, and while not negating the import of the common law mode of *stare decisis* and its technical movements between examples[4] (which comes to the fore later in this chapter as part of this book's particular jurisprudential method), it is the use of the phrase 'common law' in its most far reaching scalular sense, that is, as a mode, type or form of law, and a non-civil law form at that, that is most relevant here.[5] Further, by refusing the lure of thinking about legal 'systems' with its silencing gesture of a non-human coherent wholeness, or luxuriating in smoothly labyrinthine systemic thought, it is in this final sense of common law – not as a system per se – but as one form or shape or mode or way of law, and as one way of thinking law, that opens up the possibility of responding to concerns with the manner and conduct of jurisdictional meetings between heterogeneous ways of law, translating in the idiom of this book into a jurisprudential concern with lawful relations.

Before attending to the importance of movement, and how movement reshapes understandings of certain insidious common law problems, which is the subject

---

2 van Caenegem, 'The Common Law is Different', above, n 1.
3 Ibid.
4 *Stare decisis et non quieta movere* translates into English as 'to stand by decisions and not disturb the undisturbed', which, in practice, means that common law judges should follow precedents and not disturb settled matters. *Stare decisis* forms the crux of the doctrine of precedent, which, in turn, forms the basis of the common law method. On the critique of *stare decisis*, see, e.g., Frederick Schauer, 'Precedent' (1987) 39 *Stanford Law Review* 571; Jeremy Waldron, 'Stare Decisis and the Rule of Law: A Layered Approach' (2012) 111(1) *Michigan Law Review* 1.
5 See, e.g., Murphy, *The Oldest Social Science*, above, n 1. On the distinction between civil law and common law, see van Caenegem, 'The Common Law is Different', above, n 1.

of the next chapter, this chapter asks the more general question of how the jurist might account for and take responsibility for forms of common law practice. Why the jurist? Although there are many distinct offices for those who are legally trained, such as barrister, solicitor, proctor, judge, magistrate and coroner etc., the jurist is the one who has the capacity – as well as the responsibility – to profess, treat and therefore shape understandings of law. As such, the jurist (whether thought of as the lawyer or, more aptly, the legal scholar) has quite a distinct role in relation to the practice and conduct of law, and hence, jurisprudence, and jurisprudential thought. With common law a far from perfect practice, both materially and technically, the jurist's tasks of office include responsibilities to address ongoing and urgent problems with those practices. Amounting to a call for the responsible jurist to redress the practice of common law, which is a call that can be taken up in different ways, this chapter offers one way.

Framed as an address to the responsible jurist, there are three parts to this chapter: the first considers the challenge of lawful relations, the second recollects the office of jurist and the third explains the specific jurisprudential method of a minor jurisprudence used in this book. The first part of this chapter places lawful relations as the context, concern and normative commitment of the book. Serving as the horizon of this minor jurisprudence, 'lawful relations' is a term used to capture something other – and something more – than simply 'legal relations'. More than just a technical legal relation between two objects, whether two laws or otherwise, to be lawful attaches, transfixes, impales, and occasionally, perhaps, even enraptures. An invisible palisade, to be lawful captures both a commitment to and a responsibility for law, and for that which belongs to law. As Andreas Philippopoulos-Mihalopoulos puts it, 'there is no outside'[6] and, if this is true, which I believe it is, then without an outside, we cannot escape law. With law binding and folding our lives, we are corralled and the first task, it seems, is not to panic. The challenge then becomes learning to breathe with this potentially terrible knowledge. To do so, it helps to take seriously the responsibility we all have to live with law, and to conduct our lives with law, and endeavour to conduct that life well: a commitment to lawful relations. It is through this burdened relationship of responsibility to law, which accepts law without denying or ignoring its flaws, and accepts law without abandoning desires for revolution or radical change, that a further set of relations arise. These are relations conducted through the medium of law, including common law's relations with the earth, the living and, most significantly for this book, relations with the dead. Focusing in the first part of the chapter on common law's relations with the dead and common law's relations with indigenous laws as two examples of some of the forms lawful relations take, and how such relations are practised, I argue there is a struggle, at least in these instances, in the creation and conduct of lawful relations.

---

6 Andreas Philippopoulos-Mihalopoulos, *Spatial Justice: Body, Lawscape, Atmosphere* (Routledge, 2014) 1.

With lawful relations as context, the second part of the chapter recollects the office of jurist as both a reminder of what it means to take up and hold office and as a gathering of tasks. Recollecting, the relationship between common law and the jurist is placed as one mediated by office. In a common law country such as Australia, over and above the rights and duties of the common law subject, it is through the mechanism of office that the jurist inherits a particular relation to common law that includes a dynamic arrangement of duties, responsibilities, privileges, tasks, forms of conduct and rights of action. More specifically, these include tasks of observation, description, attendance and care. As part of their official capacities, therefore, the common law jurist takes up a responsibility for the practice of common law, which includes the conduct of lawful relations and a responsibility for the quality of that conduct. Taking seriously the question of office, in this second part of the chapter, the conduct of lawful relations is placed as part of the jurist's responsibilities of office.

Yet, in order to take responsibility for the conduct of lawful relations, the jurist must attend to the practice of common law, including how it manifests in both technical and material forms. While always a question of how one conducts office, one way is for the jurist to act jurisprudentially. The final part of the chapter explains how this is done. In a book that creates a minor jurisprudence, the method is first and foremost jurisprudential. Accepting the institution of common law, or to borrow the language of Philippopoulos-Mihalopoulos, accepting 'there is no outside',[7] this method involves thinking *with* common law, as distinct from thinking against or thinking, somehow, outside of common law. In later chapters, this 'with-ness' is performed through two case studies through practices of paradiastole (i.e. redescription), which mimic the use of the common law example.[8] Using what is described as a jurisprudential 'method of slowness' that involves the narration and redescription of two sets of quite distinct primary legal materials, this method reveals the place of movement in common law practice on a register that is otherwise often overlooked or if not overlooked, rendered meaningless.

Therefore, to summarise what is to come, this chapter introduces a context of lawful relations, recollects the office of jurist and explains the method of this book. The primary work of the chapter is to remind the jurist of their responsibilities of office, with an offering of assistance in the form of a minor jurisprudence. In this first chapter, therefore, the responsible jurist is slowly, gently, carefully and caringly nudged to the fore.

---

7 Ibid.
8 See, e.g., Quentin Skinner, *Reason and Rhetoric in the Philosophy of Hobbes* (Cambridge University Press, 1996). See also Quentin Skinner, 'Paradiastole: Redescribing the Vices as Virtues', in Sylvia Anderson, Gavin Alexander and Katrin Ettenhuber (eds.), *Renaissance Figures of Speech* (Cambridge University Press, 2007) ch 8.

1.1 Lawful relations

There are many different types of law in Australia today. It is important to understand this, as it is only by noticing the multiplicity of legal forms that it becomes possible to account for the manner in which common law is practised, and how its practice consistently operates in relation to not only other laws, but also in relation to bodies and lands. Before attending to the nature and quality of common law's relations in this broader context, that is, in relation to bodies and lands, common law's relations with other laws are introduced, followed by an explanation of why I argue laws do not seem to meet very well in Australia and why this is a question of lawful relations.

To begin, it is necessary to acknowledge, and take seriously, the existence and continued practice of multiple forms of law in Australia, today. This acknowledgement is the legal, political and ethical starting point of this book, and one I will insist on. In Australia, long before its federal birth as a nation on 1 January 1901, hundreds of distinct indigenous laws in their uniquely particular sovereign forms with deep territorial attachments were practised.[9] Despite the impacts of '"settler" colonialism' with its concomitant logic of elimination,[10] indigenous laws continue to be exercised today.[11] Yet, often such forms of law, which do not carry the status of national legal systems in the Westphalian sense of sovereign statehood, are gently but forcefully sidled away from the parameters of the word 'law'. Labelled customary law, custom or simply norm in contemporary legal, political and public discourse, there is something a little bit different, a little unique, and a little 'lesser' that undermines this linguistic arm wrestling; relentlessly placing indigenous forms of law as not-quite-law. In the common law domain, at least in settler–colonial societies such as Australia and Canada, Aboriginal law is often labelled *sui generis* (of its own genus or kind; unique) to mark this difference.[12] Yet for many indigenous

---

9 On the legal structure of modern Australia, see *Commonwealth of Australia Constitution Act 1900* (Imp) 63 & 64 Vict, c 12, s 9. On the legal structure of the *Djang*, central to some indigenous forms of law, see Bill Neidjie, *Story about Feeling* (Magabala Books, 1989). See, especially, Christine Black, *The Land is the Source of the Law: A Dialogic Encounter with Indigenous Jurisprudence* (Routledge, 2011).

10 Patrick Wolfe, 'Nation and MiscegeNation: Discursive Continuity in the Post-Mabo Era' (1994) 36 *Social Analysis* 93; Patrick Wolfe, *Settler Colonialism and the Transformation of Anthropology: the Politics and Poetics of an Ethnographic Event* (Cassell, 1999); Patrick Wolfe, 'Settler Colonialism and the Elimination of the Native' (2006) 8(4) *Journal of Genocide Research* 387.

11 See, especially, Black, *The Land is the Source of the Law*, above, n 9; Neidjie, *Story about Feeling*, above, n 9; Bill Neidjie, *Speaking for the Earth: Nature's Law and the Aboriginal Way* (Center for Respect of Life and Environment, 1991); Paddy Roe with Stephen Muecke (ed.), *Gularabulu: Stories from the West Kimberley* (Fremantle Arts Centre Press, 1983); Krim Benterrak, Stephen Muecke and Paddy Roe, *Reading the Country: Introduction to Nomadology* (Fremantle Arts Centre Press, 1984); Michael Dodson and Olivia Barr, 'Breaking the Deadlock: Developing an Indigenous Response to Protecting Indigenous Traditional Knowledge' (2007) 11(2) *Australian Indigenous Law Review* 19. See also Law Reform Commission of Western Australia, *Aboriginal Customary Laws*, Report No 94 (2006).

12 For two examples of how resonances of the label '*sui generis*' shape common law judgments, some more overtly than others, see the Canadian Supreme Court decision of *Delgamuukw v British Columbia* [1997] 3 SCR 1010, especially in relation to Justice McEachern's decision at first instance

peoples, the insistence on the word law – as well as the word sovereignty – is essential to the conduct of a lawful life; a life lived with indigenous law.[13]

In some respects, most obviously through the recognition of a multiplicity of legal forms, this book follows the well-trodden path of legal anthropology, legal pluralism and critical legal pluralism.[14] Yet this is neither a work in legal anthropology nor in legal pluralism for the following and quite straightforward reason: this is a jurisprudential work tuned into one type of law. Focusing on common law, and as a result of its cautionary approach towards lines explained in the opening walks of the introductory chapter, it is important to notice the bifurcating line between law and non-law as one that conceals possibilities.[15] Certainly the possibility of engaging in meaningful relations – especially meaningful lawful relations – diminishes when one form of law (i.e. common law) fails to recognise another form of law *as* law (i.e. indigenous law). In order to notice these possibilities, I choose not to adopt this particular line; this particular divide. It is simply not necessary. Instead, in this book, I carve out a different approach. Focusing on one specific type or mode of law, Anglo-Australian common law, my starting assumption is an acceptance that common law exists in a context of a multiplicity of legal forms which operate as different mechanisms of legal ordering, including indigenous and religious laws, irrespective of whether they may more commonly carry the naming of legal systems, customs, or religious or moral codes. While an acknowledgement of multiple forms of law is not the subject matter of this book, this acknowledgment is the horizon, and as such constitutes a normative commitment to the possibility of lawful relations. To be clear, in a jurisprudential book concerned with the form and practice of common law in the creation and conduct of lawful relations, this is an intentional and considered stance.

To illustrate the relationship between the ongoing practice of common law, and why the quality of lawful relations is at times lacking in Australia, two examples are provided. The first is the example of common law's relations with other forms of law in general, before focusing on relations with indigenous law to illustrate how laws do not meet well. The second is a distinctly different example of lawful relations that goes beyond the more obvious meeting of laws to consider how common law relates to bodies, and in particular, how common law relates to the

---

in *Delgamuukw v British Columbia* [1991] 3 WWR 97). For an Australian example, see *R v Minor* (1992) 105 FLR 180.

13 See, e.g., Audra Simpson, *Mohawk Interruptus: Political Life Across the Borders of Settler States* (Duke University Press, 2014); Larissa Behrendt, *Achieving Social Justice: Indigenous Rights and Australia's Future* (Federation Press, 2003); Black, *The Land is the Source of the Law*, above, n 9.

14 On legal pluralism and critical legal pluralism, see, e.g., Martha-Marie Kleinhans and Roderick A. Macdonald, 'What is a *Critical* Legal Pluralism?' (1997) 12 *Canadian Journal of Law and Society* 25. On legal anthropology, see, e.g., John L. Comaroff and Jean Comaroff, 'Reflections on the Anthropology of Law, Governance, and Sovereignty', in Franz von Benda-Beckmann, Keebet von Benda-Beckmann and Julia M Eckert (eds.), *Rules of Law and Laws of Ruling: on the Governance of Law* (Ashgate Publishing, 2009) ch 2.

15 On lines concealing possibilities, see Paul Carter, *Dark Writing: Geography, Performance, Design* (University of Hawai'i Press, 2009).

dead. In later chapters, especially Chapter 4 in the context of Antarctica, the argument in relation to laws and bodies is extended to how common law also struggles in relation to land. For now, however, two examples addressing common law's relations with indigenous law and the dead show how common law struggles in its relations with not only other laws but also other bodies and, as a result, why I argue the quality of lawful relations is questionable in Australia.

A problem with lawful relations: laws do not meet well

Having acknowledged the continued practice of multiple forms of law in Australia, it is now possible to attend to the meeting. How do laws meet? As with any other context where multiple forms inhabit a particular space, whether those forms are bodies, material objects, abstract ideas or, as in this case, laws, meetings tend to occur. For example, laws meet domestically. Constitutional law in Australia regulates state and federal relations, with section 109 of the *Commonwealth Constitution* regulating the rules that govern meetings between federal and state laws; the technical means by which these different forms of common law relate.[16] State laws also meet constitutionally, clashing at times in the High Court of Australia (Australia's peak court), but also meeting more literally and materially at sites of the border, whether along roads, amid rivers or misplaced railway stations.[17] Not just domestically, however, laws also meet internationally. Think of treaties, trade deals, extradition proceedings etc., as well as the movement of bodies as they locate and relocate in relation to different nations. Whether as citizen, migrant or refugee, there is a relation between international law, the status of the person and the domestic laws in place: a meeting of laws.

Laws also meet on more minor registers, irrespective of the modern state. Take the ceremony of marriage as an example. Historically governed by an ecclesiastical jurisdiction, the jurisdiction of marriage was effectively co-opted by common law in a slow move from church to state. With jurisdictional boundaries sharply debated, the definition of marriage is now a matter governed by common law and guarded by the State.[18] Yet, far from denying the role of religion in contemporary marriage, as evident in certain lines of reasoning in contemporary debates surrounding same-sex marriage, the act of marriage continues to involve a meeting of laws: religious and common. In addition to the statutory representation of common law marriage in the Australian *Family Law Act 1975* (Cth) binding two

---

16 *Commonwealth of Australia Constitution Act 1900* (Imp) 63 & 64 Vict, c 12, s 9.
17 For example, consider the various forms of co-regulation of communities located at or near state borders, such as those bordering South Australia, Western Australia and the Northern Territory where power-sharing arrangements often fluctuate but at times have included shared policing as well as combined service provision. Consider, too, the regulation of the Murray River, historically, as well as contemporary shared arrangements, such as those practised through the Murray-Darling Basin Authority.
18 See, e.g., Michael Kirby, 'Foreword', in Victor Marsh (ed.), *Speak Now: Australian Perspectives on Same-Sex Marriage* (Clouds of Magellan, 2011).

people before the state, in some ceremonies, there is also the presence and practice of a religious law, binding two people before their divinities. In such circumstances, the ceremony of marriage becomes not only the ritualised meeting of two people formalising relations under one law, but also a ceremonial meeting of laws.

More broadly, long before the modern state came to dominate (and limit) understandings of 'what law is', let alone deny meetings between laws, consider historical meetings of English common law with interlacing jurisdictions of ecclesiastical, equity, hundred, manorial, tannery, forest, merchant and admiralty laws.[19] These laws met, crossed and related in a number of ways, with common law gradually dominating in both time and space.[20] Towards the end of the eighteenth century when the Colony of New South Wales was established, except for the overhang of several of these jurisdictions, most notably equity, it seems to me that common law was no longer in the *jurisdictional habit* of meeting with other forms of law (an argument elaborated in the next chapter) and, not surprisingly, the quality of the meeting declined. When it comes to the arrival, movement and placement of common law in Australia, although having visited previously, it was not until 1788, 18 years after Britain's technical 'discovery' of the Colony of New South Wales, that English law, including common law, was introduced, and brought into relation with a land, as well as other forms of law, it had not previously engaged.[21] The 'meetings of law', therefore, is a phrase that captures a wide variety of legal meetings both domestically and internationally, as well as more informal meetings where the state is not so prescient, such as jurisdictional arrangements in early modern England, colonial ventures or even marriage ceremonies. When it comes to such varied meetings of laws, although certainly not always so, I argue that in Australia there is a pattern that tends towards laws not meeting well, which is an example of the broader problem with lawful relations. To appreciate the significance of this observation, and the depth of this sentiment, consider the example of relations between common law and indigenous laws.

While meetings between common law and indigenous laws are more than the first moments of colonisation, the first meeting haunts.[22] This is a meeting – or more aptly, a non-meeting – often narrated through the deceptively tidy story of

---

19 See, e.g., Frederick Pollock and Frederic W. Maitland, *The History of English Law Before the Time of Edward I* (Cambridge University Press, 1905). See also Frederic W. Maitland, *The Constitutional History of England* (Cambridge University Press, 1920).
20 On how these meetings are a question of jurisdiction, see Shaunnagh Dorsett and Shaun McVeigh, *Jurisdiction* (Routledge Cavendish, 2012), which is an argument expanded on in Chapter 2.
21 See Chapter 3, 3.1 for further detail on this introduction in the context of colonial New South Wales.
22 See, generally, Paul McHugh, *Aboriginal Societies and the Common Law: A History of Sovereignty, Status, and Self-Determination* (Oxford University Press, 2004); Henry Reynolds, *Aboriginal Sovereignty: Reflections on Race, State and Nation* (Allen & Unwin, 1996); Michael Mansell, 'The Bicentenary and Aboriginal Sovereignty' (1988) 62 *Law Institute Journal* 1206; Stewart Motha, 'The Sovereign Event in a Nation's Law' (2002) 13(3) *Law and Critique* 311; Paul Muldoon, 'The Sovereign Exceptions: Colonization and the Foundation of Society' (2008) 17(1) *Social and Legal Studies* 59; Peter Rush, 'Surviving Common Law: Silence and the Violence Internal to the Legal Sign' (2005) 27(2) *Cardozo*

the doctrine of discovery.²³ Offering three categories of 'discovery', that is, either conquered, ceded or settled, each category offers a different arrangement for the meeting of laws in a newly 'discovered' territory.²⁴ In the Colony of New South Wales, despite the presence of indigenous peoples and practice of indigenous laws, the doctrine of discovery came to be applied through the category of the settled.²⁵ This particular category is notoriously based on an idea of spatial and legal emptiness.²⁶ Initially intended for and applied to unpopulated lands, where the new arriver just arrives, with no one to treat or wage war, the doctrine of *terra nullius* forms the cornerstone of this 'settled' category of the doctrine of discovery.²⁷ *Terra nullius*, which colloquially translates as 'empty land' or 'land belonging to no one', was conceptually stretched and expanded in both time and space to retro-fit a land and society where the forms of law were – at least on one interpretation – not recognisable to the conqueror.²⁸ What this meant was that in Australia, the doctrine of discovery was applied *as if* it were 'settled' and interpreted in such a manner as to deny the original (and also continued) meetings of laws. For in the case of a settled colony, where it is assumed there are no other laws inhabiting the emptiness, the laws of the coloniser apply unimpeded – without meeting – unlike the categories of conquered or ceded, where colonial law is subject to some form of meeting, whether through the laws of war or diplomatic treaties. Settled, on this formal basis, at least from the point of view of English common law, supported by the law of nations (i.e. international law), there was no formal meeting of laws in the Colony of New South Wales.

Yet, there clearly was, and not only one, but multiple meetings of laws. While early nineteenth-century New South Wales Supreme Court decisions, such as *R v Ballard*, *R v Murrell* and *R v Bonjon*,²⁹ are commonly referred to as especially lucid displays of these meetings, as well as their limits, a more personal and quietly

Law Review 753; Peter Fitzpatrick, '"No Higher Duty": *Mabo* and the Failure of Legal Foundation' (2002) 13 *Law and Critique* 233.
23 See Shaunnagh Dorsett and Shaun McVeigh, 'Just So: "The Law which Governs Australia is Australian Law"' (2002) 13 *Law and Critique* 289, 294. On *terra nullius*, see Andrew Fitzmaurice, 'The Genealogy of *Terra Nullius*' (2007) 38(129) *Australian Historical Studies* 1; David Ritter, 'The "Rejection of Terra Nullius" in *Mabo*: A Critical Analysis' (1996) 18(1) *Sydney Law Review* 5. On meetings as non-meetings, see Paul Carter, *The Human Encounter and the Challenge of Coexistence* (University of Minnesota Press, 2013).
24 See, generally, Robert J. Miller et al. (eds.), *Discovering Indigenous Lands: The Doctrine of Discovery in the English Colonies* (Oxford University Press, 2010).
25 *Cooper v Stuart* (1889) 14 App Cas 286. See, generally, ibid, ch 7.
26 See, especially, Colin Perrin (ed.), *In the Wake of Terra Nullius* (Prospect Media Pty Ltd, 1998).
27 This was especially so in Australia; see, generally, Michael Connor, *The Invention of Terra Nullius: Historical and Legal Fictions on the Foundation of Australia* (Macleay Press, 2005).
28 On how this 'retro-fitting' of terra nullius came to be remembered as originary, see Fitzmaurice, 'The Genealogy of Terra Nullis', above, n 23.
29 *R v Ballard or Barrett* [1829] NSWSupC 26 ('*Ballard*'); sub nom *R v Dirty Dick* (1828) NSW Sel Cas (Dowling) 2 ('*Dirty Dick*'); *R v Murrell* (1836) 1 Legge 72; [1836] NSWSupC 35 ('*Murrell*'); *R v Bonjon* (Unreported, Supreme Court of New South Wales, Port Phillip District, Willis J, 18 April 1841) ('*Bonjon*').

pervasive example is the late eighteenth-century relationship between William Dawes, the First Fleet surveyor, and Patyegarang, a Cadigal woman. Consider the conduct of this relationship: not only a meeting of persons, this relationship was also a meeting of laws. As Paul Carter describes, present in the friendship of William Dawes and Patyegarang was a legal dramaturgy of a middle ground:

> In performances that were gestural as well as verbal, they marked out a middle ground where the laws governing both of them were placed in parenthesis, and new, provisional rules of exchange improvised.[30]

What is most interesting in Carter's exposure of Dawes and Patyegarang is the way in which partial recordings of how two people met becomes a rich and increasingly interpreted example of not only a meeting, or even a relationship, but the creation and conduct of lawful relations.[31] Not just a linguistic exchange or a deepening friendship of both use and pleasure, and potentially of the good, to use Aristotle's terms,[32] Carter notices how it was through the conduct of this relationship between an Aboriginal woman and an English man that different forms of law came into relation during the first two years of colonial settlement in Sydney.

Of course, this was not the only meeting of laws. As with Dawes and Patyegarang, who improvised rules of exchange throughout the course of their meetings, the jurisdictional coming into relation between common law and indigenous laws does not end with a single meeting of laws, neither then, nor now. Consider the series of strikingly overt recognitions of indigenous forms of law in the first decades of the Colony of New South Wales, addressed in more detail in the next chapter as questions of jurisdiction.[33] These include both the Governor and the Judge-Advocate's tentative involvement in settler–Aboriginal disputes, an explicit long-term practice of non-prosecution of intra-Aboriginal disputes, Governor Arthurs' pictorial proclamation nailed to trees, let alone more personal interactions, such

---

30 Paul Carter, 'Public Space: Its Mythopoetic Foundations and the Limits of the Law' (2007) 16(2) *Griffith Law Review* 430.
31 *Patyegarang* (Performed by Bangarra Dance Theatre, 2014); *The Spirit of Patyegarang* (Bangarra Dance Theatre, Vivid Sydney, 2014), http://bangarra.com.au/the-spirit-of-patyegarang. For a ficto-critical or speculative engagement with these notebooks, see Ross Gibson, *26 Views of the Starburst World: William Dawes at Sydney Cove 1788–91* (UWA Publishing, 2012). See also Carter, 'Public Space', above, n 30.
32 Aristotle, *Nichomachean Ethics*, Books VII–XIV.
33 See above, n 29. *Murrell* was published by George Legge using limited resources some 60 years after the decision in J.G. Legge, *A Selection of Supreme Court Cases in New South Wales from 1825 to 1862* (Charles Potter, Government Printer, 1896) vols I, II; Bruce Kercher, 'Recovering and Reporting Australia's Early Colonial Case Law: The Macquarie Project' (2000) 18(3) *Law and History Review* 659. Including a re-reporting of *Murrell*, this series of cases were initially reported in Bruce Kercher, '*R v Ballard, R v Murrell, R v Bonjon*' (1998) 3(3) *Australian Indigenous Law Reporter* 410, and more recently in Bruce Kercher and Brent Salter (eds.), *The Kercher Reports: Decisions of the New South Wales Superior Courts, 1788–1827* (Francis Forbes Society for Australian Legal History, 2009) ('*Kercher Reports*').

as Dawes and Patyegarang's, captured in letters, notebooks and diaries.[34] What becomes clear from such colonial histories of legal meetings, which others have addressed in much more detail, is that despite the doctrine of discovery, and contemporary understandings of the manner in which it was applied (settled; *terra nullius*), common law and indigenous laws met, and it was not simply a one-off meeting, but a series of meetings that continued, and continues to continue.

While meetings continue between indigenous laws and common laws, over time, with the impact of colonisation, the site of these meetings, that is, the 'meeting place' has certainly moved. Although in the legal and institutional shift from late eighteenth-century colonial New South Wales to post-federation Australia in the twenty-first century, the continued meeting of laws is still apparent, the meeting place has shifted from what could be considered 'external' to areas 'internal' to common law.[35] Consider the landmark 1992 Australian High Court decision in *Mabo, Queensland (No 2)*, which established the common law doctrine of native title for the first time in Australia.[36] No longer external to the common law, the 'internal' common law doctrine of native title can be understood as a meeting of laws, albeit one conducted solely through common law's idiom.[37] Similarly, the existence and continued practice of indigenous laws, while clearly known by those who continue to live with indigenous law, is also tacitly recognised by the common law in areas such as family law, criminal sentencing, wills and estates and education.[38] Coming in the form of common law recognition,[39] there is clearly a power imbalance. Yet despite this imbalance, these 'internal' recognitions also constitute meetings between different forms of law.[40]

While laws continue to meet, in some obvious and less than obvious ways, my point is that they often do not meet well. The failure to meet well is most explicit in the example of Aboriginal sovereignty, which is an example often returned to in this book, and one that centres on the High Court of Australia's persistent refusal

---

34 See, e.g., Governor Macquarie's Proclamation to the Aborigines, 4 May 1816 in *Historical Records of Australia* Series 1, vol 9, 141; Desmond Manderson, 'Governor Arthur's Proclamation: Images of the Rule of Law', in Oren Ben-Dor (ed.), *Law and Art: Justice, Ethics and Aesthetics* (Routledge, 2011) 288–304.
35 Shaunnagh Dorsett and Shaun McVeigh, 'Conduct of Laws: Native Title, Responsibility and Some Limits of Jurisdictional Thinking' (2012) 36 *Melbourne University Law Review* 470.
36 *Mabo v Queensland (No 2)* (1992) 175 CLR 1 ('*Mabo (No 2)*').
37 Dorsett and McVeigh, 'Conduct of Laws', above, n 35.
38 See also Law Reform Commission of Western Australia, above, n 11.
39 On the critique of recognition, see, e.g., James C. Scott, *Seeing like a State: How Certain Schemes to Improve the Human Condition have Failed* (Yale University Press, 1988); Simpson, *Mohawk Interruptus*, above, n 13.
40 On common law recognition, see, generally, Paul McHugh, *Aboriginal Title: The Modern Jurisprudence of Land Rights* (Oxford University Press, 2011); Paul McHugh, *Common Law Aboriginal Title* (Clarendon Press, 1989); John Borrows, *Recovering Canada: The Resurgence of Indigenous Law* (University of Toronto Press, 2002). On the politics of recognition, see, generally, Charles Taylor et al., in Amy Gutmann (ed.), *Multiculturalism and 'The Politics of Recognition'* (Princeton University Press, 2nd edn, 1994). On meetings between the coloniser and the colonised, see, generally, Albert Memmi, *The Colonizer and the Colonized* (Howard Greenfield trans., Earthscan, 1990) [trans. of *Portrait du Colonise Precede du Portrait du Colinisateur* (first published 1957)].

to address questions of Aboriginal sovereignty.[41] Briefly, on several occasions, the High Court has been directly confronted with the question of the continued existence of Aboriginal sovereignty.[42] On each occasion, the High Court has stated and consistently reiterated that questions of Aboriginal sovereignty are non-justiciable, that is, the issue is not subject to the jurisdiction of this particular court; another non-meeting one could say. From the initial statement in the 1979 decision of *Coe v Commonwealth (No 1)*, the High Court has consistently declared Aboriginal sovereignty non-justiciable, even since the recognition of native title in *Mabo (No 2)*.[43] Significantly, non-justiciability does not amount to a High Court claim that Aboriginal sovereignty does not exist, but rather, and more subtly, that questions of Aboriginal sovereignty are not within the realm or domain of the High Court's jurisdiction. As explored further in the next chapter, while these cases may seem to address a question of sovereignty – and hence competing or clashing sovereignties – they are, in fact, better understood as a question of jurisdiction (and also, as we shall see, questions of movement and space). Put simply, when it comes to questions of Aboriginal sovereignty, there is no common law jurisdiction. Therefore, while a meeting between laws – between common law and indigenous law – has been approached, in these instances, no meeting has occurred. Through a series of High Court judgments, Anglo-Australian common law has, in effect, 'walked away' from any such meeting under the cover of a common law procedural technique of non-justiciability. This inability to relate jurisdictionally to indigenous forms of law, and the manner and expression of this inability, is a particularly stark instance of laws not meeting well.

To summarise, from the uncertain application of the doctrine of discovery to the High Court of Australia's avoidance of consideration of questions of Aboriginal sovereignty, common law and indigenous laws do not meet well. If they meet at all, it is with unevenness, uncertainty, an often overwhelming imbalance of power and, quite frankly, for common law at least, a lack of understanding and respect for indigenous forms of law *as* law. However, it is not simply these common law meetings that are problematic. These examples are merely indicative of a broader problem with the common law practice of creating, and conducting, lawful relations. Therefore, in addition to struggling in its relation with other forms of law, as we shall see, common law also struggles in its relations with bodies too, especially the dead.

---

41 With a vast literature on theories of sovereignty, colonial sovereignty and indigenous sovereignty, including the politics of terminology, the term 'Aboriginal sovereignty' is used here to reflect the way it was used in these High Court cases.
42 *Coe v Commonwealth* (1979) 24 ALR 118 ('*Coe (No 1)*') established the common law position that Aboriginal sovereignty is non-justiciable. See also *Mabo (No 2)* (1992) 175 CLR 1; *Coe (on behalf of the Wiradjuri tribe) v Commonwealth of Australia* (1993) 118 ALR 193 ('*Coe (No 2)*'); *Walker v New South Wales* (1994) 182 CLR 45; *Thorpe v Commonwealth of Australia (No 3)* (1997) 144 ALR 677; *Members of the Yorta Yorta Aboriginal Community v Victoria* (2002) 214 CLR 422; *R v Buzzacott* (2004) 154 ACTR 37. See also *Re Phillips; Ex parte Aboriginal Development Commission* (1987) 13 FCR 384; *Commonwealth v Coe* [2002] NSWSC 94 (26 February 2002).
43 Ibid.

Introducing the dead as a topic of lawful relations

In its most general sense, to introduce is to lead or to bring something into place, position, state, condition or relation to something.[44] It is to move something into relation. In this case, the 'something' is Anglo-Australian common law and the task here is to bring the dead into relation with common law. Although, this is perhaps a little misleading as what is being introduced is, first, that there is a relation between common law and the dead and, second, that this is a relation *of* common law: a lawful relation. As will become evident, like common law and Aboriginal law, the shape and quality of relations between common law and the dead is not without its difficulties.

Who are the dead? But if 'who' implies a living subject, perhaps this is the wrong question? Yet to ask 'what' is the dead is too callous. How, then, might we talk of the dead? Defined in opposition to the living, having passed the limit of life, having moved through the moment of death, the dead are quite simply the dead. However, it is important to be clear that it is the dead, and not death, that is attended to in this book. Attending to the dead is not the same as the challenge of living with death, which is a challenge, as Zygmunt Bauman notes, not only that we know, but that we know that we know.[45] Despite the inherent uncertainties of death, including uncertainties of its time and manner of arrival, its paradoxical phenomenology as never-quite-experienced, and its unknown metaphysical and theological consequences, it is the certainty of the eventuality of death and the certainty of its materiality that is significant for the purposes of this book.[46] While much can be said on death, the concern here is not an anthropological, theological or philosophical concern with death, but a jurisprudential concern with the dead, and common law's practices in relation to the dead. For although I am sympathetic to Arthur Schopenhauer's comment that 'without death there would hardly have been any philosophizing',[47] it may be more apt, albeit with a little

---

44 Charles Talbut Onions (ed.), *The Oxford English Dictionary of English Etymology* (Clarendon Press, 1966); Robert K. Barnhart and Sol Steinmetz (eds.), *Chambers Dictionary of Etymology* (Chambers, 1998).
45 Zygmunt Bauman, *Mortality, Immortality and Other Life Strategies* (Polity Press, 1992) ch 1. See also Maurice Merleau-Ponty, *Phenomenology of Perception* (Colin Smith trans., Routledge, 1962) [trans. of *Phénoménologie de la Perception* (first published 1945)].
46 See, generally, Plato, 'Phaedo' in *Dialogues of Plato* (Benjamin Jowett trans., 1999); Plotinus, *The Enneads* (Stephen MacKenna trans., faber, 1969); Epicurus, 'Letter to Menoeceus', in Louis P. Pojman and Lewis Vaughn (eds.), *Classics of Philosophy* (Oxford University Press, 2011) ch 4; Saint Augustine, *Saint Austins Care for the Dead, or His Book De Curâ pro Mortuis* (English trans., 2nd revised edn, 1651) [trans. of *De Curâ pro Mortuis*]; Martin Heidegger, *Being and Time* (John Macquarie and Edward Robinson trans., Harper & Row, 1962) [trans. of *Sein und Zeit* (first published 1927)]; Jean Baudrillard, *Symbolic Exchange and Death* (Iain Hamilton Grant trans., Sage, 1993) [trans. of *L'echange Symbolique et la Mort* (first published 1976)]; Gillian Rose, *Mourning Becomes the Law: Philosophy and Representation* (Cambridge University Press, 1996).
47 Arthur Schopenhauer wrote, 'Death is the real inspiring genius or Musagetes of philosophy, and for this reason Socrates defined philosophy as "preparation for death". Indeed, without death there would hardly have been any philosophizing': Arthur Schopenhauer, *The World as Will*

indulgence, to rephrase this as 'without the dead, there is no common law.' Less indulgently, the point to be made is that to attend to the dead is not the same as contemplating death. More particularly, rather than a concern with law's relation to death, a jurisprudential concern with the dead is a concern with the form and conduct of common law's relations with the dead.

In a jurisprudence of movement, contemplating common law's place, why the dead? Quite simply, because it is from the dead we inherit common law. Consider time immemorial, the 'age of indefinite time'.[48] As the apparent source of common law, from somewhen before, the dead are part of the common law tradition. Without the dead, there would be no tradition: no common law tradition. Similarly, consider the doctrine of precedent as a technical device of transmission; a technique of movement that passes from the dead. As part of the common law tradition, the dead are those who came before, ordering the time of common law's past, present and future. An introduction to the dead, therefore, is a bringing into relation of common law and the dead, which is a reminder of the dead as common law's inheritance, and as part of the common law tradition. This is the dead of law; common law's dead.

To this end, it is the 'dead of law' and not the 'dead as such' that require attendance, and are addressed in this book.[49] This is the dead as inheritance and as part of the Anglo-Australian common law tradition. For an example of how the dead might figure as part of the common law tradition, consider the King's two bodies.[50] From the King's two bodies, sovereignty emanates and so too does public law. And it is on the death of the King that sovereignty passes; a transmission or movement of law between the two bodies of the King. It is on the death of the King we inherit sovereignty and through succession, the institution and ordering of public law. Likewise, this is similar for private law or at least property law. For example, consider the history of common law property. Owned by the head of the household, it was on the death of the father that property passed to the eldest son, and so too private law. Unable to be transferred in life, it was only through death that rights in private property passed: movements from the dead to the living. Although requirements for transfer have since expanded, allowing transfers between the living, it is from the dead we inherit property; the common

---

and Representation (E.F.J. Payne trans., Dover Publications, 1969) [trans. of *Die Welt als Wille und Vorstellung* (first published 1819)] vol 2, ch XLI, 463. Similarly, as Montaigne writes, 'Cicero says "that to study philosophy is nothing but to prepare one's self to die"': Michel de Montaigne, 'That to Philosophize is to Learn to Die', in Michel de Montaigne, *The Complete Works: Essays, Travel Journal, Letters* (Donald M. Frame trans., Alfred A. Knopf, 2003) Essay 20.

48 Peter Goodrich, *Oedipus Lex: Psychoanalysis, History, Law* (University of California Press, 1995) 26. See also Peter Goodrich and Yfat Hachamovitch, 'Time Out of Mind: An Introduction to the Semiotics of Common Law', in Peter Fitzpatrick (ed.), *Dangerous Supplements: Resistance and Renewal in Jurisprudence* (Pluto Press, 1991) 167.

49 See, generally, Desmond Manderson (ed.), *Courting Death: The Law of Mortality* (Pluto Press, 1999).

50 Ernst Kantorowicz, *The King's Two Bodies: A Study in Medieval Political Theology* (Princeton University Press, 1957).

law tradition of property law. This is what I mean by the dead of law, and part of the common law tradition.

Perhaps not surprisingly, common law's relations with the dead are in many ways quite complex and it could be said, at times decidedly odd. As explained in more detail in Chapter 2, categorised as neither person nor property, common law struggles to classify, regulate, govern, attach and mark its dead. Instead, in a nineteenth-century response to increased grave robbing and in unsupported support of medical demands for cadavers, common law bound that which does not slip so easily through classification, such as the shroud, sepulchre or burial site. Unable to bind the dead directly, common law now binds that which attaches to the dead. Given the status of the dead in relation to common law is not entirely clear, as neither person nor property, the dead tend to fall out of or slip through classification. In this book, this 'falling' (or this movement) is understood as a struggle to relate; common law's struggle to relate to the dead. It is important to note, however, that this struggle is not new: it is part of the common law tradition.[51] Leaving aside the precise nature or resolution of this struggle, and the complex philosophical questions it raises, it is enough to simply notice and hold onto this struggle as a part of common law practice. This is a struggle of common law, a common law struggle in relation, and more particularly in the creation and conduct of lawful relations.

In this regard, this is the question of lawfulness as a question of how to live with law: a question of conduct, which is accounted for in this minor jurisprudence by attending to the form and conduct of common law's relations with the dead. Placing the dead as part of the common law tradition, I am suggesting the relation between common law and the dead is a lawful one. The conduct of common law's relations with the dead then becomes a matter of lawfulness, in the sense of both a commitment to tradition, and as explained in Chapter 2, a responsibility for place. As such, the question of lawfulness and the question of how to live with the Anglo-Australian common law tradition demand an account of common law's relations with the dead, which I refer to as the jurist's responsibility to care for the dead. For a commitment to law includes a commitment to attend to and care for the forms and practices of common law, which includes common law's relations with the dead as one of the ways in which common law comes to be in place.

Acknowledging the lawful nature of this relation also serves as a reminder of the mythopoetic relationship we have and common law seems to have with the dead. As both tradition and mythopoesis, this locates the dead in relation to common law, and in a relation of lawfulness. With lawfulness requiring both care and attendance, it is necessary to be both careful and caring in the conduct of lawful relations with the dead. As such, for the jurist, soon to be introduced to what it means to

---

51 For an historical anthropology of the place of the dead in Roman law, see Yan Thomas, '*Res Religiosae*: On the Categories of Religion and Commerce in Roman Law', in Alain Pottage and Martha Mundy (eds.), *Law, Anthropology, and the Constitution of the Social: Making Persons and Things* (Cambridge University Press, 2004) ch 2.

take up office in the next part of the chapter, this introduction serves as preparation for the tasks of attending to common law's relations with the dead as a matter of office, which is a jurisprudential concern with the form of common law's relation with the dead and the conduct of that relation. Simply put, this can be understood as the responsibility to care for the dead as a mode of creating and engaging lawful relations. For the jurist, taking up and holding office, what this means is that the creation and conduct of lawful relations involves caring for the dead, which is a matter of practice, and one that requires practical wisdom, judgment and care.

To summarise, by introducing and bringing the dead into relation with common law, the introduction offered here has been one of the dead as part of the common law tradition. Less concerned with theological or metaphysical demands of the dead, the concern here is a jurisprudential one: a concern with the form of common law's relation with the dead and the conduct of that relation. This is a necessarily thin account of the dead, because although questions of the dead cross philosophy, theology, anthropology and more closely both the critical and social question of the dead in law, attending to the dead of common law rather than the dead as such, it is for the jurist to be both careful and caring in the conduct of relations with the dead.[52] As this book unfolds, this is framed as a responsibility to care for the dead, which is a jurisprudential concern with the technical and material forms of common law practice, and hence, the conduct of lawful relations. Directed to the jurist, and placing common law's relations with the dead as lawful, this is a reminder to care for the dead as part of the creation and conduct of lawful relations.

Therefore, in this first part of Chapter 1, the context of lawful relations has been raised as both a concern with and a commitment to common law and its practices. This included recognising multiple forms of laws in Australia, observing that these laws often do not meet well, especially common law and indigenous laws, and also accepting the dead as part of what it means to create and conduct lawful relations. The context of this book is quite simply an observation that lawful relations are problematic in Australia, and need to be attended to. In the next part of the chapter, the need to attend to common law and its practices is directed to the office of jurist.

1.2 Recollecting the office of jurist

This part recollects the office of the jurist. This is a reminder of the significance of office, and the importance of taking care to contemplate and attend to what

---

52 See Introduction. See, generally, Manderson (ed.), *Courting Death*, above, n 49. See also Peter Metcalfe and Richard Huntington, *Celebrations of Death: The Anthropology of Mortuary Ritual* (Cambridge University Press, 2nd edn, 1991); Arthur Maurice Hocart, *Kings and Councillors: An Essay in the Comparative Anatomy of Human Society* (University of Chicago Press, 1970); Robert Hertz, 'A Contribution to the Study of the Collective Representation of Death', in *Death and the Right Hand* (R. Needham and C. Needham trans., Free Press, 1960) [trans. of 'Contribution à une étude sur la représentation collective de la mort' (1907) 10 *Année Sociologique* 48 (first published 1907)]; Arnold van Gennep, *The Rites of Passage* (M. Vicedom and S. Kimball trans., University of Chicago Press, 1960) [trans. of *Les Rites de Passage* (first published 1909)].

it means or what it might mean to hold certain offices. As jurist, included in the actions of holding office is the creation, exercise and conduct of a relation with common law, which includes certain tasks and responsibilities. In the particular common law context where there are difficulties in the creation and conduct of lawful relations, these difficulties are part of the jurist's responsibilities of office. In this part, I recollect office as both a reminder and a gathering of tasks in order to develop an account of the office of jurist. To be clear, this recollection does not suggest that the office of jurist has been forgotten, rather, it offers a reminder to take care in contemplating office. Since the passing of early modern times, an account of office in its varied forms has slowly dissipated and as a result, certain understandings of role, responsibility and conduct have been lost, misplaced or simply detached from office. For the jurist, more than just a loss of understanding, there is a concomitant loss of meaning that is significant. Without an account of office that includes an account of role, responsibility and conduct it is difficult to articulate the responsibilities of the jurist. Without office, there is no responsible jurist.

Directed to the responsible jurist, the primary work of this part is to realign the relationship between the jurist and common law as a matter of office. Taking seriously the question of office, the creation and conduct of lawful relations is placed as part of the jurist's official responsibilities. To this end, this part begins by introducing the common law jurist and briefly considering how it relates to other offices. Drawing on an early modern history of office, office is understood here as a set of relations that includes a dynamic arrangement of duties, responsibilities, tasks, actions and forms of conduct. What this means is the common law jurist comes into a dynamic and very particular relation with common law, which is a relation that includes certain duties, responsibilities, tasks, forms of conduct and rights of action. Examining some of the tasks of office, including tasks of observation, description, attendance and care, I remind the jurist to attend to the technical and material forms of common law practice. In doing so, the jurist is able to take official responsibility for the creation and conduct of lawful relations, including sites of struggle. This is not an easy task.

Introducing office

Office is not simply the place we go to to work. While the term 'office' certainly evokes images of the spaces in which certain well-dressed labourers do their work, whether a room, set of rooms or a building, iconically located in a central business district although not necessarily so, this is only one way of thinking of office. In addition to describing a place of business, the term also commonly extends to staff members who work within these allocated spaces. Whether commuters on the 9–5 circuit or sole business owners working from home, office workers tend to associate this sense of office with words such as job, role, work, career etc. Yet even when associated more directly with the role or tasks of work, rather than just the concrete location of work, the spatial dominance within most contemporary uses of 'office' tends to cloud an older meaning: one associated with the conduct of taking up and holding office.[53]

What, then, is office?[54] Generally speaking, more than just architectural delights or occupations we enter and exit from at different times of the day, office also carries an older meaning referencing the elaborate weaving of duties, role, privileges, responsibilities and modes of conduct that attach through the *persona* to a particular office. However, as the modern account of office is anaemic, lacking both vigour and depth of meaning, it is often difficult to think beyond the institutional structures and concrete buildings of modernity and their spatial dimensions. In order to recollect office in this broader sense of conduct, it is helpful to consider the inheritance of office.

In the context of early modern England, Conal Condren writes:

> The office is a whole sphere of responsibilities, rights of action for their fulfilment, necessary attributes, skills and specific virtues, highlighted by concomitant vices and failures.[55]

Addressing the 'world of social offices',[56] and linking office, *persona*,[57] and social voice, Condren observes that office carries with it both 'a positive register of rights, liberties, duty, rule and service to the office and often to those protected by it' and also a 'negative register imputing neglect, oppression, licence and tyranny – in sum passionate excess'.[58] In early modern England, the act of taking up office and

---

53 For an exemplary essay on conduct and office, see Ann Genovese, 'Inheriting and Inhabiting the Pleasures and Duties of Our Own Existence: The Second Sex and Feminist Jurisprudence' (2013) 38 *Australian Feminist Law Journal* 41.
54 Marcus Tullius Cicero, *De Officiis* (Walter Miller trans., William Heinemann, 1913) [(written in 44BC and the second book to be printed using the Gutenberg printing press in 1440)]; Kantorowicz, *The King's Two Bodies*, above, n 50. See also Conal Condren, 'The *Persona* of the Philosopher and the Rhetorics of Office in Early Modern England', in Conal Condren, Stephen Gaukroger and Ian Hunter (eds.), *The Philosopher in Early Modern Europe: The Nature of a Contested Identity* (Cambridge University Press, 2006) 66; Conal Condren, *Argument and Authority in Early Modern England: The Presupposition of Oaths and Offices* (Cambridge University Press, 2006); Jeffrey Minson, 'S. Toussaint, *Humanismes Antihumanismes*, Paris, Les Belles Lettres, 2008' (2009) 14 *Cromohs* 1 (http://www.cromohs.unifi.it/14_ 2009/minson_toussaint.html); Shaunnagh Dorsett and Shaun McVeigh, 'The *Persona* of the Jurist in Salmond's *Jurisprudence*: On the Exposition of "What Law is …"' (2007) 38 *Victoria University of Wellington Law Review* 771; Dorsett and McVeigh, *Jurisdiction*, above, n 20; Shaunnagh Dorsett and Shaun McVeigh, 'Jurisprudences of Jurisdiction: Matters of Public Authority' (2014) 23(4) *Griffith Law Review* 569; Ian Hunter, *Rival Enlightenments: Civil and Metaphysical Philosophy in Early Modern Germany* (Cambridge University Press, 2001); Peter Goodrich, 'Visive Powers: Colours, Trees and Genres of Jurisdiction' (2008) 2(2) *Law and Humanities* 213; Raimond Gaita, *A Common Humanity: Thinking about Love and Truth and Justice* (Routledge, 2nd edn, 2000) ch 10.
55 Condren, 'The *Persona* of the Philosopher and the Rhetorics of Office', above, n 54.
56 Ibid, 67.
57 On *persona* and the different traces of Greek and Roman translations from Cicero to Hobbes to Agamben, see Connal Parsley, 'The Mask and Agamben: The Transitional Juridical Technics of Legal Relation' (2010) 14(1) *Law Text Culture* 12.
58 Condren, 'The *Persona* of the Philosopher and the Rhetorics of Office', above, n 54, 67.

claiming an official *persona* gained access to a particular register of speech carrying both privileges and responsibilities: a social voice. Although Condren is correct that we now live in a world in which the 'promotional rhetoric of office has a more uncertain place and a lower threshold of plausibility',[59] this is not to say we live in a world without office. Some of the most visible offices in Australia today include the Prime Minister, Chief Justice of Australia, state and federal police commissioners and other key legal figures, such as the Office of the Coroner, Office of the Director of Public Prosecutions and the Office of the Human Rights Commissioner. While also operating within institutional structures, such as a university, less visible offices include the office of jurist, jurisprudent, critic and scholar. Even less visible are those offices operating outside overtly institutional settings, such as the offices of public artist, poet and friend.

In early modern England, as Condren notes, offices also operated both within and without an institutional frame, including the 'concrete socialised offices'[60] of monarch and mayor and more elusive offices of actor, poet, rhetor and philosopher.[61] These differences are important for the simple reason that to collapse the office of poet with the office of mayor would be to corrupt what it means to think carefully about office. Clearly, part of the difference between offices is institutional form. In early modern England, for those acting in a social office outside an institution, additional work was needed to reassure others that first, there was an office and second, 'the *persona* was genuinely responsible to and representative of it.'[62] In other words, for those in more elusive offices, work was undertaken to ensure the role, responsibilities, privileges and conduct were understood *as* matters of office.

For example, consider the office of poet. While the poet laureate, crowned with laurel, appointed by government, is an office that holds a light institutional form,[63] in contemporary times work is certainly needed to link the responsibilities of the poet laureate to matters of office, let alone other poets. As Condren notes, in the current world where office has 'a lower threshold of plausibility',[64] irrespective of whether or not that office carries an institutional form, more effort is required to ensure matters of role, responsibility and conduct are understood as office.[65] This is so for the more elusive office of poet, as well as for the less elusive offices of jurist, jurisprudent, critic, coroner and soldier. In contemporary times, this is so even in circumstances where office still carries a strong institutional form. Therefore,

59 Ibid, 89.
60 Ibid, 67.
61 Ibid, 66.
62 Ibid, 67.
63 So, too, for the Nobel laureate, who, in distinction, takes up an office. Seamus Heaney, as poet laureate, who rejected one (British poet laureate) but accepted a Nobel other (Nobel Prize for Literature in 1995) is an exemplar of the contemporary office of poet. There is no poet laureate in Australia. While a call for a poet laureate occasionally arises (most recently in 2009), in April 2014, the *Australian Book Review* named David Malouf as its first ever laureate. Although, as this is a magazine, and not a government appointment, the question of office unfolds a little differently.
64 Condren, 'The *Persona* of the Philosopher and the Rhetorics of Office', above, n 54, 89.
65 Cf: Cicero, *De Officiis*, above, n 54, Book 2, XIX, 65.

despite the jurist's more recognisable institutional form when contrasted to poets or even the poet laureate, work is still needed to link the responsibilities of the jurist to matters of office.

The jurist, the coroner and the friend

Offices are not all the same. Different office carries different social duties, responsibilities and forms of conduct.[66] While various offices are addressed in this book, including the office of coroner and to a lesser extent, the friend, it is the office of jurist that is the primary concern. Yet there are different ways of understanding who the jurist is. 'Jurist' might be used synonymously with 'lawyer' to denote one who practises law, or it may be used as a matter of status to refer, somewhat reverentially, to someone particularly skilled in legal thought, while at other times the term is used to specifically refer to a judge, most often so in the USA and Canada. While these meanings may overlap, in this book I understand the jurist in a more traditional sense as a legal scholar. Broadly speaking, the jurist is a legal scholar who professes or treats of law.[67] As will be explained later in this chapter, the knowledge the jurist professes is jurisprudential.[68] This is the jurist as legal writer, who generally holds an institutional office, whether as expert, professor, academic, but may also include other less institutionalised legal writers. Jurisprudential knowledge is therefore shared through the medium of office, as it is only through office that the jurist – as scholar and writer – gains access to a social voice and is able to share legal knowledge in a particular register of speech otherwise unavailable. Clearly, the jurist inhabits a very particular and official relation to law, which is a relation that carries distinct responsibilities.

Yet, not all jurists are the same, and even in this sense of jurist as scholar, there are different types of jurist carrying markedly different relations and responsibilities to their laws. Consider the common law jurist as a legal scholar trained in common law and how this jurist differs from the civil law jurist. Each carries markedly different relations and responsibilities to their laws, most notably so in terms of their authority to create law. As is well known, both civil and international jurists have clearly established roles in law making,[69] whereas the common law jurist does not, so much so, that Raoul van Caenegem suggests the common law jurist is

---

66 Cicero, *De Officiis*, above, n 54.
67 See, e.g., John Simpson and Edmund Weiner (eds.), *Oxford English Dictionary* (Oxford University Press, 2nd edn, 1989); Peter Butt and David Hamer (eds.), *LexisNexis Concise Australian Legal Dictionary* (LexisNexis Butterworths, 4th edn, 2011); Onions (ed.), *The Oxford English Dictionary of English Etymology*, above, n 44; Barnhart and Steinmetz (eds.), *Chambers Dictionary of English Etymology*, above, n 44.
68 See, e.g., Roger Cotterrell, 'The Role of the Jurist: Reflections around Radbruch' (2013) 26:4 *Ratio Juris* 510, 511.
69 See, e.g., *Statute of the International Court of Justice* 59 Stat 1005, TS 993 (26 June 1945) art 38(1)(d).

dispensable, due in part to their lack of law-making authority.[70] While in the common law world, the authority to make law is limited to courts and parliaments, and does not extend to jurists, the common law jurist is not dispensable. Rather, as with all jurists, the place of the common law jurist is to take up office, and it must be recognised that each office is different. While the civil jurist inherits official responsibilities in relation to law-making authority, for the common law jurist, absent a clearly demarcated role in terms of creative legal authority, what it means to take up and hold office requires more detailed attendance and care.[71]

Before addressing the official responsibilities of the common law jurist, that is, the relationship between office and responsibility, two further offices that feature in this book need to be introduced: offices of coroner and friend. First, the coroner, who is an unusual legal actor. The coroner often sits in a minor or quasi-judicial role located somewhere between the judiciary and a broader understanding of the executive, at least in most Australian jurisdictions.[72] The role of the coroner has changed over the years, but the main function is to investigate suspicious deaths through the means of an inquest or inquiry. In other words, the coroner has particular responsibility to care for the dead; and this is a common law responsibility.[73] While the coroner is not the only office with responsibilities to the dead, for the care of the dead includes pastoral responsibilities that may fall within ecclesiastical, theological or familial responsibilities, as explored in Chapters 4 and 5, the coroner inherits a very particular role and responsibility in relation to common law that includes the jurisdictional responsibility to care for the dead. This is not the same office, neither is it the same relation of responsibility to the dead as the jurist. Rather, as introduced in Chapter 2 with the importance of movement, and elaborated in Chapter 5, the responsibility of the jurist to care for the dead is a responsibility of office to make inheritance possible; to transmit tradition; to move common law: a responsibility of movement. Yet, this is to race ahead.

Like the coroner, also operating on an entirely different register from the jurist is what I call the 'office of friend', which is an office that appears towards the end of this book when it steps in to perform some of the work that remains unperformed by more official legal actors.[74] Adopting an Aristotelean understanding of friendship, it is helpful to recall Aristotle's observation that there are three types of *philia* or friendship: social, political and personal.[75] For Aristotle, the first type of friendship is based on the good, the second on utility and usefulness and the

---

70 R.C. van Caenegem, *Judges, Legislators and Professors* (Cambridge University Press, 1987) 53–65. See also R.C. van Caenegem, *The Birth of the Common Law* (Cambridge University Press, 2nd edn, 1988).
71 See Hunter, *Rival Enlightenments*, above, n 54; Dorsett and McVeigh, 'The *Persona* of the Jurist in Salmond's *Jurisprudence*', above, n 54.
72 See, generally, Ian Freckelton and David Ranson, *Death Investigation and the Coroner's Inquest* (Oxford University Press, 2006).
73 On the responsibility of the coroner to care for the dead, see Chapter 4.
74 See, especially, Chapter 4, 4.4.
75 Aristotle, *Nichomachean Ethics*, Books VII–XIV.

third on pleasure.[76] While Aristotle's taxonomy of friendship is picked up and complicated in different ways through the work of Michel de Montaigne, Jacques Derrida and Giorgio Agamben, it is important to note there are different forms of friendship, some more 'official' than others.[77] Friendship is not limited to the pleasure of a personal relationship, which for Aristotle is the lowest form of friendship, but also includes forms of official friendship based on the utility of relations in the *polis* or the good of social relations. In this book, the office of friend is understood as a social office that attends to a higher form of friendship based on virtue.[78] While addressed in more depth in Chapter 4, like the office of poet or public artist, the office of friend clearly lacks an obvious institutional form and to this end, work is needed to ensure the dynamic duties, privileges and responsibilities of friendship are linked to matters of office.

So, quite simply, there are different offices, including the office of jurist, coroner and friend. Although it may sound a little trite, different offices are different and consist of different constellations of duties, tasks, responsibilities, forms of conduct and rights of action. For now, the question to be addressed is: What might it mean for the jurist to take up and hold office? The response offered is that the jurist comes into a particular and dynamic relation with common law that gives meaning to the tasks, responsibilities, forms of conduct and actions of office. In other words, the relationship between common law and the jurist is one mediated by office.

Taking up office: the jurist and matters of responsibility

Office is a set of relations, and through the act of taking up office, the jurist comes into a particular and dynamic relation with common law. Although there is more to office than responsibility,[79] this book works with the language of responsibility as a way of reminding the jurist of something too often overlooked or at times abandoned, that is, a responsibility to common law and its material practices in the creation and conduct of lawful relations. To explain what it means for the jurist to take up office, and how that links to questions of responsibility, it is helpful to consider the partially overlapping distinction between the common law subject and the common law jurist. Without delving into myriad traditions of the subject or the complexities of subjectivity, from an internal common law perspective, most simply the common law subject can be understood as one

---

76 Aristotle, *Nichomachean Ethics*, Book VIII.
77 See Michel de Montaigne, 'Of Friendship', in Michel de Montaigne, *The Complete Works: Essays, Travel Journal, Letters* (Donald M. Frame trans., Alfred A. Knopf, 2003) Essay 28, 164; Jacques Derrida, *The Politics of Friendship* (George Collins trans., Verso, 1997) [trans. of *Politiques de L'amitié* (first published 1994)]; Giorgio Agamben, 'The Friend', in Giorgio Agamben, *What is an Apparatus? And other Essays* (David Kishik and Stefan Pedatella trans., Stanford University Press, 2009) 25 [trans. of *L'amico* (first published 2007)].
78 See Chapter 4, 4.
79 Condren, 'The *Persona* of the Philosopher and the Rhetorics of Office', above, n 54.

subject to common law.⁸⁰ Governed by common law, the common law subject has a particular relation to common law that consists of certain rights, duties and responsibilities. However, the subjects' relation to common law is not the same as the jurist's, and this relation changes when the subject-as-jurist takes up office. The subject, of course, is not an incumbent of a social office, whereas the jurist is. While remaining a common law subject, the jurist takes on an additional, particular and distinct relationship with common law that is a relationship of not only rights, but also responsibilities, and one mediated by office.⁸¹

More generally, there are different ways of thinking about responsibilities of office. Peter Goodrich draws on a tradition of psychoanalysis and frames the relation between office and responsibility as one of conscience.⁸² Raimond Gaita draws on a tradition of moral philosophy and frames the relation between office and responsibility as one of truth and moral conduct.⁸³ Drawing on a sociology of law, Roger Cotterell aligns with Julius Stone by tasking the jurist with responsibilities 'to safeguard and promote law's general well-being' through practices of writing.⁸⁴ While sympathetic to the approaches of Goodrich and Gaita, as well as Cotterell's acknowledgement of writing practices, the approach taken here is wed more closely to that of Shaunnagh Dorsett and Shaun McVeigh, who draw on jurisprudential and historical traditions of jurisdiction and frame the relation between office and responsibility as a site for the conduct of lawful relations, and the conduct of lawful life.⁸⁵ In a context of problematic lawful relations, the jurist's responsibilities of office include attending to the technical and material forms of common law practice. This is a matter of conduct; the conduct of lawful relations.

How, then, might this be done? Through the tasks of observation and description, attendance and care, tasks that can be performed in various ways, the jurist attends to the responsibilities of office. For instance, writing is one way the jurist attends to common law and in doing so communicates, transmits and contributes to the movement of knowledge. Similarly, to teach others, as well as to read and contemplate are acts of office that observe, describe and attend to common

---

80 *Contra* the subject of philosophy, whether the Cartesian, Kantian, Hegelian or Marxist subject, the psychoanalytic subject in Freudian or Lacanian traditions or Heidegger's *Dasein*. Of course, there is also a long history of feminist critiques of the legal subject. For example, as Simone de Beauvoir pithily observed, 'He is the Subject, he is the Absolute – she is the Other', in *The Second Sex* (Knopf, 1953).
81 See, generally, Cicero, *De Officiis*, above, n 54.
82 See Goodrich, 'Visive Powers', above, n 54; Peter Goodrich, *'Flores Quae Faciunt Coronam* or the Flowers of Common Law', in Oren Ben-Dor, *Law and Art: Justice, Ethics and Aesthetics* (Routledge, 2011) ch 16.
83 Raimond Gaita, *A Common Humanity: Thinking about Love and Truth and Justice* (Routledge, 2nd edn, 2000) ch 10.
84 Cotterell, 'The Role of the Jurist', above, n 68. Cotterell goes on to argue that the jurist's role is to maintain 'the idea of law as a special kind of practice and enabling that idea to flourish', which Stone describes as form of 'extraversion': Julius Stone quoted in Cotterell, above, n 68.
85 See Dorsett and McVeigh, *Jurisdiction*, above, n 20; Dorsett and McVeigh, 'The *Persona* of the Jurist in Salmond's *Jurisprudence*', above, n 54.

law and contribute to the formation, distribution and passage of knowledge. Significantly, different tasks of office relate not simply to conceptual knowledge of common law content, but also to jurisprudential knowledge of forms of common law practice. In other words, the jurist's tasks of observation, description and attendance are dynamic and relational activities of office that assist in performing the jurist's responsibilities to common law. As such, the office of jurist is a dynamic site for the movement of tradition as both a matter of practice, and a matter of conduct.

Taking up the office of jurist, therefore, requires attending to and taking responsibility for the practice of the common law tradition, which requires an ability to converse in the languages of common law, including the idiom of precedent and the language of procedure. Yet it is also necessary for the jurist to take care in the conduct of office. By placing the office of jurist as a site for the conduct of lawful relations,[86] and attending to some responsibilities of this office, the jurist now has a responsibility to attend to the technical and material forms of common law practice as a way of accounting for the creation and conduct of lawful relations. The nature of these responsibilities will become more apparent as this book progresses, especially the jurist's responsibility to care for the dead, but for now it is sufficient simply to link office and responsibility to the conduct of lawful relations as a matter of practice.

To summarise, having introduced the office of jurist in this second part of the chapter, as well as the offices of coroner and friend, it is apparent that although the language of office may not hold deep meaning today, it does still hold meaning. While the jurist's relationship to common law is certainly a question of office, it is a relationship too often obscured. To recollect office therefore is an active task that ensures office is not overlooked, underestimated or forgotten, and serves as a reminder that there is a world of social offices not simply of early modern times but with contemporary resonance. For office is more than a thin account of institutional structures and concrete buildings of modernity and more than an account of profession, occupation, role, job or career. Office carries with it an elaborate weaving of duties, role, privileges, responsibilities and modes of conduct that attach through the *persona* to a particular office.

In a context of acknowledged difficulties in establishing lawful relations in Australia, it is important to take seriously the question of office. Thinking with office, as this part of Chapter 1 has shown, the relationship between the jurist and common law becomes framed as a dynamic relationship of responsibility, where the responsibilities of office include the creation and conduct of lawful relations, as well as a responsibility to care for the dead. But how might this be done? Deepening an account of what it means to live with common law, and to conduct a life with law, the next part of Chapter 1 explains how a minor jurisprudence assists the jurist with the task of attending to common law practice as part of their responsibilities of office. That is, a minor jurisprudence assists in the

86 Ibid.

performance of the jurist's official responsibilities, and addressing method, the next part explains how this might be done

1.3 A method of slowness

From the celerity of human motions to the extreme velocity of technologically enhanced speed, there are different rates of movement. Movement may be swift, rapid and ferocious or it may be languid and slow. If Paul Virilio's rate of movement is velocity and ever-increasing-speed, the rate of movement here is one of slowness.[87] Although in part a response to speed and the quickening of modernity, slowness is understood as more than simply non-speed. For a 'method of slowness' provides an opportunity for more detailed attention and more attentive description and redescription. In addition to the visual aspect of attentive detail, there is also a relation between the pace of movement and the activity of memory. Simply put, this is a material relation that suggests that a faster pace of movement quickens forgetting while a slower pace of movement leads to remembering.[88] Holding these aspects of slowness together, the jurisprudential method I adopt in this book asks the jurist to slow down and remember to attend to their responsibilities of office as a way of assisting those who may have forgotten as well as those who fail to notice, or fail to appreciate, meaning carried by the technical and material forms of common law practice. With different rates of movement, this book moves slowly.

Before attending to the importance of movement, which comes to the fore in the next chapter, in this final part of Chapter 1, I explain what it means to embrace slowness and how this assists in the creation of this minor jurisprudence. With a tone of attention and an attitude of slowness, in this book, I work carefully with materials and accept the importance of taking time as a perfectly legitimate mode of engagement. As non-speed, heightened attention and improved memory, this is slowness as both a method and ethic of conduct; a question of prudence and care.[89] A 'method of slowness' therefore is a method of attention that advocates a certain kind of care and a certain way of practising jurisprudence. In other words,

---

87 See, e.g., Paul Virilio, *Speed and Politics: An Essay on Dromology* (Mark Polizzotti trans., Columbia University, 1986) [trans. of *Vitesse et Politique* (first published 1977)]; John Armitage, 'Interview with Paul Virilio: The Kosovo War Took Place in Orbital Space' (Patrice Riemens trans.) on *CTheory* (2000): www.ctheory.net/articles.aspx?id=132.
88 See, e.g., Milan Kundera, *Slowness* (Linda Asher trans., faber & faber, 1996) 4 [trans. of *La Lenteur* (first published 1995)]. See also Karin van Marle, 'Law's Time, Particularity and Slowness', in Wessel le Roux and Karin van Marle (eds.), *Law, Memory, and the Legacy of Apartheid: Ten Years after AZAPO v President of South Africa* (Pretoria University Law Press, 2007); Franco Cassano, 'Going Slow', in Franco Cassano, *Southern Thought and Other Essays on the Mediterranean* (Norma Bouchard and Valerio Ferme trans., Fordham University Press, 2012) ch 1 [trans. of *Il Pensiero Merediano* (first published 1996)].
89 Cf: Karin van Marle's approach of slowness; van Marle, 'Law's Time', above, n 88, which follows Alan Hunt's distinction between method and approach; Alan Hunt, 'The Critique of Law: What is "Critical" about Critical Legal Theory?' (1987) 14 *Journal of Law and Society* 5.

slowness is assumed as a way of practising jurisprudence. For the jurist in office, who is responsible for the conduct of lawful relations as a matter of jurisprudence, this requires attending to common law practices in certain ways. Moving slowly and carefully with the technical and material forms of common law practice, that is, by holding onto common law, it becomes possible to deepen an account of what it means to live with and move with common law, and how we might do this well. More specifically, as a minor jurisprudence of movement, a method of slowness helps the jurist notice that common law's movements carry already instituted legal meaning and what these movements might mean. To this end, a jurisprudential method of slowness assists the responsible jurist in their conduct of office by offering a way of moving well among the movements of common law.

Therefore, having already placed lawful relations as context and directed attention towards the office of jurist, the final part of this chapter explains how this book works by articulating its method. Linking jurisprudence to office, this final part addresses one of the responsibilities of office: to act jurisprudentially. With a method that accesses and elicits certain repertoires of jurisprudential meaning, the part addresses why this is a minor jurisprudence, how this minor jurisprudence uses certain materials and the importance of slowness as a method of jurisprudential care.

A minor jurisprudence

Clearly, this is a work in jurisprudence. As such, this book offers the jurist a way of thinking with and living with common law as a matter of practice. Remembering Cicero, this is jurisprudence at its most basic – as *ius prudentia* – as an act of exercising sound judgment in practical matters of law.[90] In this regard, the jurisprudential questions asked in this book are intensely practical questions of how to live with common law, and how to do this well. Recalling that different offices carry different responsibilities, as explained in the previous part, the work of this jurisprudence can be understood as helping the jurist stay with, think with, and live with common law as part of their responsibilities of office.

While remaining critical, it must be emphasised that the task of thinking *with* common law is a jurisprudential task, and a different task from that of critique. Carrying a distinct relation to common law, one structured through particular jurisprudential methods, the office of jurist is not necessarily the office of critic. Consider the following scenario. When in office, the jurist may find herself in circumstances in which she is caught between her professional obligations and her political and ethical values, which pull in apparently opposing directions.[91] In

---

90 See Robert W. Cape Jr, 'Cicero and the Development of Prudential Practice at Rome', in Robert Hariman (ed.), *Prudence: Classical Virtue, Postmodern Practice* (Pennsylvania State University Press, 2003) ch 2.
91 Olivia Barr, Luis Eslava and Yoriko Otomo, 'In Search of Authority, Rebellion and Action' (2009) 3(2) *Sortuz: Journal of Emergent Socio-legal Studies 1*.

the case of Anglo-Australian common law with its particular colonial inheritance, its constraints are quite apparent, especially in the practice of its relations with other forms of law and the quite devastating impact of those practices. Faced with a choice of seeking an escape from the constraints of law or learning to live with those constraints is what I call 'the jurist's critical dilemma'.

Significantly, the jurist's response to this dilemma is a matter of office, and more particularly, a question of official responsibility. Faced with this dilemma, which arises again and again, the jurist's response each time involves a choice of position, whether choosing to position with common law or somewhere elsewhere and somehow beyond. But in choosing a position, the jurist also chooses a method. That is, if the jurist chooses to position with common law, this is a choice to hold onto law in order to think with, work with and learn how to live common law and in doing so take seriously the question of how to do this well. This is to think and to act jurisprudentially. Alternatively, if the jurist chooses to position beyond common law, this is a choice to seek some form of escape, and critique from a location somewhere and somehow external to common law in order think about common law, which may involve contemplating how to live with or without common law, whether living by another law or becoming lawless. These are both perfectly proper positions but offer different perspectives, and as such take up different roles and responsibilities in relation to common law, as well as different methods: one jurisprudential, one critique.

While not always so, the jurist who takes up the office of critic may at times position herself outside common law, whether through acts of transcendence or revolution as a way of gaining a perspective or a creative position that is one of less restriction or possibly unrestraint. However, to do so, to take up such a position beyond law, the jurist must abandon (at least) some of her responsibilities of office, including jurisprudential responsibilities to the form and practice of common law. Boldly put, to escape law is to abandon the office of jurist and its jurisprudential responsibilities. This is because the jurist in office is necessarily positioned with common law in order to carry out certain tasks, duties and responsibilities of common law practice.

Therefore, while certainly critical, this minor jurisprudence is not a work of critique. In this respect, while thinking with common law is certainly not the same method as a more traditional form of critique, whether Kantian or otherwise,[92] and should not be read as such, the jurisprudential method adopted here remains critical in the sense that it assists the jurist in taking responsibility for the creation and conduct of lawful relations. The critical stance here is involved not so much

---

92 For an overview of these traditions of critique, see, e.g., Michel Foucault, 'What is Critique?', in Sylvère Lotringer (ed.), *The Politics of Truth* (Semiotext(e), 2007), transcript by Monique Emery, revised by Suzanne Delorme et al., trans. into English by Lysa Hochroth. This essay was originally a lecture given at the French Society of Philosophy on 27 May 1978, subsequently published in (1990) 84(2) *Bulletin de la Société française de la philosophie* 35. See also Judith Butler's response to Foucault's essay, 'What is Critique? An Essay on Foucault's Virtue', in Sara Salih (ed.) with Judith Butler, *The Judith Butler Reader* (Blackwell, 2004) ch 12.

with overcoming law as with putting Anglo-Australian common law in its place. This involves equipping the jurist with the means to engage with the consequences of Empire and decolonisation as a matter of practice, a matter of conduct and a matter of office. Confronted with the critical dilemma, therefore, the position I take in this book is that it is for jurists to stay with and think with common law as a way of taking seriously their responsibilities to common law as a matter of office. This requires the work of jurisprudence.

More specifically, as elaborated in Chapter 2, the jurisprudential questions asked and addressed in this book concern the place of movement in common law's practices. This asks the jurist to use their practical wisdom of common law to think more carefully about how common law moves and what these movements might mean, which involves issues of technical and material practice, as well as ones of conduct. In the language of practice, this is the central question of the book: 'How does common law move?' or more carefully, 'What are some of the ways in which Anglo-Australian common law moves?' For common law is a practice, and as I explain in the next chapter, movement is part of that practice. In terms of conduct, however, this raises the ethical challenge of how to move well. Therefore, while recognising that movement is not a traditional topic of jurisprudential orthodoxy, questions of practice and conduct are properly matters of concern for jurisprudence. For the jurist, the challenge becomes one of moving well with and among the movements of common law.

However, while responding to the critical dilemma through jurisprudence, it is important to be clear this is a minor and not a major jurisprudence.[93] Reflecting its cautious approach to lines, this is not a minor jurisprudence simply through some imagined dichotomal opposition to a major jurisprudence. Rather, it is a minor jurisprudence because it accepts the institution of common law and asks how to live with common law.[94] This is a concern with how to live with a colonial form of law, which is a concern with how to live with Anglo-Australian common law, and how we might do this well. If this were a major jurisprudence, questions such as the relationship between movement and common law existence would be more fully explored. However, in asking: 'How does common law move?', I do not offer a complete scheme in response to this question. Neither do I seek the 'truth' of movement or offer a definitive juridicial, political or theological answer. Rather, as a minor jurisprudence the choice has been made to hold onto the

---

93 Cf: Goodrich, below, n 95; Minkkinen, below, n 95. For a recent and comprehensive survey of the relationship between Goodrich's and Minkkinen's minor jurisprudences, see Chris Tomlins, 'Foreword "Law As …" III – *Glossolalia*: Toward a Minor (Historical) Jurisprudence' (2015) 5 *UC Irvine Law Review* 239.

94 Cf: Peter Goodrich, *Law in the Courts of Love: Literature and Other Minor Jurisprudences* (Routledge, 1996); Panu Minkkinen, 'The Radiance of Justice: On the Minor Jurisprudence of Franz Kafka' (1994) 3 *Social and Legal Studies* 349; Edward Mussawir, *Jurisdiction in Deleuze: The Expression and Representation of Law* (Routledge Cavendish, 2011); Gilles Deleuze and Felix Guattari, *Kafka: Toward a Minor Literature* (Dana Polan trans., University of Minnesota Press, 1986) ch 3 [trans. of *Kafka: Pour une Litterature Mineure* (first published 1975)].

question of movement as a way of attending to some of the forms and modes of common law practice. As such, I do not offer a full account of Anglo-Australian common law and its movements, and neither is movement placed as a complete conceptual frame for understanding common law and its practices. Rather, this minor jurisprudence picks up and traces some of the ways in which common law moves and contemplates what these movements might mean. Endlessly moving, this minor jurisprudence asks the jurist to think about how to move well with and among the movements of Anglo-Australian common law as a matter of office. For the jurist, this places method as a method of office.

In a general sense, therefore, the task of this minor jurisprudence is to contemplate how the jurist might take responsibility for the technical and material forms of common law practice as a matter of office, and more specifically, attend to movement as part of those practices. Designed to make these practices visible, a method of slowness reveals the place of movement in the practice of lawful relations on a register that is otherwise often overlooked or, if not, rendered meaningless. This gives office its jurisprudential activity: the practice of lawful life. For the jurist, in taking up and holding office, the practice of lawful life is a responsibility to live with law. For this reason, I argue the jurist needs to pay attention to movement, which in this book is undertaken via a descriptive engagement with two sets of materials.

Redescribing practices

Following a rhetorical and critical tradition of paradiastole,[95] the mode of investigation in this book attends to and picks up certain strands of common law practice. More specifically, through a jurisprudential method of slowness that works with examples to redescribe practices, this book engages with two sets of legal materials as a way of taking responsibility for some of the forms of common law practice. The particular method of engagement with these materials is one guided by a method of slowness as well as compliant with the jurisprudential tasks of office: tasks of observation, description, attendance and care. Through narrative and redescription, this slow jurisprudential method reveals movement as part of common law's practice, and engages the tasks and responsibilities of office by offering the jurist a way of attending to common law practice.

To this end, it is necessary to explain the choice of materials and how they are used. In Chapters 3 and 4, which form the central display of the book, two case studies are developed from two sets of materials, both illustrating how common law moves. The first example is a burial party that walked in the Colony of New South Wales in 1799. This is drawn from a set of materials consisting

---

95 Quentin Skinner, *Reason and Rhetoric*, above, n 8; see, e.g., Jeffrey Minson, 'S. Toussaint, *Humanismes Antihumanismes*, Paris, Les Belles Lettres, 2008' (2009) 14 *Cromohs* 1 (http://www.cromohs.unifi.it/14_ 2009/minson_toussaint.html). See also Quentin Skinner, *Machiavelli* (Oxford University Press, 1981); Quentin Skinner, 'Paradiastole', above, n 8.

primarily of the transcript of evidence and judgment in the colonial criminal case of *R v Powell* (1799).[96] The second example concerns a death in Antarctica in 2000 and the primary materials are a coronial file.[97] Serving as exemplars, the description and redescription of these two exemplary vignettes attend to some of the technical forms and material practices of the movements of Anglo-Australian common law.

The engagement with these materials is considered; a stance. Through a careful engagement with these materials, narratives are constructed followed by redescriptions as a way of noticing and eliciting certain things about how common law works. This is not the same as using these materials to produce a detailed historiography, a work in cultural studies or legal anthropology. Why, then, engage with these materials through narrative, description and redescription? Quite simply, in a book concerned with technical and material practices of common law, mimicking common law's method assists in revealing its technical and material traces. This is because the common law method is ripe with its use of the example, narrative and description, so much so that it is arguable the use of the example is integral to the common law method.

Akin to the common law method, therefore, the approach to these materials is exemplary. This is the example as one case standing for a larger principle, most obviously so in *stare decisis* as central to common law techniques of reasoning and argument.[98] A further feature of the common law method, the extremely detailed and descriptive engagement with the example in order to address the more general deserves some attention. For instance, in one notorious Western Australian matter, after a 404-day trial, which involved the tendering of over 85,000 documents, the written reasons for judgment totalled 2600 pages in length.[99] The amount of paperwork and the intensely detailed knowledge of those involved is unfathomable. Why is it that the common law jurist *describes* in such detail? What is the purpose of this description? In providing such a detailed account, the jurist delineates; choosing between that which is described and that which is not. In making this choice, the jurist marks out the form or shape or outline of that which is being described, capturing something within the description and leaving something or some things outside. As part of their jurisprudential responsibilities,

---

96 *R v Powell* [15–16 October 1799, Court of Criminal Judicature, Dore JA] Minutes of Proceedings, State Records Office of New South Wales, NRS 2700 [X905], 298–362; *R v Powell* [15–16 October 1799, Court of Criminal Judicature, Depositions before Dore JA] Miscellaneous Criminal Papers, State Records Office of New South Wales, NRS 2702 [5/1152], 53–70. See also *R v Powell* [1799] NSWKR 7; [1799] NSWSupC 7. See Chapter 3.

97 *Findings of the Coroner in the Matter of an Inquest into the Death of Rodney David Marks Who Died at South Pole Station, Antarctica* (Unreported, Coroner's Court, Christchurch, New Zealand, Coroner Richard McElrea, 16 September 2008) ('*Findings*') and the Coroner's File in relation to the *Findings* which includes reports, depositions, questionnaires, photographs and other miscellaneous documents ('*Coronial File*'). See Chapter 4.

98 On the meaning of *stare decisis*, see above, n 4.

99 *The Bell Group Ltd (in liq) v Westpac Banking Corporation (No 9)* (2008) 39 WAR 1. See also *The Bell Group Ltd (in liq) v Westpac Banking Corporation (No 10)* (2009) 39 WAR 1.

it is the jurist's task to describe; a responsibility of office that requires the jurist give detailed accounts of the current state of the law or more commonly certain legal issues, whether it be set forth in words, written or spoken. Unfortunately, this is an account that is often tedious, and wearisomely so.

Thankfully, this micro-detailed approach that so often caricatures legal processes is not the only way of describing. To describe also carries an older meaning: to form or trace by motion or to pass or travel over a certain course or distance.[100] Relatedly, to redescribe evokes the rhetorical device of paradiastole in the sense of moving to another or the other side.[101] In this book, both meanings are embraced. Although there is certainly something particularly common law to the example, through the description and redescription of these two sets of legal materials, the method used in this book takes seriously the detail of the examples, yet remains careful not to understand the example as simply a path or a line to the general. Embracing description in its double meaning, these are acts of description and redescription that trace by motion forms of common law practice. More specifically, the book traces the technical form and material practices of common law's movements. In this respect, this book contributes to the growing body of scholarship that attends to various sites of law's material presence.[102] Attentive to the everyday material sites of common law practice, it is through redescription that this slow method reveals certain things that tend otherwise to slide by unnoticed, most notably, movement.

To summarise, following a tradition of paradiastole,[103] a method of jurisprudential redescription carefully and caringly attends to the material forms of common law's movements as a way of paying attention to certain repertoires of meaning that otherwise tend to go unnoticed. Engaging with two distinct sets of legal materials through acts of observation, narration and redescription, there is a benefit to moving slowly and for the jurist, the warning offered is to take care with how we describe. Illustrating, the second part of this book is a written performance designed to make common law practice visible through acts of redescription. That is, adopting a method of slowness reveals the place of movement in the practice of lawful relations on a register that is otherwise often overlooked or if not overlooked rendered meaningless: it reveals movement as jurisprudentially meaningful. While certainly not the most traditional jurisprudential approach, this method assists the jurist in taking responsibility for the creation and conduct of lawful relations as a matter of office. Accepting the institution of common law, this minor jurisprudence offers a reminder of why it is necessary to hold onto law and think more carefully about how to live with

---

100 Onions (ed.), *The Oxford English Dictionary of English Etymology*, above, n 44.
101 See Skinner, *Reason and Rhetoric*, above, n 8.
102 In a vast and growing field, see, especially, Philippopoulos-Mihalopoulos, *Spatial Justice*, above, n 6. See also Bruno Latour, *The Making of Law: An Ethnography of the Conseil d'Etat* (Marina Brilman and Alain Pottage trans., Polity Press, 2010) [trans. of *La Fabrique du Droit* (first published 2002)].
103 See Skinner, *Reason and Rhetoric*, above, n 8. See, e.g., Minson, 'S. Toussaint', above, n 96. See also Skinner, *Machiavelli*, above, n 95; Skinner, 'Paradiastole', above, n 8.

and move with law. Therefore, in a chapter that introduced lawful relations, recollected the office of jurist and explained the book method, the jurist has been tasked to think with common law as a way of taking responsibility for its practices, including its movements. The next chapter turns to the importance of movement.

Chapter 2

The importance of movement

> The history of the common law has always been a history of movement
> (Peter Goodrich 1990)[1]

In both obvious and less than obvious ways, common law moves. It walks, it sails, it flies, and it delves into the land, sometimes burrowing and sometimes borrowing in its attempts to attach and maintain a hold on the earth in order to find and claim its place: it moves. It also continues to move. Problematically, if noticed at all, common law's movements are often rendered meaningless. This is not only incorrect, but also potentially disastrous. As explained in this chapter, the importance of movement is not simply that common law moves, but the shapes and forms of its movements and the meanings these movements may carry. For it is not only necessary to observe that common law moves, but also to develop an appreciation that these movements carry already instituted legal meaning.

What meaning might movement carry? While there are many movements, and many meanings, most fundamentally this is movement as the institution and form of common law, and one that is given shape by jurisdiction. By moving through jurisdiction, common law creates relations across space and time and in doing so, comes into its relations and comes to be in place. This is jurisdiction as a technology of movement and it is also movement as a jurisdictional technology of the common law, shaping common law form. In a minor jurisprudence attentive to the technical and material forms of common law practice, and placing movement as part of that practice, the focus of this book is on common law's jurisdictional movements in relation to the dead. Most notably so through the institution of burial, common law's movements in relation to the dead are of particular significance in terms of common law's place. Paying attention to these movements, in this chapter, I introduce the argument that it is through the institution of burial that common law comes to be in place. Although not

---

1 Peter Goodrich, *Languages of Law: From Logics of Memory to Nomadic Masks* (Weidenfeld & Nicolson, 1990) 297.

the only way common law comes to be in place, attending to the institution of burial reveals the importance of movement. For movement puts common law in its place, and in doing so, reveals that place as temporary. For the jurist, therefore, the importance of movement provides a reminder of the jurisdictional responsibility to care for the dead as a matter of lawful relations, and as one of the ways common law moves into place. This is a matter of conduct; of how to be in place.

Having introduced the responsible jurist in the previous chapter, this chapter addresses the subject matter of this book, that is, the technical forms and material practices of common law's movements, and it does so across three parts. The first part of the chapter introduces forms of movement, which considers movement more generally before introducing some of the ways in which common law moves. The second part links movement to jurisdiction and technology as a matter of jurisprudence. Noticing a problem with place, namely, that common law's place is not as everywhere as it may seem, and noticing this problem masks jurisdiction and obscures movement, this part reveals jurisdiction as a technology of movement in the conduct of lawful relations and in the making of common law's place. The third part considers one particular form of movement. Attending to the importance of movement in placing the dead, the final part of the chapter notices the institution of burial as one of the ways in which common law moves in relation to the dead, contributing to the humanisation of the earth and, perhaps, its juridification. Placing the care of the dead as part of the responsibilities of office, therefore, the three parts of this chapter introduce the responsible jurist to the jurisprudential importance of movement.

2.1 Shaping movement

Movement is many things. Not only does it move, but although it may lead towards a destination, whether physical, figurative or normatively otherwise, movement captures more than simply that which comes before or leads towards a destination. More than just passage or progress, change in place or entry into motion, there is an action and activity to movement, and this activity comes in different forms; different shades; different shapes. Not only are there different forms of movement, but there are also different modes, techniques and practices of movement. For movement differs, changing, drifting, curving, carving, passing, impressing, wandering, altering; endlessly so. Paying attention to these different shades of movement, to the shadows and echolocations of movement shapes, as well as noticing the 'how' of movement, is to respond to the demand this book makes, that is, to pay attention to movement as a matter of jurisprudence; as part of the jurisprudential story of lawful relations.

Strangely, movement is a difficult term to define without succumbing to some form of circularity. While refraining from offering a general theory of movement, which is neither practicable nor desirable for the purposes of a minor jurisprudence, movement is understood here as simply the actions and manners of moving.² Used as a way of coming to a better understanding of common law and its technical and material practices, in a sense movement serves as a hermeneutic device for the creation of this minor jurisprudence attentive to Anglo-Australian common law and its modes of practice. Although I do not provide movement as an analytical frame, this first part of the chapter offers some guidance as to how movement is used and understood in this book. This is through an attention to different forms of common law movement.

To introduce the importance of movement, the first part of this chapter considers different forms of movement and in doing so, exposes some of the ways in which common law moves. Beginning with Aristotle as a way of unsettling, fragmenting and atomising movement in its more general sense, the part continues by attending to some of the different technical and material forms of common law movement. By slowing the pace of movement, considering different shapes of movement and exposing some of the ways in which common law moves, common law is reframed and embraced as an itinerant justice.

Unsettling movement (generally)

Movement is unsettling. It is action and activity; an entry into motion. Whether rapid or slow; perpetual, repetitive or wildly unexpected; material, conceptual, figurative or normatively otherwise, there is an action and activity present in movement. This is movement as involving a change. A change in place or position or posture or location or step or orientation; a transition, transmission, transmigration, passage. But, movement is not the same as progress or advancement, although these may also be movements. Movement may or may not be onward, it may or may not take a specific direction or head towards a specific place. It may or may not follow the line.³ To assert a destination and to hold movement to a direction is already to contain movement and limit its possibilities. Whereas movement is actually much simpler than this. Movement is the actions and manners of moving. While movement can be conceptualised in many ways, some of which will be raised here, it is Aristotle that offers an entry point to this minor jurisprudence of movement. By noticing different forms of movement, in a very general sense, Aristotle offers some useful guidance to the task of thinking more carefully about movement.

Aristotle's account of movement is more properly an account of motion. As set out in Book III of his *Physics*, Aristotle defines motion as 'the actuality (*entelechia*) of

---

2 In this respect, I take a position similar to Paul Carter, who writes in the context of meetings, 'if it is an axiom of the discourse of meeting that it must preserve the contingency of encounter, then a general theory of meeting is neither practicable nor desirable'; Paul Carter, *Meeting Place: the Human Encounter and the Challenge of Coexistence* (University of Minnesota Press, 2013). As with meetings, so too for movement.
3 See Introduction; Paul Carter, *Dark Writing: Geography, Performance, Design* (University of Hawai'i Press, 2009); Paul Klee, *Pedagogical Sketchbook* (faber & faber, 1953).

a potentiality as such' or 'the actuality of a potentiality, qua potential'.[4] Not surprisingly, this definition has been subject to much interpretation and discussion, noting its contradictions and often concluding that Aristotle erred in the use of his own terminology.[5] In this regard, Aristotle's definition of motion is not overly enlightening jurisprudentially in and of itself, as it rests heavily on the distinction between actuality and potentiality as it plays out through the work of four key Aristotelean terms: *entelechia, kinêsis, duanamis, energeia*.

This raises the not insignificant issue of Aristotelean translation. Without delving deeply, it is helpful to lightly unravel these key terms in the context of developing an understanding of different forms of movement, starting with *entelechia*, which is most commonly translated as 'actuality'. For example, as the general editor of the Oxford Aristotle translation series David Ross concludes in his interpretation of the interpretation of motion as the actuality (*entelechia*) of a potentiality as such, that '*entelechia* must here mean "actualization," not "actuality"; it is the passage from potentiality to actuality that is *kinêsis*'.[6] In other words, although *entelechia* is most often translated as 'actuality', in this context, Ross suggests it should be translated as 'actualisation', thereby raising the issue of *kinêsis*. Before addressing *kinêsis*, what is most interesting for the purposes of this book is not so much the Aristotelean debate as to what motion is but rather the difficulty of thinking carefully about movement, which is highlighted by the inconsistencies of translation. For it is not only *entelechia* that is translated liberally, shifting from 'actuality' to 'actualisation', and often used interchangeably with *energeia*,[7] but also *kinêsis*. Translated variously as motion, movement or change, a consideration of *kinêsis* more helpfully assists in noticing forms of movement.

More specifically, there is a complication of movement that arises from Aristotle's distinction between *kinêsis* and *energeia*. Related to the distinction between *duanamis* and *energeia*, where *duanamis* is a capacity to be in a different and more completed state (potentiality) and *energeia* is the exercise or completion of that potentiality

---

4 Aristotle, *Physics* (Robin Waterfield trans., Oxford University Press, 2006) 201a10–11, 201a27–29, 201b4–5.
5 With the exception of St Thomas Aquinas, who takes seriously the contradictions within Aristotle's definition of motion, the modern consensus seems to fall back on the presumption that Aristotle erred in his definition; see Louis Aryeh Kosman, 'Aristotle's Definition of Motion' (1969) 14(1) *Phronesis* 40. See also George A. Blair, 'The Meaning of "Energeia" and "Entelechia" in Aristotle' (1967) 7(1) *International Philosophical Quarterly* 101; George A. Blair, *Energeia and Entelechia: 'Act' in Aristotle* (University of Ottawa Press, 1992); Oded Balaban, 'The Modern Misunderstanding of Aristotle's Theory of Motion' (1995) 26(1) *Journal for General Philosophy of Science* 1; and, for a useful introduction, Joe Sachs, 'Aristotle: Motion and its Place in Nature' (2005) *The Internet Encyclopedia of Philosophy* (www.iep.utm.edu/aris-mot/).
6 W.D. Ross, *Aristotle's Physics* (Oxford, 1936) 537; W.D. Ross, *Physics Text with Commentary* (London, 1936) 359. See also Kosman, 'Aristotle's Definition of Motion', above, n 5, 41.
7 W. D. Ross, *Aristotle's Physics* (Oxford, 1936) 537; W. D. Ross, *Physics Text with Commentary* (London, 1936) 359.

(actuality),[8] it is in Aristotle's use of both *duanamis* and *energeia* in relation to *kinêsis* that a helpful distinction in terms of different forms of movement arises. In relation to *kinêsis*, this is *duanamis* in a slightly narrower sense of the power a thing has to produce change, where the exercise of such power to produce change is *kinêsis*. Roughly speaking, this is *duanamis* as potentiality as distinct from *kinêsis* as motion or movement. Yet, when considered in relation to *energeia*, to simply translate *kinêsis* as motion or movement is a little abrupt.[9]

In a broad sense, *kinêsis* is *energeia* (actuality) as distinct from *duanamis* (potentiality). Yet, Aristotle draws a distinction between *kinêsis* and *energeia* that complicates this broad understanding of *kinêsis*.[10] In a well-known passage, Aristotle writes:

> [A]t the same time we are seeing and have seen, are understanding and have understood, are thinking and have thought; while it is not true that at the same time we are learning and have learnt or are being cured and have been cured.[11]

Aristotle places seeing, understanding, thinking, living well and being happy as *energeia* and learning, being cured, walking and building as *kinêsis*.[12] In the combination of present and perfect tense, part of this distinction is between activities with and without a limit. This is the distinction between *energeia* as activities 'indefinitely continuable',[13] such as the ability to continue to think of something despite it having been thought, in contrast to *kinêsis* as that which is not indefinitely continuable, such as building a house, which once built can no longer continue to be built. Although an important point to keep in mind, there is more to the distinction between *energeia* and *kinêsis* than simply activities with or without a limit.

Consider walking, which is one of Aristotle's examples of *kinêsis*, and of course a central example in this book.[14] For Aristotle, in walking the 'whence and whither constitute the form.'[15] This includes the idea that no part of a walk constitutes

---

8 The distinction between *duanamis* and *energeia* is the central topic of Book Θ of *Metaphysics* and illustrated in the example of how *energeia* is to *duanamis*: 'someone waking is to someone sleeping, as someone seeing is to a sighted person with his eyes closed, as that which has been shaped out of some matter is to the matter from which it has been shaped': Aristotle, *Metaphysics* (W.D. Ross trans.), in Richard McKeon (ed.), *The Basic Works of Aristotle* (Random House, 2001) 1048b1–3.
9 See, e.g., Aristotle, 'Physics' (R.P. Hardie and R.K. Gaye trans.), in Richard McKeon (ed.), *The Basic Works of Aristotle* (Random House, 2001) 218.
10 Aristotle, Book Θ.6 of *Metaphysics* 1048b18–35.
11 Ibid, 1048b23–35. See J.L. Akrill, 'Aristotle's Distinction between *Energeia* and *Kinêsis*', in J.L. Akrill, *Essays on Plato and Aristotle* (Clarendon Press, 1997) ch 9, 142, 143.
12 Akrill, 'Aristotle's Distinction', above, n 11, 142, 143.
13 Ibid, 143.
14 This is an example used in *Metaphysics* and also in Aristotle, *Nicomachean Ethics* (Christopher Rowe trans., Oxford University Press, 2002) x. 4 [1174a29–b5]. See Akrill, 'Aristotle's Distinction', above, n 11, 149.
15 Aristotle, *Nicomachean Ethics*, above, n 14. See Akrill, 'Aristotle's Distinction', above, n 11, 152.

the same description as another part of the walk or the whole of the same walk. For example, a walk from 'home to work' only constitutes the form of a walk from home to work once it has been completed. It is only on arrival that the walker walked from home to work and, before completion, the form of the walk is different. That is, parts of the walk can be described as parts or as whole for that part, but not as the whole walk. Consider another activity, that of building, which Aristotle offers as another example of *kinêsis*. The action of building (*kinêsis*) is quite distinct from the actions of thinking (*energeia*) in the sense that it is not indefinitely continuable. Yet, even within *kinêsis* it seems that with walking, more so perhaps than with building, the complexity of the relationship between movement and limits is revealed.[16] With this in mind, consider again the walks raised in the introduction to this book, especially Francis Alÿs' walking of the Green Line, and Richard Long's artworks, both of which test these assumptions.[17] To walk, it seems, is more than to seek a destination. This is especially so when it is a being in its own end and constitutes a stroll,[18] and to walk part of the way is still to walk a walk (or to continue to stroll despite having strolled).

What is most interesting about the distinction between *kinêsis* and *energeia* is its contribution to thinking more carefully about movement and its different forms. For the distinction between *kinêsis* and *energeia* complicates the alignment of *kinêsis* and *energeia* in relation to *duanamis*. It is this complication of movement that is important for the purposes of the book. Slowing down and paying attention to movement in its varied forms, this is an attention to both forms of *kinêsis* and *energeia*. Not only does movement come in different forms, but there is an action, activity and manner of moving to walking and building, as there is an action, activity and manner of moving to thinking, seeing, understanding and living well. That is, in a book less concerned with lines and limits, let alone the perfection of a limit or destination, in this book, I understand *kinêsis* and *energeia* as different forms of movement. To this end, it is important to pay attention to the actions and manners of movement, which includes an attention to the movements of *kinêsis* as well as the movements of *energeia*.

---

16 This is not to suggest building is without its complexities. In his essay, 'Building Dwelling Thinking', Heidegger rejects a means-end schema that places building as merely a means towards dwelling and suggests building as dwelling. Placing dwelling as the basic character of Being, Heidegger concludes this essay by linking both building (*kinêsis*) and thinking (*energeia*) as inescapable from dwelling: Martin Heidegger, 'Building Dwelling Thinking' (Albert Hofstadter trans.), in Martin Heidegger, *Basic Writings* (David Farrell Krell (ed.), Harper Perennial, 2008) ch 8, 343 [first published in English 1977]. The essay 'Building Dwelling Thinking' appears in Martin Heidegger, *Poetry, Language, Thought* (Albert Hofstadter trans., Harper & Row, 1971) 145–61 [trans. of *Vorträge und Aufsätze* (first published 1954)].

17 See Introduction. See, e.g., Richard Long, *Heaven and Earth* (Tate Publishing, 2009); Richard Long, *Walking the Line* (Thames & Hudson, 2002); Francis Alÿs, *The Green Line: Sometimes Doing Something Poetic Can Become Political and Sometimes Doing Something Political Can Become Poetic* (Directed by Francis Alÿs, 2004).

18 On stroll (*spazieren*), see Kosman, 'Aristotle's Definition of Motion', above, n 5, 58.

The purpose of this brief escapade into the world of Aristotle, including his definition of motion and distinction between *kinêsis* and *energeia*, has been to note that movement can be conceptualised in different ways.[19] Without delving further into Aristotelean metaphysics and its concerns with the definition and meaning of motion, which is a distinct sensitivity and different set of questions, this jurisprudential book is concerned with how movement might assist in understanding forms of common law practice. To this end, rather than using the terminology of motion with its Aristotelean connotations, which comes layered with a more technical meaning than movement, in this book I work with the terminology of movement, but do so in a manner that learns from Aristotelean motion the importance of paying attention to movement in its varied forms. For movement has different forms as well as being a term that moves, which is inherently unsettling and for this reason it is quite reasonable to suggest there is no settled meaning of movement.[20] While not offering a concise definition of movement, later in this chapter I provide a list of some of the ways movement is used in this book (see pages 78–79). For now,

---

19 See, e.g., Robert W Sharples, *Peripatetic Philosophy: 200 BC to AD 200 – An Introduction and Collection of Sources in Translation* (Cambridge University Press, 2010); Réné Descartes, 'Principles of Philosophy', in Réné Descartes, *Descartes: Selected Philosophical Writings* (John Cottingham, Robert Stoothoff and Dugald Murdoch trans., Cambridge University Press, 1988) [trans. of *Principia Philosophiae* (first published 1644)] Part II, xxiv–xxv; Sir Isaac Newton, *The Principia: Mathematical Principles of Natural Philosophy* (I Bernard Cohen and Anne Whitman trans., University of California Press, 1999) [trans. of *Philosophiae Naturalis Principia Mathematica* (first published 1687)]; Karl Marx, *Capital: A Critique of Political Economy* (Ben Fowkes trans., Vintage, 1977) [trans. of *Das Kapital* (first published 1867)]; Paul Souriau, *The Aesthetics of Movement* (Manon Souriau trans., University of Massachusetts Press, 1983) [trans. of *Esthétique du Mouvement* (first published 1889)]; Rudolf Laban, *The Mastery of Movement* (Macdonald & Evans, 1960); Paul Virilio, *Speed and Politics: An Essay on Dromology* (Mark Polizzotti trans., Columbia University, 1986) [trans. of *Vitesse et Politique* (first published 1977)]; Henri Lefebvre, *Rhythmanalysis: Space, Time and Everyday Life* (Stuart Elden and Gerald Moore trans., Continuum, 2004) [trans. of *Eléments de Rhythmanalyse* (first published 1992)]; Edward Said, 'Traveling Theory', in Edward Said, *The World, the Text, and the Critic* (faber & faber, 1984) ch 4; Edward Said, 'Travelling Theory Reconsidered', in Robert M. Polhemus and Roger B. Henkle, *Critical Reconstructions: The Relationship of Fiction and Life* (Stanford University Press, 1994) 251; Iris Murdoch, *The Sovereignty of the Good* (Routledge, 2001); Brian Massumi, *Parables for the Virtual: Movement, Affect, Sensation* (Duke University Press, 2002); Bruno Latour and Emilie Hermant, *Paris: Invisible City* (Liz Carey-Libbrecht trans., Institut Synthélabo pour le progrès de la connaissance, 2006) [trans. of *Paris Ville Invisible* (first published 1998)] (http://www.bruno-latour.fr/sites/default/files/downloads/viii_ paris-city-gb.pdf); Eric Manning, *Relationscapes: Movement, Art, Philosophy* (MIT Press, 2009); Lauren Benton, *A Search for Sovereignty: Law and Geography in European Empire 1400–1900* (Cambridge University Press, 2010). See, especially, the work of Paul Carter, including Paul Carter, *The Road to Botany Bay: An Essay in Spatial History* (faber & faber, 1987); Paul Carter, *Living in a New Country: History, Travelling and Language* (faber, 1992); Paul Carter, *The Lie of the Land* (faber & faber, 1996); Carter, *Dark Writing*, above, n 3; Paul Carter, 'Public Space: Its Mythopoetic Foundations and the Limits of the Law' (2007) 16(2) *Griffith Law Review* 430.
20 See, e.g., Saint Thomas Aquinas, *Commentary on Aristotle's Physics* (R.J. Blackwell trans., Yale University Press, 1963) [trans. of *Commentaria in Octo Libro Physicorum Aristotelis*] 136–7 (Lib III, Cap I, Lec II, n 2); Kosman, 'Aristotle's Definition of Motion', above, n 5, 41. See, e.g., Descartes, 'Principles of Philosophy', above, n 19, xxiv–xxv.

this part continues by turning its attention from movement generally to movement as an integral part of common law practice.

Embracing the itinerant

Movement. The word movement sits so still on this page. One of the risks and occasional consequences of noticing movement is that movement stops moving.[21] To hold onto movement and allow movement to move is not an easy task. While somewhat strange to admit, yet necessary to acknowledge, it is difficult to hold onto movement; literally. Any attempt to pin down movement for the purposes of exposition and critique in an effort to account for movement risks destroying, quite precisely, the subject of that account.[22] For not only can movement not be held, but if it were to be held, it could not be held without being fixed.

In this respect, the jurisprudential task of holding movement is less one of pinning or fixing or capturing movement and more a task of noticing and paying attention to movement, and more specifically, developing an attunement to the various forms of common law's technical and material movements. As a matter of office, therefore, it is for the jurist to develop an attunement to common law forms of practice in order to know that common law moves and notice these movements, understanding common law as an itinerant justice. These are the jurist's tasks of observation and attendance and, in this regard, what is being asked of the jurist is to embrace the itinerant: a task of action, and a matter of conduct and care.

To notice movement and embrace common law as an itinerant justice requires taking the inheritance of common law seriously. Reflected in the insistent reference to 'Anglo-Australian common law', this is an understanding of common law as a tradition: an English legal tradition.[23] Yet, what is captured by insisting on common law as a tradition? Most significantly, as with other forms of law, common law is a tradition that institutes and orders life,[24] and it does so in its particular habitual common law ways that are material, technical and practical. More specifically, common law is a practical tradition; a tradition in practice; a

---

21 Cf: Said, 'Traveling Theory', above, n 19; Said, 'Travelling Theory Reconsidered', above, n 19; Murdoch, *The Sovereignty of the Good*, above, n 19; Benton, *A Search for Sovereignty*, above, n 19.
22 This is a rephrasing of Brian Massumi, who said in an interview '"[c]ritical" practices aimed at increasing potentials for freedom and movement are inadequate, because in order to critique something in any kind of definitive way you have to pin it down': Mary Zournazi, 'Navigating Movements: A Conversation with Brian Massumi', in Mary Zournazi, *Hope: New Philosophies for Change* (Routledge, 2002) ch 10.
23 See, e.g., Piyel Haldar, *Law, Orientalism and Postcolonialism: The Jurisdiction of the Lotus Eaters* (Routledge-Cavendish, 2007). See, generally, W.T. Murphy, *The Oldest Social Science? Configurations of Law and Modernity* (Oxford University Press, 1997) ch 4.
24 Paraphrasing the Justinian Code, see Peter Goodrich, *Law in the Courts of Love: Literature and Other Minor Jurisprudences* (Routledge, 1996). See, especially, Yfat Hachamovitch, 'Ploughing the Delirium', in Veronique M. Foti (ed.), *Merleau-Ponty: Difference, Materiality, Painting* (Humanity Books, 2000) ch 8. On common law as an institution characterised by codes of normative pleasure, see Haldar, *Law, Orientalism and Postcolonialism*, above, n 23.

trade, craft and a mode or way of life. Yet the jurisprudential question, as always, is one of 'how'. How, then, is common law practised? What shapes, modes and forms does it take? Further, for those living in Australia, as with the many lives lived in places formerly assembled as the British Empire, what does it mean to inherit such a tradition? Living with law, how do we conduct our lives with such an inheritance?

To ask questions of how we might conduct our lives with such an inheritance requires developing an understanding of how this inheritance materialises in everyday common law practices. As mentioned in Chapter 1, at least in its contemporary semblance as Anglo-Australian common law, common law remains a tradition that struggles in its practices in relation, and as will be explained in this chapter, one that also struggles to be in place. In this regard, two material aspects noticed in this book are the ways in which common law is a tradition practised both in relation, and in place. Addressing these problems as matters of inheritance, rather than approaching them as contemporary ahistorical concerns, the contemporary practice of the common law tradition with its troubles in the conduct of lawful relations and its uncertainties as to how it comes to be in place are not entirely surprising. For instance, consider the following observation from the often dubbed 'modern father' of English legal history, Frederic Maitland, who noted: 'From the end of the seventeenth century onwards our English law grew up in wonderful isolation; it became very purely English and insular',[25] with one of the consequences being that 'an isolated system cannot explain itself, still less explain its history'.[26] Isolation; insular; precise geographies; a loss of explanation. This loss can be seen in the manner in which common law struggles to explain its movements. Inheriting the common law tradition, and inheriting it from the late eighteenth-century with its already embedded seventeenth-century habits has contributed to the manner in which the common law tradition has been practised, as well as the troubles it faces, and continues to face in contemporary Australia.

Therefore, to notice common law as an itinerant justice requires taking the inheritance of common law seriously, and asking: how might such an inheritance materialise in everyday practices? As a practical tradition from somewhere, and somewhen, that moves and continues to move, as will be explained, an attention to movement assists in developing an understanding of how Anglo-Australian common law comes into its relations, and how it comes to be in place. Therefore, attentive to matters of inheritance, and asking how such an inheritance might

---

25 Maitland continues, 'Our lawyers seem to have known little and cared nothing about the law of foreign countries, nothing about Roman jurisprudence': Frederic W. Maitland, *The Constitutional History of England* (Cambridge University Press, 1920) 142.

26 Frederic W. Maitland, 'Why the History of English Law is Not Written', in Frederic W. Maitland, *The Collected Papers of Frederic William Maitland* (Cambridge University Press, 1911) vol 1, 480, 489. Maitland's observations are paraphrased by Pocock; the 'principal defect of the common lawyers' historical and legal thought was their ignorance of any law but their own', John G.A. Pocock, *The Ancient Constitution and the Feudal Law: A Study of English Historical Thought in the Seventeenth Century, A Reissue with Retrospect* (Cambridge University Press, 1987) 58.

materialise in everyday practices, it becomes possible to notice that common law moves: movement.

Practising movement

To introduce movement as a technical and material practice of common law, consider the perambulatory practice of beating the bounds.[27] Although the practice varies in time and place, beating the bounds generally involves a group of people walking and marking the boundaries of a parish:

> In goodly numbers the parishioners walked round the boundaries on one of the three days before Holy Thursday, or on the Feast of the Ascension, pausing with some impressiveness at the old 'Gospel trees,' stones, and other objects on the line of the boundary. At points where the boundary took a sharp turn or was vaguely marked, youths were bumped against trees and ducked in streams, or flogged at particularly undefined places, as an aid to memory. The youths also carried willow wands with which they thrashed the various objects as they went along. The tiring day was amply repaid by the evening's amusements on the village green that followed.[28]

Often accompanied by litany, the marking of the boundary by the collective physical force of walking, hitting and the repetition of sound is often described as a 'peculiar' practice.[29] However, as a ceremonial practice of lawful movement, the practice of beating the bounds is not quite so peculiar, but, rather, it serves

---

27 On beating the bounds, and the associated *writ de peramabulation facienda*, see, generally, W.S. Tratman, 'Beating the Bounds' (1931) 42(3) *Folklore* 317, 320–21; Eve Darian-Smith, 'Beating the Bounds: Law, Identity and Territory in New Europe' (1995) 18(1) *PoLAR* 63; Eve Darian-Smith, *Bridging Divides: The Channel Tunnel and English Legal Identity in the New Europe* (University of California Press, 1999) 175; Allegra di Bonaventura, 'Beating the Bounds: Property and Perambulation in Early New England' (2007) 19 *Yale Journal of Law and the Humanities* 115; John de Morgan, 'Quaint Old Customs Which Will Not Die' (1899) 11(2) *Green Bag* 53, 54–5; Bernard J. Hibbitts, 'Coming to Our Senses: Communication and Legal Expression in Performance Cultures' (1992) 41 *Emory Law Journal* 873, 932. For a reference to the office of perambulator, and in particular William Lambard, the Perambulator of Kent (1570–76), see William Renwick Riddell, 'Eirenarcha: An Ancient Law Book' (1933) 19(5) *American Bar Association Journal* 298, 298. See also Davina Cooper, *Governing Out of Order: Space, Law, and the Politics of Belonging* (New York University Press, 1998); Shaunnagh Dorsett, 'Mapping Territories', in Shaun McVeigh (ed.), *Jurisprudence of Jurisdiction* (Routledge-Cavendish, 2007) 137, 141, citing B. Bushaway, *By Rite: Custom, Ceremony and Community in England, 1700–1880* (Junction Books, 1982) 84. Cf: for a critique on the limit of Eve Darian-Smith's interpretation of the contemporary resurgence of the practice of beating the bounds in Kent, see Paul A. Passavant, 'Enchantment, Aesthetics, and the Superficial Powers of Modern Law' (2001) 35 *Law and Society Review* 709, 720–21.
28 Tratman, 'Beating the Bounds', above, n 27, 320–21.
29 See, e.g., Darian-Smith, 'Beating the Bounds', above, n 27, 63, 70; Darian-Smith, *Bridging Divides*, above, n 27, 175; de Morgan, 'Quaint Old Customs', above, n 27, 54–5.

as an example of movement as a substrate of common law practice that hints, ideationally, at common law modes of existence.

Certainly an old custom that has gone through times of revival,[30] beating the bounds is a movement that carries legal meaning. Historically, the practice of an ecclesiastical jurisdiction, beating the bounds is intrinsically linked with the institution and maintenance of lawful place. For to walk on this occasion and in this manner is more than simply an everyday ramble: it is a ceremonial walk. This ceremonial walk ensured the parish boundaries remained unencroached and in a time prior to an abundance of maps, refreshed the memory of the old and embedded memory in the young.[31] While this may be correct, there is also something else. More than just a protection from encroachment and an aid to memory, the practice of beating the bounds involves legal movements; movements of law. For to walk the boundaries in this communal ceremony not only marks the boundaries and earthly limits of the parish, but marks an ecclesiastical jurisdictional limit. Attaching to the parish, this marks the limits of certain rights and duties of parishioners, including a right to be buried in the parish churchyard. With rights and responsibilities attaching to some but not others, to beat the bounds and walk in this ceremonial manner provides legal meaning for those residing both within and without the parish.

More than just providing clarity for the assignment of rights and duties, however, to beat the bounds produces legal spaces and it does so jurisdictionally.[32] As explained later in this chapter, the jurist needs to let go of a cartographic imagination and concomitant understanding of property and pre-given space, for this is not a story of land ownership, whether personal or territorial. To beat the bounds does not produce visible spaces with permanent markers, marked and mapped in order to be owned or governed. Rather, what the beating of the bounds performs is a constant production of space through ceremony, and through its repetitions, the making of lawful place.[33] Significantly, legal meaning is created through these ceremonial movements of walking. To walk the bounds, therefore, is more than simply a physical movement but an activity, manner and movement of law.

Although beating the bounds historically relates to an ecclesiastical jurisdiction, which is a jurisdiction that has long been in dynamic relation with the common law tradition, the practice of ceremonial walking with its contribution to the production of legal spaces and places is certainly not unique to this jurisdiction, but also a continued feature of common law's technical and material practices. To appreciate the

---

30 For a description of contemporary ceremonies in Kent, see, e.g., Darian-Smith, *Bridging Divides*, above, n 27, 175–80.
31 See, e.g., Darian-Smith, 'Beating the Bounds', above, n 27; di Bonaventura, 'Beating the Bounds', above, n 27; de Morgan, 'Quaint Old Customs', above, n 27, 54–5. In contrast, fading with the advent of maps, the practice seemingly revives with community, e.g., Darian-Smith, *Bridging Divides*, above, n 27, 175–80.
32 Henri Lefebvre, *The Production of Space* (Donald Nicholson-Smith trans., Blackwell Publishing, 1991) [trans. of *La Production de L'espace* (first published 1974)]; see Chapter 2, 2.2.
33 See Chapter 2, 2.2.

beating of the bounds as a form of common law movement, consider the common law subject. As mentioned in the introductory chapter, in a context of common law's colonial movements, Sir William Blackstone wrote in his *Commentaries*:

> For it is held, that if an uninhabited colony be discovered and planted by English subjects, all the English laws are immediately there in force. For as the law is the birthright of every subject, *so wherever they go they carry their laws with them*.[34]

To carry is both to support or bear up as well as to remove or transport, including to bear a corpse for burial.[35] Taking these two meanings together, the English subject must bear and support common law as well as transport and convey. When the English subject moves, 'wherever they go',[36] whether walking the bounds, bound for colonial New South Wales, exploring Antarctica, crossing the street with or without the pedestrian guide sparkling green or red or 'in checkout lines, at cash-points, in those queues',[37] English law is carried with them. When the English subject moves, so too does common law, which includes movements such as walking, cycling, driving, flying and movements in relation to the dead. While noting that the example of beating the bounds does not arise in an overtly colonial context, from this most literal engagement with Blackstone's expression of this common law maxim, the raw observation is simply that common law moves with the physical movements of the subject, and as addressed in Chapters 3 and 4, this form of movement is not limited to the overt context of colonisation. This is a jurisdictional technology of common law's material movements, which is a form of common law movement through ceremony that travels slowly on the surface forming part of common law's practice.

Paying attention to movement and taking Blackstone's aphorism literally, this book follows the common law subject as it moves and carries common law. Recognising those walking and beating the bounds as common law subjects, this is one of the ways in which common law moves. For to ceremonially walk the bounds is not only to walk in compliance with an ecclesiastical jurisdiction but to

---

34 William Blackstone, 'Of the Countries Subject to the Laws of England', in William Blackstone, *Commentaries on the Laws of England* (Clarendon Press, first published 1765) intro, s 4 [emphasis added]. This is part of the larger rule relating to the reception of law in conquered, ceded and uninhabited countries. See Chapter 3, 3.1.
35 Charles Talbut Onions (ed.), *The Oxford English Dictionary of English Etymology* (Clarendon Press, 1966).
36 Blackstone, 'Of the Countries Subject to the Laws of England', above, n 34.
37 Seamus Heaney, 'The Tollund Man in Springtime', in Seamus Heaney, *District and Circle* (faber & faber, 2006), although, of course, the Tollund Man, who was found mummified in a peat bog in Denmark, having lived during the fourth century BC, would not be carrying English law, even with common law's origin story as existing since time immemorial (i.e. time before memory, i.e. 1066); Peter Goodrich and Yfat Hachamovitch, 'Time Out of Mind: An Introduction to the Semiotics of Common Law', in Peter Fitzpatrick (ed.), *Dangerous Supplements: Resistance and Renewal in Jurisprudence* (Pluto Press, 1991) 167.

bear and support and convey common law. This is walking as a form of common law movement; actions and manners of moving common law.[38] It is, therefore, one of the ways in which common law moves. Paying attention to distinct forms of movement, it can be observed that for the common law subject beating the bounds there are at least three forms of movement present. The first is the technical movements of common law through the jurisdictional status of the person as subject and the second is the ceremonial act of walking on the surface of the earth. The third is movements in relation to another form of law, in this instance, ecclesiastical, which is a common law technique of movement described in Chapter 3 as 'camping'.[39] Through camping, this is a form of common law movement in the creation and conduct of lawful relations. Together, these three forms of movement, active in the beating of the bounds, introduce some of the different forms of common law movement, placing walking as a common law technique of movement, and illustrating some of the meaning common law's movements may carry.

Another form of movement can be observed in common law's travelling history, which also hints at common law's historical and geopolitical movements of empire as well as its institutional movements as a matter of practice and mode of existence:

> The history of the common law has always been a history of movement, of a wandering *nomos*, a narrative of itinerant justice and itinerant justices. Its movement has been both literal and metaphysical, a question of a peripatetic court and also of laws of transmission of legal knowledge: moveable bodies become moveable signs.[40]

As Peter Goodrich notes, since the early travels of the King, the *curia regis* and the eyre circuits, common law has been an itinerant justice. From the physical movements of the King as he moved in order to hear legal disputes to the movements of the itinerant justices as they took up some of this work, common law has moved. It is important not to dismiss this as mere historical anecdote, for today, in Australia, courts and justices continue to move. From the High Court of Australia as it travels its annual circuits beyond Canberra to major cities in order to hear special leave applications to the movements of federal and state courts as they travel on circuit to towns and other remote locations, common law courts continue to move. With

---

38 On walking as juridical form, see Chapter 3, 3.3.
39 On camping as a form of jurisdictional movement, see Chapter 3, 3.4.
40 Peter Goodrich, *Languages of Law*, above, n 1. These are the first lines in chapter 9, '*Pro Persona Mori: To Die for One's Mask*', headed, 'Introduction: Laws of Movement'. Goodrich continues: 'Any intelligent discussion of the common law tradition should look to the multiple senses of legal transmission and consider the various spatial and temporal trajectories of passage of legal knowledge. Those trajectories … can be framed in diverse ways.' Goodrich frames and traces these trajectories in various ways, but primarily at the level of language from theology to law, which is a different form of tracing than the way movement is attended to in this book, that is, on a minor register of technical and material practice.

the advent of modern technology that both eases movement (such as transport) and alleviates the need for movement (such as videolink), common law courts do not stop. Despite the development of technology to a point where it is no longer necessary, courts continue to move on circuit. At the level of the institution, from historical movements of courts to modern circuits, common law is an itinerant justice. Institutionally, courts move and they do so because common law moves as a matter of practice. More than just institutional movements, these examples of beating the bounds, Blackstone's walking subject, and courts on circuit hint at movement as being part of the substrate of common law's mode of existence, both institutionally as well as ideationally.

Enlisting movement

In the first part of this chapter, some of the ways in which common law moves have been introduced. Some, however, are left to rest until they arise later in the book. As a guide, the following list lightly captures some of these different common law forms of movement and notes their major moments of feature in this book. As a word of caution, however: this list classifies some forms of movements, casting aside the relations between forms, relations the jurist ought not to overlook:

- 'Movements of empire' refer to the historical, geopolitical and empirical movements of common law between the metropole and its colonies. This is lightly touched on in this chapter and again in Chapter 4, but features most prominently in Chapter 3 in the context of the movements of common law into, in and within the Colony of New South Wales.
- 'Jurisdictional movement' is how common law moves. Linking movement, jurisdiction and technology, movement is a technique of the common law and an aspect of common law's technology of jurisdiction. In other words, this is jurisdiction as a common law technology of movement. Introduced in the next part of this chapter, jurisdiction is the preeminent common law technique of movement revealed through redescriptions of common law practice in Chapters 3 and 4.
- 'Movements in relation to the dead'; 'movements into place'. This refers to one of the ways common law moves in its relations, and into place, and raises the jurist's responsibility to care for the dead. As a material practice, common law's movements traverse the surface of the earth, which is most clearly so in its movements in relation to the dead through the institution of burial. This is a form of superficial movement introduced in the final part of this chapter on burial, noticed in Chapter 3 and complicated in Chapters 4 and 5.
- 'Movement as the substrate of common law practice'. Both ideationally and institutionally, this is a reference to movement as part of the substrate of common law's mode of existence or at least essential to that mode. Introduced in this part of the chapter, this rests quietly in this minor jurisprudence in Chapters 3 and 4, emerging lightly in the final chapter.

- 'Slow movement' refers to the time and space of movement, and its different paces. As mentioned in Chapter 1, a method of slowness is integral to the practice of jurisprudential redescription in Chapters 3 and 4.
- 'Moving well' is a normative claim that the jurist ought to pay attention to movement, in these different forms, in order to move well, both as a matter of practice and an ethics of conduct. Resting quietly, this resonates in Chapter 5.

As the jurist pays attention to movement, in all these varied ways, the task becomes one of embracing common law as an itinerant justice in order to take responsibility for Anglo-Australian common law's movements as a matter of office. This is not an easy task. In response to the difficulty of holding onto movement, in this minor jurisprudence, I choose to focus on the technical and material forms of common law's movements. As a result, the jurist is asked to pay attention not only to material practices of common law's movements, that is, not only observe *that* it moves, but also *how* it moves. In doing so, what occurs is a shift to a more minor register that not only provides the jurist with a way of accounting for the technical and material activity of common law movement, but also leads to an appreciation of certain difficulties with common law, including a problem with place. This shift in register occurs in the next part of this chapter. To this end, having introduced some of the varied shapes and forms of movement, the first part of this chapter unsettled movement and asked the jurist to embrace common law as an itinerant justice. Starting to notice the activity and manners of moving in its different forms as part of common law practice, the next part of Chapter 2 opens up ways in which the jurist may register technical forms and material practices of common law's movements.

2.2 Jurisdictional movements

With common law already moving, the next question to be asked is one of how? How does common law move? The answer this book offers is jurisdiction. Jurisdiction is the technology that gives form and shape to common law, including its movements. Drawing on recent scholarship reinvesting jurisdiction as a central concern of jurisprudence, this book contributes to this literature by linking jurisdiction with movement as a matter of jurisprudence. More specifically, this is jurisdiction as a technology of movement, as well as movement as a jurisdictional technology of the common law. Most simply, yet significant in its simplicity, this is the contention that it is through the technology of jurisdiction that common law moves.

What is jurisdiction? While quite varied definitions could be offered, as a matter of jurisprudence, the question of jurisdiction is and must always be the first question of law.[41] This is in the idiomatic sense that without jurisdiction law cannot be spoken but it is also the first question in the sense that jurisdiction is a mode of authorising law, asking whether something belongs to law – a question of what

---

41 Shaunnagh Dorsett and Shaun McVeigh, *Jurisdiction* (Routledge-Cavendish, 2012) ch 1.

is lawful – and only subsequently turning to the question of what that law is.[42] Problematically, as both authority and authorisation, the question of jurisdiction is often tied to and obscured if not consumed by questions of sovereignty, territory and the state. With jurisdictional technologies more than simply boundary-making processes, marking that which is within or without, metanarratives of sovereignty, territory and the state often work to obscure common law's technical forms and material practices, including its movements.

Always technical and never less than practical,[43] one of the benefits of 'jurisdictional thinking'[44] is that it alerts the jurist to the work of this obscuration; this sovereign consumption. In this respect, an attention to the technologies of jurisdiction reveals a problem with common law's place; the problem being that common law is not as everywhere as it may at times seem to be. Noticing the spatial aspects of this problem, a problem that stalls movement, jurisdictional thinking allows the jurist to attend to movement as a matter of jurisprudence. Choosing to work with the resources of the common law, this minor jurisprudence thinks with jurisdiction as a way of remaining within a legal idiom attentive to movement as part common law practice. As a result, the social question of law's space is separated from the jurisprudential question of how common law comes to be in place: a jurisprudential question of movement. If it is with the sovereign obscuring of jurisdiction that common law seemingly stalls, unmoving, it is by attending to common law's technologies of jurisdiction that common law moves. As a mode of authorisation, both ideationally and institutionally, jurisdiction is a technical and material practice of common law; an activity. For the jurist in office who stays with common law and thinks jurisdictionally, this places jurisdiction as an activity that gives shape to common law. As a practice that moves, this links the technologies of jurisdiction to the activities and manners of common law's movements.

Therefore, for the jurist in office, attending to the technologies of jurisdiction and noticing how common law works reveals the importance of movement as a matter of technical practice, and a matter of conduct. This is because the movement of common law reminds the jurist that common law is an activity and a technical practice. This is the work of the technology of jurisdiction. For jurisdiction is the technology that authors and authorises the activities of common law; its forms of movement. It is in this sense that this second part of the chapter on the importance of movement links jurisdiction, technology and movement, proposing that common law moves through the technology of jurisdiction. To this end, this part introduces jurisdiction as a technology, reveals a problem with common law's place, and walks alongside critical legal geography and the Lefebvrian concept of space as a way of explaining how movement, technology and jurisdiction coalesce to offer the jurist a jurisprudential question of place.

---

42 Ibid.
43 Ibid.
44 Ibid.

Jurisdiction as a technology of movement

In recent years, there has been a critical refreshing of questions of jurisdiction as a central concern of jurisprudence, most notably in the work of Shaunnagh Dorsett and Shaun McVeigh.[45] In their recent book *Jurisdiction*, Dorsett and McVeigh place 'jurisdictional thinking' as giving 'legal form to life and life to law'.[46] This is the suggestion that while technical and never less than practical, jurisdictional thinking is always also something more.[47] More than just the technical ordering of authority, and more than just a 'practical knowledge of how to do things with law', jurisdiction 'opens a domain of thought, or a jurisprudence, concerned with how to live with law and how to create and engage lawful relations.'[48] Addressing both forms of jurisdiction and a jurisdiction of form, Dorsett and McVeigh shape repertoires of jurisdiction into a jurisprudence, attending to the ways in which jurisdiction creates forms of responsibility for law.[49]

Following Dorsett and McVeigh, this book offers a contribution to the reinvestment of jurisdiction as a central concern of jurisprudence in the form of movement. This is both jurisdiction as a technology of movement, and movement as

---

45 Dorsett and McVeigh, *Jurisdiction*, above, n 41; Shaun McVeigh (ed.), *Jurisprudence of Jurisdiction* (Routledge-Cavendish, 2007); Shaunnagh Dorsett and Shaun McVeigh, 'Questions of Jurisdiction', in Shaun McVeigh (ed.), *Jurisprudence of Jurisdiction* (Routledge-Cavendish, 2007); Shaunnagh Dorsett and Shaun McVeigh, 'Just So: "The Law Which Governs Australia is Australian Law"' (2002) 13 *Law and Critique* 289; Shaunnagh Dorsett and Shaun McVeigh, 'An Essay on Jurisdiction, Jurisprudence and Authority: The High Court of Australia in *Yorta Yorta*' (2001) 56(1) *Northern Ireland Legal Quarterly* 1; Shaunnagh Dorsett, '"Since Time Immemorial": A Story of Common Law Jurisdiction, Native Title and the *Case of Tanistry*' (2002) 26 *Melbourne University Law Review* 32. See also Peter Rush, 'An Altered Jurisdiction: Corporeal Traces of Law' (1997) 6 *Griffith Law Review* 144; Peter Rush, 'Deathbound Doctrine: Scenes of Murder and its Inheritance' (1997) 16 *Studies in Law Politics and Society* 71; Peter Rush, 'Surviving Common Law: Silence and the Violence Internal to the Legal Sign' (2005) 27(2) *Cardozo Law Review* 753; Edward Mussawir, *Jurisdiction in Deleuze: The Expression and Representation of Law* (Routledge- Cavendish, 2011); Edward Mussawir, 'The Activity of Judgement: Deleuze, Jurisdiction and the Procedural Genre of Jurisprudence' (2011) 7(3) *Law, Culture and the Humanities* 463; Edward Mussawir, 'Jurisdiction of Control: Judgement and Procedural Forms in *Thomas v Mowbray*' (2010) 19(2) *Griffith Law Review* 307; Bradin Cormack, *A Power to Do Justice: Jurisdiction, English Literature, and the Rise of Common Law 1509–1625* (Chicago University Press, 2007); Haldar, *Law, Orientalism and Postcolonialism*, above, n 23; Peter Goodrich, 'Visive Powers: Colours, Trees and Genres of Jurisdiction' (2008) 2(2) *Law and Humanities* 213; Goodrich, *Languages of Law*, above, n 1; Peter Goodrich, *Oedipus Lex: Psychoanalysis, History, Law* (Berkeley: University of California Press, 1995); Goodrich, *Law in the Courts of Love*, above, n 24. See, generally, Robert Cover, 'The Folktales of Justice: Tales of Jurisdiction', in Martha Minow, Michael Ryan and Austin Sarat (eds.), *Narrative, Violence and the Law: The Essays of Robert Cover* (University of Michigan Press, 1992) ch 4; Richard T. Ford, 'Law's Territory (A History of Jurisdiction)' (1999) 97(4) *Michigan Law Review* 843; Richard T. Ford, 'Law's Territory (A History of Jurisdiction)', in Nicholas Blomley, David Delaney and Richard T. Ford (eds.), *The Legal Geographies Reader: Law, Power and Space* (Blackwell Publishers, 2001).
46 Dorsett and McVeigh, *Jurisdiction*, above, n 41, 1.
47 Ibid, ch 1.
48 Ibid, 4.
49 Ibid, ch 8.

a jurisdictional technology of the common law. To explain this contribution, a few introductory comments on jurisdiction and technology are needed before addressing some of the links between jurisdiction, technology and movement in the creation and conduct of lawful relations and the creation and conduct of common law's place, links developed slowly across this part of the chapter. As a common law technology central to both the form and conduct of lawful relations as well as the ways in which common law comes to be in place, these links suggest the technology of jurisdiction is a technology of movement giving shape and form to common law practice. This is jurisdiction as how common law moves, and it is also movement as how common law is. Attending to technologies of jurisdiction, the responsible jurist is able to register movement in accordance with the tasks of office and in doing so take responsibility for movement.

As mentioned, the question of jurisdiction is and must always be the first question of law.[50] This is most obviously so in its etymological heritage of the Latin noun *ius* (law) and verb *dicere* (to speak), which roughly translates as the saying or the speaking of law.[51] As Peter Rush explains, jurisdiction 'refers us first and foremost to the power and authority to speak in the name of the law and only subsequently to the fact that law is stated – and stated to be someone or something'.[52] This is jurisdiction as idiom, as a way of speaking and practising law. However, it is the first question of law not just in the sense that without jurisdiction, one cannot speak law, but also in the sense that 'jurisdiction asks whether law exists at all, the question of which law follows on.'[53] This is jurisdiction as both authority and authorisation.[54] As will be explained shortly in this part, it is by attending to jurisdictional modes of authorisation that a problem with common law's place is revealed; a problem which masks movement as a matter of sovereign practice.

For jurisdiction is both technical in that it is how things can be done with law, and practical in that jurisdiction is productive; crafting law. In this respect, technologies of jurisdiction create and arrange the institutional practices of law as well as creating and conducting lawful relations.[55] This is technology in the following sense:

> Technology derives from the Greek *technê*, meaning craft, art or strategy. In a classical sense, *technê* described a power or capacity to produce things whose

---

50 Ibid, ch 1. See also Rush, 'An Altered Jurisdiction', above, n 45.
51 Dorsett and McVeigh, *Jurisdiction*, above, n 41, ch 1; McVeigh (ed.), *Jurisprudence of Jurisdiction*, above, n 45, ch 1; Dorsett and McVeigh, 'Questions of Jurisdiction', above, n 45. See also Rush, 'An Altered Jurisdiction', above, n 45; Goodrich, 'Visive Powers', above, n 45, 217–18; Cormack, *A Power to do Justice*, above, n 45, 5; Emile Benveniste, *Indo-European Language and Society* (faber & faber, 1973) 392.
52 Rush, 'An Altered Jurisdiction', above, n 45, 150.
53 Dorsett and McVeigh, *Jurisdiction*, above, n 41, ch 1. See also Rush, 'An Altered Jurisdiction', above, n 45.
54 Dorsett and McVeigh, *Jurisdiction*, above, n 41, ch 3.
55 Ibid, ch 4.

eventual existence was contingent upon the exercise of that power, things whose existence was 'caused' by the craftsman. *Technê* (craft), as opposed to *epistêmê* (knowledge), connotes practical knowledge or practices ordered towards the production of something. There is, however, no strict dividing line between the two. Thus, craft is prudential because it works with, and produces, the kind of knowledge which is not scientific, but which requires judgment. For Aristotle, for example, *technê*, or craft, is also *epistêmê*, or knowledge, because it is a practice grounded in an 'account'. It is something which involves understanding (Aristotle 2002). ... [I]t is the combination of experience and technique that enables the practice of jurisdiction.[56]

This is technology in its classical sense of craft: a practical knowledge or wisdom. For the jurist, the technology of jurisdiction is a craft, practice, activity and prudence of law that requires a practical knowledge of law. Crafting law, this places technologies of jurisdiction as creating and arranging lawful relations and hence part of what it means for the responsible jurist to take up and hold office.

For example, consider the shape of the High Court of Australia's address to questions of Aboriginal sovereignty raised in Chapter 1 as a matter of lawful relations. The simple but crucial point is that the key feature of these High Court judgments, which is a feature often overlooked or underrated, is the technology of jurisdiction.[57] For the High Court has consistently held Aboriginal sovereignty 'non-justiciable'. What this means is that it was through the technology of jurisdiction that the High Court has determined questions of Aboriginal sovereignty non-justiciable; refused the question of Aboriginal sovereignty; declared it would not speak to another form of law. This is jurisdiction as a technology of the common law.

Significantly, for the jurist attending to the creation and conduct of lawful relations, it is important to recognise that common law's attempts to relate to indigenous forms of law are jurisdictional. In these High Court decisions, marked as non-justiciable, common law refused to meet with or relate to another form of law

---

56 Ibid, 55–6, with internal citation: Aristotle, *Nicomachean Ethics*, above, n 14. In a similar vein, Heidegger considers the Greek term *techne* as 'neither art nor handicraft but, rather, to make something appear, within what is present, as this or that, in this way or that way': Heidegger, 'Building Dwelling Thinking', above, n 16, 347, 361.

57 *Coe v Commonwealth* (1979) 24 ALR 118 ('*Coe (No 1)*') established the common law position that Aboriginal sovereignty is non-justiciable. See also *Mabo (No 2)* (1992) 175 CLR 1; *Coe (on behalf of the Wiradjuri tribe) v Commonwealth of Australia* (1993) 118 ALR 193 ('*Coe (No 2)*'); *Walker v New South Wales* (1994) 182 CLR 45; *Thorpe v Commonwealth of Australia (No 3)* (1997) 144 ALR 677; *Members of the Yorta Yorta Aboriginal Community v Victoria* (2002) 214 CLR 422; *R v Buzzacott* (2004) 154 ACTR 37. See also *Re Phillips; Ex parte Aboriginal Development Commission* (1987) 13 FCR 384; *Commonwealth v Coe* [2002] NSWSC 94 (26 February 2002). See Chapter 1, 1.1. See, e.g., Sean Brennan, Brenda Gunn and George Williams, '"Sovereignty" and its Relevance to Treaty-Making Between Indigenous Peoples and Australian Governments' (2004) 26 *Sydney Law Review* 307; Dianne Otto, 'A Question of Law or Politics? Indigenous Claims to Sovereignty in Australia' (1995) 21 *Syracuse Journal of International Law and Commerce* 65. *Contra* Rush, 'An Altered Jurisdiction', above, n 45.

and it did so through jurisdiction. This is in the idiomatic sense that jurisdiction authors and authorises the speech of common law, whether communicating or not with another form of law. More than just a representation of idiom, however, this is jurisdiction as the technology by which common law creates, conducts and orders lawful relations; it is how common law relates. For common law came into relation with another form of law, albeit briefly and somewhat abruptly – an instance of the questionable quality of the creation and conduct of lawful relations – but it did so through the technology of jurisdiction.[58] Marked as non-justiciable, and coming in the guise of a refusal to come into relation, this is a form of jurisdictional ordering conducted through common law's idiom. In other words, this is the technology of jurisdiction creating, arranging and ordering lawful relations and in doing so, giving form to common law practice.

This raises the jurisprudential question of movement. In the context of lawful relations, the importance of movement includes that it is through the activities of movement that common law comes into and creates relations across space and time. This includes the somewhat infantile point that moving things bump into things,[59] but also captures the more profound point that without movement there would be no lawful relations. This is because movement is how common law comes into its relations; and common law comes into its relations through the technology of jurisdiction. This is the proposal that is slowly developed in this part; that jurisdiction is a technology of movement that authors and authorises the ways in which common law comes into and conducts its relations, as well as comes to be in place. This includes relations with other forms of law and, as addressed in the final part of this chapter, common law's relations with the dead, especially through the institution of burial.

So, as illustrated in the example of Aboriginal sovereignty just examined, jurisdiction is how common law relates, and this book proposes that jurisdiction is also how common law moves. This is the proposal that jurisdiction is the technology by which common law moves, both in its relations and into place, although masked by sovereignty its movements into place are a little less obvious. Attending to technologies of jurisdiction, such as those present in these High Court cases, the jurist is able to register movement. This includes the idiomatic movement of common law as it relates to another form of law, including its movements in retreat of the unspeakable. In addition, there is a further form of movement in common law's representations of an 'everywhereness', shaping common law in such a way that it pushes out another, hinting at a problem with common law's place. So, having linked jurisdiction and technology through craft and practice to the creation and conduct of lawful relations, and suggested movement, more is needed to properly

---

58 On the quality of the conduct of lawful relations, see Dorsett and McVeigh, *Jurisdiction*, above, n 41, especially chs 6–8; Dorsett and McVeigh, 'Conduct of Laws: Native Title, Responsibility and Some Limits of Jurisdictional Thinking' (2012) 36(2) *Melbourne University Law Review* 470.

59 For a more nuanced engagement with 'bumping' as part of the ambiguity of meeting, see Paul Carter, 'The Chi Complex and Ambiguities of Meeting' (2010) 12(4) *CLCWeb: Comparative Literature and Culture: A WWWeb Journal* 1.

reveal the jurisprudential place of movement. For there is a problem with place that masks the forms of relations between jurisdiction, technology and movement. Identifying this problem assists in revealing the technical and material forms of common law's jurisdictional practices of movement, revealing jurisdiction as a technology of movement.

The problem with common law's place

Moving through the technology of jurisdiction, common law comes into its relations and these movements and relations occur somewhere. Paying attention to this 'somewhere', something particularly odd about common law's place becomes apparent. This oddness is revealed in the attempt to simultaneously hold two rival common law conceits: one enmeshed in metanarratives of the state, sovereignty and territory and the other operating on a more minor register that attends to technical and material forms of common law's movements. Paying attention to jurisdiction as a technology of movement, this book reveals a problem with common law's place. This is not a problem with authority as such, but rather its representation and actualisation. As such, the problem with place is revealed through an attentiveness to jurisdiction as a common law mode of authorisation, which is one that reveals the place of movement in forms of common law practice. The problem with common law's place is quite simply that it is not as everywhere as it may seem to be.

To illustrate the liaison between sovereignty, territory and the state, and the place of common law or more precisely its problem with place, consider again the non-justiciability of questions of Aboriginal sovereignty.[60] Generally relying on the act of state doctrine as grounds for non-justiciability,[61] the following reasoning is illuminating:

> The established legal doctrine is that the acquisition of sovereignty by the Crown is not subject to challenge in a domestic court. It is a proposition both of clear authority and logical necessity ... [I]n any legal system there must be a starting point that cannot itself be challenged within the system ... [T]his Court cannot bring into question the basic principle of law underlying its own existence that there is but one sovereignty over the geographic entity of Australia and that the exercise of that sovereignty is governed by the Constitution of Australia.[62]

---

60 See Chapter 1, 1.1; Chapter 2, 2.2.
61 The act of state doctrine provides that acts of state, such as those acts which established the sovereignty of the Australian state, cannot be challenged in courts created as a result of those acts of state; *New South Wales v Commonwealth* (1975) 135 CLR 377, 388.
62 *R v Buzzacott* (2004) 154 ACTR 37 [14] (Connolly J). This decision was affirmed on appeal: *Buzzacott v The Queen* [2005] ACTCA 7 (1 March 2005).

In this excerpt from judgment, Justice Connolly in the Supreme Court of the Australian Capital Territory, following prior High Court decisions, places the origin and continued existence of common law in Australia as fundamental, necessarily assumed and unchallengeable: unspeakable.[63] Problematically, often when questions of authority, origin or inauguration are raised, sovereignty sweeps in and occludes a consideration of jurisdiction. Yet, as already explained in this part, it is through technologies of jurisdictions that Australian courts refuse to address another law, including through this judgment. More than just a refusal to address another, however, by refusing the question asked, the Court – both Supreme and High – also refuses to explain its origins, inauguration, authority, refusing to articulate authority and authorisation. While much could be said on common law's anxious existence and its struggle to relate to indigenous forms of law as the existential condition of Anglo-Australian common law,[64] as a minor jurisprudence, the concern here is less one of existence and more a concern with technical and material practices of movement. For this reason, the jurist is asked to attend to the technologies of jurisdiction at work in the judgment.

Consider Justice Connolly's reference to the 'basic principle' that there is 'but one sovereignty over the geographic entity of Australia'.[65] Not alone in this line of thinking, for Connolly J the landmass of Australia is home to one sovereign, governed by one law; filled and full with one law: Anglo-Australian common law.[66] Of

---

63 See cases cited in Chapter 1, 1.1. In particular, note the following passage: 'The annexation of the east coast of Australia by Captain Cook in 1770, and the subsequent acts by which the whole of the Australian continent became part of the dominions of the Crown, were acts of state whose validity cannot be challenged: see *New South Wales v Commonwealth* (1975) 135 CLR 377, 388; 8 ALR 1, 28, and cases there cited. If the amended statement of claim intends to suggest either that the legal foundation of the Commonwealth is insecure, or that the powers of the Parliament are more limited than is provided in the Constitution, or that there is an aboriginal nation which has sovereignty over Australia, it cannot be supported … The contention that there is in Australia an aboriginal nation exercising sovereignty, even of a limited kind, is quite impossible in law to maintain', per *Coe vs Commonwealth (No 1)* (1979) 24 ALR 118, 129 (Gibbs J).
64 See Rush, 'Deathbound Doctrine', above, n 45. See also Kirsty Duncanson, 'The Scene of the Crime: The Uneasy Figuring of Anglo-Australian Sovereignty in the Landscape of *Lantana* (2009) 13 *Law Text Culture* 25. Cf: Juliet Rogers and Peter Rush, 'The Remains of Authority and the Trial of Saddam Hussein' (2009) 31 *Australian Feminist Law Journal* 121.
65 *R v Buzzacott* (2004) 154 ACTR 37 [14] (Connolly J).
66 See, e.g., Catriona Elder who writes, 'The fantasy of a clearly bounded and inviolable national space has underpinned many of the ideas that white Australians carry with them of what it means to be "Australian". The continually reinforced (though perpetually challenged) belief is that the nation is a singular and coherent space out to the furthermost boundaries of the sea … The fantasy of the coherence of the white Australian nation/state needs to be especially emphatic in the face of sovereign Indigenous peoples … In the Australian vision of "settler colonialism" the Indigenous peoples' prior occupation and ongoing presence directly challenges the settler fantasy. So Indigenous peoples need to be eliminated both literally and metaphorically from the space of the nation': Catriona Elder, 'Invaders, Illegals and Aliens' (2003) 7 *Law, Text, Culture* 221, 223 (citations omitted).

course, sovereignty and the operation of sovereign authority is much more complex than this.[67] Yet, given the dominance of sovereignty and the modern state in contemporary orderings of law, it is perhaps not surprising that an emphasis on the state tends to mask certain features of common law, including its forms and modes of technical and material practice. This is the collusive logic of sovereignty, territory and the state, one that tends to obscure the workings of jurisdictional technologies.

To explain, consider the place of common law represented through the language and judgment of Connolly J. With the state exercising its sovereign authority over territory, this is sovereign territory as law attaching to land; and as sovereign territorial jurisdiction, which is a common law imagining of a landmass covered by Anglo-Australian common law. This is an image and a representation of place that is one of singular common law fullness; of one empty space filled with – and only with – common law; no gaps, complete, exclusive, everywhere. Although sovereign territorial jurisdiction may appear differently for others, it emerges here as an image of a non-textured, evenly distributed, perfectly well-buttered smothering of law across land. This is a representation of common law controlling and inhabiting the geographic entity of Australia, the one and only space and, it seems, all available legal spaces.[68]

Indebted to modern understandings of the concepts of sovereignty, territory and the state, this is one understanding of the place of common law in Australia, if not the dominant understanding. While this 'everywhereness' may not be the most astounding revelation, the oddity of the observation arises in the context of a counter-image, offered in Chapter 1, which is an image arising from the acknowledgement of the existence, exercise and practice of multiple forms of law in Australia. Significantly, the representation of an 'everywhereness' of common law's place amounts to a form of spatial and legal enclosure in at least two senses. The first is that a singular and full space, completely and exclusively filled to the brim with only one form of law is a space of non-movement. So full that common law cannot move; inhibiting movement. The second is the sense that there are no longer any spaces available for the existence, practice and exercise of other forms of law, let alone the practice and conduct of lawful relations. This requires overlooking jurisdictional technologies in the creation and conduct of lawful relations.

---

67 See, generally, Michel Foucault, *Society Must Be Defended: Lectures at the Collège de France, 1975–76* (David Macey trans., Picador, 2004); Carl Schmitt, *Political Theology: Four Chapters on the Concept of Sovereignty* (MIT Press, 1985); Giorgio Agamben, *Homo Sacer: Sovereign Power and Bare Life* (Stanford University Press, 1998) and Giorgio Agamben, *State of Exception* (Stanford University Press, 2005).
68 Cf: William Edward Stanner who wrote, reflecting on this erasure, 'a view from a window which has been carefully placed to exclude a whole quadrant of the landscape. What may well have begun as a simple forgetting of other possible views turned under habit and over time into something like a cult of forgetfulness practised on a national scale. We have been able for so long to disremember the aborigines that we are now hard put to keep them in mind even when we most want to do so'. William Edward Stanner, *After the Dreaming: The Boyer Lectures 1968* (Australian Broadcasting Corporation, 1972) 25.

Yet, consider multiple forms of law in that same space. If common law is everywhere, this causes conceptual difficulties, at least spatially, for the exercise and practice of other forms of law, whether overcrowding or overlapping common law's purported place. This second image of multiple laws provides a more textured, erratic and inconsistent spatial landscaping of the spaces and places of common law in Australia. Working against the metanarratives of sovereignty, territory and the state, the second image works against the first image, challenging territorial attachments; detaching law from land.

Holding these two images together, the place of common law becomes a little unsteady. This is because on a certain register these two images, both of which are common law conceits of common law, are seemingly incompatible. In the context of multiples, what is revealed is that common law's place is not as everywhere as it may seem to be. *This is the problem with place.* On a jurisdictional register that pays attention to the technical and material practices of law, my argument is that common law simply cannot be and in fact is not everywhere. Certainly, if common law is everywhere, there are some obvious difficulties with the creation and conduct of lawful relations with other forms of law. More delicately, if in the common law imaginary, common law seems to be everywhere, if it is founded, grounded, imagined and represented on the premise it is everywhere and practised as if it were everywhere, common law necessarily carries a particular form that struggles in the creation let alone conduct, exercise and engagement of lawful relations.

Therefore, there is a problem with common law's place: common law's place is not as everywhere as it may seem. To respond to this problem and think more carefully about common law's place, it is helpful to slow down and contemplate how common law comes to be in place. This requires the jurist to notice that metanarratives of sovereignty, territory and the state tend to obscure common law's technical and practical workings, and that as a matter of office, the jurist needs to attend to common law's technologies of jurisdiction. In doing so, the jurist is then able to think more carefully about how common law comes to be in place, and the meanings this may carry. For it is through the technology of jurisdiction that common law moves into place, or at least seems to move into place; a place appearing to be everywhere.

Placing space: responding to the problem with common law's place

Integral to the problem with place is a particular imagining of a common law form, obscuring, consuming and even stopping movement. Yet, common law moves and there are different forms of movement. Addressing the relationship between movement, space and place, the jurisprudential argument developed here is that through common law's jurisdictional movements, common law produces space and comes to be (temporarily at least) in place. While noting that this argument runs alongside recent scholarship in critical legal geography, the jurisprudential concern of the jurist is not the same as the geographer's concern with space or the critical legal geographer's concern with legal space. The jurisprudential concern of the jurist is one of common law's place. More particularly, for the jurist responsible for a colonial form of law, it is a jurisprudential question of how to be in place, which is a question of conduct. To this end, the jurist is reminded that one of the jurisprudential tasks of office is to register movement and attend to common law's place. Therefore, while space is not the immediate concern of the jurist, the observation, description and redescription of space serves as a way of attending to movement, including the ways in which common law comes to be in place. This is especially so in relation to burial, which is addressed in the final part of this chapter as one of the ways in which common law moves in relation to the dead and comes to be in place.

As a jurisprudential book that occasionally crosses but largely runs alongside the no longer emergent but rather recently emerged literature falling within the rubric of 'law and geography' or 'critical legal geography', it is helpful to again briefly comment on this scholarship, raised in the introduction of this book, before considering the concept of space. Law and geography developed from an interdisciplinary unison of theoretical approaches, aiming to enrich understandings of law, space and society.[69] Published in 1994, Nicholas Blomley's *Law, Space, and the Geographies of Power*[70] is commonly attributed as beginning research in law and geography.[71] Although this is not strictly true, as both jurists and geographers have long worked across this disciplinary divide,[72] Blomley's work did initiate new strands of research. There is now a diverse range of literature addressing spatial justice,[73]

---

69 See Nicholas Blomley, *Law, Space, and the Geographies of Power* (Guilford Press, 1994) 7–26.
70 Ibid. See also Nicholas Blomley, 'Law, Property, and the Spaces of Violence: The Frontier, the Survey, and the Grid' (2003) 93(1) *Annals of the Association of American Geographers* 121; Nicholas Blomley, *Unsettling the City: Urban Land and the Politics of Property* (Routledge, 2004); Nicholas Blomley, 'Making Private Property: Enclosure, Common Right and the Work of Hedges' (2007) 18 *Rural History* 1; Nicholas Blomley, 'How to Turn a Beggar into a Bus Stop: Law, Traffic and the "Function of the Place"' (2007) 44(9) *Urban Studies* 1697; Nicholas Blomley, *Rights of Passage: Sidewalks and the Regulation of Public Flow* (Routledge, 2011).
71 See, e.g., Andreas Philippopoulos-Mihalopoulos, 'Law's Spatial Turn: Geography, Justice and a Certain Fear of Space' (2010) 7(2) *Law Culture and the Humanities* 187, 190.
72 In what arguably constitutes an earlier 'start' to critical legal geography, see Gordon Clark, *Judges and the Cities: Interpreting Local Autonomy* (University of Chicago Press, 1985). In a more general sense, the comparative questioning of the ways in which different laws exist in different locations also crosses this implicit divide; see, e.g., David Kennedy, 'New Approaches to Comparative Law: Comparativism and International Governance' (1997) 2 *Utah Law Review* 545.
73 Andreas Philippopoulos-Mihalopoulos, *Spatial Justice: Body, Lawscape, Atmosphere* (Routledge, 2015). See, e.g., Andreas Philippopoulos-Mihalopoulos, 'Spatial Justice: Law and the Geography of Withdrawal' (2010) 6(3) *International Journal of Law in Context* 201; Edward Soja, *Seeking Spatial Justice* (University of Minnesota Press, 2010).

the relationship between law and mapping,[74] scale,[75] landscape,[76] frontiers[77] and, most relevantly, the interstices of law, space and place.[78] An indication of its growing popularity and prominence is the publication of several edited collections

74 See, e.g., Dorsett, 'Mapping Territories', above, n 27; Mark Harris, 'Mapping Australian Postcolonial Landscapes: From Resistance to Reconciliation?' (2003) 7 *Law Text Culture* 71; Christopher Tomlins, 'The Legal Cartography of Colonization, the Legal Polyphony of Settlement: English Intrusions on the American Mainland in the Seventeenth Century' (2001) 26 *Law and Social Inquiry* 315; Irus Braverman, 'Hidden in Plain View: Legal Geography from a Visual Perspective' (2010) 7(2) *Law, Culture and the Humanities* 173. On the cartography of the colonial gaze, see, especially, Fraser MacDonald, 'The Last Outpost of Empire: Rockall and the Cold War' (2006) 32 *Journal of Historical Geography* 627.
75 Mariana Valverde, *Chronotopes of Law: Jurisdiction, Scale, and Governance* (Routledge, 2015); Mariana Valverde, 'The Rescaling of Feminist Analyses of Law and State Power: From (Domestic) Subjectivity to (Transnational) Governance Networks' (2014) 4(1) *UC Irvine Law Review* 325; Mariana Valverde, 'Practices of Citizenship and Scales of Governance' (2010) 13(2) *New Criminal Law Review* 216. See, e.g., Richie Howitt, 'Scales of Coexistence: Tackling the Tension between Legal and Cultural Landscapes in Post-Mabo Australia' (2006) 6 *Macquarie Law Journal* 49; Lawrence Lessig, 'The Place of Cyberlaw', in Austin Sarat, Lawrence Douglas and Martha Merrill Umphrey (eds.), *The Place of Law* (University of Michigan Press, 2003) 131.
76 See, e.g., Jane Holder, 'Law and Landscape: The Legal Construction and Protection of Hedgerows' (1999) 62 *Modern Law Review* 100; Fleur Johns, 'Private Law, Public Landscape: Troubling the Grid' (2005) 9 *Law Text Culture* 60; William Taylor (ed.), *The Geography of Law: Landscape, Identity and Regulation* (Hart Publishing, 2006); Kirsty Duncanson, '"Native" Landscapes, "Cultivated" Gardens and the Erasure of Indigenous Sovereignty in Two Recent Instances of Australian Cinematic Jurisprudence' (2012) *Law, Culture and the Humanities* 1; Duncanson, 'The Scene of the Crime', above, n 64.
77 See, e.g., Barton Beebe, 'Law's Empire and the Final Frontier: Legalizing the Future in the Early Corpus Juris Spatialis' (1998) 108 *Yale Law Journal* 1737; Rebecca Johnson, 'Blurred Boundaries: A Double-Voiced Dialogue on Regulatory Regimes and Embodied Space' (2005) 9 *Law Text Culture* 157; Annabelle Mooney, 'Keeping on the Windy Side of the Law: The Law of the Beach' (2005) 9 *Law Text Culture* 189; Jennifer Nedelsky, 'Law, Boundaries and the Bounded Self', in Robert Post (ed.), *Law and the Order of Culture* (University of California Press, 1991) 162. See, especially, Andrea Mubi Brighenti, 'Lines, Barred Lines. Movement, Territory and the Law' (2010) 6(3) *International Journal of Law in Context* 217.
78 See, e.g., Philippopoulos-Mihalopoulos, 'Law's Spatial Turn', above, n 71; David Delaney, *Race, Place, and the Law, 1836–1948* (University of Texas Press, 1998); Austin Sarat, Lawrence Douglas and Martha Merrill Umphrey (eds.), *The Place of Law* (University of Michigan Press, 2003); Ford, 'Law's Territory', above, n 45; Zoe Pearson, 'Spaces of International Law' (2008) 17(2) *Griffith Law Review* 489; Dylan Trigg, 'Place Becomes the Law' (2008) 41 *Griffith Law Review* 147; Sarah Marusek, 'Wheelchair as Semiotic: Space Governance of the American Handicapped Parking Space' (2005) 9 *Law Text Culture* 178; Renisa Mawani, 'Imperial Legacies (Post)Colonial Identities: Law, Space and the Making of Stanley Park, 1859–2001' (2003) 7 *Law Text Culture* 98; Renisa Mawani, 'From Colonialism to Multiculturalism? Totem Poles, Tourism and National Identity in Vancouver's Stanley Park' (2004) 35 *A Review of International English Literature* 31; Renisa Mawani, 'Genealogies of the Land: Aboriginality, Law, and Territory in Vancouver's Stanley Park' (2005) 14 *Social and Legal Studies* 315; Issachar Rosen-Zvi, *Taking Space Seriously: Law, Space and Society in Contemporary Israel* (Ashgate, 2004); Franz von Benda-Beckmannm, and Keebet von Benda-Beckmann, Anne Griffiths, *Spatializing Law: An Anthropological Geography of Law in Society* (Ashgate, 2009). Although not explicitly engaging with law, see, especially, Edward Soja, *Thirdspace: Journeys to Los Angeles and Other Real-and-Imagined Places* (Blackwell, 1996).

and journal themes dedicated to this amorphous field with a notable increase in publications in recent years.[79]

As with any truly interdisciplinary project, there are moments of conceptual impasse seemingly encoded within critical legal geography. If this jurisprudential book were written from the office of critic, rather than the jurist, one might observe that despite the explicit intention of critical legal geography for interdisciplinary unison, in bringing together strands of critical geography and critical legal theory something seems to get lost. What is lost tends to be either a critical tendency in the form of a sensitivity to politics and what it means to live in the *polis* or more worryingly, what is lost or lost hold of, it seems, is law. David Delaney describes this 'acknowledged intellectual impasse' as arising from the dichotomies encoded in the formulation of the field itself as law as 'legality' and geography as 'spatiality'.[80] Delaney's response to this impasse is to 'move beyond law and geography' through the offering of *nomosphericity*.[81] However, it is important to acknowledge Delaney writes from the office of geographer or critic,[82] which is not the same office as the jurist. While certainly carrying other responsibilities, neither the critic or geographer carry the same jurisdictional responsibilities as the jurist, such as the jurist's official responsibilities for the conduct of lawful relations, including the care of the dead.

Of a different genre, this minor jurisprudence is not a work of critical legal geography. As a matter of office, this minor jurisprudence works with jurisdiction as legal idiom in order to attend to the place of movement in common law practice and more particularly the ways in which common law comes into its relations and comes to be in place. Therefore, for the common law jurist, who needs to stay with common law as a matter of office, this minor jurisprudence, guided by its method

---

79 Nicholas Blomley, David Delaney and Richard T. Ford (eds.), *The Legal Geographies Reader: Law, Power and Space* (Blackwell Publishers, 2001); Jane Holder and Carolyn Harrison (eds.), *Law and Geography: Current Legal Issues* (Oxford University Press, 2003); Taylor (ed.), *The Geography of Law*, above, n 76; Desmond Manderson, 'Interstices: New Work on Legal Spaces' (2005) 9 *Law Text Culture* 1, which introduces a special edition of *Law Text Culture* dedicated to law and geography; Jane Holder and Tatiana Flessas, 'Emerging Commons' (2008) 17(3) *Social and Legal Studies* 299, which introduces an edition of *Social and Legal Studies* dedicated to the idea of commons, which substantially engages with law and geography. More recently, see the edition of (2010) 6(3) *International Journal of Law in Context*; see, especially, the recent (2011) 7(2) *Law, Culture and the Humanities*. Further, in recent years, streams of the *Critical Legal Conference* have been dedicated to critical legal geography, including the 2015 conference at University of Wrocław, Poland on the theme 'Law, Space and the Political'.
80 David Delaney, *The Spatial, the Legal and the Pragmatics of World-Making: Nomospheric Investigations* (Taylor & Francis, 2010) 8.
81 Ibid. Delaney distinguishes his neologism 'nomosphericity' from both Robert Cover's and Carl Schmitt's *nomos*. See, generally, Robert Cover, 'Nomos and Narrative', in Martha Minow, Michael Ryan and Austin Sarat (eds.), *Narrative, Violence and the Law: The Essays of Robert Cover* (University of Michigan Press, 1992) ch 3; Carl Schmitt, *Nomos of the Earth in the International Law of the Jus Publicum Europaeum* (G.L. Ulman trans., Telos Press, 2003) [trans. of *Nomos der Erde im Volkerrecht des Jus Publicum Europaeum* (first published 1950)].
82 Cf: Edward W. Soja, 'Taking Space Personally', in Barney Wharf and Santa Aries (eds.), *The Spatial Turn: Interdisciplinary Perspectives* (Routledge, 2008) ch 2.

of slowness, does not seek to move beyond critical legal geography, but rather walks alongside critical legal geography. In this sense, as one walking alongside, this minor jurisprudence is affiliated with critical legal geography, drawing on its resources and offering some jurisprudential resources in return, yet always remaining attentive to the jurist and their tasks and responsibilities of office. With this affiliation in mind, in order to assist the jurist in noticing place, and more particularly, how common law comes to be in place, it is helpful to consider the concept of space. For although space is not the immediate concern of the jurist, the observation, description and redescription of space is a way for the jurist to attend to and account for movement, including the ways in which common law comes to be in place.

Critical geographers, philosophers and social theorists have addressed the concept of space in what has become known through its interdisciplinary expansions as the 'spatial turn'.[83] Through the seminal works of Henri Lefebvre, most particularly *The Production of Space*,[84] and the 'spatial turn' more generally, there has been a conceptual shift from understanding space as fixed, apolitical and pre-given into which culture, society and life are inserted, to a more productive understanding of space as itself constituted by social action.[85] In a succinct definition indebted to the tradition of Lefebvre, Nigel Thrift writes:

> As with terms like 'society' and 'nature', space is not a commonsense external background to human and social action. Rather, it is the outcome of a series of highly problematic temporary settlements that divide and connect things up into different kinds of collectives which are slowly provided with the means which render them durable and sustainable.[86]

Thrift claims space is not a 'commonsense external background to human and social action',[87] which is a reference to what has been the predominant view of space as fixed, apolitical and pre-given. Known as abstract or absolute space, this is space as an empty vessel into which culture, society, life and law are inserted.[88] As the location in which human life and activity occurs, abstract space is not part of human and social action, but the external backdrop to it.

---

83 On the 'spatial turn', see, e.g., Nigel Thrift, 'Space' (2006) 23(2–3) *Theory, Society and Culture* 139, 139. On the 'turn' as technological, see David Wills, *Dorsality: Thinking Back through Technology and Politics* (University of Minnesota Press, 2008) 4.
84 Henri Lefebvre, *The Production of Space*, above, n 32.
85 Henri Lefebvre's influence on Marxist and critical geography and the 'spatial turn' can be substantially traced through the work of David Harvey. See, e.g., David Harvey, *Social Justice and the City* (Edward Arnold, 1973).
86 Nigel Thrift, 'Space: The Fundamental Stuff of Geography', in Sarah Holloway, Stephen Rice and Gill Valentine (eds.), *Key Concepts in Geography* (Sage, 2003) 95.
87 Ibid.
88 Nigel Thrift uses the terms absolute and relative space. Although Thrift's definition is usefully succinct, this book is conceptually indebted to Lefebvre, and prefers the terms abstract and social space; Lefebvre, *The Production of Space*, above, n 32.

Thrift continues his definition that space is the 'outcome of a series of highly problematic temporary settlements'. This includes a reminder space that cannot be understood in the absence of time.[89] Yet, a feature of abstract space as a never changing backdrop to human and social action is its imperviousness to time. What Thrift alludes to, as Doreen Massey explains, is that space is not timeless, but is in fact time-full.[90] In contrast to abstract space, Thrift explains that bringing space into the foreground of social and human action means that space is part of social and human action rather than simply the location in which life (and law) occurs. Known as social space, rather than space pre-existing social action, this is space as the outcome of social action. As Lefebvre explains, space is produced and is itself a compilation of the social relations of its production.[91]

As Lefebvre observed in 1974, to 'speak of "producing space" sounds bizarre, so great is the sway still held by the idea that empty space is prior to whatever ends up filling it.'[92] That this view of space still holds great sway over 40 years later, as it seemingly does in common law thought, is particularly pertinent to ascertaining the place of common law in Australia. Embedded within concepts such as sovereignty and territory is the apparent immovability of understandings of space as somehow existing prior to whatever jurisdictions ultimately fill those empty spaces. This reliance on such an understanding of space contributes to what this chapter has described as 'the problem with place'.

But, what about place? If the jurisprudential concern is one of place and more specifically how common law comes to be in place, which is an especially important question for the jurist trained in a colonial form of law, how does an attention to the production of space assist the jurist in attending to common law's place? Returning to Nigel Thrift's definition, it is important to notice the shift from space to place. This is the spatial production of temporary collectives 'slowly provided with the means which render them durable and sustainable'.[93] Through the actions and activities of rendering collectives durable and sustainable, this is the shift from space to place.

Drawing on the work of Lefebvre and critical geographers, and translating this into common law practice, my argument is that common law's movements contribute to the production of space. This is common law's technical and material practices of movement contributing to the production of space, as well as contributing to the making of place. For example, reconsider the declaration of Aboriginal sovereignty as non-justiciable which was raised earlier in this chapter, in spatial terms. Through the technology of jurisdiction, seen in its exclusion of another, common law produces its spaces and moves into place, or at least seems to move into place; a place appearing to be everywhere. This is the production

---

89 On time and space, see, generally, Edward Soja, *Postmodern Geographies* (Verso, 1990); David Harvey, *Spaces of Capital: Towards a Critical Geography* (Routledge, 2001).
90 Doreen Massey, *For Space* (Sage, 2005).
91 Lefebvre, *The Production of Space*, above, n 32.
92 Ibid, 15.
93 Thrift, 'Space: The Fundamental Stuff of Geography', above, n 86.

of abstract space. By declaring Aboriginal sovereignty non-justiciable, common law effectively fills all the available space and in doing so, places indigenous forms of law somewhere beyond the fullness of common law's space. This spatial hand trick is problematic. It is problematic because it places indigenous law somewhere elsewhere, yet with abstract space as territorial space filled with common law, there is no elsewhere. This is an imagining and representation of Anglo-Australian common law being everywhere, and exclusively everywhere, and as such it is hardly surprising it becomes difficult for common law to relate to other forms of law, including indigenous laws.

To imagine common law's space absent movement, therefore, is to overlook social space and fall back on abstract space. This fails to account for movement, and fails to account for the dynamic shape and form of common law practice. Attending to common law's movements, it can be seen that it is through movement that common law produces its spaces and comes to be temporarily in place, revealing the fact that common law is not everywhere. This is a more complex and mediated understanding of space as one constantly changing. In other words, the form and practice of common law's movements are activities, and productive activities that not only contribute to the making of space, but also the making of place. A place that is not permanent, but seems to be permanent, rendered durable, sustainable, immovable. Although represented as permanent through the repetition of movements, such as the repetition of walking or ceremonies of burial,[94] common law's place is neither permanent nor immovable. Common law's place is and must always be temporary. An impermanent place; a place of rest, perhaps, yet still a never-quite-permanent common law place.

In terms of common law's place, therefore, abstract space, timeless and empty, supports an understanding of the 'everywhereness' of Anglo-Australian common law. As discussed earlier on the problem with place, this is the first conceit; an image and representation of common law as completely filling up an empty vessel of timeless space, inhabiting the complete legal landscape of Australia. Not only does this incorporate abstract space into concepts such as sovereignty, territory and territorial jurisdiction but it also makes it difficult for the jurist to register movement, attend to its forms and account for common law's place.

As raised earlier in this chapter, common law moves and through its movements creates relations across space and time. This is movement as the institution and form of common law, given shape by jurisdiction. Further, as already raised, but developed throughout this book, I argue that common law comes to be in place through jurisdictional movements, which are movements that produce space and through their repetition contribute to the creation of common law's place. To this end, in order for the jurist to properly attend to the potential meaning of common law's movements, drawing on the Lefebvrian concept of space, through an affiliation with critical legal geography, serves as a way of bringing into focus the movement forms of common law practice and how this relates to

---

94 On burial, see Chapter 2, part 3. On walking, see Chapter 3, 3.3.

the jurisprudential question of place. Therefore, for the jurist, an attentiveness to jurisdiction as a common law mode of authorisation reveals the place of movement in forms of common law practice.

To conclude, by asking how common law moves, the central part of Chapter 2 has linked movement, technology and jurisdiction, placing jurisdiction as a technology of movement in the conduct of lawful relations and place-making. Noticing a problem with place, which included the masking of the technology of jurisdiction and the obscuring of movement, this part linked jurisdiction with movement as a matter of jurisprudence. For the importance of movement is not simply that common law moves but the forms of its movements and the meanings it may carry, including the production of space and common law's movements into place. To this end, this part introduced jurisdiction as a technology of movement shaping common law, revealed a problem with common law's place, affiliated with critical legal geography and drew on the Lefebvrian concept of space before concluding with an explanation of how movement, technology and jurisdiction coalesce to offer the jurist a jurisprudential question of place. The next and final part of this chapter addresses burial as one of the ways in which common law comes to be in place.

2.3 Placing burial

Moving through the technology of jurisdiction, common law comes into its relations and comes to be in place. Focusing on the form of common law's movements in relation to the dead as activities in the creation and conduct of lawful relations, this part attends to the institution of burial. Linking burial to place through common law's jurisdictional technologies of movement, this part suggests that common law's movements in relation to the dead through ceremonials of burial produce space, contributing to a temporary superficial attachment between common law and the earth and hence the making of common law's place. Having focused the bulk of this chapter on forms of movement and how, jurisdictionally, common law moves, this part shifts its attention to the meaning these movements may carry. For common law's movements in relation to the dead not only contribute to the humanisation of the earth but also, perhaps, its juridification. To this end, the book attends to and accounts for movements in relation to the dead both in and through burial as one of the ways in which common law comes to be in place or a little more delicately, how common law rests and so seems to be in place.

Introducing and following Giambattista Vico's account of the dead, especially in respect of Vico's understanding of the institution of burial contributing to the humanisation of the earth, the final part of this chapter on the importance of movement attends to movements of Anglo-Australian common law in the ceremony of burial and asks what this might mean in terms of the humanisation and juridification of the earth. While the significant question of the juridification of the earth lies beyond the scope of this minor jurisprudence and remains, perhaps for good reason, unanswered, the act of asking such a question offers the jurist some guidance towards appreciating the jurisprudential importance of movement. For one of the ways in which common law moves is through the institution of burial, which is a particularly important form of movement. This is so because the effect of common law's movements in relation to burial is common law's contribution to the humanisation of the earth, that not only produces space but also contributes to the creation of common law's place. Therefore, the importance of movements in relation to the dead, especially in relation to the institution of burial, is that such movements are one of the ways in which common law comes to be in place.

In this comparatively short third and final part of Chapter 2, the jurist is reminded that the dead are part of the common law tradition, instituting and ordering the time and space of common law. Returning to common law's struggle in relation to the dead that was introduced in Chapter 1, the jurist is asked to attend to this struggle by paying attention to movement. Noticing common law's movements in relation to the dead *as* the creation and conduct of lawful relations, the jurist is asked to contemplate the jurisprudential question of common law's place. This is a matter of office, and requires the jurist's attendance and care. Paying attention to the institution of burial and its relation to the humanisation of the earth, the final part of this chapter reveals how common law comes to be in place through movements in relation to the dead.

Movements in relation to the dead

In Chapter 1, the dead were introduced and brought into relation with common law as part of the common law tradition. It was explained that common law holds a very particular relation to the dead, and an awkward relation at that, most readily apparent in common law's odd taxonomy of the dead as neither person nor property. In order to understand the place of movement in common law's relations with the dead, it is useful to consider the uncertain status of the dead in relation to the common law categories of person and property.

Legally, the dead are not people. A person is a legal category that includes the human, but also includes legal constructions of personhood of non-human lifeforms, such as animals and corporations.[95] This is the distinction in status between the *persona* and the physical body of the living person. Although there is much debate about the legal status of those that reside on the peripheries of life and death, such as the foetus and the dying,[96] the jurisprudential question here is with the uncertain legal status of the dead and common law's movements in

---

95 On animals, see, e.g., Yoriko Otomo and Edward Mussawir (eds.), *Law and the Question of the Animal: A Critical Jurisprudence* (Routledge, 2013). On corporations, see, e.g., Joel Bakan, *The Corporation: The Pathological Pursuit of Profit and Power* (Free Press, 2004).
96 For a recent doctrinal survey see, e.g., Elizabeth Price Foley, *The Law of Life and Death* (Harvard University Press, 2011).

relation to the dead of law as a question of jurisdictional care.[97] For what is clear is that, once dead, the status of legal personhood no longer attaches: the dead are not legal persons. For this reason, it is not so much the change in status from life to death that is the concern, but rather jurisdictional movements in relation to the dead that are momentarily revealed through this change in status, raising the jurisprudential challenge of how to care for the uncertain dead.

If not legal persons, then are the dead captured within the common law classification of property? Can the dead be owned? Are there rights of possession in relation to the dead? Generally speaking, there is no property in human corpses.[98] Historically the subject of an ecclesiastical jurisdiction over the dead and their burial, common law began its address to the dead by attending to those outside the parameters of an ecclesiastical jurisdiction. Contributing to a slow desacralisation of the dead, common law came to address those buried in unconsecrated ground, untouched by an ecclesiastical jurisdiction: the unregulated dead. In nineteenth-century England, this address continued when in response to a developing demand for cadavers for medical research, a burgeoning commercial industry of grave robbing emerged. Yet, to steal a corpse was not an act of theft, for the dead were not property and therefore not capable of being stolen. Maintaining its attachment to the principle that the dead were not property, common law regulated that which was clearly property: the shroud, the coffin and the earthly bounds of the burial site: surfaces.[99] This superficial regulation continues today. As distinct from regulating the dead directly, common law regulates that which surrounds the dead. Regulating the shroud etc., common law can, albeit indirectly and somewhat awkwardly, regulate the corpse within.

An example of this awkwardness that seemingly characterises common law's relations with the dead manifests in the High Court of Australia judgment in *Doodeward v Spence*, which involved a 1908 dispute over the rights to a preserved body of stillborn conjoined twins that had been retained for over 40 years as a

---

97 On the jurisprudential care of the dying, see Shaun McVeigh, 'Subjects of Jurisdiction: The Dying, Northern Territory, Australia, 1995–1997', in Shaun McVeigh (ed.), *Jurisprudence of Jurisdiction* (Routledge-Cavendish, 2007) ch 11.

98 The written origin of this principle is not entirely clear, but is most often attributed to a decision of Edward Coke in *Haynes's Case* (1614) 12 Co Rep 113; 77 ER 1389 or his *Institutes*: Edward Coke, *The Third Part of the Institutes of the Laws of England: Concerning High Treason, and Other Pleas of the Crown, and Criminal Causes* (M. Flesher, for W. Lee, and D. Pakeman, 1644) 203; see Dorsett and McVeigh, *Jurisdiction*, above, n 41, ch 5. Clearly established by the time of *Exelby v Handyside* (1749) 2 East PC 652, the principle is of continuing contemporary relevance; see Prue Vines, 'Bodily Remains in the Cemetery and the Burial Ground: A Comparative Anthropology of Law and Death or How Long Can I Stay?', in Desmond Manderson (ed.), *Courting Death* (Pluto Press, 1999) ch 6; Prue Vines, 'The Sacred and the Profane: The Role of Property Concepts in Disputes about Post-Mortem Examination' (2007) 29 *Sydney Law Review* 235; Ngaire Naffine, '"But a Lump of Earth?" The Legal Status of the Corpse', in Desmond Manderson (ed.), *Courting Death* (Pluto Press, 1999) ch 5.

99 On Roman practices regulating the spaces of the dead, see Yan Thomas, '*Res Religiosae*: On the Categories of Religion and Commerce in Roman Law', in Alain Pottage and Martha Mundy (eds.), *Law, Anthropology and the Constitution of the Social* (Cambridge University Press, 2004) ch 2.

'curiosity'.[100] In a case often cited as legal authority for the continuation of the 'no property principle' and the creation of an exception based on work, care and skill, the High Court held this particular dead was capable of being property because it had been embalmed and preserved with care and skill, yet the High Court did not directly address the question of whether absent care and skill the dead can be property.[101] In a short but revealing judgment considering the legal ramifications of the work and skill performed on the dead, Griffith CJ, Barton and Higgins JJ indirectly attended to the question of burial, determining that this uncertain corpse had acquired some attribute differentiating it from a corpse awaiting burial, and could therefore constitute property no longer awaiting burial. Noticing the place of burial in defining the dead and its contribution to the jurisdictional care of the dead, and noting the lack of address as to whether in the absence of work, care and skill the 'uncared' for dead are property, it seems there is an awkwardness concerning common law's relations with the dead. This includes its inability to bury the dead, an inability to place the dead, a struggle with place; common law's place.

But what of movement? Given common law's ambiguous relation as neither person nor property, and remembering this book takes Blackstone's aphorism literally and follows the common law subject as it carries common law, what happens to common law in the movements between life and death? That is, in the transition and change from life to death the living subject of law – the legal person – becomes a non-subject (or at least an awkward subject) of law as neither person nor property. Simply put, given the ambiguity of common law's awkward relation to the dead, it seems unlikely that common law carried in life remains with the body of the (former) subject in death, or more precisely, beyond death. In terms of movement, what this means is that if common law moves with the living as they move, yet struggles to attach to or mark the dead after death, then something has altered, something has changed. This is a form of common law movement. Assuming common law is with the body of the living subject in some manner, whether it be in, on, nearby or attached, then in the moment of death common law moves, somehow departing. As picked up in Chapter 3, although common law may remain close by, common law is not with the dead, at least not in the same manner it is with the living. Therefore, if common law is with the body as it lives yet is not with the dead, paying attention to movement may be worthwhile.

Illustrated through the awkward classification of the dead as neither person nor property, common law struggles in its relations with the dead. Noticing, and leaving aside any attempt to resolve, it is enough to try and hold onto this struggle. By holding onto common law's struggle in relation to the dead, what

---

100 *Doodeward v Spence* (1908) 6 CLR 406.
101 See Prue Vines, 'The Sacred and the Profane: The Role of Property Concepts in Disputes about Post-Mortem Examination' (2007) 29 *Sydney Law Review* 235, 238. Cf: Rohan Hardcastle, *Law and the Human Body: Property Rights, Ownership and Control* (Hart Publishing, 2009) 28.

becomes apparent is that it is for the jurist to take responsibility and care for common law's lawful relations, including common law's relations with the dead as matter of inheritance, and as a matter of common law practice. This requires an attention to movement. Clearly, common law's movements in relation to the dead are not the only way common law moves, but they are of particular importance for what they reveal about the ways in which common law comes into its relations, and the place of common law. To this end, paying attention to movements in relation to the dead and attending to the institution of burial assists in deepening an account of the form of common law and its practices of movement. Focusing on the acts, actions and activities of burial, the question raised is: what might it mean to bury the dead for common law? To contemplate this question, the remainder of this part addresses the form and potential meaning of common law's movements in relation to the dead through the ceremonial act of burial.

Burial and common law's movements into place

Tracing movement and delving into this awkward relation a little further, the question to be asked is: what might common law's movements in relation to the dead have to do with common law's place? To delve means to dig or to make a hole by digging, including to turn up the ground with a spade.[102] More than the act of digging, however, to delve carries an older meaning that shifts from the act of digging to the act of placing. For to delve also means 'to put or hide in the ground by digging', especially to bury a corpse.[103] To consider what common law's movements in relation to the dead might mean in terms of place-making, this part continues by asking: what happens to common law when the dead are buried, if anything at all? With the assistance of Giambattista Vico, attending to the institution of burial and more specifically to common law's movements in relation to burial, and noting the earthly movements that result from the use of a spade, in this chapter I do this delving literally.

Giambattista Vico was an Italian jurist who wrote in philosophy, philology, rhetoric and jurisprudence in the late seventeenth and early eighteenth centuries.[104] In part a response to René Descartes, Vico created in his major work, *The New Science*,[105] a form of knowledge not predicated on Cartesian clarity, linearity and a priori deductions. Structuring civil society around the presence of three

---

102 On the plough as the instrument of institution and attachment, see Hachamovitch, 'Ploughing the Delirium', above, n 24. See also Yifat Hachamovitch, 'The Ideal Object of Transmission: An Essay on the Faith Which Attaches to Instruments' (1991) 2(1) *Law and Critique* 85.
103 Onions (ed.), *The Oxford English Dictionary of English Etymology*, above, n 35.
104 See Giambattista Vico, *The Autobiography of Giambattista Vico* (Thomas Goddard Bergin and Max Harold Fisch trans., Cornell University Press, 1944) [trans. of *Vita di Giambattista Vico Scritta da se Medesimo* (first published 1725–31)].
105 Giambattista Vico, *The New Science of Giambattista Vico* (Thomas Goddard Bergin and Max Harold Fisch trans., Cornell University Press, 1967) [trans. of *Principi di una Scienza Nuova* (first published 1725)].

basic human institutions: religion, burial and matrimony, and attending to the second institution, Vico explains:

> The second human institution is burial. (Indeed *humanitas* in Latin comes first and properly from *humando*, burying.) This institution is symbolized by a cinerary urn, placed to one side within the forest, indicating that burial goes back to a time when men ate fruit in summer and acorns in winter. ... The urn indicates also the origin among the gentiles of the division of the fields, to which is to be traced the distinction of cities and peoples and finally of nations. ... By long residence and burial of their dead they came to found and divide the first dominions of the earth, whose lords were called giants, a Greek word meaning 'sons of the earth,' i.e., descendants of those who have been buried. Hence they considered themselves noble, justly ascribing their nobility in that first state of human institutions to their having been humanly engendered in the fear of the divinity. From this manner of human engendering and not from anything else, what is called human generation took its name. The houses which had branched out into several families thus formed were called the first gentes because of such generation.[106]

As Robert Pogue Harrison summarises, Vico places the institution of burial as the 'generative institution of human nature'.[107] This is the dead as ordering the time and space of humanity and further, this is burial as the institution that orders the relations between time and space, that is, place. For the jurist, this becomes significant in terms of attending to common law's place. Vico's poetics of the dead are picked up in Harrison's, *The Dominion of the Dead*.[108] Focusing on the institution of burial and referring to the same passage from Vico's *New Science*, Harrison explains:

> [H]umans bury not simply to achieve closure and effect a separation from the dead but also and above all to humanize the ground on which they build their worlds and found their histories ... [H]umanity is not a species (*Homo sapiens* is a species); it is a way of being mortal and relating to the dead. To be human means above all to bury. Vico suggests as much when he reminds us that, '*humanitas* in Latin comes first and properly from *humando*, burying' (*New Science at 12*). By *properly* he means essentially and irreducibly.[109]

To bury the dead is to humanise the earth. With different ceremonial manifestations, humans tend to bury their dead, including covering the dead with earth.[110]

106 Ibid, 8–9.
107 Noting 'nature' is from *nasci* meaning 'to be born', Robert Pogue Harrison, *The Dominion of the Dead* (University of Chicago Press, 2003) xi.
108 Ibid.
109 Ibid, xi.
110 See Peter Metcalf and Richard Huntington, *Celebrations of Death: The Anthropology of Mortuary Ritual* (Cambridge University Press, 2nd revised edn, 1991).

This material act is carried through in our language of human, humus and humic. To bury the dead is to humanise the earth, and it is through this humanisation the living can then dwell and in dwelling can build their present, found their histories and imagine their future.[111] Less concerned with dwelling, it is the link between the institution of burial and the humanisation of the earth that is of interest. This is the importance of Vico for the book. That is, in the relation between the institution of burial and the humanisation of the earth, what this book notices is movement.

Consider the materiality of burial. Quite obviously, in placing the dead in the earth in an act of burial there is material contact between the dead and the earth. In time, the dead return more completely to the earth, breaking down into the humus, returning to the earth. Ashes to ashes, dust to dust. We understand this, but we need to know the depth of the materiality of this. When we bury the dead they become the earth, and the earth we inherit, as well as what authorises this inheritance is the dead. The dead are our inheritance and as humus, so is the earth. Attending to common law's movements in relation to the dead, especially through burial, the book suggests common law is turned towards the earth. As revealed in Chapter 3, common law's aspects, its sides and its surfaces, are in a sense turned towards the earth as it traverses the surface of the earth. More than just traversing, however, it is towards the earth that common law moves in its attempts to mark and attach and create and hold its space; rest, coming into place, most poignantly so in the act of burial. For it is towards the earth that common law has practical bearing. As such, the jurist must notice these forms of movement and their potential meaning. In this respect, one of the jurisprudential contributions this book makes is the suggestion that the act and manner of burying the dead involves a movement of common law that tends towards the earth. In common law's movements towards the earth, especially through burial, the practical effect is more than just the production of space but also the contribution to the creation of common law's place. These places are impermanent, though rendered through ceremony and its repetitions, they seem a little more permanent.

What, then, might it mean to bury the dead for common law? Through the institution of burial ordering the relation of time and space, and through movements of humanisation, common law's movements between the dead and the earth are redescribed in Chapters 3 and 4 as movements of common law place-making. For the dead not only humanise the earth but also, through common law's movements in relation to the dead, are one of the ways common law comes to be in place, raising the question of the juridification of the earth. In this respect, the jurisprudential importance of burial is that it is one of the ways in which common law moves into place. For common law, to bury the dead carries particular meaning regarding how common law moves and how it comes to be in place, yet it is always already a dynamic place and one that is inherently impermanent. This means

111 Harrison, *The Dominion of the Dead*, above, n 107, whose reading of Vico is influenced by his reading of Heidegger.

the importance of burial and burying the dead for common law is, therefore, intricately and intimately linked with the place of common law: with where it is and how it comes to be.

With burial in place, what might this mean for the jurist in the conduct of their responsibilities of office? As mentioned in Chapter 1, common law's relation with the dead is placed in the book as a lawful one, and it is for common law and the jurist to be both careful and caring in its relations with the dead. This is the practice of being lawful, and it is through this practice that lawful relations are conducted. For the responsible jurist, therefore, the importance of movement encompasses more than the tasks of accounting for and registering movement, which are primarily tasks of attention and observation, but also involves responsibilities of action and care. For it is through movement that common law comes into its relations with the dead; through movements in ceremonies of burial common law comes to be or at least seem to be in place; and through movement common law creates and conducts lawful relations with the dead.

Therefore, through the official practices of noticing and attending, as well as the practices of caring and doing, it is for the jurist to care for the dead. Of course, it is not solely for the jurist to care. As addressed in Chapters 4 and 5, and already raised in Chapter 1, the office of coroner also has a responsibility to care for the dead but this is a responsibility of a different office that manifests in different ways. Concerned with the place of Anglo-Australian common law, especially the place of its colonial form, it is for the jurist as a responsibility of office to care for the dead as a matter of common law inheritance. With burial as one of the ways in which common law comes to be in place, to care for the dead requires more than simply attending to the activities of burial, but also attending to and caring for common law's place. This requires accounting for aspects of common law as it is turned towards the earth, to care for its attachments and relations and to care for the earth. From practice to conduct, more than simply attending to place, therefore, to care for the dead is to conduct lawful relations with the dead. In this respect, the care of the dead is an important mode of creating, engaging and conducting lawful relations. For to care for the dead is a jurisdictional practice in lawfulness; to attend to and care for the form and conduct of lawful relations. As a practice of living with common law, this is the question of how we might live this life well. This is a matter of conduct, and to conduct lawful relations with the dead is to live lawfully; to conduct a lawful life.

To conclude, in many respects, in this book I follow the work of Vico and Harrison in their account of the dead, burial and humanisation of the earth, but in doing so, I offer a jurisprudential contribution through an attention to the movements of Anglo-Australian common law in the institution of burial, considering what this might mean in terms of the humanisation and juridification of the earth as well as how common law moves into place. For one of the ways common law moves is through the institution and ceremony of burial. The effect of these movements is, in part at least, not only a contribution to this humanisation but also the temporary attachment between common law and the earth, contributing to the production of space and common law's place and its potential juridification. This is the importance of movement: movement puts common law in its place, and reveals that place as temporary. Placing the dead through the institution of burial, what this requires of the jurist is attention and care.

Therefore, having noticed common law's awkward relation with the dead as part of the common law tradition, the final part of this chapter began the process of attending to the dead of law by paying attention to common law's movements in relation to the dead, focusing on the institution of burial and how this relates to common law's movements into place. In doing so, something else also occurred. With the care of the dead placed as a responsibility of office, the focus altered from a concern with the jurist's responsibilities of observation and attendance, which were of concern earlier in this chapter, to the jurist's responsibilities of action and care. In this respect, at the conclusion of these first two chapters, there is a responsible jurist in office alert to the jurisprudential importance of movement as part of common law's technical and material practices. For the purposes of creating a minor jurisprudence of movement, this concludes Part I of the book, which continues in a very different manner in Part II. Starting with the next chapter, Part II of the book is introduced, which substantially shifts registers from a mode of explanation – the overarching mode so far – to a manner of performance as a way of revealing movement through redescription. In this regard, in Part II of the book, a jurisprudential performance is offered, which begins with a burial party that walks.

Part II
Performing jurisprudence

Figure PII.1 Shaun Gladwell, *Apologies 1–6* (2007–2009)
Single-channel digital video, colour, sound, 27 minutes 10 seconds Museum of Contemporary Art Australia, donated through the Australian Government's Cultural Gifts Program by Andrew and Cathy Cameron, 2011

Image courtesy of Museum of Contemporary Art Australia and Anna Schwartz Gallery © Shaun Gladwell

Chapter 3

A burial party walks

As empire expands, a colony's status as conquered, ceded or settled regulates the manner and extent of law's movements into colonial spaces. However, law's inaugural movements into colonies tend to collapse into metanarratives of sovereignty, territory and territorial jurisdiction. In this collapse, what becomes lost is an account of jurisdiction: an account of the techniques and practices of law's movements. What also becomes lost are accounts of other, more minor, forms of legal movement. One such form is the practice of walking. Illustrating this practice, in 1799, 11 years after the Colony of New South Wales was established, a burial party walked into the woods beyond an emergent frontier settlement in order to locate and bury two men. Paying attention to modalities of movement as the burial party walks, it becomes possible to notice some of the ways in which common law moves. Walking to bury the dead, this chapter reveals how the laws of empire moved. For movement is integral to the laws of empire, both between the metropole and the colonies, and within the colonies themselves.

While it may not be so everywhere, although it may well be so elsewhere in the former British Empire, in Australia at least, it is through the movements of common law that the laws of empire move. Without movement, there are no laws of empire. To ensure these movements are not rendered meaningless, this chapter asks the responsible jurist to contemplate what these movements might mean, especially in terms of how common law comes into its relations and through its relations, how it comes to be in place. However, rather than providing advice to the jurist, such as how to account for movement as part of their tasks of office, which was the approach taken in the first two chapters of the book, both this chapter and the next shift registers from one of advice giving to one of jurisprudential performance. That is, to assist the jurist in their task of paying attention to movement, this chapter takes up the task of this minor jurisprudence, narrating, describing and redescribing some of the technical and material forms of common law practice as a way of accounting for movement and revealing its jurisprudential significance. Through the performance of a minor jurisprudence of movement, therefore, this chapter illustrates how the laws of empire move.

There are four parts to this chapter. The first part provides a short introduction to movements into the Colony of New South Wales, before focusing on movements within the colony, which is the subject of the rest of the chapter. Moving within, the second part of the chapter constructs a narrative vignette of a burial party that walked in 1799 while the third and fourth parts of the chapter redescribe this vignette, revealing how the movements of a burial party constitute two related forms of common law movement: walking and camping. More specifically, this is an attention to movements of common law practised through, first, the juridical form of walking and, second, movements towards burial through a jurisdictional device described as camping with the dead.

Attending to movements of common law within the Colony of New South Wales, what is revealed in this chapter are some of the techniques and material practices of common law's movements, including how common law moves in relation to the dead. This is important because it is through this relation that we accumulate obligations to the dead and, perhaps less intuitively, it is through this relation that common law moves and comes to be in place. In walking with empire, therefore, and moving common law into place, the question for the jurist becomes one of how to move responsibly: a question of conduct. In walking with empire, the question for the jurist becomes: how are we to move well?

Why might this matter? By placing walking as a juridical form of movement, what this means is that the common law subject actively partakes in and actively practises this form of common law movement each and every time they walk. *This is the importance of movement.* This requires the jurist, in taking up and holding office, to take responsibility for the forms of colonialism, including common law's movements. In doing so, the question that arises is one of how to walk responsibly with common law. Carrying the laws of empire as we move, including as we walk, how might we walk with dignity, delicacy and prudence? What does it mean – or what might it mean – to walk with common law, and walk well? Remembering that the motivating concern in this book is one of how to live with common law and, moreover, how to live this life well, in this chapter, these are questions of conduct reframed as matters of responsible walking.

To this end, this chapter serves as a reminder of the importance of paying attention to how we walk. For if we romanticise walking, if we ramble, walking becomes mere physical action and we lose hold of walking as a material practice of common law. Without walking as legal action, the movements of common law become static and frozen as authority – as sovereignty and territory – leaving no room for a dynamic account of the multiple devices of legal movement and transmission: an account of jurisdiction. Further, if we lose hold of walking as juridical form, we not only risk losing hold of the forms of colonialism, we also risk losing sight of common law moving in space and shaping place. As such, we will continue to struggle to take responsibility for these movements, and without movement, we will continue to struggle to take responsibility for forms of common law practice.

3.1 Movements into, movements within

In the expansion of the British Empire, including the eighteenth- and nineteenth-century expansions into various colonies established on what has since become known as Australia, the laws of empire moved, and they continue to move. In a context of a recent American Revolution, and fears of a French Revolution crossing the Channel, the reasons for these particular colonial expansions are manifold.[1] In addition to a fear of losing control, major drivers included a burgeoning prison population with a very practical need for transportation and long-term storage, coupled with the desire to pin down a strategic trade location while preventing other European nations from gaining a permanent foothold in the south. As part of this particular expansion of the British Empire, English common law started to move into the partially mapped Colony of New South Wales.[2] Yet it did not do so all at once. Providing legal, historical and geopolitical context, this first part of Chapter 3 introduces the doctrine of discovery, comments on some movements between the metropole and one specific colony, and provides the foundation for noticing movements within the Colony of New South Wales.

By the eighteenth century, the doctrine of discovery was a well-established and central tenet of the law of nations and one that remains foundational in contemporary international law.[3] Offering three main categories of discovery, the acquisition of sovereignty through the taking of 'new' lands by European powers were configured as actions of conquering, ceding, or settlement, and depending on the category, the process of obtaining sovereignty unfolded quite differently. In short, if the new land you desire is inhabited and already occupied by people, the choice is either to conquer through warfare (and if you win, your law applies unimpeded) or to treat (and if so, the terms of cession govern what combination of laws apply). Alternatively, if the new land you desire is uninhabited (i.e. there are no humans), then you may settle with the added bonus of your law applying in full, unimpeded by the law of another. Although the story is more complex, the Colony of New South Wales, which was the first British colony in what is now Australia, was ultimately addressed under the category of 'settlement', rather than

---

1 See Alan Atkinson, 'The First Plans for Governing New South Wales 1786–1787' (1990–1991) 24 *Australian Historical Studies* 22, 22–4. See also Merete Falck Borch, *Conciliation – Compulsion – Conversion: British Attitudes Towards Indigenous Peoples 1763–1814* (Rodopi, 2004) ch 3. See, generally, Andrew Fitzmaurice, *Humanism and America: An Intellectual History of English Colonisation, 1500–1625* (Cambridge University Press, 2003).
2 See, generally, Governor Phillip's First Commission, 12 October 1786, in Frederick Watson (ed.), *Historical Records of Australia, Series 1, Governor's Despatches to and from England* (Library Committee of the Commonwealth Parliament, 1914–1925) ('*HRA*') vol I, 1; Governor Phillip's Second Commission, 2 April 1787 in *HRA*, vol I: at 2; Instructions to Arthur Phillip, 25 April 1787 in *HRA*, vol I: at 2.
3 For the historical position on the Doctrine of Discovery, see Grotius, below, n 5. For a survey of contemporary positions, see, e.g., Miller, below, n 4.

conquer or cession, and this was *in spite of* the presence of indigenous peoples and the lack of uninhabited land.[4]

How did this work? Consider the planting of the flag as an iconic image of proclamations of sovereignty. In the late eighteenth century, the accepted international legal position recognised by the British government, and reflected in English common law rules, was that ceremonial performances of possession such as planting a flag or burying a jar of coins was not enough in and of itself to claim sovereignty. Rather, such ceremonies acquired an inchoate title only. To perfect sovereignty, in addition to the ceremony, actual possession was needed.[5] In the case of so-called 'uninhabited' land, the acquisition of sovereignty is a two-step process. Step one involves a proclamation (the planting of the flag, for example) and the flagbearer acquires an unfinished or 'inchoate' title over certain tracts of land. To finish the job, step two requires actual occupation of the land. It is only when both steps are completed that sovereignty is acquired.

Both of these steps matter yet the second step is often forgotten in modern tellings of Australian histories, seemingly replaced with nationalistic flag raising and swashbuckling narratives of scurvy-riddled voyages in the name of 'discovery'. Whether told as stories of flags, coins, boats or the transmission of letters, it is important to note that the modes and manners of empirical movements are messier than the neatly spliced categories of the doctrine of discovery.[6] This is especially so in Australia. With European visitors since the beginning of the seventeenth century, including the Dutch since 1606 and the British since 1688, and with the French and Spanish on the shoreline, it was not until Lieutenant (later Captain) James Cook's ceremonial activities in 1770 that Britain began, yet did not complete, its claim for sovereignty.[7]

As is well known, armed with secret instructions from the British Admiralty to claim 'new' lands, Cook's instructions of 30 July 1768 included a responsibility

4 See, e.g., Larissa Behrendt, 'The Doctrine of Discovery in Australia', in Robert J. Miller et al. (eds.), *Discovering Indigenous Lands: The Doctrine of Discovery in the English Colonies* (Oxford University Press, 2010) ch 6.

5 For the international legal position, see Hugo Grotius, *The Freedom of the Seas or the Right Which Belongs to the Dutch to Take Part in the East Indian Trade* (R. van Damen Magoffin trans., Oxford University Press, 1916) [trans. of *Mare Liberum Sive de Jure Quod Batavis Competit ad Indicana Commercia Dissertatio* (first published 1609)]. For Britain's recognition of this position, see Shaunnagh Dorsett and Shaun McVeigh, 'Just So: "The Law Which Governs Australia is Australian Law"' (2002) 13 *Law and Critique* 289, 294.

6 See, generally, Lauren Benton, *A Search for Sovereignty: Law and Geography in European Empires, 1400–1900* (Cambridge University Press, 2010). See also Behrendt, above, n 4; Stuart Banner, *Possessing the Pacific: Land, Settlers, and Indigenous People from Australia to Alaska* (Harvard University Press, 2007) ch 1, although on the place of *terra nullius*, see Andrew Fitzmaurice, 'The Genealogy of *Terra Nullius*' (2007) 129 *Australian Historical Studies* 1.

7 On the Spanish in the Colony of New South Wales, see Robert J. King, *The Secret History of the Convict Colony: Alexandro Malaspina's Report on the British Settlement of New South Wales* (Allen & Unwin, 1990). On the French on the shoreline, see, e.g., Philippe Godard and Tugdual de Kerros, *1772: The French Annexation of New Holland: The Tale of Louis de Saint Aloüarn* (Odette Margot, Myra Stanbury and Sue Baxter trans., Western Australian Museum, 2008).

to cultivate friendships with the 'Natives'. In these precise words, Cook was instructed to:

> [O]bserve the Genius, Temper, Disposition and Number of the Natives, if there be any and endeavour by all proper means to cultivate a Friendship and Alliance with them, ... and Shewing them every kind of Civility and Regard.[8]

Additional instructions authorised Cook to make a choice. This was a choice *governed* by the doctrine of discovery and therefore *conditional* on whether he found inhabited land (i.e. cession) or uninhabited land (i.e. settlement):

> You are also with the Consent of the Natives to take the possession of Convenient Situations in the Country in the Name of the King of Great Britain: Or: if you find the Country uninhabited Take Possession for His Majesty by setting up Proper Marks and Inscriptions, as first discoverers and possessors.[9]

Despite the known presence of indigenous peoples that was clearly evident in his own notebooks, Cook chose the second. That is, despite finding inhabited land, Cook chose to act *as if* he found 'the Country uninhabited'. This is not unknown and, both legally and politically, Cook's choice continues to have major ramifications for indigenous peoples.[10] In the context of this sadly familiar story of dispossession, I want to draw your attention to three specific moments in Cook's first voyage to open up stories of movement. These include his violent first steps on land, a burial at Stingray Bay and a ceremony at Possession Island.

On 29 April 1770, Cook reached the east coast of the 'Continent or Land of great extent',[11] and landed at Stingray Bay, later named Botany Bay.[12] As Cook wrote in his own journal, describing his first landing, humans already inhabited the land:

> Saw, as we came in, on both points of the bay, several of the Natives and a few hutts; Men, Women, and Children on the South Shore abreast of the Ship, to which place I went in the Boats in hopes of speaking with them, accompanied by Mr. Banks, Dr. Solander, and Tupia. As we approached the Shore they

---

8 'Secret Instructions for Lieutenant James Cook Appointed to Command His Majesty's Bark the Endeavour 30 July 1768' in J.M. Bennett and Alex C. Castles (eds.), *A Source Book of Australian Legal History: Source Materials from the Eighteenth to the Twentieth Centuries* (Law Book Company, 1979) 253 (http://www.foundingdocs.gov.au/item-did-34.html).
9 Ibid.
10 Cook's choice, and the ramifications it had for indigenous people in Australia, is well known, and one only needs to read *Mabo* to see how this plays out legally.
11 Ibid.
12 See Paul Carter, *The Road to Botany Bay: An Essay in Spatial History* (faber & faber, 1988).

all made off, except 2 Men, *who seem'd resolved to oppose our landing*. As soon as I saw this I order'd the boats to lay upon their Oars, in order to speak to them; but this was to little purpose, for neither us nor Tupia could understand one word they said. We then threw them some nails, beads, etc., a shore, which they took up, and seem'd not ill pleased with, in so much that I thought that they beckon'd to us to come ashore; but in this we were mistaken, for as soon as we put the boat in *they again came to oppose us, upon which I fir'd a musquet* between the 2, which had no other Effect than to make them retire back, where bundles of their darts lay, and *one of them took up a stone and threw at us, which caused my firing a Second Musquet,* load with small Shott; and altho' some of the shott *struck the man*, yet it had no other effect than making him lay hold on a Target. *Immediately after this we landed*, which we had no sooner done than they throw'd 2 darts at us; this *obliged me to fire a third shott*, soon after which they both made off, but not in such haste but what we might have taken one; but Mr. Banks being of Opinion that the darts were poisoned, made me *cautious how I advanced into the Woods*. We found here a few small hutts made of the Bark of Trees, in one of which were 4 or 5 Small Children, with whom we left some strings of beads, etc.[13]

Inhabited, unbeckon'd: a landing opposed. Three shotts, a man struck, one stone; a tactical withdrawal, cautious steps, a few beads in the Woods; a struggle to relate. Captured in this terribly efficient account of the first British landing in Australia, the creation and conduct of lawful relations is already of questionable quality.

Remaining moored in the bay for one week, Cook and his men explored the area, searching for water, cataloguing plants and largely avoiding interactions with the Gwiyagal of the Tharawal nation.[14] During this time, Cook wrote:

> Last night Forby Sutherland, Seaman, departed this Life, and in the A.M. his body Was buried ashore at the watering place, which occasioned my calling the south point of this bay after his name[15]

During this first landing an Orkney sailor was buried in what is remembered as the first British burial ceremony in Australia. As poet Henry Kendall wrote some 90 years later in 'Sutherland's Grave':

---

13 James Cook, *Captain Cook's Journal during His First Voyage Round the World Made in H M Bark 'Endeavour' 1768–71* (Elliot Stock, 1893) entry for 29 April 1770 (emphasis added).
14 This nation is also commonly referred to as Gweagal/Gwiyagal of the Dharawal/Tharawal. As representative bodies, I have followed the practice of the Tharawal Aboriginal Corporation and Tharawl Land Council.
15 Cook, above, n 13, entry for 1 May 1770. See Carter, *The Road to Botany Bay*, above, n 12.

> There tread gently – gently, pilgrim; there with thoughtful eyes look round;
> Cross thy breast and bless the silence: lo, the place is holy ground!
> Holy ground for ever, stranger![16]

Having fired three times at indigenous men in the first meeting in an effort to clear the land, and having explored and mapped the land, with the dead 'carried on shore, and decently interred',[17] the *Endeavour* sailed north, continuing to map the coastline. On the evening of 22 August 1770, on an island in the Torres Strait, Cook performed a ceremony of possession:

> Before and after we Anchor'd we saw a Number of People upon this Island, Arm'd in the same manner as all the others we have seen, Except one man, who had a bow and a bundle of Arrows, the first we have seen upon this Coast. From the appearance of the people we expected they would have opposed our landing; but as we approached the shore they all made off, and left us in peaceable possession of as much of the Island as served our purpose. After landing I went upon the highest hill.
>
> Having satisfied myself of the great Probability of a passage, thro' which I intend going with the Ship, and therefore may land no more upon this Eastern coast of New Holland, and on the Western side I can make no new discovery, the honour of which belongs to the Dutch Navigators, but the Eastern Coast from the Latitude of 38 degrees South down to this place, I am confident, was never seen or Visited by any European before us; and notwithstanding I had in the Name of his Majesty taken possession of several places upon this Coast, *I now once More hoisted English Colours, and in the Name of His Majesty King George the Third took possession of the whole Eastern coast* from the above Latitude down to this place by the Name of New Wales, together with all the Bays, Harbours, Rivers, and Islands, situated upon the said Coast; after which we fired 3 Volleys of small Arms, which were answer'd by the like number from the Ship.
>
> This done, we set out for the Ship.[18]

Named Possession Island in the Torres Strait Islands, the raising of the flag and firing of guns in this British ceremony of possession was a performance aimed at acquiring inchoate title to the whole of the east coast of Australia; the first step in obtaining territorial sovereign possession. Despite the presence of indigenous peoples, the obvious problem of inhabited land, and unresolved questions of whether this performance was sufficient to claim possession of what the British sought to

---

16 Henry Kendall, 'Sutherland's Grave', in Henry Kendall, *The Poems of Henry Kendall* (Angus & Robertson, 1920).
17 Sydney Parkinson, *Journal of a Voyage to the South Seas, in His Majesty's Ship, The Endeavour* (London, 1773) entry for 6 May 1770.
18 Cook, above, n 13, entry for 22 August 1770.

possess, there is a further difficulty. It was not until 18 years had passed before the British attempted 'effective occupation' (i.e. 'step 2'). Yet, between 1770 and 1788, despite the absence of the necessary second step perfecting sovereign acquisition, Britain asserted legal authority over these 'new' lands through technologies of jurisdiction in at least two respects.

First, instructions to Captain Phillip as first Governor of the Colony of New South Wales conferred jurisdiction over the eastern half of the continent.[19] This was an area 'considerably larger than that claimed by Cook' and included unmapped coastlines yet to be subjected to the colonial gaze.[20] Second, civil and criminal courts were established in 1787 (i.e. before 1788) through the *Charter of Justice 2 April 1787 (UK)* claiming jurisdiction over this yet to be acquired sovereign territory.[21] Together, these two actions suggest the empirical movement of common law into the Colony of New South Wales is a much more complex story than ceremonial performances, instructions to a governor or lines on a map. Not only a story of flawed sovereignty, this is also a story of moving jurisdiction, both into the Colony and within.

It was not until 1788 that the Colony of New South Wales started to mark its place with the arrival of several ships, taking up of the task of 'effective occupation' through the physical activities of a small penal population, military order and a few second sons. With the Governor of New South Wales as commander-in-chief and its courtly institutions established by letters, armed with Emmerich de Vattel's *Law of Nations*, William Blackstone's *Commentaries* and a Handbook for Magistrates, a non-legally trained colonial judiciary moved into the Colony of New South Wales. With the establishment of parliament not until 1823,[22] sovereign authority in the first years of the colony was exercised by the Governor and Judge-Advocate; two military officers taking up offices of the Crown to exercise jurisdiction. Moving from Botany Bay to Sydney within days of arrival, within a decade after its establishment, the colony had slowly expanded beyond the bounds of Sydney town; movements within.

Within 10 years, not surprisingly, the 'settlement' had slowly stretched across land, and not necessarily uninterrupted. The remainder of this chapter focuses on a specific place that is now located approximately 70 kilometres outside Sydney's CBD on the edge of metropolitan Sydney approximately one to two hours drive.

---

19 This included 'from Cape York' to 'the Southern Extremity of the said Territory of New South Wales' and 'all the Country Inland to the Westward as far as the One hundred and Thirty fifth Degree of East Longitude'. Instructions to Arthur Phillip, 25 April 1787 in *HRA*, above, n 2, vol I, 11. See also Governor Phillip's First Commission, 12 October 1786 in *HRA*, above, n 2, vol I, 1; Governor Phillip's Second Commission, 2 April 1787 in *HRA*, above, n 2, vol I, 2.
20 Dorsett and McVeigh, above, n 5. On the cartography of the colonial gaze in the most recent expansion of the British Empire, see Fraser MacDonald, 'The Last Outpost of Empire: Rockall and the Cold War' (2006) 32 *Journal of Historical Geography* 627.
21 *New South Wales Charter of Justice, Letters Patent 2 April 1787* (UK).
22 *New South Wales Act 1823* (UK) 4 Geo IV, c 96. The Third Charter of Justice established the Supreme Court of New South Wales, *Charter of Justice 13 October 1823* (UK).

Yet in 1799, while still located northwest of Sydney at the foot of the Blue Mountains, Hawkesbury was a dispersed series of settlements a two-day journey from Sydney, whether by road via Parramatta or by boat north along the coast and up the Hawkesbury River. Although a substantial distance (i.e. approximately 1000 kilometres) from the 'actual' frontier, namely the 135th meridian marking the formal western inland boundaries of the Colony, as historians have long observed, the movement of English law into the Colony of New South Wales was much more stuttered, incoherent and incomplete than lines on a map.[23] In 1799 Hawkesbury *was* the colonial frontier; a dynamic, moving, incomplete common law place.

By paying attention to movement in its different forms, and having been attentive to some of the historical, geopolitical and empirical movements of common law between the metropole and its colonies and within the colony itself, this part has addressed some of the forms of common law's empirical movements both into the Colony of New South Wales, but also introducing movements within; movements which come to the fore in the next part of the chapter. The remainder of this chapter illustrates how even very small and localised movements of common law are also part of the European appropriation of the New World, constituting movements of a European *nomos* that impose both order and place.[24] While this imposition occurs in many places, and often noticed on grander scales of sovereignty, this imposition was especially so for places imagined to be located beyond international and public law, and somehow beyond common law, such as Hawkesbury in 1799.

3.2 Death in the woods beyond

On 14 October 1799 Constable Edward Powell, Simon Freebody, James Metcalfe, William Timms and William Butler appeared before the New South Wales Court of Criminal Judicature in response to a charge: 'For wantonly Killing Two Native Men of this Territy'.[25] Judge-Advocate Richard Dore and a six-member military

---

23 See, e.g., Bruce Kercher, *An Unruly Child: A History of Law in Australia* (Allen & Unwin, 1995); Henry Reynolds, *The Other Side of the Frontier: Aboriginal Resistance to the European Invasion of Australia* (Penguin, 1982); Henry Reynolds, *Aboriginal Sovereignty: Reflections on Race, State and Nation* (Allen and Unwin, 1996), although problematically Bruce Kercher's 'eucalyptus tang', coupled with a personification of the land, strips bare any texture of place, while the imagery of Henry Reynolds' cloak muffles the middle ground. Cf: Paul Carter, 'Public Space: Its Mythopoetic Foundations and the Limits of the Law' (2007) 16(2) *Griffith Law Review* 430.
24 Drawing on Carl Schmitt's account of sovereignty, see Dorsett and McVeigh, above, n 5, 292.
25 NRS 2700 [X905] 329. This chapter is indebted to the work of Bruce Kercher through the Kercher project, which has transcribed colonial records of the Court of Criminal Judicature, including this (now reported) case *R v Powell* [1799] *NSWKR* 7. However, rather than working from the more recent and summarised case report, this chapter works primarily with original materials from the records of the Court of Criminal Judicature to ensure a linguistic resonance is not lost as well as, more significantly, to cater to the fact that the reported *R v Powell* derives from two different yet incomplete sources. Although the Kercher reporting of *R v Powell* is a highly attentive amalgamation of these two incomplete sources, the task of constructing a colonial case report and the use of

jury of the New South Wales Corps constituted the Court,[26] and all five accused were convicted. Handing down the Court's decision, one of the members of the Court, Captain Waterhouse, added, 'that by his Opinion he means not to affect their Lives, because it is the first instance of such an offence being brought before a criminal Court and therefore the prisoners were not aware of the consequences of the Law.'[27] On the basis of a majority consensus, which was the applicable judicial standard at the time rather than unanimity, the case was reserved 'by special Verdict until the sense of his Majesty's Ministers is Known upon the subject'.[28] The New South Wales' Governor John Hunter wrote to the Colonial Office, seeking advice from the metropole.[29] Bail was granted, the convicted prisoners were

testimonial evidence to construct a minor jurisprudence of movement are not the same. The original court records are complemented by Bruce Kercher and Brent Salter (eds.), *The Kercher Reports: Decisions of the New South Wales Superior Courts, 1788–1827* (Francis Forbes Society for Australian Legal History, 2009) ('*Kercher Reports*') ix, *HRA*, above, n 2, and archival research in relation to Colonial Office documents at the National Archives in England. The secondary literature on *R v Powell* is slight, but in a different genre has been addressed by Lisa Ford. Writing from the office of the critic (see Chapter 2, 2.2), and writing in a context of legal pluralism concerned with post-1763 practices of Anglophone settler sovereignty, Lisa Ford focuses on the accused's arguments of self-defence, provocation and retaliation and engages with *R v Powell* as an exemplary moment of a discourse of colonial lawlessness constructed to fall within legitimising parameters of colonial lawfulness. Cf: Lisa Ford, *Settler Sovereignty: Jurisdiction and Indigenous People in America and Australia 1788–1836* (Harvard University Press, 2010) ch 4. Also, for a short summary of the case and its potential import for legal history, see Brent Salter, 'Early Interactions Between Indigenous People and Settlers in Australia's First Criminal Court' (2009) 83 *Australian Law Journal* 56, 57–9. For other minor commentary on this case and surrounding events, see Peter Turbet, *The First Frontier: The Occupation of the Sydney Region 1788 to 1816* (Rosenberg Publishing, 2011); Jan Barkley-Jack, *Hawkesbury Settlement Revealed: A New Look at Australia's Third Mainland Settlement, 1793–1802* (Rosenberg Publishing, 2009); Grace Karskens, *The Colony: A History of Early Sydney* (Allen & Unwin, 2009).

26 Richard Dore was the third Judge-Advocate of the Colony of New South Wales (1798–1800). Preceding him were David Collins (1788–1796) and Richard Atkins (1796–1809, except 1798–1800 and 1808). The first Judge-Advocate, David Collins, was a marine officer with no formal training in law. The second Judge-Advocate, Richard Atkins, was a younger son of an aristocratic family, who fled England to escape creditors and had a severe drinking problem. Richard Atkins also had no legal training and was replaced by Richard Dore (1798–1800) and again as a result of the rebellion in 1808. Richard Dore was the first judicially trained judge, who arrived as a result of the Governor's pressing England for a professional judge. See Kercher, *An Unruly Child*, above, n 23, 47–8. The military members of the jury were Captain Henry Waterhouse, Captain John McArthur (a central figure in the overthrow of Governor Bligh in 1808), Lieutenant John Shortland, Lieutenant Neil McKellar, Lieutenant Matthew Flinders and Lieutenant Thomas Davies. The bench, therefore, consisted of naval officers Waterhouse, Shortland and Flinders and NSW Corps' MacArthur, McKellar and Davies; Turbet, *The First Frontier*, above, n 25, 115.

27 Captain Henry Waterhouse NRS 2700 [X905] 362.

28 NRS 2700 [X905] 361. The Court was unable to agree on an appropriate sentence, with three members sentencing corporal punishment and four members, including the Judge-Advocate, determining the case be specially reserved. In capital cases, the *Charter of Justice* required a majority of five out of seven members of the Court concur or proceedings be transmitted to England. See note in *HRA*, above, n 2, vol II (1797–1800) 735.

29 Although the Governor had the power to grant pardons, as this case was contentious and seen to be the 'first' of its kind, Governor John Hunter sought advice from the metropole.

released with sureties pending instructions from London and the 'Court disapproving the Conduct of Powell as a Constable do order him to be sus-pended'.[30] Only three years later, in 1802, Lord Hobart, the Secretary of State for War and the Colonies, pardoned all five men, although the conditional emancipations were later cancelled by the then New South Wales Governor King.[31]

During the five-day trial from 14 to 18 October 1799, the Court heard evidence from 16 witnesses and received written and oral submissions from the accused. Before embarking on the narrative proper, a few peculiar eighteenth-century legal rules and procedures need to be explained to avoid collapsing the content or operation of this case with modern understandings of how criminal trials operate. First, the content of *R v Powell* is not the same as a modern judgment. While contemporary case reports focus on conclusions rather than processes; publishing the Court's judgment and reasons for decision, and only rarely summarising evidence or counsel's argument as part of the final court report, this 1799 case is different. In *R v Powell*, the substance of the 'case report' is a transcript of testimonial evidence provided by witnesses, and only the final few lines of a 25-page report include the Court's judgment and abrupt reasons for decision. Second, in accordance with the rules of evidence, the legal standards of the time prohibited Aboriginal witnesses from providing evidence in court.[32] In addition to carrying an uncertain legal status as non- (or not-quite) English legal subjects, the logic behind this prohibition was that as non-Christian 'heathens', Aboriginal people were deemed incapable of swearing the (Christian) oath in Court and thus incapable of providing evidence.[33] In a case concerning the killing of two Aboriginal

---

30 NRS 2700 [X905] 361.
31 Lord Robert Hobart, 4th Earl of Buckinghamshire, was a member of the House of Lords from 1801 to 1804. He served as the Secretary of State for War and the Colonies (a telling combination of title). This was a British cabinet position responsible for the army and all British colonies, except for India. Created in 1801, Lord Hobart was its first Secretary – before being split into two (i.e. one army, one colony) in 1854. In relation to these events, Lord Hobart ultimately granted pardons received by the third Governor, Captain Philip Gidley King, Robert Hobart, 'Letter from Lord Hobart to Acting-Governor King (acknowledged 30 October 1802)' in *HRA*, above, n 2, vol III (1801–1802) 366, 372, 592. However, 'Conditional Emancipations' rather than 'Free Pardons' were granted; see note 13 June 1802 in *HRA*, above, n 2, vol III (1801–1802) 626. Further, the conditional emancipations were prepared but cancelled, and 'the men affected were pardoned only for their colonial crimes, and allowed to work out their original sentences of transportation', *HRA*, above, n 2, vol III (1801–1802) 785.
32 See *R v Fitzpatrick and Colville* [1824] NSWKR 2. See also Alex C. Castles, *An Australian Legal History* (Law Book Company, 1982) 532–4.
33 The question of how and when Aboriginal people became subjects of the British Crown is complex, uncertain and ultimately vexed. On the one hand, subjecthood in this sense is often remembered as occurring at the moment of 'settlement', for example: 'That the Aborigines were British subjects seemed to have been conclusively settled, so far as colonial courts were concerned, by the various proclamations and statutes establishing the Australian colonies', Australian Law Reform Commission, *Recognition of Aboriginal Customary Laws*, Report 31 (1986) [39]–[40]. On the other hand, various later moments, often circulating around the institutional formalisation in the 1820s and 1830s (such as the Supreme Court), are also touted as the originary moment of 'subjecthood'. See, e.g., *New South Wales Act 1823 (UK)*; *Australian Courts Act 1829* (UK) 9 Geo IV, c 83, s 3, 24;

boys, all witnesses were therefore non-Aboriginal. Third, compared with current standards of evidentiary relevance that require witnesses to remain strictly on-topic (or at least the legal topic), although certainly not unusual for trials in the late eighteenth century, the evidence provided in *R v Powell* went far beyond the direct subject matter of the trial, namely: the criminal responsibility of the accused for the death of two Aboriginal boys.[34] For example, rather than denying the killing of the two Aboriginal boys, the defence sought to justify their killing by reference to several possible sources of authorisation including the Governor, the Lieutenant-in-Charge of Hawkesbury, a recent widow of one of the men killed in the woods beyond, and an argument based on a natural (or legal) order.[35] As a result, in the process of providing evidence in relation to the killing of two Aboriginal boys, most witnesses provided testimony that ranged widely in both time and space, covering a series of events in and around Hawkesbury in preceding months and years. By tracking these events through the witnesses' words, an opportunity arises to materially and visually reveal some common law movements in and around Hawkesbury at the close of the eighteenth century.

Where is Hawkesbury? Today the City of Hawkesbury is a local government area on the metropolitan fringes of Sydney, a sprawling urban city covering roughly 1800 square kilometres, with a population of nearly 5 million people. In 1799 Hawkesbury was a colonial settlement at the geographical and legal frontier of the Colony of New South Wales. New settlers had moved, and continued to move to the 'uninhabited' outskirts beyond the new city, taken land (often without formal authorisation from the colonial administration), built dwellings and planted crops.[36] A number of violent confrontations occurred between Aboriginal people and 'settlers', including shootings, spearings and 'property' theft (corn in particular) as the colony 'stretched'. With reports of both Aboriginal and non-Aboriginal people having been killed, the non-Aboriginal witnesses often reasoned, albeit not surprisingly, that no violence had been 'committed on the natives at the Hawkesbury or elsewhere without provocation being given.'[37] Witnesses provided various estimates of death tolls in the region.[38]

Proclamation of Governor Hindmarsh (28 December 1836) which extends 'the same protection to the native population as to the rest of His Majesty's subjects': Bennett and Castles, *A Sourcebook of Australian Legal History*, above, n 8, 258.

34 See, e.g., Kercher, *An Unruly Child*, above, n 23.
35 Prisoners' defence NRS 2700 [X905] 309. See also Ford, *Settlor Sovereignty*, above, n 25.
36 This narrative uses the testimonial terminology of 'settlers', cf: Albert Memmi, *The Colonizer and the Colonized* (Howard Greenfield trans., Earthscan, 1990) [trans. of *Portrait du Colonise Precede du Portrait du Colinisateur* (first published 1957)].
37 Lieutenant Thomas Hobby NRS 2700 343. Cf: 'Letter from Lord Hobart to Acting-Governor King (acknowledged 30 October 1802)' in *HRA*, above, n 2, vol III (1801–1802) 366.
38 For different estimates, see Lieutenant Thomas Hobby NRS 2700 [X905] 344 (two white, two Aboriginal in two months); Robert Braithwaite NRS 2700 [X905] 345 (four white, five Aboriginal in 12 months); Jonas Archer NRS 2700 [X905] 349 (12 white, 20 Aboriginal in five years); John Molloy NRS 2700 [X905] 361 (26 white, unknown Aboriginal in 4.5 years). See also Jan Barkley-Jack, *Hawkesbury Settlement Revealed*, above, n 25, 318–26; Turbet, *The First Frontier*, above, n 25, 118.

In this time and place, certain events occurred: some known, many unknown. The following story is a narration of events reconstructed solely from the evidence provided in *R v Powell (1799)*. As will be explained in more detail after the narration, the task here is not an attempt to reconstruct historical truth and, if such truth occurs, it is a welcome by-product. Rather, by piecing together evidence through the spoken words of witnesses, the task of this narrative is a jurisprudential one. Tracking how the court hears, this narrative sets the scene for tracing jurisdictional movements of common law that occurs through acts of redescription in the final parts of this chapter.

Narrating R v Powell (1799)

In a context of ongoing violence, during the winter of 1799, a rumour circulated in Hawkesbury that it was 'the intention of the natives to Come down in numbers from the Blue mountains to the Hawksbury and to murder some of the white People and particularly some of the Soldiers.'[39] Little thought appeared to be given to any potential reasons behind this 'Resolution of the Natives',[40] although the Commanding Officer of Hawkesbury, Lieutenant Hobby, suggested the 'Resolution' was 'in con-sequence of a native woman and Child being put to death by a Soldier.'[41] A prior violence, and a prior violence by soldiers.

In the same period as this rumour circulated, an ex-soldier turned free settler, William Goodall, was 'working on his Grounds'[42] when he was 'alarmed'[43] by a 'Pty of Natives'.[44] In what was described as a triggering event for what was to come, according to Goodall, this was a 'desperate attack',[45] 'without the smallest provocation'.[46] Despite reports of his death, Goodall survived several spear wounds and testified as a defence witness.[47] As a result of Goodall's attack, and several other unspecified attacks on travellers using Parramatta Road between Hawkesbury and Parramatta, coupled with the 'Resolution of the Natives',[48] Lieutenant Hobby sought the advice of the Governor in relation to the perceived

---

39 Lieutenant Thomas Hobby NRS 2700 [X905] 340.
40 Ibid, 343.
41 Ibid.
42 William Goodall NRS 2700 [X905] 352. According to Peter Turbet, his grounds were located on what is now 'Old Windsor Road, near Bingara Crescent, Bella Vista'; Turbet, *The First Frontier*, above, n 25, 108.
43 Ibid.
44 Ibid.
45 Ibid.
46 Ibid.
47 Lieutenant Thomas Hobby NRS 2700 [X905] 341. See also William Goodall NRS 2700 [X905] 352. William Goodall had been a sergeant who was originally responsible for the Hawkesbury store, but had become a 'free settler' in April 1797; Turbet, *The First Frontier*, above, n 25, 108. Goodall survived his wounds, living another 30 years, before his death at Windsor in 1828; Turbet, *The First Frontier*, above, n 25, 109.
48 Lieutenant Thomas Hobby NRS 2700 [X905] 343.

increase in violence.⁴⁹ According to Lieutenant Hobby's testimony, the Governor 'appeared much displeased at the Conduct of the natives'⁵⁰ and told him 'something must be done'⁵¹ and to 'act discretionally agst the natives'.⁵² Lieutenant Hobby interpreted the Governor's vague comments somewhat more precisely and explained to the Governor 'his Intention that if the natives should still continue their violent outrages of sending out a party of the military to kill five or six of them wherever they were to be found.'⁵³

On or about 7 August 1799, the location of an Aboriginal group allegedly present at the spearing of Goodall was reported to the military. As Lieutenant Hobby testified, he ordered several soldiers to 'go in pursuit of them immediately. and desired the natives might not be fired upon unless they made resistance – in which Case to bring them in Dead or alive or words to that effect.'⁵⁴ Having gone out in pursuit, the military party returned the following day with an Aboriginal man referred to as Charley. Although Charley denied any involvement beyond being present at the spearing of Goodall, he was escorted from Hawkesbury to Sydney 'by a Pty of Soldiers as a Prisoner',⁵⁵ and taken before the Governor. Noting distinct juridical textures of different legal places, as well as the patterns of lawful movements between those places, Corporal Peter Farrell, who escorted Charley to Sydney, recalled his conversation with the Governor, and testified:

> [T]hat His Excellency made Enquiry of the witness Who he had go there that the Witness answer 'it was a Native who was known to have been at the Spearing of Goodall & committing several barbarous Depredations'. that the Governor said 'Well, what am I to do with him. Why did not your own Commanding Officer of Hawkesbury do something with him' That the witness answered he supposed it was from a wish to make a more public Example of this Native that his Excellency replied it was not in his Power to give orders for the hanging or shooting of such ignorant Creatures who could not be made sensible of what they might be guilty of therefore could not be treated according to our Laws. That the witness then Requested to know what was to be done in the present Case when the Governor told the Witness that immediate Retaliation should be made on the Spot or words to that effect as it was the only mode his Excellency said he could think upon that some Bystander observed that was impossible as the Natives always took

---

49 Ibid, 340–42.
50 Ibid.
51 Ibid.
52 Ibid.
53 Ibid, 341.
54 Ibid. This occurred at Lieutenant Hobby's quarters, located 'near today's George Street, Windsor, opposite Arndell Street', per Turbet, *The First Frontier*, above, n 25, 110.
55 William Goodall NRS 2700 [X905] 352.

advantage of the time & place 'Then' replied his Excellency 'so soon as they can be Caught'[56]

Charley was 'admonished … as to his future Conduct'[57] by the Governor, discharged without punishment, escorted back to the Hawkesbury and returned 'to Mr Cumins with whom he had long lived as servant to be further admonished'.[58] Corporal Farrell 'Returned to the Hawkesbury and made report verbally to his Comanding Officer of what had been done which he publicly also repeated among the Settlers'.[59]

Not long afterwards, it became known that two white men, Hodgkinson and Wimbo, had been killed in the woods while on a hunting expedition.[60] Details of their deaths were told to Jonas Archer, a settler, by an Aboriginal referred to as Yellowgowy. Yellowgowy reported that Hodgkinson and Wimbo had been camping in the woods with several Aboriginal men and were killed by an Aboriginal man known as Major White as well as one or two other unnamed Aboriginal men. As Jonas Archer testified:

> Quest. by Court. Did you understand from the Native Yellowgowy that the native Major White attended the deced HodgsKinson and Wimbo as friends in the Woods. Yes. Yellowgowy said that White met the deced HodgsKinson and Wimbo in the Woods and asked them if they had got any Pheasants being answered No, they made a fire and the native made another being Even. about Sundown which the natives invited them to do observing they would get Pheasants the next day, that in the night the said Natives put them to death as before stated.[61]

According to Jonas Archer, Yellowgowy described to him 'the manner in which said murder was Comitted said that White and other native Run their Dowels (a sort of Spear) in to said Hodgskingson & Wimbo'.[62] After receiving this information from Yellowgowy, Jonas Archer told another Aboriginal referred to as Jemmy that Major White had Hodgkinson's gun, and Jemmy agreed to retrieve the gun and return in a few days.[63] On the evening the two Aboriginal boys were killed, approximately one month after the deaths of Hodgkinson and Wimbo,

---

56 Corporal Peter Farrell NRS 2700 [X905] 315 cf: 355.
57 Ibid, 355 cf: 315.
58 Ibid, 355 cf: Corporal Peter Farrell NRS 2700 [X905] 315 where there is no reference to 'servant'. Cumins, it seems, might have been Lieutenant Cummings, Turbet, *The First Frontier*, above, n 25, 111.
59 Ibid.
60 Also referred to as 'Wimbow' and 'Wimbolt'.
61 Jonas Archer NRS 2700 [X905] 347–8. The reference to 'pheasants' is a reference to lyrebirds.
62 Ibid, 347.
63 Ibid.

Isabella Ramsay offered the following account of a conversation that occurred in her house concerning the deaths in the woods beyond:

> [T]hat about the time the above natives were killed she believes the evening of the same day the said three Natives came into her dwelling house at the Hawkesbury with the musket of Thomas Hodgskinson who had been lately killed by the natives in the woods and delivered up said Musket. That Freebody and another Pson then came into the house of the Witness and questioned the natives as to what manner said Hodgskinson had been killed. They in the best manner they could explained he was killed for the sake of the victuals he had with him and that there were three of them in the Killing of him – that the night preceeding the murder three other natives slept with him – that they passed part of the next day together and toward the even. made a fire and eat, after which the said Hodgskinson and Wimbolt laid them down under the Covering of Blankets that the said three other natives afterwards secured their two Muskets and put said Hodgkinson and Wimbolt to death with their Waddys.[64]

In support of the reference to victuals as part of the reason as to why Hodgkinson and Wimbow might have been killed, Jonas Archer added:

> What was the reason do you supose that the said natives put them to death. Possibly for the sake of their provisions or because Wimbo had the daur of the Comrade of said White living with him. Do you mean to say the said natives daur was forcibly detained by Wimbo. No. I know she might have left him had she Chused.[65] [...]
>
> Are not the settlers or their Men in the habits of taking the women from the natives and that the native men are prevented taking them away thro fear of their Fire Arms. In two Instances I remember lately, but cannot say whether the Women were detained by force – but were taken away agst the Inclination of their native men – and I Know that said two women were Companions to the white men from choice.[66]

According to Jonas Archer, Hodgkinson and Wimbo were killed either for victuals or because Wimbo had the daughter of the comrade of Major White living with him. Although Jonas Archer was of the view this particular daughter was not kept by force, this may not have been the view of Major White. Of course, it must be emphasised that the relationship between these killings and Aboriginal law is – and should remain – unclear. Whether the deaths of Hodgkinson and Wimbo

---

64 Isabella Ramsay NRS 2700 [X905] 333. Apparently the house is 'on the river to the east of Archer's, just north of today's Deerrubben Park', Turbet, *The First Frontier*, above, n 25.
65 Jonas Archer NRS 2700 [X905] 348.
66 Ibid, 350.

were in accordance with or breach of Aboriginal law is a matter that can only be determined by the relevant form of indigenous law. Not only is the practice and reasoning of Aboriginal law beyond the parameters of common law's internal logic, in these circumstances, the role of Aboriginal law in these events certainly cannot and should not be determined by the evidence of white witnesses in a 1799 trial for the killing of two Aboriginal boys.

A burial party

In response to these deaths, a burial party was organised by some of the Hawkesbury settlers to head into the woods and locate and bury the bodies of Hodgkinson and Wimbo. Before the burial party departed, Lieutenant Hobby arranged for soldiers to accompany them:

> Quest. by Powell: What orders did you give to a Party of Soldiers who went out to bury the Body of Tho. Hodgskinson who had been Killed by the Natives.
> My orders to the Soldiers were to got out with the Men who were going out to bury the Bodies of Hodgskinson and Wimbolt (who were murdered by the natives about two months since) 'That if they fell in with any Natives on the Road either going or returning to fire in upon them.'[67]

In his evidence, Lieutenant Hobby testified he meant the order to apply to both settlers and soldiers, and explicitly for that expedition only, although this may have been misunderstood:

> Quest. When you sent a Pty of Soldiers out in pursuit of the natives were they accompanied by Settlers or any other descript. of Persons.
> Yes they were and I believe by several.
> Did you when you gave orders to the Pty to go out and shoot any of the native they shod meet with consider these orders extending to the Settlers or others that accompanied the Pty.
> Yes I did upon that Excursion only.
> Are you positive that your orders were so explicit as that the whole Pty understood they were only to attack the Natives whilst on that excursion.
> The orders I delivered to the Serj were. but its possible they might be misunderstood.
> Do you Know that any of the prisoners now arraigned were present on the above Pty.

---

67 Lieutenant Thomas Hobby NRS 2700 [X905] 340. Confirmed by Jonas Archer NRS 2700 [X905] 349; William Fuller NRS 2700 [X905] 351–2. Also supported by Isabella Ramsay's evidence of Constable Powell's comments NRS 2700 [X905] 334.

I do not possitively know but have reason to supose they were from a remark made to me by Metcalf that had I seen the bodies of Hodgkinson and Wimbolt that I should have thot. nothing of the Natives being put to death.[68]

The burial party located the bodies of Hodgkinson and Wimbo and buried them in the woods. One of the witnesses, William Fuller, who 'resides at Richmond a free man and lives by his labor'[69] confirmed that at least two of the accused, namely Metcalf and Freebody, were part of the burial party.[70] Further, according to Jonas Archer, prior to being located by the burial party, the dead had not been properly buried:

> Did you go out with Pty who went to Bury the bodies of the dead Hodgkinson Wimbo and in what state did you find them
> Yes I did go out, and saw said two Bodies naked covered by wood and both were Speared in the Body's and otherwise mangled their Cloaths provisions and Arms and Blankets were taken from them[71]

For a number of witnesses, the treatment of the dead was a significant concern. Consider this account provided in defence by several of the accused, William Timms, Simon Freebody and William Butler:

> It's well known by many of the Gentlemen present that they are a Treacherous Evil minded Blood Thirsty set description of Men that they will be Familiar, and be with People for a Considerable time until perhaps they have received the 9/10th of a loaf of Bread and then for the last tenth they will Murder, two or three who before were their Friends to get it – many Instances of a Similar kind are known – again it was generally understood that it was a standing order, or at least it was so issued from the Commanding Officer to Kill any of the Natives found in their way, particularly after the Barbarous Cruel and Inhuman Murder of the unfortunate Hodgkinson and Wimbow, a Murder the most horrid to have beheld. Any Gentlemen to have seen the Mangled Bodies of the Deceased would have shuddered and ever bore an Antipathy against the Cruel Natives in general, and that it behoves every Man to be on his guard against them and their Intentions, never to give them any Encouragement for it's the Indulgences they have received makes them so knowing.[72]

---

68 Lieutenant Thomas Hobby NRS 2700 [X905] 343.
69 William Fuller NRS 2700 [X905] 350.
70 Ibid, 351–2. Although not clear on the primary materials, according to Turbet, *The First Frontier*, above, n 25, 116, Fuller was also part of the burial party.
71 Jonas Archer NRS 2700 [X905] 348.
72 William Timms, Simon Freebody and William Butler NRS 2700 [X905] 312.

Events then came to a head. On the afternoon or early evening of 18 September 1799, approximately one month after the return of the burial party, three Aboriginal males, including Jemmy, voluntarily attended the dwelling of Isabella Ramsay to return Hodgkinson's gun, as requested by David White.[73] The circumstances of Hodgkinson's death were explained by the three Aboriginal males, reiterating he had been killed by Major White (not present in the dwelling).[74] In addition to the potential reasons already offered as to why Hodgkinson and Wimbo might have been killed – for victuals or in response to an Aboriginal female living with Wimbo under unclear circumstances of consent – a further reason was offered, that is, the behaviour of soldiers or a soldier in particular:

> Metcalfe then questioned them again Concerning the Murder of Hodgkinson and Wimbow on the Mountains their answers was 'not angry with any more white Men, but very bad Soldier, very bad them'[75]

Throughout the evening, an increasing number of settlers attended this dwelling and discussed what should be done with the three Aboriginal males, who were no longer voluntarily remaining in the dwelling.[76] Constable Edward Powell suggested they should be killed as he understood it was the Governor's orders to kill.[77] Entering with a 'bright Cutlass', William Butler asked 'what sentence shall we pass on these blackfellows? I will pass sentence myself. They shall be hanged.'[78] After some discussion and apparent consensus, rope was collected from another dwelling and the three Aboriginal males had their hands tied behind their back, rope twisted around their necks[79] and were escorted from the dwelling by a number of men.[80] Approximately 15 minutes later, two musket shots were fired.[81] Soon after the shots were fired, William Timms returned to Isabella Ramsay's house and requested a spade.[82]

The following day, the bodies of two Aboriginal Darug males were located. They had been buried, but were 'dug ... up and left the Bodies laying on the Ground', before being examined.[83] Both bodies had their hands tied behind the

---

73 John Pearson NRS 2700 [X905] 337; Prisoners' defence NRS 2700 [X905] 309.
74 John Pearson NRS 2700 [X905] 337; Jonas Archer NRS 2700 [X905] 347.
75 Prisoners' defence NRS 2700 [X905] 309. See also William Bladey NRS 2700 [X905] 359.
76 See Isabella Ramsay NRS 2700 [X905] 333–5; John Pearson NRS 2700 [X905] 337–8; Prisoners' defence NRS 2700 [X905] 309–10.
77 Isabella Ramsay NRS 2700 [X905] 334; Thomas Rickerby NRS 2700 [X905] 331; Lieutenant Thomas Hobby NRS 2700 [X905] 339; Prisoners' defence NRS 2700 [X905] 312.
78 Isabella Ramsay NRS 2700 [X905] 333; cf. John Pearson NRS 2700 [X905] 338.
79 This was after having collected rope from a dog's lead, John Pearson NRS 2700 [X905] 338; David White NRS 2700 [X905] 346; Isabella Ramsay NRS 2700 [X905] 334.
80 See John Pearson NRS 2700 [X905] 338; Isabella Ramsay NRS 2700 [X905] 334.
81 Isabella Ramsay NRS 2700 [X905] 334; Thomas Lambourne NRS 2700 [X905] 336; John Pearson NRS 2700 [X905] 338; David White NRS 2700 [X905] 346.
82 John Pearson NRS 2700 [X905] 338.
83 Thomas Rickerby NRS 2700 [X905] 330; Prisoners' defence NRS 2700 [X905] 310–11.

back.[84] The smaller and younger had died as a result of a cutlass wound while the older one had been shot 'thro the body by a Musket Ball'[85] and had cutlass wounds to the extent that 'the head was nearly severed from the Body'.[86] The smaller body was Lule Geo or Little George,[87] who was estimated to be approximately 11 or 12 years old.[88] The larger body was Jemmy, who was approximately 15 or 16 years old.[89] Jemmy had returned Hodgkinson's gun, as requested.[90]

A decent burial?

During the five-day trial, the Court was told of these events. The Court was also informed that later in the evening of 18 September 1799, after the shots had been fired, two of the accused, Simon Freebody and William Timms, told David White that Edward Powell had fired at one of the captured Aboriginal males while William Butler held a rope around his neck, but that particular captive had escaped.[91] According to David White, Simon Freebody said he had killed one of the other Aboriginal males with a cutlass and the third Aboriginal male had been held by James Metcalf and shot through the body.[92]

As Chief Constable Thomas Rickerby explained, the investigation into these killings began after being told by Mary Archer:

> [T]wo Native boys having been Killed … the night before, and … that Edward Powell the Constable, Simon Freebody, James Metcalfe, William Butler, William Timms, Thomas Sanburn & Bishop Thompson were all together when they were Killed, but that Sanburn, Thompson and Pearson had nothing to do with the murder, that in Consequence of this Information the Witness being Chief Cons. at the Hawkesbury went up to Powells with two more Constables with him namely David Browne and John Soare, that Powell was from home, but in his house were Metcalf, Thompson, (and he believes Timms) and Sanburn making enquiry of them if they Knew any thing about the Boys being murdered they made answer one and all that they Knew nothing about it. But that Sanburn said they were as decently buried as any of the white people that were Killed by the Natives. the Witness asked said Sanburn if he would shew him where they were buried,

---

84 Robert Braithwaite NRS 2700 [X905] 344; Thomas Rickerby NRS 2700 [X905] 330–31; Lieutenant Thomas Hobby NRS 2700 [X905] 339.
85 Thomas Rickerby NRS 2700 [X905] 331.
86 Lieutenant Thomas Hobby NRS 2700 [X905] 339. See also Thomas Rickerby NRS 2700 [X905] 330–31; Robert Braithwaite NRS 2700 [X905] 334.
87 John Tarlington NRS 2700 [X905] 358.
88 Ibid.
89 Ibid.
90 John Pearson NRS 2700 [X905] 337; Prisoners' defence NRS 2700 [X905] 309.
91 David White NRS 2700 [X905] 346.
92 Ibid.

who told him no. that on leaving Powells house he met with Powell of whom he made the like enquiry about the murder, who said he Knew nothing about it he had Killed none of them nor did he Know who had. That Powell refused to inform the Witness where the said bodies were buried but on a search he discovered and with assistance dug them up and left the Bodies laying on the Ground while he went up to the Comanding Officer at the Hawkesbury Lieut. Hobby, who went with Mr Braithwaite and the witness, and the Bodies were examined[93]

Confirming this situation, Constable David Browne 'Deposeth to have seen the Bodies of the said deced Natives which appeared to him to have been murdered and he was ordered to take Care of them until they were buried.'[94] Likewise, recounting the same events, the defence submissions included:

William Timms, Simon Freebody & William Butler Positively Declare that they heard of the Natives being at the house of Robert Foster, and they went as did many others to see them being (as was said) the Natives which Murdered Hodgkinson and Wimbow, they left them after some little time and proceeded to their different homes; the next Day William Timms went to see where the Natives were Buried as did many others. Timms said, Ah my Poor Master (Hodgskinson) was not Buried like this, he was Cut into Pieces with a Tomahawk and a Death Spear run through his Yard and came thr'u the back part of his neck, on thos words the said Timms was taken into Custody and the others likewise on Similar words were taken up also[95]

Finally, after five days of hearing the evidence and defence submissions, the Court held the accused severally guilty of murdering two Aboriginal boys without provocation.[96] The case was reserved by special verdict, Edward Powell suspended as Constable and bail granted to all the accused,[97] although, ultimately, the accused were pardoned.[98]

---

93 Thomas Rickerby NRS 2700 [X905] 330.
94 David Browne NRS 2700 [X905] 335.
95 Evidence of William Timms, Simon Freebody and William Butler NRS 2700 [X905] 311–12.
96 NRS 2700 [X905] 361–2.
97 Ibid, 361.
98 Lord Hobart ultimately granted pardons received by the third Governor, Captain Philip Gidley King, Robert Hobart, 'Letter from Lord Hobart to Acting-Governor King (acknowledged 30 October 1802)' in *HRA*, above, n 2, vol III (1801–1802) 366, 366, 372, 592. However, 'Conditional Emancipations' rather than 'Free Pardons' were granted; see note 13 June 1802 in *HRA*, above, n 2, vol III (1801–1802) 626. Further, the conditional emancipations were prepared but cancelled, and 'the men affected were pardoned only for their colonial crimes, and allowed to work out their original sentences of transportation', *HRA*, above, n 2, vol III (1801–1802) 785.

Moving court; locating law: a question of jurisdiction

As should be clear from the narrative just provided, legal issues before the Court of Criminal Judicature were more complex than simply determining the criminal responsibility of the accused men. Significantly, legal issues included the question of whether or not common law even applied: a question of jurisdiction.[99] Did this Court have jurisdiction, and if so, did the Court have jurisdiction over all of these different narrated events, actions, bodies and lands? Was the Court able to 'speak' its law to each of these bodies, and over the complete fullness of these lands? If so, how did this work, and by what means did this actually occur? These are not only important questions of jurisdiction, they are also questions of common law's place. Before redescribing this narrative with the aim of locating common law and attending to its movements, it is helpful to address the most obvious location of law in this narrative, that is, the jurisdictional site of the speakers: the Court.

The Court of Criminal Judicature was convened in a series of buildings in Sydney in 1799. Often housed in the Governor's House or a schoolroom, even in the absence of the architectural surrounds of an English-styled courthouse, the familiar courtroom mechanics were constructed: defined roles, demarcated spaces and informal codes of etiquette and conduct: a legal deliberation set in a colonial attempt of a very English environment.[100] Across five days in October, the hearing of this criminal matter involved witnesses testifying, the accused offering some comments in response and submitting a collective letter in defence, and the deliberation and judgment (albeit a judgment in deferral) of Judge-Advocate Dore and his military bench. Clearly, the Court of Criminal Judicature exercised jurisdiction: they conducted a hearing and made a decision according to English criminal law. But where, and when, and most importantly, how was this jurisdiction exercised? The first question of where is quite straightforward: a courtroom within a courthouse, the prototypical site of law, and also a very material site of legal activity. The second question of when, however, is a little more complex. On the one hand, the exercise of jurisdiction occurred on 18 October 1799 (i.e. date of judgment), when Judge-Advocate Dore clearly spoke the law, judging all of the accused guilty of murder and deciding to defer a decision on sentence by referring the matter to London for further advice. Yet, as raised in Chapter 2, jurisdiction is not only judgment, but also deliberation, and for this reason, the 'when' of the exercise of jurisdiction also includes the dates of the full hearing from 14 to 18 October, rather than simply the date of judgment. The location of this exercise of jurisdiction therefore was in a courtroom in Sydney for five days in October 1799.

While the when and the where of jurisdiction are relatively clear, what remains unclear is the question of how jurisdiction works? How was jurisdiction exercised,

---

99 See Chapter 2, 2.2.
100 On relations between law and architecture in the context of courthouses, see Linda Mulcahy, *Legal Architecture: Justice, Due Process and the Place of Law* (Routledge, 2011).

and what did this exercise actually amount to? Remembering jurisdiction is exercised in relation to its subjects, whether person, property or thing, who or what were the subjects of jurisdiction here? Consider the exercise of jurisdiction in relation to persons. Within the courthouse, the five accused men – Constable Edward Powell, Simon Freebody, James Metcalfe, William Timms and William Butler – were all persons subject to the Court's criminal jurisdiction. Brought before the Court to stand trial for alleged crimes, the Court exercised jurisdiction in relation to their activities, casting judgment in determining their guilt for killing two Aboriginal boys. Yet it is not just the five male accused who are the subjects of jurisdiction in this narrative, but also, albeit in a different manner, the witnesses. Whether called to court by a formal summons or attending on their own accord, each witness spoke in an environment highly regulated by English law. Speaking as a body subject to the laws populating the space of the courtroom, that is, English criminal and evidentiary law, these bodies were also heard as English legal subjects. With jurisdiction inherently relational, requiring a speaker and its other, the bodies of the witnesses were spoken to and in a sense, were 'jurisdictionally called to' by the bench (the Judge-Advocate; the military jury), as well as being jurisdictionally heard. Not just the accused, the witnesses therefore were also subject to an exercise of jurisdiction due to their presence in the specific conflation of time and space of this courtroom.

Yet this is not sufficient, and far too constrained: the exercise of jurisdiction is not only limited to the time and space of the courtroom. A legal subject is always a legal subject 'wherever they may go'.[101] Whether inside or outside a court, each body carries a particular jurisdictional status. Jurisdictional activity therefore engages not only the body in court, but also actions outside court. How then might we think jurisdictionally about events such as Charley's activities, the spearing of Goodall, attacks on the road, and the burial party? Spoken in court, how might the exercise of jurisdiction in those five days in October relate *jurisdictionally* to these prior activities that occurred beyond the newly marked colonial spaces of Sydney?

The Court of Criminal Judicature clearly exercised jurisdiction across five days in October, and through this exercise marked the bodies in the courtroom. Yet in the same time and space, the Court also engaged a series of prior events into the common law tradition, narrated as they were through witness testimony provided in the courtroom. In this jurisdictional embrace, it seems arguable that these prior actions, bodies and lands, spoken as evidence in a courtroom in October 1799, became marked as or located within common law. Through a courtly exercise of jurisdiction which heard of events in prior times and distant places, including a burial party that walked into the woods beyond Hawkesbury, these events become captured within a common law idiom, bringing them into some form of common law being. By speaking in court, and speaking under oath in testimonial speech, what this means is that a jurisdictional

---

101 Blackstone, below, n 103.

embrace *retrospectively* marks these prior events *as* common law. Therefore, across five days in a Sydney courtroom, a series of events that occurred elsewhere in time and space were marked, and marked jurisdictionally, by English common law. From the physical ground of a temporary courtroom, common law moved in time and space, retrospectively marking prior bodies, activities and potentially even lands.

This analysis of jurisdictional movement from the courtroom back in time resonates with a rather more traditional approach that beneficially avoids certain awkward issues of legitimacy and authority in terms of common law's place: 'retrospectivity'.[102] In common law traditions, there is a general rule or rebuttable presumption against retrospectivity. When new laws are created, they apply from that point of time onwards. If this were not the case, and new laws applied before they came into being, certain behaviour previously legal at the actual time of the behaviour becomes subsequently – whether one week, two years or several decades later – illegal, creating an archetypal moment of injustice. In *R v Powell*, while the accused did argue that the killings were authorised, and therefore not contrary to any existing law at the time, this is not what I mean by invoking the term 'retrospectivity'. Rather, in the moment of the trial – in October in the courtroom – evidence was provided, stories told, and events narrated of activities occurring outside and *prior to* the time and space of the courtroom. In this spatial translation across time, in the telling of old events in the now-ness of the courtroom – in that October present – these prior events were marked as common law. This is what I mean by retrospectivity: a technique of common law movement. Carried on testimonial words, this was a retrospective marking as common law travelled back in time, moving into prior places far beyond the Sydney courtroom of this hearing. But was this the first marking of these events *as* common law?

While noticing the exercise of jurisdiction through the Court's practices of deliberation and judgment, an exercise of retrospectivity, the more interesting question – at least in the terms of this book – is whether there was an earlier jurisdictional movement *before* the technique of retrospectivity sent common law 'back in time'. What happened before this courtly embrace? Were the activities spoken in testimony – these bodies as well as these lands present in these prior activities – already marked as 'common law' at the time of these events, that is, in the months or years before the trial in October 1799? For example, where was common law *as* the burial party walked? Was it already 'there'? Or did the jurisdictional marking occur only after – but not *as* – the burial party walked?

As we shall see in the next parts of this chapter, while common law moves

---

102 Retrospective rule making can encompass corrective laws, interpretive regulation, and judicial decisions. A rational justification for retrospectivity requires a reconsideration of the nature of law and the rule of law, and might reveal new insights into the nature of law and the limits of societal order: see Charles Sampford, *Retrospectivity and the Rule of Law* (Oxford University Press, 2006).

retrospectively through the exercise of jurisdiction in the hearing and judgment of *R v Powell* itself, marking prior bodies, events and even possibly lands, this is not the only jurisdictional movement occurring. Jurisdiction operates in a variety of ways, and does not require a courtly institution to actively and directly wield it. Rather than focusing on this jurisdictional time travelling in reverse, what is needed is an attention to the place of common law *before* the exercise of jurisdiction by the Court of Criminal Judicature.

If we step aside from a court-centric understanding of jurisdiction and its concomitant retrospective legal story, it becomes easier to appreciate different ways in which common law moves, and moves anyway and in any event, with or without the instigation or oversight of a mortared institution. The purpose of the forthcoming redescription is to remind the jurist how to notice common law techniques and practices in their varied forms. For far too long understandings of common law practice have been overly institutionally bound, but this is not the only way common law works. Although common law is certainly authorised through the material practices of its formal institutions, the sites and places of law lie not only with judicial organs, or with bodies inside and outside court, but also take up residence in the land. The question of how and when common law takes up residence, whether moving through bodies or lands, is the question that motivates this chapter.

To this end, the rest of the chapter zooms in and focuses on the burial party, reconfiguring the practices of walking and camping as jurisdictional techniques of movement. Walking. Touching the surface of the earth. Jurisdiction. Movement. This is a more fragile and textured movement of common law than the more obvious movements of a courtly claim, yet it is in their simplicity of form that their significance rests. Boldly put, these material forms of movement contribute to and may even authorise the later jurisdictional movements emanating from and bound to the Court. More temperately, while the courtly exercise of jurisdiction certainly contributes to common law's movements, in order to understand the place of law, it is important to pay attention to the practice of common law and notice its different forms of movement, even movements before (in time) rather than before (in space) the Court.

Therefore, while the Court of Criminal Judicature clearly exercised jurisdiction during five days in October 1799, to simply frame the jurisdictional issue in this criminal case as a matter of whether or not English common law applied misses the legal practice of movement and in doing so, overlooks something quite important about how common law works, namely, how common law moves into place. To this end, this chapter attends to common law's techniques and material practices and tracks the institution of common law by tracing its movements. Paying attention to testimony, and through the practice of redescription, or paradiastole, it becomes possible to illuminate, illustrate and think more carefully about how common law moves, relates and comes to be in place jurisdictionally. Therefore, having temporarily rested with common law's courtly institution, and hinted at movements prior to court, it is time to walk with a burial party.

3.3 Juridical walking

In 1799, 11 years after the Colony of New South Wales was established, a burial party walked into the woods beyond the emergent frontier settlement of Hawkesbury in order to locate and bury two men: they walked to bury the dead. In doing so, the laws of empire moved. Paying attention to the modes and forms of movement as the burial party walks, it becomes possible to notice some of the ways in which common law moves. This is the task of the remainder of this chapter, which redescribes the movements of the burial party, noticing the form and conduct of common law practice and attending to movement as part of those practices. The material form of movement attended to in this part of the chapter is walking, while in the final part the material movement attended to is camping. For a burial party *walks*. And as this burial party walks, they do so in an unsynchronised, idiosyncratic, temperate repetition of footfall after footfall after footfall. To begin, this part slows down its movements and notices the pace of the burial party as it walks, and notices each step; each footfall; each foot*fall* ... Falling, yet never quite fallen. Always maintaining or regaining balance and in doing so, grounding; touching. A momentary attachment of body to earth, of sole to the surface of the earth: humus; humic; human. A fleeting attachment, yet one that leaves traces, no matter how slight. In noticing the action and activity as the burial party walks, this part attends to these motions and redescribes walking as a movement of common law. This is walking as juridical form.

A burial party walks, and as this burial party walks, common law moves. By naming walking as a juridical form, this part reveals one of the ways in which common law moves. Through the common law imagining of the subject carrying common law as they move, and through the utilisation of jurisdiction as a relatively low-level technology that attaches to the surface, I argue that the institution of common law occurs through the movements of the burial party as it walks. Significantly, this is prior to the institutional marking of these events through the exercise of jurisdiction by the Court of Criminal Judicature in *R v Powell*. By following the burial party as it walks, and in doing so, paying attention to a minor register of technical and material practice, an account of common law's movements is developed. Most clearly, there is repetition: the repetition of footfall after footfall after footfall ... In addition to repetitions within walking, there are also repetitions of walking, movement, death, burial. As a consequence of recognising walking as a form of lawful action, what this chapter reveals is the horrific, dynamic, repetitious nature of common law's colonising movements: as the burial party walks, the laws of empire move.

The task of this part of the chapter is to illustrate walking as a basic technology and material practice of common law movement, and what these movements might mean in terms of common law's place. To notice the juridical form of walking, this part redescribes the movements of the burial party by considering who the burial party consisted of, how it walked, what laws it might have carried, how it carried common law and the potential effect of walking with common law. By attending to how the burial party walked, the jurisprudential redescription in this part reveals a juridical mode of walking, placing walking as a common law form of movement. In this respect, this part serves as a reminder of the importance of paying attention to how we walk.

So, a burial party walks.

Textures of place: walking into the woods beyond

Remembering Blackstone's aphorism insisting that wherever common law subjects go they carry common law with them, the claim that 'English laws are immediately *there* in force' needs to be carefully contemplated.[103] Where is this 'there' that is a place where English laws are immediately in force? Taken literally, if common law is carried in order to be planted, English law cannot be 'there' before being carried to the place called there. For instance, does this 'there' include the woods beyond; the woods the burial party walked into? Surely to imagine the woods beyond as already 'planted'[104] by English subjects is, for the burial party at least, a little premature. For this reason, I insist on paying attention to and tracking empirical forms of common law's movements within the Colony of New South Wales. One way of tracking is to attend to the burial party and think more carefully about how it walked, why it walked, and what legal consequences might flow from walking.

In 1799 a burial party walked into the woods beyond the emergent frontier settlement of Hawkesbury in order to locate and bury the dead, and in walking to bury the dead, it walked beyond. Not found in other Germanic languages, the literal meaning of the old English term *begeondan*, which is the etymological root of beyond, is 'on yon side, on the farther side'.[105] In walking beyond, a burial party walked on yon side, on the farther side. This is more than simply walking from a position – from the nascent settlement – in a forward direction to a further side that although it may well be in sight, remains somewhere elsewhere. The beyond of the burial party is not merely a geographical or topographical beyond, neither is it a beyond of a binary between a progressive civilisation and an odious nature. The beyond of the burial party is more complicated than the traverse of boundaries and binaries, and more complicated than walking a line. In walking beyond, a burial party walked to bury the dead, and in doing so, the laws of empire moved.

---

103 See Chapter 2, 2.1. For ease of reference: 'For it is held, that if an uninhabited colony be discovered and planted by English subjects, all the English laws are immediately *there* in force. For as the law is the birthright of every subject, so wherever they go they carry their laws with them', William Blackstone, 'Of the Countries Subject to the Laws of England', in William Blackstone, *Commentaries on the Laws of England* (Clarendon Press, first published 1765) Introduction, Section 4 (emphasis added).

104 Ibid.

105 Charles Talbut Onions (ed.), *The Oxford Dictionary of English Etymology* (Clarendon Press, 1966); Robert K. Barnhart and Sol Steinmetz (eds.), *Chambers Dictionary of Etymology* (Chambers, 1998).

A burial party walked into the woods beyond: on yon farther side; somewhere elsewhere; beyond. Before the burial party walked beyond, what becomes apparent in the evidence provided in *R v Powell* is that common law was subject to some limitation or restraint of movement, seemingly unable to move into the woods and beyond the boundaries of this eclectic, ever deviating, never stable frontier. An intangible limit, always shifting, seemingly never quite known, yet the presence of the limit is known, revealed in several disparate testimonial glimpses including the physical mass of the burial party, the gradation of farms, the mythopoetic woods, the Governor's treatment of Charley and Lieutenant Hobby's extraordinary order. These glimpses and subtleties of testimonial phrases reveal that before the burial party walked beyond, before the burial party could travel on yon farther side, something was needed to ease the constraints, to lift the limits for the burial party to pass through and traverse into the beyond. The argument I ultimately develop is that the nature of this something was the responsibility to care for the dead; for it was the deaths of Hodgkinson and Wimbo that enabled common law to move beyond. Before we can attend to the dead, however, it is necessary to attend to the beyond, and to think more carefully about how, why, and to what legal consequences a burial party walked into the beyond.

The burial party consisted of a group of men. A physical mass of male bodies, both military and civilian, walking at their own individual rate, pace, tread. Stepping, striding, walking, marching, the burial party was more than one; a pack. There is a weightiness to the physical mass that walked into the woods beyond. A mass of movement and of inconsistent footfalls, cracking the debris, marking their movements, spreading traces: a cacophony. As a party, there is 'safety in numbers', whether from ongoing colonial–indigenous violence or from the woods beyond or, perhaps, both. Remaining with the materiality of the sheer physical mass of movement of the burial party, the presence of a group in and of itself suggests something to be overcome: a limit, a restraint, a hesitation. More specifically, the burial party was a group of male settlers, or at least it was to begin. For the burial party that walked were a group of settlers accompanied by soldiers; in the company of soldiers. A companionship that again suggests, perhaps, a limit. This may be a limit to safety, a protective mechanism to ensure the safety of the settlers, but also hints at a more complex limit. A hesitation that required a physical mass to move, and not just any physical mass, but the sheer mass of both settlers and soldiers walking into the woods beyond. Together, into the woods beyond.

Echoing James Cook's journal entry narrating his first violent steps, 'cautious how I advanced into the Woods',[106] there is an impression that emerges from the testimonial evidence in *R v Powell* that places the woods as an ominous place beyond, a place not yet governed, not yet controlled by common law. There is

---

106 Cook, above, n 13, entry for 29 April 1770. See also Katrina Schlunke, 'Entertaining Possession: Re-enacting Cook's Arrival for the Queen', in Kate Darian-Smith and Penelope Edmonds (eds.), *Conciliation on Colonial Frontiers: Conflict, Performance, and Commemoration in Australia and the Pacific Rim* (Routledge, 2015) ch 13.

an impression that something more is needed before being able to walk into the woods beyond, which emanates, in part, from the reference by several witnesses to 'the woods' in their evidence.[107] In addition to the linguistic and idiomatic capture of a certain time and place – for the woods is certainly not a contemporary reference to the Australian bush (or in the language of tourism: 'the outback') – there is something in the manner of the phrase that is suggestive of its difference. Not just its material, geographical and aesthetic difference, but also its legal difference, which is, more specifically, a difference in legal place as well as a difference in the texture of legal places.

The first witness for the defence William Fuller opened his evidence: 'That sometime before Wimbo the deceased went into the woods.'[108] The dramatic tension arises from the suggestion that had Wimbo *not* gone into the woods … However, it is not simply going or being in the woods that exudes a dramatic tension, but also an intimacy of companionship when in the woods:

> Question from prisoner Metcalf. Did I not tell you when I brought the natives in with Hodgskinson's piece that the said three natives had acknowledged sleeping with Hodgskinson in the woods the night before he was Killed?[109]

More than a suggestion of a known association between Hodgkinson and Wimbo and the Aboriginal boys that were executed as some sort of justification for their killing, there is an intimacy of sleeping together in the woods, of sleeping with, that relates to the location of being in the woods, somewhere out of reach, somewhere beyond:

> Question by court. Did you understand from the Native Yellowgowy that the native Major White attended the dec'd HodgsKinson and Wimbo as friends in the Woods?
> … Did you personally know this native Called Major White? Yes I knew him well and he was under engagement to accompany me in the Woods at the time he Killed Hodgskinson and Wimbo.[110]

There is a companionship, a friendship, a togetherness of being in the woods that appears to be one of fragile solidarity. As such, to break this solidarity after attending 'as friends in the Woods'[111] is seen as a betrayal of sorts; a betrayal intimately connected with being in the woods, of being beyond. It makes little sense to transpose these events out of the woods into the emergent Hawkesbury settlement,

---

107 Jonas Archer NRS 2700 [X905] 347–8; William Fuller NRS 2700 [X905] 350; Isabelle Ramsay NRS 2700 [X905] 333–4.
108 William Fuller NRS 2700 [X905] 350–1.
109 Isabella Ramsay NRS 2700 [X905] 334.
110 Jonas Archer NRS 2700 [X905] 347–8.
111 Jonas Archer NRS 2700 [X905] 347. For more detail on the office of friendship, see Chapters 2 and 4.

because there is something to the place of the woods and of being 'in' the woods that is somewhere other.[112] Whether 'as friends' or engaged to 'accompany', there is an implicit suggestion that the woods are not the place of settlement; not a settled place. The trope of city as civilisation and dichotomous nature in need of taming is not new, and a trope certainly present in the time and place of the burial party. More than just a trope of the untamed, Giambattista Vico's structuring of the forest as the poetic site of the institution of the *polis* resonates with these suggestive references to the woods, for it places the woods beyond as a site necessary for the placement of the settled in the *polis* as the non-beyond.[113] Without over-extracting from these testimonial references to 'the woods', the suggestion is that for the new residents of Hawkesbury in 1799, the woods held a particular place in the civic imagination, and this place was one of not just a material beyond, but also a poetical and mythopoetical beyond.

Placing the site of woods as a mythopoetical beyond means the woods are more merely a beyond of the material manifestations of settlement, patiently awaiting their temporal taming and inevitable conquest through a slowly rapid transformation from wild abandon into farms, roads and other architectural displays of the city, but the woods are also a mythopoetic beyond of common law. As I argued in Chapter 2, the place of common law is not everywhere, and certainly not everywhere then.[114] In 1799, despite lines on a map boldly suggesting otherwise, the place of common law was much more limited, and did not stretch into the woods beyond. In concert with legal historians who have long suggested the colonial movements of law into and in Australia were more complex and messier than a series of proclamations reflecting lines on a map, the series of events in and around Hawkesbury in 1799 suggest likewise.[115] Throughout the proclaimed areas of the Colony of New South Wales in 1799, there was no consistent covering or smothering of common law. Instead, the place of common law was (and still is) much more temperate, disparate, messier and incomplete. The place of common law was limited; subject to bounds.

The limited place of common law occasionally reveals itself, and does so, in this case, if we take seriously the proposition that different places carry different legal textures. The legal manifestation of place, and the different intensity to these manifestations, are most easily recognised in places subject to bounds, and the legal regulation – whether explicit or implicit – of those bounds. Some of these implicit legal bounds and their (de)gradations are revealed in Robert Braithwaite's evidence regarding the placement of different farms in and around Hawkesbury:

---

112 See Robert Pogue Harrison, *Forests: The Shadow of Civilization* (University of Chicago Press, 1992).
113 Giambattista Vico, *The New Science of Giambattista Vico* (Thomas Goddard Bergin and Max Harold Fisch trans., Cornell University Press, 1967) [trans. of *Principi di una Scienza Nuova* (first published 1725)]. See also ibid.
114 See Chapter 2, 2.2.
115 See Chapter 3, 3.1.

What is the state of security or danger of the settlers of the Hawkesbury with respect to the natives? I conceive the property of the Settlers on the front farms to be and perfectly secure in popular situations. Those of the back farms and above the Creek in remote situations are exposed to great danger from the natives and he thinks the Persons of the people are insecure both on these farms and when they may be travelling on the Roads, and the Witness knows the several single persons have been attacked on the Road by the natives altho' such Persons have been armed.[116]

Although it is not entirely clear where the front and back farms were in relation to the movements of the burial party, what is interesting about these comments is the differentiation between places. Commenting on colonial 'safeness', Robert Braithwaite offers an account of different places, including the front farms ('perfectly secure'), the back farms and 'above the Creek' ('great danger') and the Roads ('insecure').[117] Coupled with Lieutenant Hobby's testimony that there was a 'Resolution of the Natives' to 'Come down in numbers from the Blue mountains', it is possible that the great danger above the creek was also the place from which they might 'come down'.[118]

Speculative, granted, but regardless of where the physical woods were in relation to the location of the front and back farms, the reference to the back farms as insecure is suggestive of the insecurity of the woods beyond. More importantly, there is a clear distinction between different places and different levels of security that reveal these different places as different legal sites; as different legal places. For the lack of security is for those carrying common law and is a lack in the sense of an insecurity, uncertainty or anxiety in the place of common law, especially its place beyond. While walking with common law, the place of common law in the woods beyond is an uncertain place.[119]

The different legal textures of common law places, including its absence (i.e. a place of non-common law, or a common law non-place),[120] is further evident in the movements and non-punishment of Charley, who was captured and taken before the Governor. In a conversation that preceded the burial party, a limitation or restriction on the movements and places of common law can be detected in the Governor's comments regarding the punishment of Charley as provided in the evidence of Corporal Peter Farrell. Although quoted earlier in this chapter,[121] for ease of reference and to notice the texture of place, this testimony is quoted again:

---

116 Robert Braithwaite NRS 2700 [X905] 345–6.
117 Ibid.
118 Lieutenant Thomas Hobby NRS 2700 [X905] 340–1.
119 See Chapter 3, 3.3.
120 On non-places, see Marc Augé, *Non-places: Introduction to an Anthropology of Supermodernity* (Verso, 1995) although this is not a non-place in the same sense.
121 See above, n 56.

> [T]he Governor said 'Well, what am I to do with him. Why did not your own Commanding Officer of Hawkesbury do something with him' That the witness answered he supposed it was from a wish to make a more public Example of this Native that his Excellency replied it was not in his Power to give orders for the hanging or shooting of such ignorant Creatures who could not be made sensible of what they might be guilty of therefore could not be treated according to our Laws. That the witness then Requested to know what was to be done in the present Case when the Governor told the Witness that immediate Retaliation should be made on the Spot or words to that effect as it was the only mode his Excellency said he could think upon[122]

Commenting on this conversation, as reported on the return of Corporal Farrell and one of the private soldiers, Lieutenant Hobby offers a similar account:

> [T]he said native was according to orders taken before the Governor, who expressed himself in the hearing of the Guard of Soldiers that he could not take upon himself to punish the native in Cool blood but that the Commanding Officer at the Hawkesbury should have punished him upon the Spot where he was taken.[123]

In these accounts of the unsuccessful attempt to punish Charley, a distinction emerges between the site of capture and site of attempted punishment. Charley was captured by Corporal Farrell at the house of John Burne, after having been sighted as part of an Aboriginal party near the farm of Joseph Phelps.[124] Although it is not clear precisely where this farm was, and whether it was a 'front farm' or 'back farm' in terms of Robert Braithwaite's distinction, it was a Hawkesbury farm and may have been 'perfectly secure', 'insecure' or a place of 'great danger'. When going to locate Charley, Corporal Farrell is likely to have wandered through some of these different locations. The importance of this distinction becomes easier to detect if these varied places are compared to the second site: the Governor in Sydney.

The Governor spoke to Charley, presumably but not necessarily at the Governor's residence, but clearly somewhere in the town of Sydney, and expressed the opinion there was nothing to be done, nothing could be done; a limit to the Governor's authority to punish Charley here. For it was 'not in his power' to punish Charley by death as Charley 'could not be made sensible' of what he might be guilty of and so Charley 'could not be treated according to our Laws', that is, common law, or at least not so here, in Sydney, at the Governor's residence.[125] This is a recognition of a limit to the application of common law; it does not apply here, to this person, these actions in this place. The Governor clearly distinguishes

---

122 Corporal Peter Farrell NRS 2700 [X905] 315 cf 354–5. See also Chapter 3, 3.1.
123 Lieutenant Thomas Hobby NRS 2700 [X905] 341–2.
124 Peter Farrell NRS 2700 [X905] 354.
125 Ibid, 354–5.

between an inability to punish Charley at the physical and symbolic heart of colonial settlement in Sydney, while acknowledging that Charley could have been punished 'on the Spot' at the site of capture.[126]

There are different common law places. In Sydney, the Governor could not punish Charley 'in Cool blood', whereas elsewhere Charley could have been dealt with 'on the Spot'.[127] This may refer to certain extraordinary orders, but also elicits a difference in the placing of common law: a difference in legal places. The Governor's suggestion that Charley could not be dealt with here, but could have been dealt with there 'as that was the only mode he could think upon',[128] suggests Hawkesbury as the beyond or at least the edge of the beyond: common law's beyond. The location of the beyond is always, by its nature, somewhere elsewhere. For those in Sydney in 1799, quite possibly the whole of Hawkesbury was 'beyond' whereas for those in Hawkesbury, such as Robert Braithwaite, there was a more textured patterning making some places more beyond than others. There is a distinction between the places of common law and this is a difference of the beyond.

The beyond is always relative to where one stands. The Governor spoke in a place where common law applied. Without Charley understanding the nature of the offence (among other reasons why common law might not apply to Charley), common law applied here in this place, and as such Charley cannot be punished. In contrast, over there, somewhere elsewhere beyond, common law does not apply, at least not obviously so, and Charley can be punished. Although there are other grounds for the punishment of Charley 'on the Spot', including natural law, a military order or the laws of war etc., the purpose of considering the non-punishment of Charley is to observe the different textures to the place of common law. Part of the difference between these sites is a difference in the place of common law. At times less overt or not there at all, there are different common law places hosting different textures of common law. In particular, for some sites, being those beyond, there is, it seems, a limit, hesitation or boundary, acting as a hold on common law's movement. This is a distinction between places of common law; of texture; of how common law is written into the land (geography); a difference of the beyond.

The difference in common law's place, its limits and difficulties in common law's movements beyond is also revealed within Lieutenant Hobby's extraordinary order to the burial party, 'that if they fell in with any Natives on the Road either going or returning fire in upon them'.[129] In addition to the grossly indiscriminate application of this order, in that it applied to any or all Aboriginal people the burial party 'fell in with', or as it was rephrased in a question to Lieutenant Hobby,

---

126 Lieutenant Thomas Hobby NRS 2700 [X905] 341–2.
127 Ibid.
128 Peter Farrell NRS 2700 [X905] 354–5.
129 Lieutenant Thomas Hobby NRS 2700 [X905] 340.

'shoot any of the natives they should meet with',¹³⁰ what is particularly stark about this order is the recipients of the authorisation. It applied to both soldiers and settlers alike.¹³¹ As Lieutenant Hobby acknowledged, not only did this order apply to non-military members of the burial party, it was also quite possible that this order was not understood to apply *only* to the movements of the burial party. Although Lieutenant Hobby accepted that he made it clear to the Serjeant that the order applied only to 'attack the natives whilst on that excursion',¹³² he also accepted the possibility that this might have been 'misunderstood'.¹³³ It clearly was. Several witnesses testified that they understood the order to kill to operate beyond the confines to the burial party's excursion to locate and bury the dead.¹³⁴ The temporal and spatial expansion of this 'sovereign' order – authorising the right to kill – beyond the confines of the burial party hints at its extraordinary purpose.¹³⁵ However, even before its (mis)interpretation to operate beyond the burial party, its application to both military and non-military members of the burial party was extraordinary.¹³⁶ Its extraordinariness arose because of the need for the burial party to walk into the woods beyond, to walk to a differently textured place; to walk in order to bury the dead.

Therefore, I have argued that there was some sort of limitation to common law's movements prior to the movements of the burial party. Before the physical mass of the burial party, and the Lieutenant's extraordinary order, common law was subject to some limitation or restraint of movement, seemingly unable to move

130 Ibid.
131 Ibid.
132 Ibid.
133 Ibid.
134 See, especially, Jonas Archer NRS 2700 [X905] 349; William Timms, Simon Freebody and William Butler NRS 2700 [X905] 312. See also William Goodall NRS 2700 [X905] 352–3; Isabella Ramsay NRS 2700 [X905] 334; Lieutenant Thomas Hobby NRS 2700 [X905] 339; Thomas Rickerby NRS 2700 [X905] 331. See, generally, Lieutenant Neil McKellar, member of the Court, NRS 2700 [X905] 360.
135 On the sovereign as the right to kill, see, e.g., Thomas Hobbes, *Leviathan* (Andrew Crooke, 1651); Samuel Pufendorf, *Two Books of the Elements of Jurisprudence* (Liberty Fund, 2009); Samuel Pufendorf, *Of the Law of Nature and Nations: Eight Books* (L. Lichfield, 1703); Giorgio Agamben, *Homo Sacer: Sovereign Power and Bare Life* (Daniel Heller-Roazen trans., Stanford University Press, 1998).
136 But see Lieutenant Neil McKellar, member of the Court, NRS 2700 [X905] 360. In an evidentiary and procedural anomaly, while sitting in judgment on the case of *R v Powell*, Lieutenant McKellar provided evidence in response to questions asked by the accused and other members of the bench that when he had previously spent time in Hawkesbury as Commanding Officer (that is, Lieutenant Hobby's position) he had issued standing orders 'To destroy them whenever they were to be met with after their being guilty of outrages, except such native children who were domesticated among the settlers'; NRS 2700 [X905] 360. It is unclear from Lieutenant McKellar's 'evidence' whether the order he gave while in command at the Hawkesbury authorised non-military settlers to kill or whether it was limited to soldiers. What is clear, however, is that as far as Lieutenant McKellar was aware, his orders had not been countermanded, and were given on authority from verbal orders of the Governor, orders which Lieutenant McKellar understood as continuing in force.

beyond the boundaries of the emergent frontier settlement into the woods. This is a limit hinted at in references to the woods as an ominous place beyond, a place that is not yet governed – not yet controlled – by common law. It is also a limit suggested in the sheer physical mass of the burial party, as settlers accompanied by soldiers, and a limit suggested by the need for an extraordinary order. There is an impression that something more is needed before being able to walk into the woods beyond. Whether this is friendship, companionship or an Aboriginal guide, or whether this is an extraordinary military order, there is a need for something else, something other, before walking into the woods beyond. For the burial party, as will be shown, it was the deaths of Hodgkinson and Wimbo and, in particular, the need to locate and bury the dead, that enabled common law to move beyond, a beyond it could not otherwise move into.

How the burial party walked

The burial party comprised men who walked from Hawkesbury to the woods and back again. Their bipedal motions were invigorated by their purpose to locate and bury the men who died beyond. However, it is an oversimplification to assume a fixed purpose and fixed, although unknown, destination meant their physical movements were linear. The movement of walking is much messier than the lines we imagine between beginning and end; intention and execution; purpose and completion. Although the purpose of the burial party's walk is important, and addressed in the next part of the chapter, in order to ensure the material and juridical act of walking itself is not overlooked or subsumed by its purpose, it is important to consider the material actions of the burial party's walk, absent its purpose. While we know the burial party walked, and it walked for one or more purposes, how did the burial party walk, and what legal meaning or meanings might this walk carry? In order to work towards an answer to these questions, we must consider whether there were different legal *personae* collected in the party; that is: who actually constituted the burial party?

The burial party were a group of men, both settlers and military. Lieutenant Hobby, for instance, testified that the burial party were not just soldiers but accompanied by several other persons, although whether 'settlers or any other description of persons' is not clear.[137] Even with this hint, the knowledge of who was in the burial party is scant. It is clear that several witnesses were in the burial party, including Jonas Archer and 'free man' William Fuller.[138] It is also apparent that at least two of the accused were members of the burial party: James Metcalf and Simon Freebody.[139] Beyond these details, and this basic configuration of

---

137 Lieutenant Thomas Hobby NRS 2700 [X905] 343.
138 Jonas Archer NRS 2700 [X905] 348; William Fuller NRS 2700 [X905] 351.
139 Jonas Archer NRS 2700 [X905] 348; Lieutenant Thomas Hobby NRS 2700 [X905] 343.

settlers and soldiers, little more is known.[140] Of the non-military contingent in the burial party, the settlers may or may not have been convicts, serving or emancipated, although it is likely that some of the settlers were ex-convicts. Given the time and place, it is unlikely that there were any women.

Although it is unclear precisely who constituted the burial party, it is a lack of clarity accounted for as well as possible in this chapter. In addition to noticing the possible configurations of gender and occupation that may have constituted the burial party, class is also relevant. There is something in the way the dead are referred to or more precisely, how the dead are *not* referred to, that hints at the need to account for class. What is quite apparent in the evidence is that although the burial party seek two dead, Thomas Hodgkinson and John Wimbo, it is principally Hodgkinson who is sought. While generally referred to as 'Hodgkinson and Wimbo', witnesses often refer simply to Hodgkinson, seemingly forgetting Wimbo. For instance, in Isabella Ramsay's description of the conversation in her dwelling the evening the two Aboriginal boys were killed, Wimbo is seemingly forgotten:

> [T]he biggest of the natives got up for a drink of water, to whom Powell said you shall have no water here, you have killed a Good fellow and you shall not live long. John Pearson a neighbour then came in, when the same native got up a second time for a drink of water, when Freebody gave him some water, and Powell said they should be killed for they have killed a worthy goodfellow and it will be a pity to see them go away alive. Butler soon after came in to the house of the witness with a bright Cutlass and asked if the natives were there, saying what sentence shall we pass on these blackfellows. I will pass sentence myself. They shall be hanged. Metcalf came into the house of Witness with several others, who said we will not Kill them, we will carry them out as the means of finding the natives who Killed Hodgskinson.[141]

Hodgkinson; a good fellow; a worthy good fellow. In a question asked by Constable Edward Powell, one of the accused, to Lieutenant Hobby, the failure to remember there was more than one dead to bury was corrected in response:

Question by Powell. What orders did you give to a party of soldiers who went out to bury the body of Thomas Hodgskinson who had been killed by the natives? My orders to the soldiers were to go out with the men who were going out to bury the bodies of Hodgskinson and Wimbolt[142]

---

140   While inconclusive, archival research at the National Archives in Kew, England yielded little detail on the members of the burial party.
141   Isabella Ramsay NRS 2700 [X905] 333–4.
142   Lieutenant Thomas Hobby NRS 2700 [X905] 340.

Hodgkinson was a free settler.[143] It seems Wimbo was not.[144] Again, although it is not entirely clear what status John Wimbo (or Wimbow or Wimbolt) carried, there was less concern for his death than the death of Hodgkinson and my suspicion is that this was due to differential class. Wimbo had been a convict and it seems most likely that, in 1799, Wimbo was either still an indentured convict allocated to Hodgkinson for the period of his transportation sentence (or extended sentence) or Hodgkinson's free man servant-companion. With master–servant relations not uncommon,[145] as well as the practice of indentured convict-labour in the early years of the Colony of New South Wales, it seems likely that Wimbo was in some way contracted to Hodgkinson. This proposition garners some support from the testimonial phrasing, for in moments when Wimbo is not forgotten, reference is always to 'Hodgkinson and Wimbo', never 'Wimbo and Hodgkinson'. Given this potential relationship between Hodgkinson and Wimbo, it is possible that the burial party included similar master–servant configurations of free settlers and their convict or ex-convict servant-companions among the non-military contingent of the burial party.

It is also not clear whether there were any Aboriginal members of the burial party. The only hint of a suggestion comes from Jonas Archer, who was a member of the burial party, and had previously engaged Major White 'to accompany me into the woods'.[146] Given Major White was generally referred to as the person who killed Hodgkinson and Wimbo, it seems highly unlikely that Major White accompanied Jonas Archer on this excursion into the woods to locate and bury Hodgkinson and Wimbo. It is possible, however, that the burial party was accompanied by other unnamed Aboriginal men or women. The silencing of Aboriginal companions and guides in colonial records and colonial literature is well known and it is not clear whether the silence here was a silence of physical

---

143 Although not conclusive, there is no convict record for Thomas Hodgkinson, which, when coupled with testimonial evidence, strongly suggests at the time of his death, Hodgkinson was a settler. This is supported by Lisa Ford, who refers to 'a local settler named Hodgkinson and his settler guide', Ford, *Settlor Sovereignty*, above, n 25, 98. Although Ford repeats the pattern and briefly mentions these particular killings, Ford leaves the 'settler guide' unnamed and focuses on Hodgkinson. Peter Turbet describes Thomas Hoskisson as a 'game shooter' and 'a married man with two young children and a third on the way: Turbet, *The First Frontier*, above, n 25, 106.

144 Although not conclusive, there is a convict record for John Wimbo. Cf: Ford, *Settlor Sovereignty*, above, n 25, 98; Salter, *Early Interactions*, above, n 25, 57, which incorrectly refers to the 'murder of another settler named Hodgkinson and an Aboriginal acquaintance named Wimbo'. According to Peter Turbet, John Winbow was found guilty of highway robbery at the Winchester Assizes in October 1789. His sentence of death was commuted to seven years' transportation, and he arrived in the Colony of New South Wales with the Second Fleet (aboard *Scarborough*) in 1790, per Turbet, *The First Frontier*, above, n 25, 106, citing M. Flynn, *The Second Fleet: Britain's Grim Convict Armada of 1790* (Library of Australian History, 1993) 619.

145 See, e.g., John Tarlington NRS 2700 [X905] 356–7, who references his 'free man servant'. See also Prisoners' defence NRS 2700 [X905] 311; Peter Farrell NRS 2700 [X905] 355; Robert Braithwaite NRS 2700 [X905] 345.

146 Jonas Archer NRS 2700 [X905] 348.

absence or one of present absence.[147] While unclear whether there were any Aboriginal members, guides or companions to the burial party, given the content of Lieutenant Hobby's extraordinary order, it seems highly unlikely that there were any Aboriginal members.

More than just a mix of settlers and military, the burial party may or may not have been English. It is quite possible that a non-military member or members of the burial party were from other parts of the British Empire, such as Ireland. Without delving deeply (or even lightly) into the politics of the British Empire, some key events precipitated the establishment of the Colony of New South Wales, contributing to and shaping its constitution, and its early years, including events leading up to and including the Irish Rebellion of 1798.[148] The relevance of the Irish Rebellion is twofold. First, it meant that a number of those transported to the Colony of New South Wales in its early years were Irish, some having been involved in the Irish Rebellion.[149] Second, more than just placing the Irish in the Colony of New South Wales, and therefore possibly in the burial party that walked from Hawkesbury in 1799, this provides an insight into the technology of the common law imagining as captured in Blackstone's aphorism, that is, of jurisdiction as one of the key devices of common law movement.

Speculating, imagine one of the members of the burial party that walked into the woods beyond in 1799 was a male Irish convict, which may or may not have been true. This Irish convict, sentenced by English law to transportation is deemed a British subject and through the *persona* of the British subject carries English law, including English common law. Having been convicted, sentenced and transported in accordance with English common law, this Irish male is clearly marked and legally masked as a British subject. This is so regardless of whether or not this imagined Irish convict recognises the authority of the English or English law. In other words, even had this imagined person been part of the Irish Rebellion of 1798 or was one of those who may yet become part of the Castle Hill Rebellion (where Irish convicts in the Colony of New South Wales separated from the British Empire, creating New Ireland and appointing Phillip Cunningham as sovereign on 6 March 1808), this Irish wore the legal mask of a British subject. This is the insidious significance of the common law imagining of the common law subject for the ways common law moves. Irrespective of whether or not this

---

147 See, generally, Carter, *The Road to Botany Bay*, above, n 12; Paul Carter, *The Lie of the Land* (faber & faber, 1996); Paul Carter, *Living in a New Country: History, Travelling and Language* (faber, 1992). See also Julie Evans, Patricia Grimshaw, David Phillips and Shulee Swain, *Equal Subjects, Unequal Rights: Indigenous Peoples in British Settler Colonies, 1830–1910* (Manchester University Press, 2003). Cf: Ilbijerri Theatre Company, *Coranderrk: We Will Show the Country* (Ilbijerri and Minutes of Evidence Project, 2010–current); University of Melbourne, *Minutes of Evidence Project: Promoting New and Collaborative Ways of Understanding Australia's Past and Engaging with Structural Justice* (ARC Linkage-Project Grant, current).
148 See Chapter 3, 3.1.
149 See, e.g., Mark McKenna, *The Captive Republic: A History of Republicanism in Australia 1788–1996* (Cambridge University Press, 1996) 13–15.

Irish male subjectively recognises the authority of English law, including English common law, once marked as a British subject, a common law subject, common law moves with the movements of the subject. When this imagined Irish male walks, he carries and moves English common law.

As both settlers and military, the burial party carried different forms of law as they walked. Most significantly, they carried the laws of empire, including common law. Yet, common law was not all they carried. For instance, taking up the office of the soldier, the military members of the burial party also carried military law, including its various privileges, duties and regulations. As a collective whole, the burial party carried military law as well as natural law, presumably various religious laws (i.e. Catholic, Protestant etc.), and English common law.[150] What this means is that the burial party walked as a collection of *personae* and in doing so, the burial party's non-linear movements as they walked were not simply material movements but also legal movements as they carried various forms of law; lawful movements.

Walking as juridical form

To accept this partial redescription of the burial party demands a shift from appreciating walking as mere physical action to walking as legal form. For more than a material, technical and ethical practice, the argument being developed is that walking is also a jurisprudential practice; a practice in jurisprudence. This is walking as an intimate technical and practical action and a productive activity of common law practice. Further, this is the substrate of the proposition that as a material practice of common law, walking is a jurisdictional device that authorises common law's movements. This is the central contention of this part; this is walking as juridical form.

As juridical form, walking emerges from and returns to common law practice. This raises an important question: what is the relationship between the movements of the burial party as they walk and movements of common law? What has rested quietly in the background is an assumption that there is a relationship – and a particular relationship – between common law and the body of the subject. In order to contemplate the relation between the burial party as it walked, and movements of common law, consider the *persona* as the literal mask. Visualise the burial party as common law subjects, masked, carrying common law on the surface of the mask, on the surface of the walkers' bodies, as they walk. Whether picked up or placed on, this masking institutes the common law subject as an assemblage of rights, duties, responsibilities etc. In this image, in this conceit, what is starkly emphasised are the simultaneous movements of walking and common law. There is a togetherness of the surface: the surface of common law, touching the surface of the mask, resting on the surface of the common law subject, as the subject walks on the surface of the earth.

150 See Chapter 1, 1.2.

If common law moves with subjects as they walk, then how does it move? The form of the relation between movements of walking and movements of common law as the burial party walks is superficial: a relationship of the surface. Surface; the outermost boundary of any material body, immediately adjacent to the air or empty space, or to another body.[151] Bodily complications of social theory and philosophy aside,[152] the form of the relation between walking and common law suggested in this book is one of or on the surface. As raised in Chapter 2, although common law may carry meaning, it does not tend to carry deep meaning (such as answers to ontological dilemmas) but rather carries meaning on the surface (such as processional or procedural guidance). This is what I mean by the superficiality of common law and a superficiality of its material practices. For although common law may attach to the body of the subject in a variety of other ways, such as attachments contributing to the construction of certain forms of subjectivity (Lacanian, Freudian, or otherwise) this does not negate the proposition that at the level of technique and practice, common law is practised on the surface. On a minor register of technical and material practice, common law forms of movement are both movements on and movements of the surface. Significantly, these superficial movements engage both the surface of the subject and the surface of the earth. What must be addressed then is the possibility of movement not only on the surface, but more significantly, from the surface. The question of movement from the surface is a question of transmission.

What is the effect of juridical walking? Does walking, in its juridical form, act as a device of legal transmission? Walking and carrying common law, producing space, the burial party move common law from the frontier settlement of Hawkesbury and into the woods beyond. Whether common law returns with the burial party on its return, or whether in some manner or form common law somehow remains in the woods beyond is a possibility that requires some attention. For instance, is walking a movement device of common law, which transmits common law from body to land? Following the burial party as it walks beyond the frontier settlement of Hawkesbury into the woods beyond and then back again, and following common law as it attaches to the surface of the burial party as it walks (or the surface of each member of the burial party as they walk), how might we know whether there are any common law movements from the surface? Let us consider the materiality of the burial party's actions. There is clearly a materiality to walking that emanates in the gait, the tread and the stride of the walker – of each member of the burial party – as the heel swings towards the ground, touching, rolling, transferring, lifting, swinging, landing, touching, rolling, again and again and again. In leaving material tracks, trace patterns

---

151 Onions (ed.), *The Oxford English Dictionary of English Entymology*, above, n 105; Barnhart and Steinmetz (eds.), *Chambers Dictionary of Entymology*, above, n 105. Cf: Chapter 2, 2.2.
152 See, e.g., Maurice Merleau-Ponty, *The Visible and the Invisible* (Alphonso Lingus trans., Northwestern University Press, 1968) ch 4 [trans. of *Le Visible et L'invisble* (first published 1964)].

and trails as the burial party walks, it is at least possible that when common law moves, it also marks the land.

Yet, the answer remains unclear. There are at least two distinct possibilities: either common law stays with the body, not touching the land (or at least not remaining with the land), or it moves from the body and stays with the land. Each will be considered. The first possibility is that common law remains with the subject as they walk, not transmitting either onto or into the earth. For the burial party, this would mean that when it walked beyond, common law also moved beyond, but when it returned to the frontier settlement, common law returned and nothing remained beyond. That is, although there may be material marks of the movements of the burial party as it walked in the woods beyond, there are no common law markings: nothing remains. The difficulty with this, however, is that it not only fails to capture how common law moves and continues to move as it comes to rest in place, and it not only fails to capture the technical and material activity of common law movement as a mode and manner of place-making as well as the resonance of common law's place, but it also renders movement jurisprudentially meaningless and in doing so, overlooks how common law comes to be in place. With the juridical form of walking, these oversights are problematic but become more prominent in the next part of the chapter, which notices movements towards burial as a further form of movement that contributes to the becoming of a common law place.

Another possibility is that something remains. This the position I take, and the possibility the final part of this chapter and the next chapter explore. As the burial party walks, it leaves traces, tracks and trails as it treads, tromps, travails, traverses. Yet, this is not only material traces of footprints, treaded earth, crunched leaves, squished debris, but also legal traces: traces of common law. As the burial party walks, carrying common law, marking the land with its physical movements, I argue it also marks the land with common law. While not a permanent marking, it is a marking that contributes to the production of common law spaces and through repetitions, such as repetitions of walking into the woods beyond which makes the beyond somewhat less beyond, also contributes to temporary common law markings and makings of place.[153]

Therefore, while it remains possible that the burial party walks without a common law trace, this book takes the position that through the juridical practice of walking, common law does leave a trace, although it may not always be that easy to see. This is walking as juridical form serving as one of the ways common law moves, leaving its trace; marking place. However, there is a limit. For me, it seems that although common law may wander in and out of the woods, and may ruffle the surface as it did with the burial party as it walked, and as it did with the walking of Hodgkinson and Wimbo, and the walking of others, it does not seem to stay: at least not permanently. Yet walking is only one materialisation of common law movement, and while it may only leave temporal traces, it can be seen that

---

153 See Chapter 2, 2.2.

to walk with empire is not jurisprudentially meaningless. As illustrated in the next and final part of the chapter, other forms of movement linger, both temporally and spatially.

Therefore, to bring this walk to some form of temporary rest, it must be remembered that for those subjected to common law and named as common law subjects, such as the members of the burial party, to walk is to carry and move common law. And to walk is an endless repetition, both within a technology of bipedal movements but also on a scale of humanity: humans walk; common law subjects walk, and we will continue to walk and in walking, we will produce space, leaving jurisprudential traces. This is where the ramifications lie. Repetition. For to walk is to move common law: repeat; repeat; repeat. This is the enormity of what seems a relatively insignificant common law technique of movement. This is the horror of walking; the shuddering and shimmering; the ruffling of the surface; the marking of the land: to walk is to move common law.

Repeat.

3.4 Camping with the dead

Having walked with the burial party, and noticed the ruffling of the surface as common law moves, the previous part redescribed the movements of the burial party and revealed the juridical form of walking. This is walking as a jurisdictional device that authors and authorises common law's movements, which places walking as a material practice of common law. Most simply, and most boldly, this is walking as one way common law moves in the material world. However, this is not the only way common law moves. In this part, a further form of common law movement is revealed. Paying attention to the repetition of walking as a juridical form of movement, it becomes possible to contemplate how common law comes into its relations through movement. For as the burial party walks, and as common law moves with the walking of the burial party, common law also moves in relation to the dead. Paying attention to the responsibility to care for the dead and how this responsibility is integral to the movements of the burial party, including how and why it walks, the final part of this chapter redescribes the movements of the burial party as instituting and ordering lawful relations between common law and the dead, and in doing so, both moving and placing common law in the woods beyond.

This part therefore addresses the burial party's responsibilities to the dead, which is a responsibility that is primarily taken up and practised through the ceremony of burial. While ceremonies of burial enact and perform a lawful relation between common law and the dead, in a sense the series of burials in and around Hawkesbury in 1799 are burials that never quite happen. Irresolvable, while the burial party might walk into the woods beyond, akin to Polynices in *Antigone*, the dead are never quite buried properly.[154] What this means is that it is not burial

---

154 Sophocles, *Antigone*, see below, n 178.

per se, but rather movements towards burial that become significant. This is because it is in common law's struggle to bury the dead – a struggle present in its movements towards burial – that common law's technical and material practices of movement are revealed.

Focusing on movements towards burial as one of the ways in which common law moves in its struggles to relate to the dead, this final part notices how common law comes into its relations with the dead through what is described as a jurisdictional technique of 'camping'.[155] Gilles Deleuze in his final work with Felix Guattari, *What is Philosophy?*, contrasts French philosophical tendencies to build structures, German tendencies to lay foundations and English tendencies to 'camp' (to move and inhabit).[156] Likewise, rather than lay foundations or build structures, paradigmatically of English philosophy, English common law moves and inhabits; it camps. Taking up Deleuze and Guatarri's concept of camping, I argue that the practice of 'camping' is a jurisdictional technique of movement that creates and conducts lawful relations, including, in this specific instance, lawful relations between common law and the dead. Noticing the requirement of burial as a responsibility to the dead, and a lawful responsibility integral to the movements of the burial party, this final part redescribes movements towards burial as movements of common law; lawful movements. For the burial party, these movements take the form of common law camping with the dead.

In this regard, in addition to the juridical form of walking addressed in the last part, the second form of movement attended to is movement towards burial. Attending to the burial party as it walks into the woods beyond to bury the dead, this part addresses the burial party's responsibilities to the dead, and the form or forms of lawful relations between the burial party and the dead. Through this jurisprudential attention, what is revealed in this part is how common law moves in its relations by camping with the dead, and in doing so, continues to rustle and ruffle the surface of the earth as it moves, or at least seems to move, into place.

So, a burial party walks to bury the dead.

Responsibilities to the dead: burial

Having considered the nature of the beyond, and noticed different textures to common law's places, including its non-places, in Hawkesbury in 1799 common law was subject to some sort of hesitation or restraint, unable to move into the woods beyond. Yet, despite this restraint, the burial party was able to walk, and walk beyond. Contemplating the purpose of the burial party, that is, why the burial party walked, it becomes apparent that the burial party walked as a way of taking responsibility for the dead. The question of how the burial party walked

---

155 Gilles Deleuze and Felix Guattari, *What is Philosophy?* (Hugh Tomlinson and Graham Burchell trans., Columbia University Press, 1994) ch 4 [trans. of *Qu'est-ce que la Philosophie?* (first published 1991)].
156 Ibid, especially 105–6.

still remains to be addressed, though it will ultimately be suggested that while carrying common law, the burial party walked not because of any common law rights or duties, but rather, in response to a jurisdictional call to care for the dead; a practice of common law camping with the jurisdiction of the dead.

For now, however, the question is, superficially at least, more simple: why did the burial party walk? Quite obviously, the burial party walked to locate and bury the dead. But was this the only purpose? Implicit within the testimonial language of several of the witnesses, there are multiple or perhaps intermingled purposes, namely burial or the pursuit of 'natives'. With different emphases, some witnesses refer simply to the need to bury the dead, such as a 'party of Soldiers who went out to bury the Body of Tho. Hodgkinson who had been Killed by the Natives',[157] 'men who were going out to bury the Bodies of Hodgkinson and Wimbolt',[158] 'excursion to bury the deceased'[159] or a 'party who went to bury the Bodies of the deceased Hodgkinson and Wimbo'.[160] Another witness fails to mention burial: 'a party of soldiers out in pursuit of the natives',[161] while others offer a more mixed description, including 'the party of Soldiers and others who went out in pursuit of the natives and to bury the two Bodies of Hodgkinson and Wimbo'.[162] On these testimonial words, the purposes of the burial party ranged from a party of men who went to bury the dead, or at times 'a' dead (due to the relative import of Hodgkinson and lack of import of Wimbo), to a party of men who had the dual purpose of burying the dead and pursuing 'natives', to a party of men simply in pursuit. Given this uncertainty, it is plausible that the burial party had a mixed purpose of both burial and pursuit, yet this is not my suggestion. While recognising the ignominy resting behind 'pursuit', a form of human-hunting, it seems to me that the relationship between these two purposes is not collegial.

Without undermining the severity of the extraordinary order granted to the burial party, including its overt colonial violence, religious overtones and the problematic of 'pursuit', absent the dead, without the need for burial, the burial party would not and arguably could not walk in the way it did and where it did. There is something very particular, something significant and intensely fundamental, to the need to locate and bury the dead. So even though it is plausible that both purposes might have been present, without the dead, there is no burial party; and certainly no reason for the burial party to walk. This was the overriding purpose: to take responsibility for the dead through the ceremonial practice of burial. This is implicit in the institution of the burial party, as the act of organising a burial party – in and of itself – reveals the importance of burial. Why, then, did the burial party walk into the woods beyond to bury the dead? In other words, why is it important to bury the dead and what is it about burying the dead that

157 Question by Edward Powell to Lieutenant Thomas Hobby NRS 2700 [X905] 340.
158 Lieutenant Thomas Hobby NRS 2700 [X905] 340.
159 Jonas Archer NRS 2700 [X905] 349.
160 Ibid, 348.
161 Lieutenant Thomas Hobby NRS 2700 [X905] 343.
162 William Fuller NRS 2700 [X905] 351.

authored and authorised the burial party to walk beyond? Placing the purpose of the burial party as one of burying the dead, it becomes possible to attend to the form of the relation between common law and the dead as a lawful one.

Although burial is not a universal activity, it is an activity that arises in various ceremonial guises in different times and places. As Richard Huntington and Peter Metcalf explain in *Celebrations of Death*, although there are a variety of rituals celebrating death, the desire to bury the dead tends to be central to those rituals.[163] This includes the English, where a central responsibility to the dead is the obligation to bury.[164] Whether burial is integral to what it means to be human, as Vico and Harrison suggest,[165] or whether it is more subtle in its cultural manifestations, as Huntington and Metcalf suggest,[166] for the members of the burial party – even if the men constituting the party were from mixed cultural and legal backgrounds[167] – the desire to bury the dead is evidently part of the context in which the party walked, and also the reason *why* it walked.

More explicitly, the importance of burial is also revealed in testimonial comments concerning the failure to properly care for the dead. For instance, in the combined defence submissions by Timms, Freebody and Butler, the perceived ill treatment of the dead was viewed as grounds for further killings:

> [A]gain it was generally understood that it was a standing order, or at least it was so issued from the Commanding Officer, to Kill any of the Natives found in their way, *particularly after* the Barbarous, Cruel and Inhuman Murder of the unfortunate Hodgskinson and Wimbow, a Murder the most horrid to have beheld. Any Gentlemen to have seen the Mangled Bodies of the Deceased would have shuddered and ever bore an Antipathy against the Cruel Natives in general [emphasis added].[168]

What the accused are referring to is the need, or at least a justification for, an elevated response 'against the Cruel Natives in general'.[169] It is not clear whether this call for an elevated response responded to the 'Barbarous, Cruel and Inhuman' murders of Hodgskinson and Wimbo, that is, the way they were killed or to the treatment of the dead; the 'Mangled Bodies'. Whether it was the manner of murder, or manner in which the dead were treated, what was clearly important was having witnessed the bodies of the dead.[170] Jonas Archer suggests

---

163 Richard Huntington and Peter Metcalf, *Celebrations of Death: The Anthropology of Mortuary Ritual* (Cambridge University Press, 1991).
164 Ibid.
165 Vico, *The New Science of Giambattista Vico*, above, n 113; Robert Pogue Harrison, *The Dominion of the Dead* (University of Chicago Press, 2003). See also Chapter 2, 2.3.
166 Huntington and Metcalf, *Celebrations of Death*, above, n 163.
167 See Chapter 3, 3.3.
168 Prisoners' defence NRS 2700 [X905] 312.
169 Ibid.
170 Ibid. Cf: John Tarlington NRS 2700 [X905] 357.

the dead were left unburied,[171] describing the mangled dead, 'naked covered by wood' with 'Cloaths provisions and Arms and Blankets' removed, which suggests Hodgkinson and Wimbo may not have been buried in the ground, although the covering of wood is ambiguous.[172] Yet, even if covering the dead with wood was a ceremonial form of burial, it was not a form of burial recognised by the members of the burial party. This much is clear from the intensity of the testimonial reports concerning the treatment of the dead, where the ill treatment of the dead was used to justify dramatically accelerated violent responses, including the execution of two Aboriginal boys known *not* to have been responsible for the killings of Hodgkinson and Wimbo. For instance, resonating with the above comments of the accused, Metcalfe commented to Lieutenant Hobby, 'had I seen the bodies of Hodgskinson and Wimbolt that I should have thot. nothing of the Natives being put to death'.[173]

That the concern is not just that death has occurred, but also with the treatment of the dead and the importance of burying the dead properly is most apparent in a comment made by one of the accused men, Thomas Sanburn, to Constable Thomas Rickerby. In a not-entirely successful effort to deny knowledge of the killing of the two Aboriginal boys, Sanburn stated that 'they were as decently buried as any of the white people that were Killed by the Natives.'[174] A decent burial; a proper burial. Decently and indecently, the two Aboriginal boys killed by the accused were buried, but as Thomas Rickerby explained, he 'with assistance, dug them up and left the Bodies laying on the Ground'[175] before the bodies were inspected at some later time. Left 'laying on the ground', it is not known whether the bodies of these two young dead boys were buried again: a decent burial; a proper burial? Hodgkinson and Wimbo were also left laying on the ground, 'covered by wood',[176] and although the details of their final burial are also unknown, what is known is that a burial party walked into the woods beyond to bury the dead; to ensure the dead were buried properly.

Clearly, there is something to burial.[177] Not only is there a cultural responsibility or even a decency, perhaps, that is captured in the need and concomitant responsibility to bury the dead (i.e. the reason *why* the burial party walked), but I argue that the responsibility to bury the dead is also a lawful one. This is *how* the burial party moved. As mentioned previously, before the physical mass of

---

171 Jonas Archer NRS 2700 [X905] 348.
172 Ibid.
173 Lieutenant Thomas Hobby NRS 2700 [X905] 343. See also Robert Braithwaite NRS 2700 [X905] 344–5 referring to a conversation with Constable Edward Powell regarding the killing of the two Aboriginal boys; 'The witness observing that it was a very cruel way of killing them even had they been detected in committing any act of depredation. Powell replied had the witness seen the bodies of Hodgkinson and Wimbolt how they had been murdered by the natives, that he would not have thought it so inhuman.'
174 Thomas Rickerby NRS 2700 [X905] 330.
175 Ibid.
176 Jonas Archer NRS 2700 [X905] 348.
177 See Chapter 2, 2.3.

the burial party and the Lieutenant's extraordinary order, common law was subject to some limitation or restraint of movement, seemingly unable to move beyond the boundaries into the woods. The deaths of Hodgkinson and Wimbo enabled common law to travel beyond, and having considered why, the question remains: but how? In the remainder of this chapter, I argue that the burial party responded to a call to uphold its relations with the dead to ensure the dead were buried lawfully. By complying with the jurisdiction of the dead through 'camping', I argue that the burial party walked, carrying and moving common law into the beyond.

Antigone: jurisdictional responsibilities

To illustrate how the responsibility to bury the dead is also a lawful one, consider the relation between Antigone and Polynices in Sophocles' *Antigone*.[178] In the opening scene, Antigone tells her sister Ismene of King Creon's decree to deny the burial of Polynices.[179] Of course, it is Creon's refusal to bury Polynices, and the maintenance of this order that is central to this tragedy. In the opening discussion between Antigone and Ismene, the authority of Creon's order is questioned by Antigone as being in conflict with another order of law: the laws of the gods. For Antigone, the depth of Creon's refusal of burial, which carries a punishment of death by stoning for anyone attempting to bury Polynices is unacceptable. A few scenes later, having attempted – without Ismene's support – to

---

178 Sophocles, 'Antigone' in Sophocles, *The Theban Plays: King Oedipus, Oedipus at Colonus, Antigone* (E.F. Watline trans., Penguin, 1947) (*Antigone*). Obviously the secondary literature on Antigone is vast, but for Antigone in a jurisprudential context, see, especially, Costas Douzinas and Ronnie Warrington, 'Antigone's Law: A Genealogy of Jurisprudence', in Costas Douzinas, Peter Goodrich and Yifat Hachamovitch (eds.), *Politics, Postmodernity and Critical Legal Studies: The Legality of the Contingent* (Routledge, 1994) ch 6, 187; Bonnie Honig, 'Antigone's Two Laws: Greek Tragedy and the Politics of Humanism' (2010) 31(1) *New Literary History* 1. For contemporary jurisprudence, Antigone often features, albeit often quite briefly, as a parable of conflict; Costas Douzinas and Ronnie Warrington, 'Antigone's Law', 196. This conflict generally manifests as either a conflict between the laws of man and the laws of the gods; positive law and natural law; the laws of family and the laws of the city etc., and Antigone is then often read as a political, ethical or legal actor navigating these conflicts. In this book, Antigone is understood as a legal actor subject to multiple forms of law on the basis that in Sophocles' *Antigone*, as suggested by Costas Douzinas and Ronnie Warrington, the two dichotomous poles of natural law and positivism are 'placed in their unceasing circulation, they create an economy of conflict and of revolving hierarchies, which becomes the history of law and of law's consciousness – jurisprudence'. Less concerned with jurisprudence as law's consciousness and more concerned with jurisprudence as the practical wisdom of law, it is Antigone's unequivocal desire to bury Polynices, and the material manifestations of that need to bury, that are of interest to this minor jurisprudence. In this regard, while Antigone is understood to be subject to multiple forms of law, such as natural law and positive law, the laws of man and the laws of the gods, rather than focusing on the dichotomous poles of natural law and positivism, what is noticed is the relation between the living and the dead as a lawful one.
179 Sophocles, *Antigone*, above, n 178, (21–38). In this chapter, citations for Sophocles, *Antigone* are to line numbers.

bury Polynices by covering the body with a light layer of earth, then brought by a sentry to Creon, Antigone challenges the authority of Creon's order.[180] To refuse to bury the dead, even if it is a rule proffered by a sovereign, is one in breach of another form of law: the laws of the gods. There is something horrifically raw about Creon's decree to leave the body of Polynices unburied, which is something even Creon later acknowledges, albeit tragically too late to prevent the spiral of irresolvable burials. This something may resonate on different religious and moral registers, but what is most interesting is that there is something to the baseness of Creon's decree that requires attendance. To refuse to bury the dead is not merely culturally or personally offensive, but something more, and the something more has something to do with law. More particularly, it has something to do with the form of the relationship between the living and the dead as a lawful one, that is, as relation that is guided, connected or perhaps bounded by law.

For Antigone, the need to bury the dead, her '*must*',[181] was expressed as a need to comply with another law; the laws of the gods. Yet it is necessary to shift away from this image of competing laws with inconsistent demands, for while this image has much to say, and to say jurisprudentially, this tells only part of the law story but not all.[182] What is also significant for this particular jurisprudential tale – a minor tale of movement – is Antigone's relation to the dead. While there is something particular to the fraternal relation between Antigone and Polynices that requires Antigone to act as she did, especially as expressed in her choice of the irreplaceable brother in her final lament,[183] for Antigone's actions to be rendered as just a personal relation between siblings, misses something important. It is not simply Polynices as her brother that demands Antigone's actions, but Polynices as the dead that also demands. Part of the need to bury Polynices for Antigone was her relation to the dead, and not just to her dead brother Polynices, but the dead more generally: to Hades.

In *Antigone*, the duty to bury is constructed as a duty to the dead. It is not the same as a duty to the formerly living. In this respect, what Antigone makes clear in the context of the treatment of her two brothers, Eteocles and Polynices, is that it is not for those still living to assess the honourable quality of the acts of the formerly living and determine the manner in which each specific dead ought to be treated.[184] As Antigone acknowledges, although the dead may well be differentiated in Hades, it is not for the living to determine this. Rather, the task and responsibility of the living is to bury the dead. This is what Antigone means (or at

---

180 Ibid, 418, 443, 449, 451–508.
181 See Douzinas and Warrington, 'Antigone's Law', above, n 178 at 188, citing Sophocles, *Antigone*, above, n 178, 44, 45, 98–9.
182 See Chapter 1.
183 Sophocles, *Antigone*, above, n 178, 891–967. Cf: Thucydides, 'Funeral Oration of Pericles', in Thucydides, *The History of the Peloponnesian War* (Richard Crawley trans., Project Gutenberg, 2008) Book II, ch VI.
184 Sophocles, *Antigone*, above, n 178, 522–5.

least part of what she means) when she acknowledges that in 'the country of the dead, that may well be law' but for the living, there is 'a duty to the dead'.[185]

The duty to the dead is a relation of responsibility: it is a duty or responsibility to Hades, not the former living, and includes a responsibility to bury. One way of visualising the form of this relation of responsibility, as illustrated in the relation between Antigone and her dead brother Polynices (and Hades), is that Antigone responds to the call of the dead: a call to bury. This is the call of the dead; a call to care for the dead, to respect the dead, to take responsibility for the dead and uphold the duty of the living to the dead, which includes a duty to bury. Yet, despite the temptation, to frame this as a 'call' is somewhat problematic. It is problematic because if Antigone is taken to respond to the call of the dead, then what is being asked of the dead is to call to the living – to speak – which is a great burden not only on the dead, but also on the living. Leaving aside other ways in which the dead may speak, such as through faith or memory,[186] on a register of technical and material practice, the dead cannot speak and to ask the dead to do so is problematic.

If the dead do not speak, then how might we explain the relation between the living and the dead? While remaining problematic, the call of the dead hints at the way in which the dead communicate to the living. Despite the inability of the dead to orally call to the living, the naming of the call offers a reminder that the relation between the living and the dead is a lawful one. Antigone responds to the lawful call of the dead, abiding by the duties to the dead to ensure the dead are buried, and buried lawfully, which is the duty to respond to the call of the dead as a matter of lawfulness; lawful duty. This is crucial because the relation between the living and the dead is not only lawful, but also jurisdictional, created and conducted through responsibilities of burial.

For lawful relations between the living and the dead are conducted through jurisdiction. As explained in Chapter 2, this is jurisdiction as a relational device; as a mode and manner of creating and conducting lawful relations. Working with jurisdiction offers a different jurisprudential reading of *Antigone* than the more common 'competing laws' narrative. That is, the relation between Antigone and the dead is a jurisdictional relation conducted between Antigone and Hades; between the living and the dead. In this respect, the duty to bury the dead is jurisprudentially reframed and placed as a duty to respond to the jurisdictional call of the dead and comply with the lawful responsibilities to care for the dead. Jurisdictionally speaking, the duty Antigone was bound to follow to ensure Polynices was properly buried, regardless of the consequences she may and did suffer, was a duty of law; a lawful duty. The intense desire, the 'must' of Antigone, was a must of obedience and compliance with the jurisdictional responsibility to care for the dead. For *Antigone*, in the genre of tragedy, there was an irresolvable responsibility to care for the dead, resulting as it did for Sophocles with the failed

---

185 Ibid.
186 Cf: Harrison, *The Dominion of the Dead*, above, n 165.

burials of both Polynices and Antigone. Yet, even despite the irresolvable, it is the 'must' of Antigone to respond to the jurisdictional call of the dead as a way of taking responsibility for the dead, and caring for the dead, that is significant because it offers an understanding, and recognition, that there is a lawful relation between the living and the dead, and that the form of this relation is jurisdictional. This is what I refer to as the 'jurisdiction of the dead'.

Having considered the site of jurisdiction in Sophocles' *Antigone*, it is helpful to reconsider and redescribe the movements of the burial party as it walked to bury the dead. For the burial party, like Antigone, there is also a lawful relation with the dead. More specifically, this is a jurisdictional relation between common law and the dead created and conducted *as* the burial party walked into the woods beyond to bury the dead.

Walking to camp: camping with the jurisdiction of the dead

Before the physical mass of the burial party and Lieutenant Hobby's extraordinary order, common law was subject to some limit, seemingly unable to move beyond the boundaries into the woods. As the burial party walked beyond, the burial party encountered land as it touched the earth, treading, step-by-step. Carrying common law as it walked, the burial party walked in order to uphold a duty to bury the dead and in doing so, heeded the call of the jurisdiction of the dead. For it was the deaths of Hodgkinson and Wimbo that enabled common law to travel beyond because, most simply but also most significantly, the dead needed to be buried. To this end, the burial party responded to a call to uphold their lawful relations to the dead and ensure the dead were buried properly, and not as Polynices was. Responding to this jurisdictional call, the burial party walked and walked beyond to bury the dead as a matter of lawful responsibility.

As previously noticed, common law was subject to some limitation or hesitation of movement, unable to move beyond and as such, it was not common law that authored and authorised the burial party to walk beyond. Rather, it was a responsibility to care for the dead that authored and authorised the burial party to walk, and walk beyond. More specifically, walking to ensure the dead were buried lawfully, the burial party responded to a jurisdictional call to take responsibility and care for the dead; to uphold their lawful relations to the dead. This is *how* the burial party walked. This is significant because the act and actions of the burial party, responding to this call while carrying common law, meant the burial party walked in *compliance* with the jurisdiction of the dead. This is important. Responding to the call of the dead, although still carrying common law, the burial party carried common law while walking in *compliance* with the jurisdiction of the dead. In other words, the burial party responded to a jurisdictional call creating and conducting lawful relations between common law and the dead. Walking in compliance with the jurisdiction of dead, the burial party moved common law through the institution and exercise of technologies of jurisdiction.

By recognising the form of relation between common law and the dead as a lawful one conducted through technologies of jurisdiction, it then becomes possible to contemplate *how* the burial party walked in compliance with the jurisdiction of the dead. My suggestion is that the particular jurisdictional technique by which the burial party walked may be best described as 'camping'. As mentioned, Deleuze and Guattari contemplate geophilosophy, contrasting philosophical tendencies to build structures (French), lay foundations (German) and to move and inhabit by camping (English).[187] Paradigmatically of English philosophy, my proposal is that common law camps; tending less towards the building of structures or laying of foundations than towards the techniques and practices of moving and inhabiting. This is not to lay claim to an exclusive technique, for at times common law does build structures and does lay foundations, yet when it does, they are never quite permanent. This is because common law's mode of existence is one of movement, or at least movement is integral to that mode.[188]

This can be detected in the movements of the burial party. For the burial party, the relationship between common law and the dead is quite aptly described as camping. The previous restraint on movement beyond was eased because the burial party carried common law as it *camped* with the jurisdiction of the dead. This is not simply an affective restraint of not wanting to walk beyond, but a common law restraint. Without camping, both the burial party and common law were subject to some restriction of movement. It was only through common law camping with the jurisdiction of the dead that the burial party was able to walk beyond, carrying common law as it walked, in order to locate and bury the dead. This is common law movement in the form of camping with the dead. Therefore, through the jurisdictional technique of camping, I argue that common law moves with the walking movements of the burial party, which moves in compliance with the jurisdiction of the dead.

There are two related ramifications. The first is that, in addition to attending to walking as a form of common law movement, the redescription of the burial party revealed the responsibility to bury the dead as another form of common law movement. For it is only through the responsibility to care for the dead and the requirement to bury that the burial party walked. This places the requirement to comply with the jurisdiction of the dead, including the duty to bury, as a mode of authorisation for certain forms of common law movement. For as the burial party walks beyond to bury the dead, common law moves. Therefore, in addition to walking, the responsibility to bury the dead is one of the ways in which common law moves, and the form of that movement is camping.

The second ramification is that the form of common law movement exhibited by the burial party walking to bury the dead through the technology of camping takes the form of a lawful relation. Here, the form of that relation is camping as common law moves and inhabits the jurisdiction of the dead. Leech-like,

---

187 Deleuze and Guattari, above, n 155, ch 4, especially 105–6.
188 See Chapter 2, 2.1.

attaching to the surface of another form of law, such as the jurisdiction of the dead, in order to move beyond, where movement may otherwise be difficult. This is a lawful relation between common law and the dead: the device of this relation is jurisdiction, the form of this relation is camping. In other words, the jurisdictional technique of camping is one way in which common law relates to the dead. To this end, camping is also a form of lawful relations.

Therefore, as illustrated throughout this chapter, one of the ways in which common law moves in relation to the dead is through a responsibility to bury. That is, these movements to bury constitute movements of common law as it camps with the jurisdiction of the dead. It was therefore a jurisdictional movement through camping with the dead that common law moved into the woods beyond. Without the need to respond to the lawful call of the dead, and without common law camping with the jurisdiction of the dead, not only would common law and the burial party not have moved, and not have been able to move into the woods beyond, there would also not have been the creation and conduct or the institution and ordering of lawful relations.

To conclude, the task of a minor jurisprudence of movement has been taken up in this chapter through the redescription of a burial party that walked into the woods beyond to bury the dead. Narrating then redescribing some of the technical forms and material practices of common law movement, this chapter revealed how the laws of empire move and in doing so, placed movements within the Colony of New South Wales as jurisprudentially significant. More specifically, it was revealed that it was through the juridical form of walking and camping with the dead, as two distinct material forms of movement, that common law moved into the woods beyond. This chapter also raised the jurisprudential question of how to move well by placing movement as a matter of conduct. Walking with empire, the chapter has offered a reminder of the importance of paying attention to how we walk. In the next chapter, the performance of this minor jurisprudence of movement continues through a second vignette which narrates and redescribes movements in relation to the jurisdiction of the dead in the polar South.

Figure 4.1 Connie Samaras, *Dome and Tunnels, V.A.L.I.S. (vast active living intelligence system)* (2005–2007) (archival inkjet print from film, 60 × 48", edition of 5)

Figure 4.2 Connie Samaras, *Buried Fifties Station, V.A.L.I.S. (vast active living intelligence system)* (2005–2007) (archival inkjet print from film, 40 × 32", edition of 5)

Chapter 4

Jurisdiction of the dead

> The death of Dr Rodney Marks has highlighted an investigative and jurisdictional void for deaths in Antarctica, in some circumstances.
> (Coroner Richard McElrea, *Findings*)[1]

Dr Rodney David Marks died in Antarctica. An Australian astrophysicist working at the Amundsen-Scott South Pole Station, he died in unusual circumstances. It was not simply the manner of Rodney Marks' death that was unusual, but also the place of his death. With an historical absence of a living population, the coming of the living to Antarctica – as explorers and then scientists – has also meant the coming of the dead. For in a sense, Antarctica is populated by a history of dead explorers, which is a history that continues with the death of scientists. In this regard, what is unusual in this instance is not simply that a scientist died in Antarctica, but the precise location of this death. For Marks died at a scientific research station at the centre of Antarctica, located only metres from the south pole: a fascinating juridical place.

Described by a New Zealand coroner as a 'jurisdictional void',[2] this image and its attendant common law imagining is interrogated in this chapter by paying attention to the movements of common law. Through these movements, it becomes possible to account for and develop an account of the creation and conduct of lawful relations in the polar South. Narrating and redescribing the death, burial and reburial of Rodney Marks, this chapter reveals that despite the apparently unusual circumstances, common law's movements in relation to this particular dead were surprisingly usual.

So, how does common law move in Antarctica? This is the central question asked in this chapter. However, before attending to this question, an anterior question needs to be addressed: that is, why Antarctica? For a minor jurisprudence of

---

1 *Findings of the Coroner in the Matter of an Inquest into the Death of Rodney David Marks Who Died at South Pole Station, Antarctica* (Unreported, Coroner's Court, Christchurch, New Zealand, Coroner Richard McElrea, 16 September 2008) 43 ('*Findings*').
2 Ibid.

movement that attends to the movements of Anglo-Australian common law, the relevance of Antarctica may not be immediately obvious. For the following three reasons, however, the turn to Antarctica assists in the further elaboration of this minor jurisprudence. Each of these three reasons revolves around thinking of the South: literal, methodological and chthonic.[3]

First, this chapter quite literally locates itself at the geographical south pole and asks, from this most southerly of places, how might we account for and develop an account of some of the ways in which common law moves? From movements in relation to other forms of law to movements in relation to the dead, such an account attends to common law practices of movement and notices the ways in which common law comes into its relations and comes to be or at least seems to be – or perhaps seems not to be – in place. By locating at the most southerly place on earth, which is also Australia's most southerly place by virtue of the Australian Antarctic Territory, this literal engagement with the South opens up the possibility of accounting for movements and relations of the laws of the South.

Second, in a more ambitious engagement with the South, in order to develop an account of the movements of and relations between different laws of the South, this chapter engages with international law on a register that might be considered somewhat southerly. That is, attending to the place of law in the polar South, while recognising the presence of several international treaties that provide for the structure and ordering of laws in Antarctica,[4] this chapter operates on a register that rests somewhere beneath this overarching legal architecture. For there is more to the everyday practices of law in Antarctica than mere administration, and central to these everyday practices of law is the movement of common law. This chapter pays attention to the ways different forms of law move in order to think through how these different forms may or may not relate, both to one another and to the dead. Seeking out a southerly register of international law reveals some of the techniques used by different forms of law, especially different forms of common law, to move, pattern and place; creating spaces of a lawful South.

Third, and forcing the southerly theme further, the central narrative developed in this chapter concerns jurisdictional difficulties governing the dead in Antarctica. To this extent, this chapter notices movements of different forms of common law as they seek out a chthonic place in attempts to dwell in or beneath the surface of the earth in order to govern the dead in Antarctica. The particular difficulties of this struggle to move-into-and-below-the-earth become oddly apparent in this

---

3 On laws of the South, see especially the special edition by Richard Johnstone, Shaun McVeigh and Christine Black, 'Of the South' (2007) 16(2) *Griffith Law Review* 299. On movement and the South, see generally Franco Cassano, *Southern Thought and Other Essays on the Mediterranean* (Norma Bouchard and Valerio Ferme trans., Fordham University Press, 2012) [trans. of *Il Pensiero Merediano* (first published 1996)]; Franco Cassano, 'Southern Thought' (2001) 67 *Book Eleven* 1.

4 See Chapter 4, 4.1. As will be explained, these treaties are collectively known as the 'Antarctic Treaty system'.

unusually ambiguous not-quite-earthly place where there is an abundance of ice and the land-is-not-quite-land.

Through this trebled and troubled engagement with the laws of the South – literal, methodological and chthonic – this chapter contributes to an ongoing discussion of how we might account for and develop an account of lawfulness in the global South and what such an account might mean for how we move with and how we live with the laws of the South.[5] However, an account of the laws of the South is a much larger project than the specific concerns of this book and is certainly not resolved, neither is a resolution attempted here. Instead, as with the rest of this book, the primary task of this chapter is a related but more modest one, and pays attention to how common law moves in the polar South as a way of contributing to the creation of a minor jurisprudence of movement, and understandings of common law's place. Focusing on the threshold practices of common law's movements in the polar South, it becomes clear that at times, common law struggles to move in Antarctica. By locating meaning in the ways in which common law moves, relates and places, including its struggles, the task is to think more carefully about how common law creates and conducts lawful relations in the polar South, including its techniques of movement and practices of care. Working with a distinct set of legal materials arising from a coronial inquest, including the formal Coronial Findings and aspects of the accompanying Coronial File, this second performance of a minor jurisprudence unfolds in the following way.

There are four parts to this chapter. The first part introduces movements in the polar South and provides the necessary context by addressing movements in history, law and architecture in Antarctica. The second part of the chapter concerns the death, burial and reburial of Rodney Marks, who died at the south pole in 2000. The third and fourth parts of the chapter redescribe this coronial narrative, revealing some of the different forms of movement in the polar South. To this end, the third part of the chapter attends to movements of Anglo-Australian common law and its struggle to come into relation with the dead in the polar South. The final part of the chapter addresses the office of the coroner and the more successful movements of a New Zealand coronial jurisdiction that instituted lawful relations in the polar South, as well as the office of friend that buried; instituting burial.

Across these four parts, this chapter illustrates how common law moves in relation to the dead. As suggested in earlier chapters, this is how we accumulate obligations to the dead and for common law; this is especially important for it is through this relation common law moves and comes to be in place. Having already placed the care of the dead as a jurisprudential matter of office, this chapter continues the work of the previous chapters, noticing common law's repetitions in its technical and material forms of movement. In doing so, however, this chapter adds something, well, two things: burial and office.

---

5 See especially Johnstone, McVeigh and Black, 'Of the South', above, n 3.

Unlike the previous chapter, in which the dead were left lying on the ground, never quite buried properly, in this chapter, the dead are buried – twice. Remembering Giambattista Vico who placed burial as the institution that humanises the earth,[6] this chapter attends to the multiple burials of Rodney Marks: the first in Antarctica and the second in Australia. Taking seriously common law's movements in relation to the dead as jurisprudentially meaningful, this chapter attends to these movements and notices the institution of burial as one way common law moves into place and in doing so, contributes to the humanisation and, perhaps, juridification of the earth. As well as the institution of burial, in a minor jurisprudence concerned with movements in relation to the dead, what this chapter adds is an attention to different offices and their relation to different methods of care. Introducing the office of coroner and its relation to methods of care, the office of friend also features, illustrating how different offices host different methods and modes of caring for the dead.

Asking how common law moves, this chapter pays attention to the repetition of certain technical and material practices, notices the continued colonial form of common law's southern movements and adds office and its relation to different methods of care, revealing the jurisprudential significance of movement. While the question of conduct again rests quietly before emerging as ethos in Chapter 5, it is important to mention the place of conduct in this chapter. By returning the question of movement to jurisprudential practice, the question of conduct – of how we might move with common law, and how we might move well – becomes a question of jurisprudential concern. What this means is that having walked with empire in the last chapter, and asked how to walk well, it must be remembered that we continue to walk with empire, throughout the global North, and the global South. We also continue to camp. To this end, this chapter camps with the dead in the sense that it camps with common law as it camps with the jurisdiction of the dead, asking how we might camp well.

4.1 Movements in the polar South

Holding onto law in Antarctica is a challenge. Despite the risk of both movement and law seemingly slipping and sliding away, this chapter accounts for lawful movements in the polar South. To this end, this part introduces some of the major forms of movement in the polar South as a way of introducing the place of law in Antarctica. Addressing movements in history, law and architecture in Antarctica, this first contextual part of the chapter includes a brief overview of the history of exploration, role of science and legal frameworks authored through international and domestic instruments in Antarctica, plus some unusual geographical aspects surrounding the south pole. Challenging relations between territory and land, this

---

6 Giambattista Vico, *The New Science of Giambattista Vico* (Thomas Goddard Bergin and Max Harold Fisch trans., Cornell University Press, 1967) [trans. of *Principi di una Scienza Nuova* (first published 1725)]. See Chapter 2, 2.3.

part places movement in relation to the polar South, setting the scene for a narrative and its jurisprudential redescription in the following parts of the chapter.

Moving histories

The history of Antarctica begins in the imaginary as a counter-balance to the weight of the North. One of 'geography's most ancient assumptions',[7] it was long reasoned that a large landmass in the southern hemisphere was necessary in order to balance the combined landmasses of the northern continents.[8] Called by various names, this imaginary was illustrated on maps as *terra australis incognita*: 'unknown land of the South'.[9] One of these early names was *Antarktos*, which marks the etymological origin of Antarctica as the coupling of the Greek terms *anti* and *arktos*. Translated as both 'the opposite of north'[10] and 'against or opposite the bear',[11] the reference to bear is a reference to the constellation Ursa Major, also known as 'the Great Bear',[12] which 'appears to skim the Arctic Circle, the line of latitude that marks the line of the midnight sun'.[13] Both directly and indirectly, Antarctica was named in opposition to its north.

Mythologised, romanticised and gendered as both masculine and feminine,[14]

---

7 Laurence M. Gould, 'Emergence of Antarctica: The Mythical Land', in Richard S. Lewis and Philip M. Smith (eds.), *Frozen Future: A Prophetic Report from Antarctica* (Quadrangle Books, 1973) 11–12.
8 See, generally, Paul Simpson-Housley, *Antarctica: Exploration, Perception and Metaphor* (Routledge, 1992) ch 1. See, e.g., ibid; Paul Shepheard, *The Cultivated Wilderness, or, What Is Landscape?* (MIT Press, 1997) 72; Bill Manhire (ed.), *The Wide White Page: Writers Imagine Antarctica* (Victoria University Press, 2004) 9; Emilio J. Sahurie, *The International Law of Antarctica* (New Haven Press, 1992) xxi; Maria Pia Casarini, 'Activities in Antarctica Before the Conclusion of the Antarctic Treaty', in Francesco Francioni and Tullio Scovazzi (eds.), *International Law for Antarctica* (Kluwer Law International, 2nd edn, 1996) 627–8.
9 Simpson-Housley, *Antarctica*, above, n 8, 1, citing J.G. Hayes, *Antarctica: A Treatise on the Southern Continent* (Richards Press, 1928) 4. See also Gould, 'Emergence of Antarctica', above, n 7, 11–12.
10 Simpson-Housley, *Antarctica*, above, n 8, ch 1.
11 Ibid.
12 Shepheard, *The Cultivated Wilderness*, above, n 8, 60–61.
13 Ibid.
14 There is an emerging feminist literature on polar exploration that raises a number of important issues in relation to the changing associations of masculine and feminine in historical and contemporary engagements with Antarctica. As the South to the Arctic's North, defined in the negative as not-North, Antarctica has often been constructed as the feminine opposite to a masculine Arctic. Yet, as an icescape host to 'fields of endeavour for male explorers', awaiting penetration, both Antarctica and the Arctic are often also constructed as feminine, Elizabeth Leane, 'Placing Women in the Antarctic Literary Landscape' (2009) 34(3) *Signs: Journal of Women in Culture and Society* 509, 510. In contrast, Antarctica also figures as a 'masculine space of the imperial frontier as opposed to the feminized space of domestic colonial settlement': Christy Collis, 'The Australian Antarctic Territory: A Man's World?' (2009) 34(3) *Signs: Journal of Women in Culture and Society* 514, 514. See also Jennifer H. Laing and Geoffrey I. Crouch, 'Lone Wolves? Isolation and Solitude within the Frontier Travel Experience' 91(4) *Human Geography* (2009) 325. For a useful introduction to this emerging literature, see the special edition by Victoria Rosner (ed.), 'Comparative Perspectives Symposium: Gender and Polar Studies' (2009) 34(3) *Signs: Journal of Women in Culture*

the history of the Antarctic imaginary is complex.[15] Yet, whichever version is taken up, central to this imaginary is the ambiguous nature of land in Antarctica. Today, this complex imaginary continues and is captured, to a certain extent, in the colloquial naming of Antarctica by scientists, tourists and others as simply, 'the Ice'.[16] Yet, before 'the Ice', which comes to the fore shortly, the standard historical recital of Antarctic history begins with references to Greek philosophers (albeit with some inconsistencies), although generally including Pythagoras' belief that the earth was round[17] and Aristotle's reasoning that the symmetry of a sphere required balance by an inhabited or inhabitable southern region,[18] before accelerating chronologically to Captain James Cook's voyage in 1773 when the Antarctic Circle was crossed.[19] Some recitals also refer to Herodotus' account of a Phoenician voyage in 700BC,[20] and occasionally to a Maori war canoe captained by Hui Te Rangiora in 650 that travelled south until it reached the frozen waters of what is now known as the Ross Sea.[21] Despite this earlier Maori voyage and the importance it continues to hold,[22] it was the Englishman Captain James Cook whose voyage trumpets the beginning of the 'age of exploration'.[23]

The age of exploration involved numerous journeys aimed at discovering and exploring Antarctica, devolving into national competitions for the right to claim various 'firsts', including the first to cross the Antarctic Circle (Cook, British Royal Navy, 1773); the first to sight Antarctica (disputed: Fabian Gottlieb von

---

and Society 489. See, especially, Victoria Rosner, 'Gender and Polar Studies: Mapping the Terrain' (2009) 34(3) *Signs: Journal of Women in Culture and Society* 489; Klaus Dodds, 'Settling and Unsettling Antarctica' (2009) 34(3) *Signs: Journal of Women in Culture and Society* 505. See also Elena Glasberg, *Antarctica as Cultural Critique: The Gendered Politics of Scientific Exploration and Climate Change* (Palgrave, 2012). For a careful consideration of the gendered constructions of colonial lands in the context of colonial exploration and the sublime in the sixteenth and seventeenth centuries, see Judith Grbich, 'The South, International Law and the Apocalyptic Sublime' (Paper presented at the South of International Law, Melbourne Law School, University of Melbourne, 8–9 July 2010).

15 See, generally, Simpson-Housley, above, n 8.
16 See, e.g., *Findings*, above, n 1, 2; Jeff Rubin, *Lonely Planet Guide to Antarctica* (Lonely Planet, 3rd edn, 2005) 314; Stephen Pyne, *The Ice: A Journey to Antarctica* (Arlington Books, 1987).
17 Although arguable whether this idea originated with Pythagoras, by the time of the Pythagorean School it was generally accepted in ancient Greece that the earth was round. See, e.g., Gould, above, n 7, 11, 12.
18 See, e.g., Simpson-Housley, *Antarctica*, above, n 8, 1.
19 See, e.g., ibid; Philip W. Quigg, *A Pole Apart: The Emerging Issue of Antarctica* (New Press, McGraw-Hill Book Company, 1983) 8–9.
20 See, e.g., Rubin, *Lonely Planet Guide to Antarctica*, above, n 16, 21.
21 See, e.g., ibid, 21–22.
22 See, e.g., the first reading by Rahui Katene of the Maori Party, Member for Te Tai Tonga, of the parliamentary debate for the stalled Antarctica (Environmental Protection: Liability Annex) Amendment Bill 2009 (NZ); New Zealand Parliament, *Parliamentary Debates*, House of Representatives, 20 August 2009, 5769 (Rahui Katene, Te Tai Tonga).
23 Antarctica literatures often classifies into ages, including a mythical age, heroic age of discovery and exploration and an age of science. See, e.g., Gould, 'Emergence of Antarctica', above, n 7, 11, 11.

Bellingshausen, Russian Imperial Navy, 1820; Edward Bransfield, British Royal Navy, 1820; Nathaniel Palmer, American sealer, 1820); and the first to land on mainland Antarctica (disputed: John Davis, American sealer, 1821). Yet it was not simply a sense of nationalism that pushed towards these discoveries but also commerce in the form of seal trade.[24] Whether driven by national or commercial urges, accompanying these various events of the 'first' was an insatiable appetite for naming, which continues today.[25]

After the waves of shipping discoveries abated, competition turned to physical modes of land-based movements. This included another series of 'firsts', including the first to reach the magnetic south pole (T.W. Edgeworth David and Douglas Mawson, Nimrod Expedition, 1907); the first to climb Mount Erebus, which was then the highest but now the second highest volcano in Antarctica (T.W. Edgeworth David, Nimrod Expedition, 1907);[26] the first to traverse the Ross Ice Shelf (Ernst Shackleton, 1908–1909); the first to traverse the Transantarctic Mountain Range (Ernst Shackleton, 1908–1909); the first to set foot on the South Polar Plateau (Ernst Shackleton, 1908–1909); and the first to reach the geographic south pole (Roald Amundsen, 14 December 1911).

One of the most sought after 'firsts' was the geographic south pole (see Figure 4.3). Yet in a collective memory that renders the meaning of this particular first somewhat unusual, Roald Amundsen's accomplishments of 14 December 1911 are often coupled with, if not overwhelmed by, a more memorable second in the well-known telling of the 'ill fated' Scott expedition.[27] This 'second' can be seen often, and is actually quite difficult not to see at the current south pole, especially during the exuberant centennial celebrations that ceremonially marked the anniversary of both arrivals on 14 December 2011 (Amundsen) and 17 January 2012

---

24 See Shepheard, *The Cultivated Wilderness*, above, n 8, 78–79. See also Quigg, *A Pole Apart*, above, n 19, 9.

25 Although beyond the scope of this chapter, there is a fascinating history of nomenclature in Antarctica, including places named Mount Terror and Mount Eribus (the god of darkness), both nominally named after ships. The process of naming in Antarctica is now bureaucratised, governed by US policy and though the grounds of legal authority are unclear, the United States Board on Geographic Names establishes a set of criteria matching the importance of natural features with the importance of personal names to ensure an 'appropriate' match, United States Geological Survey, 'Policy Covering Antarctic Names' on *United States Board on Geographic Names* (2010), http:// geonames.usgs.gov/antarctic/index.html. It was through this US process that a mountain in Antarctica was named after Rodney Marks; see Chapter 4, 4.2. Cf: Paul Carter, *The Road to Botany Bay: An Essay in Spatial History* (faber & faber, 1987).

26 The highest volcano in Antarctica is Mount Sidley, which was discovered by Richard E. Byrd while on a plane in 1934. However, due in part to its remoteness, Mount Sidley is still 'overshadowed' by its junior in height, Mount Erebus, which is located on Ross Island, near scientific bases, and continues to feature as a desired mountain to climb. The highest mountain in Antarctica is Vinson Massif, which was first identified in 1958 then climbed in 1966.

27 See, especially, Roland Huntford, *Scott and Amundsen: The Last Place on Earth* (Random House, 1999). See also Francis Spufford, *I May Be Some Time* (faber & faber, 1996); Harry King (ed.), *South Pole Odyssey: Selections from the Antarctic Diaries of Edward Wilson* (Rigby, 1982); Quigg, *A Pole Apart*, above, n 19, 25–8.

Figure 4.3 Pierre R. Schwob, 'Sign at the (Ever Moving) South Pole' (2006)

(Scott). From the naming of the hyphenated Amundsen-Scott South Pole Station, to the current south pole marker, Amundsen and Scott are equally proclaimed,[28] most visually so in the famous south pole sign, quoting both men (see Figure 4.3).[29]

With the firsts abating, although for the creative record seeker, never quite ending,[30] the ages seemingly changed, and after the explorers came the scientists, often referred to as 'modern-day explorers'. The repetition of the discourse of the age of exploration continues in many ways, including a desire for firsts, and

28 The 2012 geographic south pole marker is a spinning dial that depicts Amundsen on one side with Scott on the other; see United States Antarctic programme, *Antarctic Photo Library*, http://photolibrary.usap.gov.
29 Pierre R. Schwob, 'Sign at the (Ever Moving) Actual Geographical South Pole (a Few Feet Away from the Ceremonial Pole)', in Pierre R. Schwob, *PRS Trip to Antarctica, Jan 2006* (2006), http://www.classicalarchives.com/prs/astro/Antarctica/index0004.html (Figure 4.3). Taken in 2006, this was the sign in 2000, but has since been replaced in 2011 for centennial celebrations by a newer, larger sign containing the same details, although with fonts. The new sign was made in the desert of Las Vegas and photographed next to a Saguaro cactus by its makers before departing to the south pole. G. Ethan, 'The Mobile Marker', in G. Ethan, *Ethan's Vivifying Adventures* (10 December 2011), http://ethansvivifyingadventures.blogspot.com.au/2011/12/mobile-marker.html. I am especially grateful to Pierre R. Schwob for allowing me to publish his photograph.
30 See, e.g., William J. Spindler, 'Winterover Statistics', in *Amundsen-Scott South Pole Station* (2000), http://www.southpolestation.com/trivia/00s/2000.html, which includes a list of firsts for those who winter-over at the Station.

obsessive naming. It also continues with the adoption of diaristic tendencies.[31] Across the British Empire and its empirical movements, the genre of diaries has a particular relation with a colonial form of travel writing.[32] In addition to the English gentleman in India,[33] coastal explorers in colonial New South Wales,[34] those seeking the inland sea,[35] as well as those in search of the Great Southern Land and, later, the south pole,[36] the genre of diaries as a colonial form of travel writing is inseparable from the history of Antarctic exploration.[37] For instance, from Scott to Shackleton to Mawson, personal journals were edited and published, reverse-funding the exploration, and these books remain rampantly popular, especially in small town second-hand bookstores.[38]

Although both the form and expectations of exploration have changed from voyages of classical discovery to searches for scientific knowledge, the genre of diaries remains intrinsic to present day Antarctic exploration. Like their predecessors, scientists tend to keep diarised accounts of their time on 'the Ice'. A number of these are published on websites, often directly linked with the research institute attached to the scientific project undertaken in Antarctica. With the increased availability of technology, and increased use and popularity of public writing through blogs etc., the contemporary revival of this older genre of travel writing is embedded in the everyday practices of scientists in Antarctica and, to a lesser extent, tourists. From group emails to online blogs, these are not just personal memoirs, but travel writing in the form of a diarised public record. Often linked to a university or scientific research centre, this is a form and practice of a certain mode of institutional knowledge, and a practice that is attended to in this chapter.

In addition to histories of moving ships, roaming explorers and more sedentary scientists, it is important to recognise the increasing role of tourism. There is a Lonely Planet Guide to Antarctica, currently in its fifth edition with a sixth

---

31 See Chapter 4, 4. 2.
32 See, especially, Piyel Haldar, *Law, Orientalism and Postcolonialism: The Jurisdiction of the Lotus Eaters* (Routledge-Cavendish, 2007); Carter, *The Road to Botany Bay*, above, n 25; Paul Carter, *Living in a New Country: History, Travelling and Language* (Faber, 1992). See, generally, Paul Longley Arthur, *Virtual Voyages: Travel Writing and the Antipodes 1605–1837* (Anthem Press, 2010).
33 Haldar, *Law, Orientalism and Postcolonialism*, above, n 32.
34 James Cook, *Captain Cook's Journal during His First Voyage Round the World Made in H M Bark 'Endeavour' 1768–71* (Elliot Stock, 1893); Sydney Parkinson, *Journal of a Voyage to the South Seas, in His Majesty's Ship, The Endeavour* (London, 1773) entry for 6 May 1770; Carter, *The Road to Botany Bay*, above, n 25.
35 John Oxley, *Journals of Two Expeditions into the Interior of New South Wales: Undertaken by Order of the British Government in the Years 1817–18* (John Murray, 1820); Carter, *The Road to Botany Bay*, above, n 25, ch 3; Julie Evans, *Edward Eyre: Race and Colonial Governance* (University of Otago Press, 2005).
36 See, e.g., Roald Amundsen, *The South Pole: An Account of the Norwegian Antarctic Expedition in the 'Fram', 1910–1912* (A.G. Chater trans., J. Murray, 1912) [trans. of *Sydpolen* (first published 1912)]; Robert Falcon Scott, *Scott's Last Expedition* (MacMillan, 1913) ch 20.
37 Ibid.
38 Amundsen, *The South Pole*, above, n 36; Scott, *Scott's Last Expedition*, above, n 36.

expected in 2017.[39] The great unknown is now known and accessible to those able and willing to pay for the pleasure.[40] A raft of tour operators, cruise ships, charter flights and various adventure specialists offer an 'Antarctic experience'. Tourism, it seems, is the major industry in Antarctica.[41] Yet, with no single government controlling Antarctica, there are no visa requirements for visitors.[42] In this respect, the regulation of Antarctic tourism through the twin efforts of international law and the private sector has been described, in another first, as 'the first real test' for the Antarctic Treaty system.[43]

There is, therefore a concern with the juridical form of the movements of tourists, and as explained shortly, this is a jurisprudential concern with the practices and conduct of lawful movement that is neither answered nor sufficiently addressed by reference to international cooperation, private international law or diplomacy.[44] Remembering that common law moves with the movements of the subject, as explained in Chapter 2 and illustrated in Chapter 3, the question that arises, then, is one of movement.[45] For instance, when persons of various nationalities move around Antarctica, what laws are present? For those carrying common law, how do they move; how do they walk, and what does this mean for the movement and place of common law?

So, in a scenario of cruise ship passengers and crew, airline attendants and commercial yachts, and, of course, scientists, what does it mean to think carefully about the place and movements of different laws in Antarctica? Paying attention to movement, especially movements of common law (Anglo-Australian common law and also a New Zealand coronial jurisdiction), this chapter shows how it is possible to hold onto law in the polar South and avoid the vacuum-packed

---

39 See Rubin, *Lonely Planet Guide to Antarctica*, above, n 16. The current edition is the 4th edition (2008). There is no *Rough Guide to Antarctica*.
40 See, e.g., Shepheard, *The Cultivated Wilderness*, above, n 8, 60–61.
41 Tourism numbers have dramatically increased in recent years and according to the 2009–2010 statistics from the International Association of Antarctic Tour Operators, the number of 'landed' tourists in Antarctic for that one season was 36,875. For statistics and a brief introductory history of tourism in Antarctica, see 'Tourism Overview: Scope of Antarctic Tourism – A Background Presentation', in *International Association of Antarctic Tour Operators* (2012), http://iaato.org/tourism-overview. See, generally, Debra Enzenbacher, 'Antarctic Tourism Policy-Making: Current Challenges and Future Prospects', in Gillian Triggs and Anna Riddell (eds.), *Antarctica: Legal and Environmental Challenges for the Future* (British Institute of International and Comparative Law, 2007) ch 8; Murray P. Johnson and Lorne K. Kriwoken, 'Emerging Issues of Australian Antarctic Tourism: Legal and Policy Directions', in Lorne K. Kriwoken, Julia Jabour and Alan D Hemmings (eds.), *Looking South: Australia's Antarctic Agenda* (Federation Press, 2007) ch 7.
42 See Alexis Averbuck and Jeff Rubin, *Antarctica* (Lonely Planet, 2012).
43 Gillian Triggs and Anna Riddell, 'Introduction', in Triggs and Riddell (eds.), *Antarctica*, above, n 41, xi.
44 On the regulatory challenge of tourism for international law, see, generally, Triggs and Riddell, *Antarctica*, above, n 41, xv–xvi. See also Enzenbacher, 'Antarctic Tourism', above, n 41; Johnson and Kriwoken, 'Emerging Issues', above, n 41.
45 See Chapter 2, 2.1; Chapter 3, 3.3, 3.4.

172 Performing jurisprudence

sensation of a 'jurisdictional void'[46] that apparently arises 'in some circumstances'.[47] This is the task undertaken in this chapter: to account for and develop an account of some of the practices of lawful movements in the polar South. To this end, having introduced some of the moving histories, an introduction to moving laws follows.

Moving laws

Antarctica exists without a state. While remaining an international legal site, questions of sovereignty and territory in Antarctica have effectively been absolved through the mechanisms of the 1959 *Antarctic Treaty*,[48] which sets aside disputes over territorial sovereignty to focus on international scientific cooperation and environmental preservation for the 'common heritage of mankind'.[49] Australia, New Zealand and the United States of America, which all feature in this chapter, are signatories to the *Antarctic Treaty*, as are many other countries.[50] While international law overtly governs Antarctica through a series of treaties known as the 'Antarctic Treaty system',[51] the presence of the continuing performance of territorial claims coupled with everyday legal practices reveal something a little bit different about the movement and place of law in Antarctica. It is not only international law that is present and lightly placed in Antarctica, but also common law in its various national guises (see Figure 4.4).

Despite the *Antarctic Treaty* and broader 'Antarctic Treaty system', which place territorial claims in abeyance, states continue to maintain their territorial claims to specific parts of Antarctica, including, for example, Australia's claim to the Australian Antarctic Territory and New Zealand's claim to the Ross

---

46 *Findings*, above, n 1, 43.
47 Ibid.
48 *Antarctic Treaty*, opened for signature 1 December 1959, 402 UNTS 71 (entered into force 23 June 1961) ('*Antarctic Treaty*').
49 See Gillian Triggs, *International Law and Australian Sovereignty in Antarctica* (Legal Books, 1986) ch 9; Gillian Triggs, 'Australian Sovereignty in Antarctica: Traditional Principles of Territorial Acquisition Versus a "Common Heritage"', in Stuart Harris (ed.), *Australia's Antarctic Policy Options* (Centre for Resource and Environmental Studies, 1984) ch 2.
50 There is a hierarchy attached to signatories of the *Antarctic Treaty*, above, n 48, with different benefits attached to different types of signatory. Australia, New Zealand and the USA were three of the original 12 signatories to the *Antarctic Treaty* and as such also consultative members able to vote. There are currently 50 members (29 consultative, 21 acceding).
51 The 'Antarctic Treaty system' refers to a series of related agreements that collectively 'govern' Antarctica, including the *Antarctic Treaty*, above, n 48, *Agreed Measures for the Conservation of Antarctic Fauna and Flora*, signed 2 June 1964, 17 UST 996 (entered into force 1 November 1982), *Convention for the Conservation of Antarctic Seals*, opened for signature 1 June 1972, 29 UST 441 (entered into force 11 March 1978), *Convention for the Conservation of Antarctic Marine Living Resources*, opened for signature 20 May 1980, 1329 UNTS 48 (entered into force 7 April 1982) and *The Protocol on Environmental Protection to the Antarctic Treaty*, opened for signature 4 October 1991, 30 ILM 1455 (entered into force 14 January 1998).

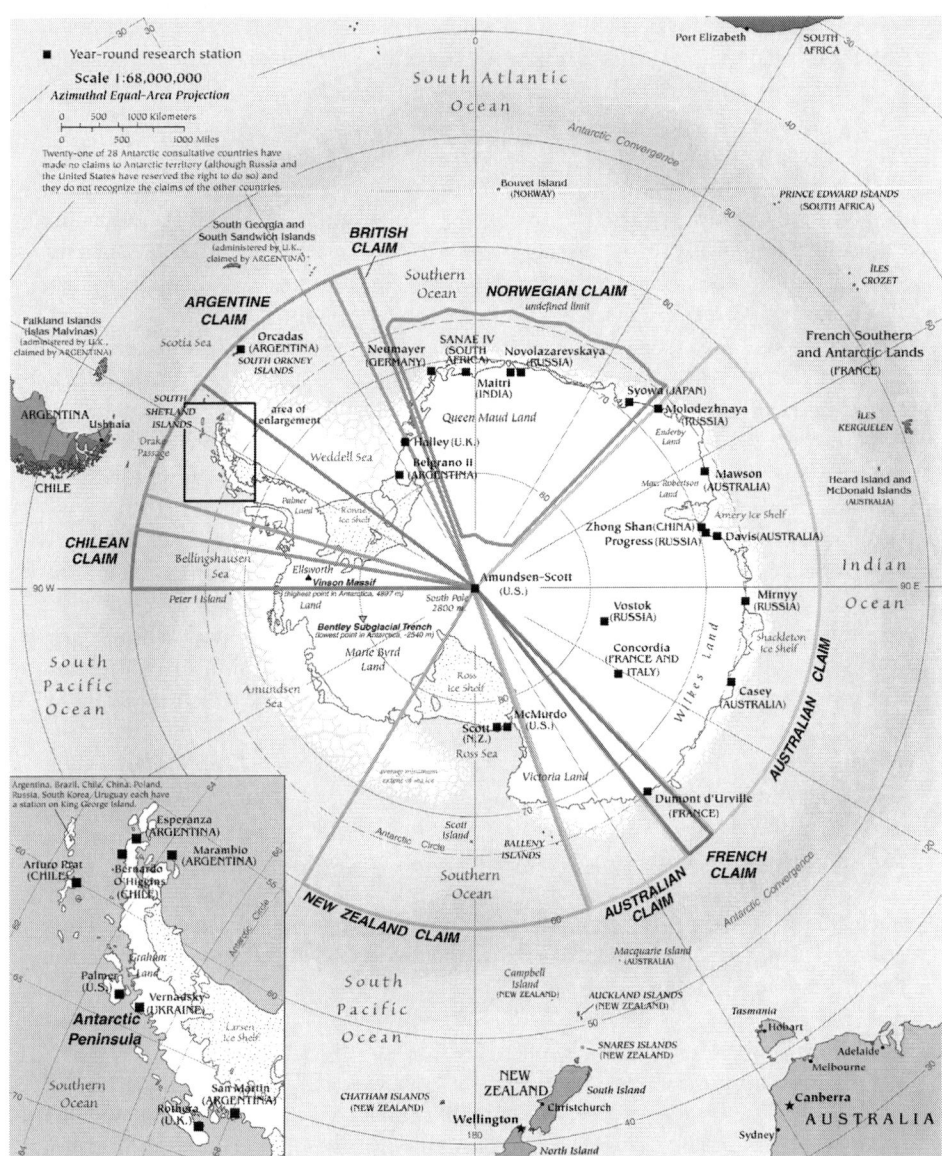

Figure 4.4 CIA, 'Map of the Political Antarctic Region', *The World Factbook 2013–14*
© Central Intelligence Agency, Washington, DC, 2013

Dependency.⁵² As can be seen from the map in Figure 4.4 of territorial claims in Antarctica, all territorial claims follow lines of longitude and converge at the south pole, which visually carves the landmass into an unevenly sliced pie.⁵³

As with other maps of Antarctica, this map of the Antarctic region does not follow the contemporary cartographic convention of placing north at the top. In this instance, north is not up and south is not down but instead, south is the centre. In the case of Antarctic cartography, rather than reading a map horizontally and vertically, a map must be read with an appreciation that all that tends towards the centre is south and all that tends away from the centre is north. Put simply, a map of Antarctica is a movement in and out of a southern centre.

An accepted international standard, the map in Figure 4.4 is produced in the USA by the CIA, and includes not only territorial claims but also the location of permanent scientific research stations. Australia's claim is in two sections separated by a French claim, and alongside the New Zealand claim. Notice, however, there is no territorial claim by the USA. Although reserving a right to claim in the future, and despite this cartographic production, the USA does not recognise the validity of any territorial claims. This makes the role of a domestic American intelligence agency authoring this international legal cartography somewhat surprising. Yet notice the various scientific research stations run by different states, scattered across the continent, including an American proliferation of scientific research stations across numerous territorial claims. In particular, notice the Amundsen-Scott South Pole Station ('the Station'), which is located at the centre of the map – the centre of these territorial claims – precisely at the point of convergence of these territorial claims tracing meridian lines towards their south pole nexus. The precise legal location of the Station then becomes an interesting question: Is the Station located in one or multiple territorial claims? What might this mean for the creation and conduct of relations between different laws?

As should be apparent, in this most southerly of locations, there is an interesting relation between territorial claims and the broader international legal architecture authored through the Antarctic Treaty system. As Victor Prescott and Gillian Triggs observe:

> Antarctica's international boundaries may be distinguished from the international boundaries of other continents in five ways. First, all the claimed boundaries coincide with meridians that meet at the south pole … Second, there are no bilateral agreements dealing with national claims to the continent. However, Australia, Britain, France, New Zealand and Norway have ensured that their adjoining claims are conterminous. Third none of the

---

52 On territorial claims in Antarctica, see, generally, Donald R. Rothwell, *The Polar Regions and the Development of International Law* (Cambridge University Press, 1996) ch 3. On Australia's claim to territory, see Chapter 4, 4.3.

53 Central Intelligence Agency of the United States of America, 'Antarctic Region Map' on *World Factbook: Antarctica* (3 May 2012), https://www.cia.gov/library/publications/the-world-factbook/geos/ay.html (*Map of Claims Figure 4.4*).

boundaries in Antarctica have [sic] been demarcated. Fourth, none of the countries that claim territory enforce [sic] any restrictions on the movements of people or goods at the limits of their territory. The issue of sovereignty was placed in abeyance by Article 4 of the Antarctic Treaty.[54]

Given the location of the Station at the nexus of multiple territorial claims, the fourth point raised by Prescott and Triggs matters. Due to a lack of enforcement of territorial claims, there are no restrictions on the movement of people in Antarctica. So people move, wandering in and out, across and around different non-demarcated territorial claims and within nationalised research stations, while carrying different laws, including common law. This uncertain territorial basis provides an opportunity to attend to some of the ways in which common law moves and places or fails to move and place in Antarctica. While the overarching legal architecture in Antarctica is constructed through international law and its mechanisms, in the absence of sovereignty and territory, how does this actually work? This is a question of the technologies of jurisdiction and there are two registers of response: the first concerns the operation of personal jurisdiction attaching to status and the second concerns the continued practical insistence of state territorial claims despite their effective legal abeyance.

First, as set out in the *Antarctic Treaty*, in the absence of sovereignty and territory, a system of personal jurisdiction based on citizenship status operates. Article 8(1) of the *Antarctic Treaty* provides that persons in Antarctica are 'subject only to the jurisdiction of the Contracting Party of which they are nationals in respect of all acts or omissions occurring while they are in Antarctica for the purpose of exercising their functions'.[55] This means that those in Antarctica, such as scientists and tourists, are effectively governed by their own state laws.[56] In an age of scientific cooperation, this means that people of different nationalities living and working at scientific research stations are governed by various domestic laws. However, not all states are signatories to the *Antarctic Treaty*. This means that certain persons (i.e. citizens of non-signatories) are therefore not governed by article 8(1) of the *Antarctic Treaty*. This raises some important questions. With a roving population of cruise ship passengers and research scientists, how does law work in Antarctica? More specifically, what is the everyday practice and movement of laws in Antarctica? Remembering Blackstone and thinking of the movements of subjects as they carry their state laws *as* movements of different forms of law,[57] can this tell us something about the movements, relations, shapes and patterns of laws in the polar South?

---

54 Victor Prescott and Gillian D. Triggs, *International Frontiers and Boundaries: Law, Politics and Geography* (Martinus Nijhoff, 2008) 383.
55 *Antarctic Treaty*, art. 8(1).
56 *Antarctic Treaty*, art. 8(1) provides for a limited form of personal jurisdiction, though its interpretation and extent of its reach has been subject to debate. See, e.g., Tim Stephens and Ben Boer, 'Enforcement and Compliance in the Australian Antarctic Territory: Legal and Policy Dilemmas', in Kriwoken, Jabour and Hemmings (eds.), *Looking South*, above, n 41, 54, 58–9.
57 See Chapter 2, 2.1; Chapter 3, 3.3.

Second, although sovereignty and territory may be in abeyance, states continue to 'maintain' their territorial claims through various activities. These include efforts to ensure the requirement of 'effective occupation' is met for the purposes of sovereign acquisition through activities such as the establishment of scientific research stations and continuation of scientific research, as well as practices such as stamps and postal services.[58] Conversely, practices indicating the failure of states to recognise their own territory may also be important to the status of their territorial claims, such as the notorious statement by the New Zealand government that New Zealanders in the 1979 plane crash at Mount Erebus in the Ross Dependency (New Zealand's territorial claim to Antarctica) were 'outside their home territory'.[59] Another activity potentially contributing to a future case for sovereign acquisition is the passing of state legislation intended to govern territory claimed in Antarctica. Even though this legislation may effectively be 'in abeyance', it is interesting to consider what role such legislation might serve. The position of Australia and New Zealand are central in this respect, both maintaining territorial claims in Antarctica.[60]

Without delving further into the activities of states in Antarctica, it is important to recognise that the ordering of laws in Antarctica is more complex than an international treaty that sidesteps sovereignty and territory in favour of a structuring of personal jurisdiction. The overarching legal architecture is provided through several treaties, yet the day-to-day operation of law in Antarctica, it could be said, is principally administrative. However, if so, the place of law in Antarctica is rendered purely administrative, meaning there is no place for law and in effect, there is a 'jurisdictional void … in some circumstances'.[61] I do not agree. To counter this conceit, and dismantle the image of a lawless void, this chapter shifts to a southerly register of techniques and practices,[62] and takes an interest in the particular form of international law that occurs in Antarctica: one without a state. For, in Antarctica, in the absence of sovereignty, territory and clearly delineated state boundaries, the operation of law is effectively stateless. As subjects carry their state laws, they interact and relate, forming patterns of law that are both intra- and international, but on a personal, rather than on a state or territorial level.

Therefore, although territorial claims are under moratorium while the treaty system continues to operate, the continued maintenance of such claims

---

58 See, e.g., Stuart Harris, 'Foreword', in Kriwoken, Jabour and Hemmings (eds.), *Looking South*, above, n 41, v-vi. In relation to the use of legislation as an act of maintaining sovereign claims, see Stephens and Boer, 'Enforcement and Compliance', above, n 56. See, generally, Sahurie, *The International Law of Antarctica*, above, n 8, 17–9. On the doctrine of discovery, see Chapter 3, 3.1.
59 Sahurie, *The International Law of Antarctica*, above, n 8, 19, quoting New Zealand Royal Commission to Inquire into the Crash on Mount Erebus, *Report of the Royal Commission to Inquire into the Crash on Mount Erebus, Antarctica of a DC10 Aircraft Operated by Air New Zealand Limited* (1981).
60 Note, however, that the US does not recognise either claim. This is not unusual, for most other treaty nations do not recognise territorial claims in Antarctica, although of those states claiming territory, some recognise territorial claims of others.
61 *Findings*, above, n 1, 43.
62 See the introduction to this chapter at above, n 3.

by Australia and New Zealand, for example, impacts the everyday workings and movements of laws in Antarctica. This provides an opportunity taken up in this chapter to pay attention to the techniques and practices of common law in the polar South. In other words, in the absence of sovereignty and territory, Antarctica provides an opportunity to pay attention to jurisdiction, including its technologies. However, it is first necessary to introduce one final form of movement. As well as Antarctica's moving histories and laws, there is also the challenge of moving architecture and ice.

Moving ice; moving architecture

Ice moves. In Antarctica, there are three major forms to these icy movements: seasonal, circumnavigational and sedimentary. First, and most obviously, each winter Antarctica effectively doubles in size as the surrounding oceans and seas slowly freeze and Antarctica stretches and expands beyond, before returning through a geographical retreat with the warmer change in seasons to the comfort of a more obvious land. The second form of movement is circumnavigational. With the earth spinning as it does, it slowly shifts ice away from the geographic south pole towards the Weddell Sea. On the CIA map of Antarctica, this is a movement spinning outwards from the south pole towards the coast of the Argentinian claim. Yet this movement evolves at different paces, since ice moves more rapidly near the coast. Annually, and in relation to the first movement of seasons, ice may move up to two kilometres near the edge of Antarctica, while movements at the south pole are much less, approximately 10 metres per year plus an additional anisotropic stretch of about 15 centimetres a year, all towards the Weddell Sea.[63] With Antarctica effectively doubling in size each winter as the ice freezes, ice moves both faster and further at the edges than near the centre of Antarctica. The third form of movement is a movement in the depth of the ice. With each seasonal accumulation of snow, layer upon layer, compacting on the surface, ice slowly builds, moving upwards, engulfing that which may have been before. Slowly buried, this 'sinking' is most graphically so in the architectural remnants of both scientific and exploration remains, as is apparent in the two photographs by Connie Samaras that opened this chapter.[64] The first is a photograph of the decommissioned Dome while the second is a photograph of the earlier 1950s' station, buried. Forming part of her series, *V.A.L.I.S. (vast active living intelligence system)* (2005),[65] alongside the play on transcendence and technology through its

---

63 A material, such as ice, is anisotropic if its response differs according to the direction of the loading, such as the 'weight' of light.
64 Connie Samaras, 'Dome and Tunnels', *V.A.L.I.S. (vast active living intelligence system)* (2005–2007) (archival inkjet print from film, 60 x 48", edition of 5) above, at page 186 (Figure 4.1); Connie Samaras, 'Buried Fifties Station', *V.A.L.I.S. (vast active living intelligence system)* (2005–2007) (archival inkjet print from film, 40 x 32", edition of 5) above, at page 187 (Figure 4.2).
65 Connie Samaras, *V.A.L.I.S. (vast active living intelligence system')* (2005) on *Connie Samaras* (2011), http://www.conniesamaras.com/VALIS.html

Philip K. Dick's reference, Samaras uses the technique of 'deadpan' framing to hold onto material fragments of place in the polar South, challenging the romanticism of the polar sublime that is so attentive yet inattentive to place. Attending to the relation between architecture and movements in the ice, Samaras captures in these photographs a momentary hold of movement; slow movement. In a sense, what Samaras also captures is a rhythm of the polar South; the slow movements of ice constantly remaking place in the polar South.[66]

With these three interlacing forms of movements in the ice in Antarctica – seasonal, circumnavigational and sedimentary – what this means is everything in or on 'the Ice' also moves, including, for example, the bodies of Scott and members of his party who died on their return from the geographic south pole in 1912: 'I am just going outside. I may be some time.'[67] Buried in ice, resting at camp with Oates beyond, their bodies remain held in a form of stasis, unable to decompose. Yet, the bodies of Scott and his men slowly move with the movements of the ice, drifting away from the south pole and sinking deeper below the surface. In time, these movements will place the dead in a segment of ice no longer supported by land and their bodies will be released into the water beneath the ice. From the original burial site, frozen in camp, scientists have tracked the movement of these dead and made projections about when and where they will be released from the ice and returned to the sea:[68]

> These data suggest that the last camp may reach the position of the current ice front in around the year 2250; some 340 years after the journey began. It will then be about 100 metres deep in the ice shelf, and well below sea level. These calculations are subject to several uncertainties. The largest of these, when the last camp might reach the Ross Sea, involves the calving of the ice front, which means that it is extremely unlikely that the bodies will emerge from a submerged part of the ice shelf, but instead, will be carried off within an iceberg when they get close enough to the ice front. Their final resting place will then be dependent on the ocean currents, the size of the iceberg, how it melts and breaks, whether the piece that holds the bodies ever capsizes, and other imponderables. In any event, it seems certain that the bodies of Scott, Wilson and Bowers, followed in due course by those of Oates and Evans, will ultimately be committed to the deep.[69]

With the dead of the 'last camp'[70] moving in an uncertain legal place with an overarching legal architecture subject to different territorial claims, this raises the

---

66 Cf. Cassano, 'Southern Thought', above, n 3, 2.
67 As Captain Lawrence Oates spoke, 'I am just going outside. I may be some time', Scott, *Scott's Last Expedition*, above, n 36.
68 See Olav Orheim, 'The Present Location of the Tent that Roald Amundsen Left Behind at the South Pole in December 1911' (2011) 47(3) *Polar Record* 268; R.K. Headland, 'Captain Scott's Last Camp, Ross Ice Shelf' (2010) 47(3) *Polar Record* 270.
69 Ibid, 270.
70 Ibid.

question of the jurisdiction of the dead. Particularly, in their icy movements, have these particular dead crossed or they will cross different territorial claims, different legal hosts?

Something similar has already occurred. Sir Vivian Fuchs was an English explorer and leader of the Commonwealth Trans-Antarctic expedition, completing the first overland crossing of Antarctica in 1958. The trek took 99 days and started at the Weddell Sea, crossing the south pole and ending at the Ross Sea at Scott Base. In the tradition of travel journals, once finished, Fuchs and Edmund Hillary spent eight weeks writing a book of the expedition to recuperate costs (in this case, successfully).[71] In 1991 a large iceberg calved, separating from Antarctica, a common occurrence. Less commonly, this particular iceberg had on its surface an entire former base used by Fuchs in his since famous overland expedition.[72] A British remnant, drifting.

The detachment of Fuchs' base on a calving iceberg demonstrates illustrates the continuous movements of ice, which moves slower near the centre and faster near the edges of Antarctica.[73] The obvious question to be asked is: Who has jurisdiction over the iceberg containing the architectural memorabilia of Fuchs' expedition? Would it be Britain's or whoever's territory the iceberg was last in before it broke from 'the Ice', or whoever's marine territory it floats through? Or is this the common heritage of mankind? An earlier example was captured by the American Navy Icebreaker *USS Edisto* on 24 February 1963 in the Ross Sea, when members of the crew noticed, in the midst of a tabular iceberg roughly 150 by 450 metres, the remains of part of a research station. Known as the 'Little America Station', it had been built by Admiral Richard E. Byrd, in five iterations, between 1929 and 1959 and was found floating approximately 300 miles from its original site in the Bay of Whales on the Ross Ice shelf. According to reports: 'The break had bisected the Station, exposing the interiors of two stations. Cans and equipment placed neatly on shelves were clearly visible. Five telephone poles supported by guy wires with antenna-type fittings and two bamboo marker poles were still in place.'[74] A helicopter from the ship landed on the iceberg, but the station was covered with 75 metres of snow, which meant no one was able to enter the camp.

Both Fuchs' cabin and the floating remnants of the Little America Station illustrate the difficulties of locating law in Antarctica in the shadows of metanarratives of sovereign territory and territorial jurisdiction, especially where the land is ice and constantly moves. Not surprisingly, then, in the midst of all this movement, there is also a desire for stability:

---

71 Vivian Fuchs and Edmund Hillary, *The Crossing of Antarctica: The Commonwealth Trans-Antarctic Expedition, 1955–58* (Cassell, 1958).
72 Arthur Watts, *International Law and the Antarctic Treaty System* (Cambridge Grotius Publications limited, 1992) 112.
73 Ibid.
74 For a news report, including some stunning photographs, see 'Little America Station Sighted at Sea', *Bulletin of the U.S. Antarctic Programs Officer* (Volume 4, Number 7), April 1963 19–20. See also http://www.southpolestation.com/trivia/igy1/la3.html.

No one clears things away on Antarctica, so Scott's hut has been standing since his disastrous exhibition of 1912 and has now, by default, become a piece of English heritage.[75]

But, as with Fuchs, what would it mean if and when this piece of English heritage breaks away from 'the Ice' in the form of an iceberg? Who would have jurisdictional authority to speak for this heritage? This is the question of jurisdiction that animates this chapter.

In contrast to the iconic monuments of the early explorers that are protected and placed in stasis, like the versions of the Little America Station, Antarctica's architectural structures of science are upgraded, updated and subject to successive renovations. Although at times remnants of past buildings are also kept, this is perhaps less a part of a nation's heritage and more a heritage of 'global' science. With a large number of scientific research stations, as seen in the earlier CIA map, one of these architectural structures of science is located at the south pole. In 2000 this is where Rodney Marks died.

The South Pole Station

The Amundsen-Scott South Pole Station is a US research station that consists of several disparate and isolated buildings located near the geographic south pole in Antarctica. At an altitude of 2900 metres, the Station is located within a few hundred metres of the south pole.[76] Since it was first constructed in 1956, the Station has been rebuilt several times. The original building lasted until 1975, when it was replaced by the Dome (1975–2003) and, since 2003, the Elevation Station is the main building at the Station. Figure 4.5 is an image of the entrance to the Dome in 2007, after it was decommissioned, but before it was dismantled.[77] What is noticeable in Figure 4.5 is the Dome appears to be indented, sitting low, having sunk in the ice. Although what has actually occurred is a slow build-up of ice over the years, slowly rising around the Dome, necessitating the constant removal of ice to keep the entrance open until it was replaced in 2003 and finally removed in 2010.[78]

Although Station buildings have changed since the original Station in 1956 (now buried), the Station consists of a scattering of buildings separated by various

---

75 Shepheard, *The Cultivated Wilderness*, above, n 8, 59.
76 See, e.g., Michael C.B. Ashley et al., 'Near-Infrared Sky Brightness Monitor for the South Pole' (1995) 2552 *Society of Photo-Optical Instrumentation Engineers* 33, 33.
77 Special thanks are owed to Rachel Shephard and David Rootes of Antarctic Logistics & Expeditions (www.adventure-network.com) for providing me with, and other images of the south pole displayed in this chapter.
78 See also Samaras, *Dome and Tunnels*, above, n 64; Samaras, *Buried Fifties Station*, above, n 64; Center for Astrophysical Research in Antarctica and Greg Griffin, 'A Panoramic View Just as You Get off the Plane', in *Virtual Tour – South Pole* (2 May 2000), http://astro.uchicago.edu/cara/vtour/pole/arrival_pan_small.jpg.

Figure 4.5 B&C Alexander, 'The Main Entrance to the Geodesic Dome' (2006)
Built in 1975, the Dome gradually became buried by ice and was replaced by a new elevated station in 2008

© B&C Alexander/Antarctic Logistics & Expeditions

distances, up to several kilometres apart. In 2000 the Dome was the main building. A silver geodesic dome, quite visually distinctive, and also noticeable in Figure 4.6, the Dome included the mess and staff living quarters.[79] The aerial photograph of the Station in Figure 4.6 was taken by CARA, University of Chicago. Apart from the Dark sector, which falls outside this image, this aerial photograph shows most of the buildings that constituted the Station in 2000. Most importantly, it clearly illustrates how the Station consists of several buildings located at some distance from each other.

Reading Figure 4.6 from top to bottom, notice the following three details. First, located near the top left corner, just below the Dome (which looks like a golf ball) are the Archways, which is the straight line just below but tangential to the Dome. The Archways include Biomed, a gymnasium and the carpenter shop, and it is also possible to detect the sunken entrance. Second, directly below

---

79 Figure 4.6 is available online, including: U.S. National Oceanic and Atmospheric Administration, 'Aerial View of the South Pole Station' (1983), (Figure 4.6). https://commons.wikimedia.org/wiki/File:Pole-from-air.jpg#filelinks. See also Center for Astrophysical Research in Antarctica, 'Aerial View of the South Pole Station', in *Virtual Tour – South Pole* (1983), http://astro.uchicago.edu/cara/vtour/pole/pole-from-air.jpg.

Figure 4.6 'Aerial View of the South Pole Station' (1983)

the Archways and the entrance to the Dome, approximately half-way down the image, is the ceremonial south pole. Locate two rectangles near the left-hand border, then look for a small marking directly to the right. On close inspection, notice a small semicircle of flags. These flags surround the ceremonial south pole (see Figure 4.7). Third, in the bottom left corner, notice some text with a 'warning' triangle, which marks the true geographic south pole as at 1 January 1985.

As shown in Figure 4.6, there is more than one south pole. Depending how you count, there are at least five, if not seven, south poles.[80] Two south poles are of particular interest here. The first is the geographic south pole, which is the 'actual' south pole where the earth's axis of rotation intersects with its surface at the fixed position of 90° S and the lines of longitude converge. This is a point

80 The south poles include the geographic South Pole (90°S), ceremonial south pole (photo opportunity), South Magnetic Pole (magnetic field at right angles to surface of earth located north of the Antarctic circle in the Southern Ocean some 2825 kilometres from the geographic south pole), South Geomagnetic Pole (mathematical abstraction where the magnetic pole would be if it worked like a bar magnet), pole of inaccessibility (furthest point from the Antarctic coast, approximately 870 kilometres from the geographic south pole and marked by a bust of Lenin), the south of rotation (the point the earth actually spins around located within 20 meters of the geographic south pole and constantly rotating around the geographic pole over 435 days, with the geographic pole being the average of the rotational pole), the South Celestial Pole (a line between poles to the sky; cf: North Star) and, albeit with some generosity, the south pole of Cold (the place where the lowest temperature on earth has been recorded which is currently the Russian Vostok research base).

Jurisdiction of the dead   183

Figure 4.7 Ben Cooper, 'The Ceremonial South Pole' (2007)
© Ben Cooper/Antarctic Logistics & Expeditions

established annually using Geological Survey Doppler positioning techniques, and marked by a silver pole with a medallion atop. The second is the ceremonial south pole, which is more audacious; a metallic chromium globe on a plinth surrounded by 12 flags of the original signatories to the *Antarctic Treaty*. Located close to the Station, currently 100 metres or so from the geographic south pole, the ceremonial pole is a photographic opportunity placed within walking distance of the Station.

Taken in 2007, Figure 4.7 is a relatively recent photograph of the sign, both poles (one obvious, the other hidden behind the sign, just seen peaking out below the US flag) surrounded by flags. A perfect photo opportunity. Yet the white backdrop, which in all probability aligns more readily with preconceived notions of what the south pole looks like, actually belies the proximity of the multiple south poles to the buildings that make up the Amundsen-Scott South Pole Station. Turning our sight in the other direction, and also taken in 2007 is another aspect of the south poles, captured in Figure 4.8, of the current Elevated Station, which was opened in 2003. Figure 4.8, the ceremonial south pole is the red and white striped barber's pole in the centre, surrounded by flags of the original signatories to the *Antarctic Treaty*, with the US flag especially prominent. In the (very close)background is no longer the white icy vistas of Figure 4.7 but rather the new elevated main Station that replaced the Dome. Despite the impossibility of judging distance from such a photograph, the main building of the Station

184 Performing jurisprudence

Figure 4.8 'Amundsen-Scott South Pole Station' (2007)

is located surprisingly quite close to both the ceremonial south pole (shown in Figure 4.8) and the geographic south pole, which is located where Figure 4.8 is taken from.[81]

Not only is there more than one south pole, but the *south pole moves*. To counteract movements in the ice, the geographic south pole is relocated on 1 January each year. Each year a new geographic pole is created with a new medallion marker and a ceremony performed as it is placed in its temporarily correct location.[82]

---

81 Amundsen-Scott South Pole Station in August 2007, available at Wikimedia commons, https://commons.wikimedia. org/wiki/File:Amundsen-scott-south_pole_station_2007.jpg. See also National Science Foundation, 'NSF Dedicates New South Pole Station' (Press Release, 15 January 2008), http://www.nsf.gov/news/news_images.jsp?cntn_id= 110961&org=NSF; J. Dana Hrubes, 'Some Panoramas' (March 2005, South Pole and North Pole, photograph) on *Polar Winter* (2005), http://www.polarwinter.com/2005/mar-05-pics/panorama-3-23-05-5s-opt.jpg.
82 See, e.g., Center for Astrophysical Research in Antarctica, 'Moving the South Pole' (26 December 1993), http://astro.uchicago.edu/cara/outreach/resources/other/movepole.html; William J. Spindler, 'The 2011 Pole Marker', in *Amundsen-Scott South Pole Station* (2011), http://www.southpolestation.com/trivia/2010marker.html.

Figure 4.9 Devon McDiarmid, 'South Pole ceremony' (1 January 2015)
Station personnel pass the US flag, from its drifted location to the newly surveyed location beside the 90° South marker
© Devon McDiarmid/Antarctic Logistics & Expedition

Figure 4.9 shows a recent south pole ceremony where the flag, and then new marker were passed from hand to hand as it moved towards to its new location, some 10 metres from the previous marker.[83] Although it is not possible to see in this particular photograph, markers from previous geographic south poles are left in the ice for several years, receding into the distance, before eventually being taken into storage. This means that not only is there a ceremonial south pole and a geographic south pole, but there are also markers of former geographic south poles providing a visual assurance of the annual movements of the ice. Unlike the geographic south pole, the ceremonial south pole is allowed to drift, and occasionally moved to keep it within walking distance of the Station.

The Station also moves

Built as it is on a glacier that moves 10 metres a year towards the Weddell Sea and currently located approximately 100 metres from the geographic south pole,

---

83 See also Peter Rejcek, 'A Good Point: South Pole Geographic Marker Changes with the Times', in *The Antarctic Sun* (1 January 2010), http://antarcticsun.usap.gov/features/contenthandler.cfm?id=1998; Alex Kiefer, 'South Pole Marker', in *TrekEarth* (2005), http://www.trekearth.com/gallery/photo284509.htm. For an art installation interpreting these movements, see Xavier Cortada, 'The Markers' (South Pole, 2007).

the Station drifts approximately 10 metres each year towards the geographic south pole, heading slowly towards the Weddell Sea. Among all these different forms of movement, what is the place of law and the location of territorial claims? As displayed earlier in the Map of Claims (Figure 4.4), which shows Antarctica sliced into a jurisdictional 'pie', what is particularly interesting about the Station, with its multiple buildings located several kilometres apart is that, as with the rest of Antarctica, the Station also moves. Visualise the Map of Claims (Figure 4.4) super-imposed on Figure 4.4, which was the aerial photograph showing the various buildings that make up the South Pole Station.[84] With Antarctica's jurisdictional centre radiating out from the geographical south pole, which is located amongst the Station buildings and with buildings scattered across a large area, in different directions, a jurisdictional intrigue arises. While the specific details are not entirely clear and the precise location of territories are not definitively demarcated, *different buildings at the Station appear to be located within different territorial claims*. This includes the likely location of the Dome in Australian claimed territory, at least part of the main Station building in New Zealand claimed territory and the ceremonial pole in the territory claimed by the United Kingdom, Chile or Argentina.

Proving to be an increasingly popular location with both scientists and tourists, for more effective coordination of activities in the area, the Amundsen-Scott South Pole Station was formally adopted as Antarctic Specially Managed Area ('ASMA') No 5 by Measure 2 at the 30th Antarctic Treaty Consultative Meeting in 2007 in Delhi.[85] This includes an interesting response to the 'problem' of movement I have raised, that is, the problem of the relationship between moving between the south poles and the apparent territorial jurisdictions 'claimed' by various states:

> Due to the movement of the ice sheet in the geographic location of the ASMA will move approximately 10 m per year; the area is centered on the elevated South Pole Station, and all sectors are relative to this location. Treaty parties may consider shifting the Area if it becomes appropriate in the future.[86]

---

84 For a visual representation of this jurisdictional issue, see an online map produced by the United States Antarctic programme which has the unauthorised addition of territorial claims superimposed on the map; Jan S. Krogh, 'The Land Borders of Antarctica – The South Pole', in *Jan S Krogh's GeoSite* (22 November 2010), http://geosite.jankrogh.com/borders/ant/index.htm.

85 Thirtieth Antarctic Treaty Consultative Meeting – Tenth Committee on Environmental Protection Meeting, ATCM XXX (New Delhi, 30 April 2007–11 May 2007). http://www.ats.aq/devAS/ats_meetings_meeting.aspx?lang=e. Each year the USA reports to the Antarctic Treaty Consultative Meeting. For example, the USA reported to the XXXIV Antarctic Treaty Consultative Meeting in Buenos Aires: United States of America, 'Amundsen-Scott South Pole Station, South Pole Antarctic Specially Managed Area (ASMA No 5) 2011 Management Report' (Report presented at the XXXIV Antarctic Consultative Meeting, ATCM XXXIV, Buenos Aires, 20 June–1 July 2011).

86 United States Antarctic programme, *Management Plan for Antarctic Specially Managed Area No 5: Amundsen-Scott South Pole Station, South Pole* (Measure 2, Annex A), s 6(i).

Jurisdiction of the dead 187

In a complete detachment of land and territory, the institutional and international response to the 'problem' of movement is to shift the protected area; to move territory so that it catches up with movements of the icy land. This has not yet occurred.[87]

With everything moving, including south poles and buildings, in time, it is possible that Station buildings may move between different territorial claims, potentially ending up in one singular claim as the geographic south pole is annually relocated and the Station slowly drifts towards, then away from the south pole, heading to the Weddell Sea. This raises some intriguing questions about the place of law in the polar South, especially where the relation between land and territory is constantly in flux.

With movements in the ice, and movements of architecture, where multiple forms of law also move, the question of the place of law – of how laws move and come to be in place – as well as the creation and conduct of lawful relations as a way of caring for place, requires some attendance. Therefore, having introduced some of the movements of history, law and architecture as context, the next part of this chapter builds on this context by providing a narrative of the death of a scientist at the south pole. For a minor jurisprudence of movement, the rest of this chapter practises an attention to lawful place.

4.2 A death at the south pole

With movements in the polar South – movements in histories, laws, architecture and, of course, ice – it is difficult to place the dead in this apparent 'jurisdictional void' of a non-place where land and territory do not rest together well.[88] Yet, the dead are located in the polar South, and the dead require care. While this care may come in different forms, whether through material or memorial practice or different forms of law and lawful practices, it is for the jurist taking up and holding office to attend to and account for movement and in doing so, take seriously the responsibility to care for the dead. Other offices also carry responsibilities, including the coroner, which continues to have quite particular jurisdictional responsibilities to the dead despite its relatively low-level judicial positioning. To this end, this part narrates the death, burial and reburial of Rodney Marks, which is a narrative constructed primarily through the lens of the institution investigating the cause of his death: the office of the coroner.

As with the last chapter, where the narrative of a burial party was created using certain historical legal materials not for the purpose of developing an historiography but to develop a vignette of jurisprudential significance, this chapter

---

87 The most recent update to the maps constituting the 2007 ASMA Management Plan were made in 2011; see, e.g., the website providing information on management measures, 'Antarctica Specially Managed Area No 5: Amundsen-Scott South Pole Station, South Pole, e.g. http://www.southpole.aq/maps/.
88 *Findings*, above, n 1, 43. On non-places, see Marc Augé, *Non-Places: Introduction to an Anthropology of Supermodernity* (Verso, 2008).

works with select contemporary legal materials for the purposes of exploring the jurisprudential significance of common law's movements in relation to the dead in the polar South. These materials arise from a coronial inquest. Engaging with coronial materials in this manner is quite distinct from a doctrinal analysis or developing a narrative that aims to establish the 'truth' of a series of events. This is especially so given, in the coronial materials relating to the death of Rodney Marks, there is an important absence of information, making the task of truth-seeking impossible in any event.

Contemporary coroners, as a matter of jurisdiction, are tasked with determining the cause of death. In this particular case, the coronial investigation skipped over a number of events that occurred after his death, most noticeably so in terms of the six-month period between Rodney Marks' death at the south pole and the coronial investigation in New Zealand. To track events occurring during this six-month period, events not of interest to a coroner but certainly of interest here, coronial documents are read in conjunction with a medley of often unverifiable materials, including media reports, scientist's travel diaries, blogs and memorial websites.

To be clear, the following narrative of the death of Rodney Marks is incomplete, and necessarily so. First and foremost, the primary coronial materials used in this chapter come with significant limits. Arising from the coronial investigation into the death of Rodney Marks conducted by the Christchurch coroner in New Zealand, the primary materials are the *Findings of the Coroner* ('*Findings*'),[89] and parts of the coronial file made available for this book ('*Coronial File*'), such as witness depositions, reports, maps and photographs.[90] Most significantly, these primary materials are restricted by coronial orders made under the now-repealed (yet still applicable in these circumstances) s 25(2)(b) of the *Coroners Act 1988 (NZ)*, prohibiting publication of certain evidence provided at the inquest.[91] Further, my access to the *Coronial File* was restricted (quite properly so) for reasons of personal privacy and to ensure international relations were not prejudiced. As a result, the version

---

89 *Findings*, above, n 1. The *Findings* are in most respects a contemporary court report, and consist of the formal findings, which is a very short summary conclusion, a series of recommendations to different governmental authorities and the Coroner's reasons for decision. Of course, there are differences, most noticeably that a coronial report does not carry the same judicial weight as other court decisions, as it is often placed in an administrative or quasi-judicial role in court hierarchies, and hence its contribution to *stare decisis* is limited. Further, the coronial method is not the usual common law adversarial standard, but rather inquisitorial, resulting in findings and recommendations that are advisory and non-binding. Finally, while a public document, they are not readily available, and these *Findings* were obtained on request.

90 The Coroner's File in relation to the *Findings of the Coroner in the Matter of an Inquest into the Death of Rodney David Marks Who Died at South Pole Station, Antarctica* (Unreported, Coroner's Court, Christchurch, New Zealand, Coroner Richard McElrea, 16 September 2008) (*Coronial File*). Documents in the *Coronial File* are cited by reference to the specific document title and also, where available, the exhibit number. Materials in the *Coronial File* include reports, depositions, questionnaires, photographs and other miscellaneous documents.

91 In addition to these legislative restrictions, there are also additional and more specific restrictions prohibiting the publication of certain information from the *Findings*, ibid.

of the *Coronial File* relied on in this chapter is incomplete, and includes significant gaps, including a large number of withheld documents, while other documents were only partially released, subject to either substantial or minor redactions.[92] In this respect, I use these coronial materials in a manner that complies with all orders and prohibitions, but in addition, I have also chosen to further anonymise all witnesses. By using inquest documents as the material base of this chapter, important silences result from this institutional focus. So, while it is true that documents such as institutional communications between Australia, the USA and New Zealand, and a report on this unexpected death at the south pole produced by the United States Antarctic programme, would certainly thicken the following narrative and redescription, the fact of their absence remains jurisprudentially productive.

What follows is not a complete chronology and does not claim historical accuracy, but is a narrative developed through a reading of the *Findings* and an incomplete *Coronial File*, coupled with an engagement with scientists' travel diaries where helpful. To this end, the limits of materials and incompleteness of this narrative serves as an integral aspect of this chapter, particularly by suggesting the role and limitation of official institutions in the jurisdictional movements and places of common law in Antarctica but also, importantly, in its silent gesture towards jurisdiction as a technique of lawful communication.

A narrative

Rodney Marks was an Australian astrophysicist working at the Amundsen-Scott South Pole Station in 2000.[93] During the astral winter, which includes a six-month period of complete darkness between the sun setting on the March equinox and it rising again on the September equinox,[94] the Station continues to operate and a smaller crew remain for what is known as the 'winter-over'. During this period, which is approximately March to November each year, the Station is effectively closed with planes unable to fly in or fly out. Staff members remaining for the winter-over are physically isolated for eight months or so, and in 2000, approximately 100 staff remained for the winter.[95] Although isolated physically, winter staff remain in contact with persons outside the Station by various means of communication, including regular but (at least in the year 2000) only intermittent

---

92 These included 'Report on Unexpected Death at South Pole Station: United States Antarctic Program', *Coronial File*, above, n 90, exhibits 12–13; 'E-Mail Exchanges NZ Police USA Govt Officials', *Coronial File*, above, n 90, exhibits 17–25; 'Questionnaire Correspondence with Officials in the USA', *Coronial File*, above, n 90, exhibits 26–31; 'Email Exchanges with USA Government Officials – NZ Police Exhibit', *Coronial File*, above, n 90, exhibits 33–35 and 'NZ Police Exchanges with American Representative NSF', *Coronial File*, above, n 90, exhibits 36–7.
93 *Findings*, above, n 1, 3, 45.
94 Although less extreme in other parts of Antarctica, at the south pole the sun rises and sets only once a year on the September and March equinox, although atmospheric refractions mean the sun is above the horizon for four days at each equinox, with the light or darkness slowly fading over several weeks.
95 *Findings*, above, n 1, 3, 45. A

internet and satellite transmissions.⁹⁶ On 12 May 2000, during the astral winter, Rodney Marks died suddenly.⁹⁷ At the time, his cause of death was unknown,⁹⁸ and it was a further six months until an autopsy determined he had died from methanol poisoning.⁹⁹ Yet the question of how Marks came to ingest methanol has never been conclusively determined.¹⁰⁰

Due to a lack of evidence as to how or why Marks came to ingest methanol, the question of whether Marks died as a result of an accident, suicide or murder remains unresolved. The formal *Findings of the Coroner* in full, were:

> Rodney David Marks, an Australian National temporarily residing at Amundsen-Scott South Pole Station, Antarctica, Astrophysicist died on 12 May 2000 at Amundsen-Scott South Pole Station as a result of acute methanol poisoning (152 mg/100ml in blood, femoral), the methanol overdose being undiagnosed and probably occurring one to two days earlier, he being either unaware of the overdose or not understanding the possible complications of it, the medical assistance to him being compromised by an Echtachem blood analyzer being inoperable, death being unintended.¹⁰¹

In these complete, yet brief, formal *Findings* the Coroner concluded 'death being unintended'.¹⁰² However, in the reasons for decision, also contained in the *Findings*, the Coroner elaborated this conclusion, indicating a clear preference for accidental death rather than suicide or death by someone else's intent.¹⁰³ Ultimately, however, the case remains uncertain and rumours that this was 'first murder in Antarctica' continue to circulate.¹⁰⁴

Before his death, Rodney Marks was an astrophysicist whose research expertise related directly to the technology used at the Station. Having graduated with first class honours from the University of Melbourne,¹⁰⁵ his doctoral thesis in astrophysics from the University of New South Wales was completed in 1998, one year prior to heading to Antarctica in November 1999.¹⁰⁶ Having previously worked at the Station for the summer of November 1994 to February 1995, and again

---

96 Ibid, 33.
97 Ibid, 3, 23–30, 45.
98 Ibid, 3, 10.
99 Ibid, 11–15.
100 Ibid, 31–40, 45.
101 Ibid, 45.
102 Ibid.
103 Ibid.
104 Ibid.
105 Office of Legislative and Public Affairs, 'NSF Press Release: Antarctic Researcher Dies' (12 May 2000) National Science Foundation, http://www.nsf.gov/od/lpa/news/press/00/pr0032.htm.
106 *Findings*, above, n 1, 3; Rodney David Marks, *Antarctic Site Testing – Microthermal Measurements of Surface-Layer Seeing at the South Pole* (PhD thesis, University of New South Wales, 1998).

for the summer and 'winter-over' of November 1997 to November 1998, this was Marks' third trip to Antarctica.[107]

For the summer and winter-over of 1999 to 2000, Rodney Marks worked in the Martin A. Pomerantz Observatory, a building known as 'MAPO'.[108] Located several kilometres from the Dome in the Dark sector, an area protected from minimal light and electromagnetic interference for scientific research, this was a separate building operating as a scientific venue for astrophysical research and observation.[109] About eight scientists worked at MAPO during the winter-over of 2000 and, as it was a decent walk, in harsh conditions, would often stay for several days at a time rather than return to their sleeping quarters in the Dome.[110] According to one coronial witness' deposition:

> Rodney worked at 'MAPO'. It was an observatory – it was all science. There was about 8 people working there. It is about a kilometre from the dome. ... Often beakers (scientists) would stay there for 4 or 5 days at MAPO ... I didn't go out there after I fell, it was too far to walk.[111]

Marks had previously worked on the 'South Pole Infrared Explorer', which was an 'infrared telescope' known as Spirex.[112] While not entirely clear, on his second trip to Antarctica, Marks was most likely a university employee. It seems Marks was employed as a postdoctoral research fellow at Harvard-Smithsonian Centre for Astrophysics connected to the Smithsonian Astrophysical Observatory (Smithsonian Institute and Harvard University). In particular, it seems he was working as their 'winter-over scientist' on AST/RO ('Antarctic Submillimetre Telescope and Remote Observatory') as part of a larger scientific research grant through – or in collaboration with – the Center for Astrophysical Research in Antarctica ('CARA') at the University of Chicago.[113] With complex layerings of legal and institutional responsibilities at the Station, as an employee of a university (whether Australian or American), Marks was certainly not an employee of one of the public or private US organisations responsible for running the Station.[114]

---

107 *Findings*, above, n 1, 3; 'Statement of REH' *Coronial File*, above, n 90. The fact that Marks had previously spent a winter-over in Antarctica was relevant to counter the suggestion that 'over-winter syndrome' implied that the cause of death was suicide. As Paul Shepheard writes: 'It's a sort of lethargic claustrophobia similar to suicidal despair.' Shepheard, *The Cultivated Wilderness*, above, n 8, 57–8.
108 *Findings*, above, n 1.
109 See Ashley et al., 'Near-Infrared Sky', above, n 76, 35.
110 'Deposition of RST', *Coronial File*, above, n 90.
111 Ibid.
112 *Findings*, above, n 1, 17.
113 Ibid, 16–7; cf: Office of Legislative and Public Affairs, above, n 105; cf: a message from the National Science Foundation Manager Bill Coughran, 'Rodney Marks', in William J. Spindler, *Amundsen-Scott South Pole Station* (13 May 2000), http://www.southpolestation.com/trivia/blueflash/billc.html.
114 Ibid; 'Deposition of WJS', *Coronial File*, above, n 90.

Before his fatal illness, Marks had been at the Station for nearly six months without any health issues, and apart from an initial health check, had only seen the Station doctor on one other occasion. This was a week or so earlier, on 2 May 2000, when he complained of shortness of breath, which is a fairly common health complaint at the Station due to the extremely high altitude in Antarctica (often two to three kilometres above sea level) and more specifically, the Station (the south pole's elevation is roughly 2835 metres (9301 feet)). Marks' next visit to the Station doctor was 10 days later, on 12 May 2000, when Marks' girlfriend called to report that Marks had 'thrown up blood' and was told to come into the clinic immediately.[115] Symptoms continued to develop over the day. Although central to the coronial inquest, the details of Marks' physical deterioration leading up to his death are not relevant to this chapter and need not be recounted.[116] What is relevant, however, is that at the time of Marks' illness and death, the cause of death was unknown to all at the Station. As the Coroner explained in the *Findings*:

> At the hearing (day 1) [the Station doctor] was asked whether, at the time of the death, he had any theories as to why Dr Marks had died. ... He said there was no one medical condition that explained what happened to him that day. 'Every event or thing I can think of leaves a gap or loophole.'[117]

The standard of medical care provided by the Station doctor to Rodney Marks was criticised in the *Findings*.[118] While it was not suggested this amounted to anything more intentional or sinister than professional oversight or possibly incompetence, criticism directed towards the standard of medical care related particularly to the failure of the Station doctor to maintain certain medical equipment.[119] Specifically, it was significant that a particular piece of medical equipment, called an Echtachem analyser, had been out of action for a lengthy period during the winter-over, including the days of Marks' illness and death.[120] If functioning, this Echtachem machine would normally have been used to conduct certain tests. Further, had this machine been used, the *Findings* suggested the cause of Marks' illness was quite possibly identifiable prior to his death and, depending on the timing of the identification, potentially treatable.[121] Although the reason this machine was out of action was in dispute and highly contentious, later tests on the machine determined the machine had actually been operational at the time, but had not worked due to the failure of the Station doctor to replace a lithium battery, a battery that was in stock at the Station.[122]

115 *Findings*, above, n 1, 24.
116 Ibid, 24–30.
117 Ibid, 10.
118 Ibid, 33–45.
119 Ibid.
120 Ibid.
121 Ibid.
122 Ibid.

Rodney Marks died in a building known as 'Biomed', which was the medical facility at the Station. Located in the Archways and linked to the Dome via tunnels was a separate building. As the Station doctor explained: 'At the base I lived at Biomed. It is an 1100 square foot building. It is a separate building connected to the dome by a tunnel.'[123] After Marks was formally declared dead, the winter site manager explained, 'We put the body in a body bag. I took him down to a secure area in the fuel arch.'[124] As the Station doctor confirmed: 'the manager had removed his body into a bag and put him outside. It was probably for about an hour.'[125] When the satellite reconnected about an hour later, as part of its regular cycle of connection and disconnection, communications concerning the death of Rodney Marks were conducted with unknown institutional others, including communications with 'Denver', presumably the headquarters of Raytheon, at the time being the US organisation responsible for the daily operations of the Station.[126] As a result of these communications, Marks' body was collected from outside and brought back into Biomed for tests, before again being placed outside in a storage area located in a tunnel that connects Biomed with the central Station building, the Dome.[127]

As it was May and the middle of the winter-over, there was no possibility of removing Marks' body from the Station until the first flight out at the end of winter. In early November 2000, Marks' body was taken on the first flight out to McMurdo Station and then to Christchurch, New Zealand.[128] Due to a longstanding diplomatic arrangement between the USA and New Zealand for the purposes of the United States Antarctic programme,[129] the direction of flights from the Station run only to Christchurch, New Zealand via McMurdo Station, which is another US research station located on Ross Island, Antarctica within New Zealand's Ross Dependency. This diplomatic arrangement had a very explicit impact on the movement of the body of Rodney Marks, in that it meant his body was taken to Christchurch, New Zealand rather than, for example, his home: Australia.

Although there is little information in the *Findings* or the *Coronial File* addressing the remaining months of the astral winter, what is clear is that Rodney Marks was temporarily buried near the south pole.[130] This temporary burial was organised and conducted by friends and colleagues who remained at the Station for the winter-over, seemingly buried without any institutional support. Having died on 12 May 2000, Rodney Marks was buried on 3 July 2000. During the intervening eight weeks before burial, his body remained in storage in the tunnels.

In November 2000, at the end of the winter-over, Marks' body was disinterred from his south pole grave, removed from 'the Ice' and placed on the first flight out

---

123 'Deposition of RST', *Coronial File*, above, n 90.
124 'Statement of SEH', *Coronial File*, above, n 90.
125 *Findings*, above, n 1, 33.
126 Ibid.
127 Ibid.
128 Ibid, 3.
129 Ibid.
130 See Chapter 4, 4.4.

of the Station to McMurdo Station and then to Christchurch, New Zealand.[131] Although the question of precisely when is unclear (yet jurisprudentially significant), at some point the Christchurch Coroner *assumed* jurisdiction and began an inquest into the cause of death.[132] In November 2000 an autopsy was performed. As flights left the south pole, various staff members, having wintered-over at the Station, travelled through Christchurch and were interviewed by the New Zealand police as part of the coronial investigation.[133] Later in 2000, after initial inquest hearings had begun, the results of an autopsy performed in Christchurch and accompanying toxicology report determined Marks had died as a result of methanol poisoning, and that the methanol had been ingested.[134] The coronial inquest then sought to determine how Marks may have come to ingest methanol.

During a long police investigation (from 2000 to 2007), the limits of police investigative powers and the limits of New Zealand's coronial jurisdiction were pronounced. Difficulties in accessing information from the US government, the agency responsible for the United States Antarctic programme (National Science Foundation) and the subcontractor responsible for the Station (Raytheon) meant that much information was unknown to the New Zealand coronial and police investigations.[135] For example, information as basic as a list of staff members at the Station for the winter-over was never provided by any American government agency or private organisation involved with the management and operation of the Station. Despite this high-level diplomatic blocking, in an act of mundane subversion, a staff list was ultimately obtained some time later by the New Zealand police from an internet site, which remains publicly available, at least in 2015.[136] Any internal US investigations, whether conducted by government agencies or any of the private companies involved, including any information in relation to staff, the nature of Marks' work station or personal quarters etc., were never provided to the New Zealand police or the Christchurch Coroner. The USA, it seems, did not recognise the jurisdiction of the Coroner or at least as a matter of diplomacy, chose not to cooperate. Suffice it to say, a lengthy, institutionally frustrating and ultimately unsatisfactory New Zealand coronial and police investigation ensued.[137]

Despite these impediments, in September 2008 the Coroner delivered the *Findings* for the inquest into the death of Rodney Marks.[138] This was over eight years after Marks had died. The Coroner determined Marks had died from methanol poisoning but was unable to determine how Marks had come to ingest methanol. Whether he ingested methanol by mistake or by another's intent was unclear, although the

131 *Findings*, above, n 1, 3.
132 Ibid, 3–4. See Chapter 4, 4.3, 4.4.
133 Ibid, 3–4, 6–9.
134 Ibid, 11–15.
135 Ibid, 3, 5–9, 35–8, 41–2.
136 Ibid, 7–8. See William J. Spindler, 'South Pole Winter 2000', in *Amundsen-Scott South Pole Station* (2000), http://www.southpolestation.com/trivia/00s/2000.html.
137 *Findings*, above, n 1, 41–2.
138 Ibid.

Coroner considered suicide less likely, especially given his recent engagement to his girlfriend who was a colleague at the Station. Although rumours suggesting that this was the 'first murder' in Antarctica continue to circulate, an absence of information means that this is unlikely to amount to more than mere speculation.[139]

Acknowledging the difficulty of conducting an inquest in a context of jurisdictional uncertainty and lack of mutual assistance obligations, the *Findings* include the following jurisdictionally ambitious recommendation:

> That the New Zealand government considers the appropriate means of ensuring the full, open and accountable investigation of all deaths that occur in Antarctic territory and takes steps to promote such outcomes.[140]

Obviously, the Christchurch Coroner's power to make recommendations was limited to the New Zealand government and did not extend beyond the borders of Aotearoa to other countries. At this stage, nearly eight years after the *Findings* were released, while not possible to identify whether there have been any diplomatic communications between New Zealand and other states, such as Australia or the USA, as this is privileged information and by definition inaccessible, there does not appear to be any mention of this issue in any major international forum, such as the annual meetings of the Antarctic Treaty system.

In other ways, Rodney Marks is remembered. In 2001 a plaque was erected at the base of Marks Mount, a mountain in Antarctica named after him.[141] Marks Mount is an Antarctic mountain in the Worcester Ranges located at 78° 47' S, 160° 35' E, with a height of 2600 metres.[142] Also in 2001, the annual marker of the geographic south pole, traditionally designed and made at the Station by

---

139 See, e.g., Will Cockrell, 'A Mysterious Death at the South Pole', in *Men's Journal* (28 December 2009), http://www.mensjournal.com/death-at-the-south-pole; Robert Neff, 'Murder at the South Pole: Antarctic Scientist's Death Investigated' in *Ohmynews* (21 December 2006), http://english.ohmynews.com/articleview/article_view.asp?at_code=381541; Golden Fleece, 'Is Rodney Marks Antarctica's First Murder?' in *Above Top Secret.Com: Deny Ignorance* (5 April 2009), http://www.abovetopsecret.com/forum/thread452350/pg1.
140 *Findings*, above, n 1, 43.
141 United States Geological Survey, 'Geographic Names Information System: Antarctic Feature Detail, Marks, Mount', in *United States Board on Geographic Names* (2010), http://geonames.usgs.gov/antarctic/index.html. See also https://www1.data.antarctica.gov.au/aadc/gaz/display_name.cfm?gaz_id=136196. The description provided is as follows: 'A broad ice-covered mountain rising to 2600 m 5 mi NNW of Mount Speyer in Worcester Range. Named after Rodney Marks (1968–2000), an Australian citizen who died while conducting astrophysical research as a member of the 2000 winter party at the NSF South Pole Station. He was employed by the Smithsonian Astrophysical Observatory, working on the Antarctic Submillimeter Telescope and Remote Observatory, a research project of the University of Chicago's Center for Astrophysical Research in Antarctica ("CARA"). He previously had spent the 1998 winter at the Pole as part of CARA's South Pole Infrared Explorer project.' According to this entry, the decision to name 'Marks, Mount' was made on 1 January 2001, the name was entered into the Geographic Names Information System on 23 December 2002 and last modified on 15 January 2004.
142 United States Geological Survey, above, n 141.

winter-over staff, was made in memory of Rodney Marks by his friends, Dave Pernic and Mike Boyce, engraved with a scorpion resting on top of the continent of Antarctica, the dedication 'For Rodney Marks, 1968–2000' around the edge, and the phrase, 'not without peril'.[143] As with all south pole markers, the 2001 marker was placed in ceremony and has since drifted; removed and placed in storage.

Marks' burial site at the south pole continues to be marked with a memorial: an Australian flag. The flag is replaced annually by one of Marks' friends who act as 'unofficial stewards, making sure there is always a Commonwealth Star waving at Marks's last resting place in Antarctica.'[144] As Schneider, one of the 'unofficial stewards', observes:

> The NSF hates it and continually fights to get rid of it. I guess they don't want there to be a reminder of the incident. But I want that flag there, and Rodney's family likes the fact that that point in the ice is marked. The fact that the flag moves farther away from the base each year, as the ice moves, is a very graphic reminder of the passage of time since this terrible event in our lives. At some point it might die, but the ephemeral nature of it makes it a powerful memorial.[145]

Having been buried at the south pole, and removed from his south pole grave and taken to New Zealand for an autopsy, the body of Marks was moved one final time and returned to Australia. Reburied in Geelong at a coastal site overlooking the ocean, Rodney Marks was buried with a southern orientation.

4.3 Struggling to move

Dr Rodney David Marks died in Antarctica; a fascinating juridical place. A continent and place of land that is covered by ice and surrounded by waters, Antarctica is a physically ambiguous place. Lacking the littoral, Antarctica challenges understandings of the often assumed binary opposition of land and sea. In this respect, Marianne Moore's well-known poem about the sea, called 'A Grave', opens with a helpful visual image.[146] This is one we can all imagine, and have most probably experienced: a person on a coastline, looking out across an ocean in quiet contemplation. For Moore, this image is coupled with an observation of a human tendency to want to place themselves in the centre, whether the centre of an object, location, or in the language of this book, a place. We have already seen this human tendency played out in Antarctica. Consider, for example, the race to be the 'first' to reach the south pole. What is particularly powerful about Moore's image of coastal contemplation, which is otherwise admittedly a somewhat inoccuous image, is

---

143 For a photograph of this image see, e.g., Stephen Hudson, 'Geo Pole' on *Stephen Hudson* (25 January 2001), http://www.stephenhudson.net/SPole/GeoPole1.html.
144 Cockrell, *A Mysterious Death at the South Pole*, above, n 139.
145 Ibid.
146 Marianne Moore, 'A Grave', in Marianne Moore, *Complete Poems* (faber & faber, revised edn, 1981) 49.

her meditation on the human impossibilitity of actually seeing the sea. As Moore writes, no matter how much we might desire to place ourselves in the centre or the middle of an object, it is impossible to 'stand' at the centre 'of this'.[147] The 'this' for Marianne Moore is the sea. However, the 'this' for this chapter is Antarctica: an ambiguous place that is not-quite-land and not-quite-sea. Not quite either, its land is covered by ice that moves and its seas freeze and expand and contract in archaic seasonal non-patterns. Frozen. A land of ice. Not quite sea, but also, not quite land.

It was standing in the middle of 'this' that Rodney Marks died. His body was temporarily buried in the icy ground, before being removed to the sanctity of land, or at least the sanctuary of a land less ambiguous that it is land. In the context of Moore's poem, Rodney Marks was both standing and temporarily buried in the middle of 'this'. Is the 'this' of Antarctica different or different enough from Marianne Moore's 'this' of the sea? The question of 'this' is a question of whether Antarctica provides a sufficiently 'earthly foundation' for the placing of law.[148] As introduced in the first part of the chapter, it is not only relations between land and sea that are complicated in the polar South, but also relations between land and territory, which is part of the challenge of Antarctica. In thinking of the place of common law – of thinking common law – in Antarctica, an understanding of nature based on the distinction between land and sea becomes a little unsteady and in this unsteadiness, what also loosens, perhaps, is an understanding of how common law moves, including how it struggles to move into place.

Moore's poem, which was originally called 'A Graveyard in the Middle of the Sea', clearly and evocatively refers to the sea as a grave.149 In a sense, this is also the case for Antarctica, where bodies are laid bare in the ice and can be uncovered by digging, but there are also important differences between burials in Antarctica and burials at sea. Not only is it difficult to excavate in Antarctica as the ice continually builds up and moves, making it difficult to uncover the dead, but in contrast to burials in land or at sea, the dead in Antarctica do not decompose. Instead, there is a stasis that, in effect, amounts to a suspended burial. What is important to recognise is that the nature of the land in Antarctica means it is difficult to bury the dead, which makes it difficult to properly care for the dead. Yet, there are different methods and practices of caring for the dead, some more careful and more attentive than others.

In these final two parts of the chapter, a redescription of the burial and reburial of Rodney Marks reveals different forms of movement as well as different practices

---

147 Ibid. See also Robert Pogue Harrison, *The Dominion of the Dead* (University of Chicago Press, 2003) 6–8.
148 Ibid, 7.
149 Moore, above, n 146, 49. Interestingly, the published version of this poem was a revision of Moore's earlier, unpublished, and differently titled poem: 'A Graveyard in the Middle of the Sea'. This earlier work was written between 1916 and 1918, and revised by Ezra Pound in 1932. See Jeredith Merrin, 'Re-Seeing the Sea: Marianne Moore's "A Grave" as a Woman Writer's Re-Vision', in Patricia Willis (ed.), *Marianne Moore: Woman and Poet* (Orono, ME: National Poetry Foundation, 1990) ch 3.

of care. In this third part of the chapter, the movements of common law are attended to in relation to the places of burial and reburial and what is revealed is that Anglo-Australian common law struggles to move in relation to this dead. Struggling to move and establish lawful relations with this particular dead in the polar South, Anglo-Australian common law establishes lawful relations through the second burial in Victoria. Yet, unable to bury the dead in the polar South, the struggle to move in relation to the dead in the polar South also reveals a struggle to care. To this end, this part focuses on the movements of Anglo-Australian common law in Antarctica, paying particular attention to the difficulties of movement that arise in relation to the first of the two burials of Rodney Marks. The difficulty to move and establish lawful relations in the polar South is examined by first contemplating Anglo-Australian common law's general movements into and in Antarctica, before turning more specifically to movements in relation to the death, burial and reburial of Rodney Marks. While Anglo-Australian common law moves in different ways in relation to territory, persons and the dead, what is revealed in this part is that despite different techniques of movement, Anglo-Australian common law struggles to move in relation to the dead of the polar South, and ultimately fails to move, and to (properly) care.

Territorial movements: mapping Anglo-Australian common law into the polar South

Where did Rodney Marks die? In whose territorial claim, and in the vicinity of which laws? In the *Findings*, the Christchurch Coroner dismissed location as irrelevant, but did acknowledge the oddity of the investigation.[150] Somewhat dismissively, the Coroner reasoned that Rodney Marks:

> [U]ndoubtedly died at South Pole Station. During the investigation the question arose as to whether Dr Marks had died in Antarctic territory historically claimed by New Zealand. The US does not recognise such claims. This issue was not relevant in this case to jurisdiction by a New Zealand Coroner. For the record it would seem that Dr Marks died marginally within the Australian sector.[151]

Unlike the Coroner, for this minor jurisprudence of movement, the place of death, site of burial and grounds for jurisdiction are intensely relevant. Intriguingly, the Coroner suggested Rodney Marks may have died in Australian territory, although the reasoning for such a suggestion is not explicit in the *Findings*.[152] However, the implicit suggestion in the accompanying *Coronial File* is that the Biomed building in which Marks died was, at the time at least, located in the Australian Antarctic

---

150 *Findings*, above, n 1, 4.
151 Ibid, 4.
152 Ibid, 4, 8; 'Deposition of GKW', *Coronial File*, above, n 90; 'Antarctic Territory – Book Diagrams', *Coronial File*, above, n 90, exhibits 15–16.

Territory.[153] So, Marks was an Australian citizen who may or may not have died in the Australian Antarctic Territory. There was no Australian coronial investigation and, as far as it is possible to tell from the public record, no other institutional or formal legal action beyond diplomatic communications between Australia and New Zealand (and perhaps the USA). Silenced through diplomatic privilege, at some point, Australia seems to have acknowledged, conceded or consented to New Zealand, and the Christchurch Coroner's jurisdiction. While the office of the coroner is not introduced until the next part, it is quite clear that an Australian coroner would have had jurisdiction over the body of Marks once it reached mainland Australia, having travelled from the south pole via New Zealand for reburial.[154] However, despite this possible jurisdiction, triggered at least from the time of return for reburial, there was no coronial inquiry or inquest conducted in Australia. The more interesting matter, however, is Anglo-Australian common law's relation to the dead prior to the return for reburial. This requires an attention to Australian legislation and a technique described as 'jurisdictional re-mapping'.

Australia has the largest Antarctic territorial claim. Inherited from Britain in 1933,[155] Australia's claim covers 6.5 million square kilometres, which covers approximately 42 per cent of Antarctica,[156] and is named the Australian Antarctic Territory ('AAT').[157] From an Australian perspective, the AAT is governed by Anglo-Australian common law.[158] Domestic legislation creates and recognises the 'Government of the Australian Antarctic Territory', but it does not actually establish a law-making body or a new body of law. Instead, Anglo-Australian common law comes to be in, that is, to move and to place in the AAT through a fairly simple, historically familiar common law technique that can be thought of as 'jurisdictional re-mapping'. Effectively, the AAT is 're-mapped' into the Australian Capital Territory ('ACT') on the mainland and occasionally, for criminal matters, into Jervis Bay Territory (Australia's smallest mainland territory, which serves as a port for the capital, Canberra). This is a two-way movement. First, in the common law imaginary, the AAT is geographically relocated into the Australian mainland for the purposes of placing common law and providing a common law presence. Simultaneously, through this jurisdictional technique, common law moves from

---

153 Ibid.
154 For contemporary legislative provisions in Victoria, see *Coroners Act 2008* (Vic) ss 4–5, 14–5, 52. See also Chapter 4, 4.4.
155 First claimed and named Victoria Land by the United Kingdom in 1841, this inheritance was formalised through the enactment of the *Australian Antarctic Territory Acceptance Act 1933* (Cth), transferring territory between meridians 160° E and 45° E that was south of 60°.
156 Julia Jabour, Alan D. Hemmings and Lorne K. Kriwoken, 'Introduction', in Kriwoken, Jabour and Hemmings (eds.), *Looking South*, above, n 41, 1.
157 *Australian Antarctic Territory Acceptance Act 1933* (Cth). See also *Australian Antarctic Territory Act 1954* (Cth) s 4; Sahurie, *The International Law of Antarctica*, above, n 8, 14.
158 See, e.g., Joint Standing Committee on the National Capital and External Territories, *Antarctica: Australia's Pristine Frontier – Report on the Adequacy of Funding for Australia's Antarctic Program* (Commonwealth of Australia, 2005) 2. See, generally, Triggs, *International Law and Australian Sovereignty in Antarctica*, above, n 49.

the ACT to the AAT. In order to illustrate the significance of these jurisdictional techniques for the movements of Anglo-Australian common law, it is necessary to add some detail to the legislative context.

In 1954, prior to the establishment of the Antarctic Treaty system, the *Australian Antarctic Territory Act 1954* (Cth) was passed. As indicated in the Act's long title, this was an Act 'to provide for the Government of the Australian Antarctic Territory'.[159] The effect of this Act meant that laws in force in the ACT were deemed to apply to the AAT. This Act has since been amended and several accompanying pieces of legislation passed, especially since the introduction of the Antarctic Treaty system, however, the basic governing structure remains.[160] Technically, at least according to domestic legislation, the AAT is governed by common law present in the ACT. In the utilisation of a familiar common law technique, this means the AAT is effectively re-mapped and relocated in the legal imaginary as the ACT, which is certainly more efficient than developing a body of law directly applicable to the AAT, especially given the uncertainty of its effectiveness in the context of the Antarctic Treaty system.

There are a number of interesting provisions in the federal legislation authoring and authorising the movement and place of Anglo-Australian common law in Antarctica, especially in relation to other laws, and especially in relation to their erasure.[161] For instance, with the passing of the *Australian Antarctic Territory Act 1954* (Cth), the 'laws in force' in the AAT, except for laws of the Commonwealth already in force in the AAT, ceased to be in force.[162] What these existing 'laws in force' might be or might have been is unanswered by the legislation, except for the direction that these are existing laws 'not being laws of the Commonwealth in force in the Territory'.[163] In the absence of an indigenous population, there is no law indigenous to Antarctica. However, in 1954, there may have been the presence or at least the risk of a presence of other state laws resulting from prior attempts to claim sovereignty or territory. Similarly, there may have been customary international law or at least a possibility of such a presence. In any event, it is likely that this was a matter of caution, ensuring that if there were any other laws present in Antarctica, the legislative declaration meant they were no longer present, which is, in effect, a jurisdictional technique enacted through legislation declaring that other unnamed laws cease to be; an ordering of laws. Rather than a coming together through meeting, negotiation and other forms of legal communication, absolute unilateral erasure by means of deeming and declaration

---

159 *Australian Antarctic Territory Act 1954* (Cth). See also Sahurie, *The International Law of Antarctica*, above, n 8, 16.
160 See Triggs, *International Law and Australian Sovereignty in Antarctica*, above, n 49, ch 7.
161 See *Australian Antarctic Territory Act 1954* (Cth) ss 5–6. See also s 8 (federal laws do not apply in the AAT unless expressly stated to do so), s 10 (ACT courts have jurisdiction 'in and in relation to' the AAT) and ss 11–3 (the structure of ordinances governing the AAT place the Governor in a central role).
162 *Australian Antarctic Territory Act 1954* (Cth) s 5.
163 Ibid.

exhibits a lack of quality and care in the creation and conduct of lawful relations. Reframed, this moment of common law's erasure of other forms of law serves as a way of clearing the ground before moving into place; *tabula rasa*.

With the eradication of other laws, Australian federal legislation effectively seeks to impose a body of Anglo-Australian common law in Antarctica, governing the AAT. For example, section 6 of the *Australian Antarctic Territory Act 1954* (Cth) operates, in effect, as a technical form of jurisdictional and geographical movement which locates and relocates the AAT for various purposes. Somewhat strangely, for civil law the AAT is part of the ACT yet for criminal law the AAT forms part of Jervis Bay Territory: both located on mainland Australia.[164] What this means is the Australian Antarctic Territory is not actually located in Antarctica; at least not legally or in the common law imaginary. Rather, for criminal activities and criminal law, the AAT is deemed to be part of Jervis Bay Territory, which is a small detached federal enclave providing a naval port for the ACT (65 square kilometres of land and 9 square kilometres of marine reserve), surrounded in all directions by New South Wales. For the purposes of governing criminal activity, therefore, the AAT is placed in a bay on mainland Australia, several hours drive south of Sydney. In contrast, for the purposes of non-criminal activity, the AAT is placed in the ACT (again, several hours drive southwest from Sydney). With the division between criminal and civil laws, these are movements that locate and relocate the AAT, rearranging legal topographies and measures of distance between Antarctica and mainland Australia. Through large-scale jurisdictional re-mapping, therefore, these statutory provisions locate and relocate the AAT from the icy ground of Antarctica to stretches of sandy coastline and limestone plain on Australia; jurisdictional movements of territory.

Moving persons: placing Anglo-Australian common law in the polar South

Forms of movement introduced so far have focused primarily on territory, however Anglo-Australian common law also moves in the polar South through the jurisdictional status of the person. In other words, common law moves not only through the jurisdictional re-mapping of territory, but also through attachments to the jurisdictional status of the person. As mentioned, utilising the technique of 'deeming', Australian federal legislation places common law in parts of Antarctica by rearranging a cartographic imagination for various legal purposes. While on the surface attending to territory, this legislation has been interpreted in a more limited manner. As a matter of interpretive practice, largely for purposes of policy and diplomacy, this seemingly territorial-based legislation has been read down so that Anglo-Australian common law applies not to the AAT per se, but rather, applies only to Australian citizens in the AAT. Therefore, although the declared legislative intent is to govern territory, the legislation is effectively read down to govern Australian citizens in Antarctica thereby reflecting the legal choreography

---

164 *Australian Antarctic Territory Act* (Cth) s 6

of the Antarctic Treaty system of persons, not territory. Yet, as explained in Chapter 2 and illustrated in Chapter 3, common law moves with or without institutional support, including movements prior to deliberation and judgment. In this respect, what is jurisprudentially significant about this legislation is how it authors and authorises ways in which common law moves into and within the AAT, and ways in which the AAT moves into and within the Australian mainland continent through jurisdictional technologies of re-mapping. Irrespective of whether this federal legislation will ever be interpreted or applied to non-Australian citizens located in the AAT, and in direct conflict with the practical attachment to persons, it is the jurisdictional imagining that common law attaches to territory contained within these legislative provisions, and the way this territorial imagining is remapped to a more obvious land that is important.

Since the passing of the *Antarctic Treaty*, the domestic legislative response in Australia adjusted and is captured in a short piece of legislation, the *Antarctica Treaty Act 1960* (Cth), which contains four sections and includes the text of the *Antarctic Treaty* as an appendix. Section 4 of the *Antarctic Treaty Act 1960* (Cth) contains provisions giving effect to the *Antarctic Treaty* and makes two interesting moves. First, Australian citizens in Antarctica are subject to the laws in force in the AAT whether they are in the AAT or other parts of Antarctica.[165] That is, for the purpose of governing Australian citizens in Antarctica, regardless of where they may actually be materially located, they are deemed to be in the AAT. Second, and conversely, a person who is not an Australian citizen is not subject to the laws in force in the AAT, whether they are in the AAT or other parts of Antarctica.[166] What this means is that s 4 puts into effect the *Antarctic Treaty* abeyance of sovereignty and territory in regards to persons other than Australian citizens, while at the same time maintaining (or at least not letting go of) the representation of a body of law placed in the polar South that governs the AAT by somehow jurisdictionally attaching to the 'land'.

It is not only land that is jurisdictionally remapped, but also persons. Although Australian citizens are governed by Australian law as common law subjects, while in Antarctica – wherever they might be located in Antarctica – Australian subjects are jurisdictionally re-mapped into the AAT. Whether on a boat in the Weddell Sea off in the Argentinian claimed territory to the 'west', or at the American-run McMurdo Station on the New Zealand-claimed Ross Ice Shelf in the 'south', an Australian citizen is deemed to be located in the AAT in order to be governed by the laws in force in that territory. This means for activities governed by criminal law, Australian subjects in Antarctica are first deemed to be in the AAT then by virtue of s 6 of the *Australian Antarctica Territory Act 1954* (Cth) they are then deemed to be in Jervis Bay Territory. While for civil law, the same common law subjects are first deemed to be in the AAT then swiftly relocated via an act of jurisdictional re-mapping into the ACT. As with the re-mapping of territory, this is a material

165 *Antarctic Treaty Act 1960* (Cth) s 4(2).
166 Ibid, s 4(1).

practice of a jurisdictional technology that moves, remaps and re-places the location of persons in relation to territory and in doing so, authorises, enables and effects the movement of common law in Antarctica.

Despite the re-mapping of territory and persons, movements of Anglo-Australian common law are not movements of law that provide for a consistent covering (or smothering) of law in and over the AAT. It is a much more textured movement and patterning of law. In concession to the Antarctic Treaty system, common law present in the AAT only applies in the sense that it only touches and attaches to Australian citizens. It does not apply to non-Australian citizens, who remain governed by their own laws. Australian citizens anywhere in Antarctica are deemed to be located in the AAT, and therefore the ACT or Jervis Bay, in order to be governed by Anglo-Australian common law. This is a movement of common law that stretches beyond the AAT in order to attach to Australian subjects as they move in other parts of Antarctica. This provides an intriguing visual patterning of the movements of Anglo-Australian common law in Antarctica as it attaches to some and disregards others. Importantly, this illustrates Anglo-Australian common law's movement as techniques of jurisdictional re-mapping not only in relation to territory but also in relation to the jurisdictional status of the person.

Unmoved: failing to care for the dead in the polar South

The difficulty and limitations of these movements that jurisdictionally re-map the place of common law in Antarctica, whether through re-mapping territory or re-mapping persons, is revealed by attending to Anglo-Australian common law's movements in relation to the death, burial and reburial of Rodney Marks. More specifically, this is especially so in the context of burial, and in the context of common law's struggle to move in relation to the dead and produce a lawful space at the burial site at the south pole. As we know, but need to keep in mind, Rodney Marks was an Australian citizen who may or may not have died in the AAT. With the techniques of jurisdictional re-mapping of both territory and persons, irrespective of where Marks actually died, in the common law imaginary, he would have been cartographically moved and deemed to have been located within the AAT; at least, he would have been deemed to be so when he was alive. But, as mentioned in Chapter 1, common law has a long history of a fairly awkward engagement with the dead: as neither person nor property.[167] In this instance, as will be revealed, Anglo-Australian common law struggles and arguably fails in its ability to move in relation to the dead; a failure in the creation and conduct of lawful relations.

Rodney Marks died at Biomed, which was a building located in the Archways and linked via tunnels to the main building, the Dome. But where, more precisely, was Biomed? Whose territory? Which jurisdiction? Not now, but in 2000? Well, in 2007 it seems that Biomed was located in the AAT, at least according to the

---

167 See Chapter 1, 1.1; Chapter 2, 2.3.

Findings, although whether this assertion has a rigorous basis is markedly uncertain.[168] Yet, even if this was true, this was seven years after Marks' death, which means there has been at least 70 metres of icy movement so near to the convergence of territorial lines of claim, which may or may not be significant. So while possible Marks died while Biomed was located in the AAT, it remains possible that Biomed, at least in 2000, was located in territory claimed by New Zealand or France (which both holding neighbouring claims) and that Marks died within one of those territorial claims. However, regardless of where Marks was located – whether in or out of the AAT – as an Australian citizen and common law subject, Anglo-Australian common law would have attached to Rodney Marks; at least until the moment of death. Why, then, did Anglo-Australian common law fail to apply to and govern this dead? As neither person nor property, the problem is one of common law's relation with the no-longer-person after death. Further, what this means is that the techniques of jurisdictional re-mapping as they relate to the status of the person ultimately struggle to move the dead. In relation to the site of death in the polar South, therefore, unable to re-map the dead into the AAT or if Marks was already in the AAT, unable to attach to the dead as neither person nor property, Anglo-Australian common law struggles to move in relation to the dead.

If Anglo-Australian common law struggles to move in relation to dead at the site of death, what about movements in relation to the place of burial near the south pole? Again, the precise location of the burial site in relation to territorial claims is unclear, except that it was near the south pole, making the territorial location even more uncertain. However, what is clear is that the location was either inside or outside the AAT. If the burial site was outside the AAT, then Anglo-Australian common law was, again, unable to move beyond the landscape of its proclaimed territorial confines in the absence of a living common law subject; it simply cannot attach to other land. However, if the first burial site was within the AAT, then even if common law failed to attach to the dead – as not quite person and not quite property – then Anglo-Australian common law through its territorial pretensions and jurisdictional techniques of re-mapping the AAT into mainland Australia and vice versa, could have governed the burial site. Yet, it did not.

Anglo-Australian common law did not govern this dead, at least not in the polar South. With no coronial jurisdiction, police investigation, courtly proceedings or any exhibitable form of institutional care, whether Marks died or was buried within or without the AAT, Anglo-Australian common law struggled to move in relation to this dead. Anglo-Australian common law struggled, and in a sense failed, to care for this dead. This is not to overlook a later form of care through movements in relation to the dead in the second burial in Victoria, movements contributing to a humanisation of the earth.[169] It is also not to overlook the possibility that Anglo-Australian common law moved in relation to this dead through its jurisdictional technique of camping, introduced in the last chapter. Although in this case, rather

168 See Chapter 4, 4.2, especially ASMA Map 4.
169 See Chapter 2, 2.3.

than camping with the dead, this would have involved Anglo-Australian common law camping with a New Zealand coronial jurisdiction that was able to move in relation to the dead and take responsibility for the care of the dead in the polar South. Yet, due to diplomatic privilege and the privacy of any relevant jurisdictional communications, while possible Anglo-Australian common law moved in relation to the dead in this manner, camping with the coroner, this is entirely speculative. What is less speculative is that at the south pole, at least on the surface, Anglo-Australian common law failed to move in relation to the dead at the south pole burial site, unable to establish lawful relations with the dead. This is so regardless of whether the burial site was in the AAT or elsewhere in Antarctica.

Part of the failure to move in relation to the dead and care for this dead seems to relate to common law's need for and lack of an earthly ground. Despite its territorial pretensions, Anglo-Australian common law certainly does not govern the whole of the AAT. Rather, it operates through the jurisdictional status of the person by attaching to the bodies of Australian citizens as ones subject to Anglo-Australian common law. But, by moving through the jurisdictional status of the person, as it does so elsewhere and as it will continue to do so, Anglo-Australian common law struggles to attach to the dead. While this struggle is often circumnavigated by common law governing that which surrounds the dead, such as the shroud or the burial site, Anglo-Australian common law is less able to govern that which surrounds and attaches to the dead in the polar South. Therefore, the challenge that arises in the context of Anglo-Australian common law and its movements in relation to the death, burial and reburial of Rodney Marks is the challenge of moving to and caring for the dead in order to establish lawful relations and in this process, form an attachment to the earth and produce a lawful place.

More than just a side-effect of the Antarctic Treaty system that places territorial sovereignty in abeyance, the failure of Anglo-Australian common law to move in relation to the dead in the polar South relates to the nature of the not-quite-land of Antarctica and its relation to technologies of jurisdiction as technologies of movement. In relation to the death and burial of Rodney Marks, and with the notable exception of the later earthly reburial, Anglo-Australian common law failed to govern this dead. This failure is, in part, a result of the challenge of juridical attachment in an ambiguous land. For in order to attach, hold and produce lawful spaces, and to move into place, common law needs an earthly foundation; it needs unambiguous land. In Antarctica, with an abundance of ice, always moving, Anglo-Australian common law struggles to attach, hold and produce lawful spaces, at least through the technology of jurisdictional re-mapping as it moves in relation to territory or persons. Certainly in relation to the burial of Rodney Marks at the south pole, Anglo-Australian common law was unable to attach to the burial site, even if this was a site located within the AAT. This is because Anglo-Australian common law, despite its territorial pretensions, moves through an attachment to subjects and not an attachment to an ambiguous land in the polar South. When the subject is dead, Anglo-Australian common law fails to move in the polar South and as such, fails to take responsibility for and care for the dead.

This part noticed different forms of movement of Anglo-Australian common law in relation to territory, persons and the dead in the polar South. By focusing on the threshold of these movements, it became clear that common law struggles to move in the polar South, and at times fails to care. Reaching its threshold in relation to the dead and an earth that is not quite earth, despite its techniques of jurisdictional re-mapping, Anglo-Australian common law failed to move in relation to the dead; failed to hold onto and attach to the land of Antarctica and in doing so, failed to care for the dead. Others, however, were more successful in their techniques of movement and practices of caring for the dead, as revealed in the next and final part of the chapter.

4.4 Instituting lawful relations

With Anglo-Australian common law failing to care for this dead in the polar South, the question then becomes one of who cares, how do they care, and how are these practices of care connected to other forms of law? These are question of legal and institutional care, which are not questions of personal and emotional care. No longer addressing Anglo-Australian common law, my attention turns primarily to New Zealand common law, while other common laws and other forms of law also momentarily feature. With the focus shifting beyond Australia, the final part of this chapter attends to two different offices, one more obviously 'official' than the other, and two different modes of care, both of which institute lawful relations with the dead in the polar South. The first is the office of coroner. Attending to the office of the coroner, and its contemporary inheritance of a medieval jurisdictional responsibility to care for the dead, what is revealed in this part is a jurisdictional technique of movement that allows a coroner in New Zealand to create and conduct lawful relations with the dead in the polar South. Despite these movements, however, the coroner's technical and material practices of legal and institutional care are limited; unable to bury the dead in the polar South; unable to properly and finally care. Yet, the second office attended to in this final part of the chapter also cares for and takes responsibility for the dead, practising a form of care quite distinct from that of the coroner through the institution of burial. Practising a form of care that is more personal, less institutional, yet nevertheless lawful, this is the office of friendship; and it is through those taking up and holding the office of friend that Rodney Marks was buried in the polar South. With different offices practising responsibilities of care in distinct ways, together, these two offices – that of coroner and that of friend – move in relation to the dead, collectively taking responsibility and caring for the dead in the polar South.

Office of coroner

How did a New Zealand coroner come to assume and exercise jurisdiction? Remembering that Rodney Marks was an Australian citizen who died on unknown territory, which may or may not have been territory claimed by Australia, while working at a US-run research station, then, the obvious question needs to be asked: why this coroner? Clearly, there is no coroner in Antarctica, but why not an Australian coroner or a coroner in the USA? From a close reading of the *Findings* and the *Coronial File*, it is difficult to precisely ascertain how and when the Christchurch coroner assumed jurisdiction. At no point in the *Findings* or in the *Coronial File* is any explicit reasoning provided as to why the Christchurch coroner had jurisdiction in relation to the death of Rodney Marks, apart from the reasoning quoted earlier in the chapter that the place of death was not relevant to the coroner's assumption of jurisdiction.[170] The silence on the manner in which jurisdiction was obtained is significant, particularly given that the coroner found there was a 'jurisdictional void for deaths in Antarctica, in some circumstances'.[171] If there was a jurisdictional void, then how did the Christchurch Coroner have jurisdiction in order to recognise such a void? Obviously, the fact that there was an inquest means there cannot be a void, although the awkwardness of the coronial inquest does suggest difficulties in the movement, place and exercise of a New Zealand coronial jurisdiction in the polar South.

Before responding more specifically to the question of 'why this coroner', it is important to appreciate the particular nature of a coronial jurisdiction in a common law country. An understanding of the history of the coroner will assist in unravelling the quite particular relationship between the office of coroner and the dead, shedding some light on why it is a coroner and not some other office or institution that established lawful relations with this dead. In England, the office of coroner has had a continuous existence for over 800 years. As with common law more generally, coronial jurisdictions formed part of the empirical and geopolitical movements of empire that moved in the expansion of the British Empire between the metropole and its colonies.[172] In former British colonies, such as Australia and New Zealand, the office of coroner is very much a product of this inheritance. Although there have been some intriguing debates as to the precise origin of the coroner, especially the contributions of Maitland and Charles Gross towards the end of the nineteenth century,[173] R.F. Hunnisett quite convincingly places the origins of the office of coroner in September 1194,[174] when chapter 20 of the articles of the eyre 'ordered the election in every county of three knights and a clerk as keepers of the pleas of the crown'.[175] The formal title for the 'keepers of the pleas of the crown' was '*custos* (or occasionally *conservator*) *placitorium corone*' and

---

170 *Findings*, above, n 1, 4; Chapter 4, 4.3.
171 *Findings*, above, n 1, 43.
172 See Chapter 2, 2.1; Chapter 3, 3.1.
173 See Charles Gross, 'The Early History and Influence of the Office of the Coroner' (1892) 7(4) *Political Science Quarterly* 656 and response by Maitland, F.W. Maitland, 'Review of "The Early History and Influence of the Office of the Coroner" by Charles Gross' (1893) 8(32) *The English Historical Review* 758.
174 R.F. Hunnisett, 'The Origins of the Office of the Coroner: The Alexander Prize Essay' (1958) 8 *Transactions of the Royal Historical Society* 85; R.F. Hunnisett, *The Medieval Coroner* (Cambridge University Press, 1961) ch 1.
175 Hunnisett, 'The Origins of the Office of the Coroner', above, n 174, 86. See also Hunnisett, *The Medieval Coroner*, above, n 174, ch 1.

used throughout the Middle Ages, but, according to Hunnisett, the 'shorter forms *coronarius*, which was confined to a short period around 1200, and *coronator* rapidly gained greater currency. The English form was 'coroner' or 'crowner',[176] which is the origin of both the office and name of 'coroner'.

The medieval office of the coroner was an office subject to a number of changes in duties and responsibilities, even in its early years:[177]

> Throughout the Middle Ages the coroner could be ordered to perform almost any duty of an administrative or inquisitorial nature within his bailiwick, either alone or with the sheriff, but there were other duties which belonged more specifically to his office and which he performed without being ordered. These consisted of holding inquests upon dead bodies, receiving abjurations of the realm made by felons in sanctuary, hearing appeals, confessions of felons and appeals of approvers, and attending and sometimes organising exactions and outlawries promulgating in the county court. These were the 'crown pleas' which the coroner had to 'keep', and he kept them in four ways: by taking the actions just mentioned, attaching or arresting witnesses, suspects and others, appraising and safeguarding any lands and goods which might later be forfeited, and by recording all the details.[178]

Importantly, in addition to various administrative or inquisitorial duties the medieval coroner may have been ordered to undertake, the medieval coroner had some very particular responsibilities of office, inherent responsibilities not requiring external orders, including a responsibility to hold inquests in relation to the dead.[179] Prior to September 1194 such duties were performed by other local officials.

Although there are a number of aspects of the office of medieval coroner that form an important part of the inheritance of the contemporary office of coroner, including the inquisitorial nature of a coronial jurisdiction, for this redescription, it is sufficient to consider the relationship between the coroner and the initial finding of a dead body.[180] If a dead body was found, there was a duty on the finder and others, including the hundred, to raise a 'hue and cry' (*hutesium et clamor*).[181] There was also a duty on the finder to inform the coroner and protect the body until the coroner arrived. To ensure this protection occurred, it was an offence to move the body. Significantly, this meant the medieval coroner went to the dead. This is a

---

176 Hunnisett, *The Medieval Coroner*, above, n 174, 1, after citing the Latin phrase for chapter 20 of the articles of eyre, '*Praeterea in quolibet comitatu eligantur tres milites et unus clericus custodes placitorum coronae*' from W. Stubbs (ed.), *Select Charters of English Constitutional History* (Clarendon Press, 9th edn, 1913) 254.
177 Hunnisett, *The Medieval Coroner*, above, n 174.
178 Ibid, 1.
179 Ibid.
180 See, generally, ibid.
181 Ibid; Hunnisett, 'The Origins of the Office of the Coroner', above, n 174.

pattern of movement that contrasts with how the body of Rodney Marks moved, where it was the dead that moved from the polar South to the Christchurch Coroner. In modern times, it seems the coroner no longer moves to the dead, but, rather, that the dead move to the coroner. Despite the change in direction of movement between the dead and the coroner, it is important to recognise that since the origin of the medieval coroner in 1194, it has been the office of coroner that has institutional responsibility for the dead.

Having briefly considered the historical origins of the office of coroner, it is apparent that the answer to 'why a coroner' rather than some other institution or office is that the office of coroner has institutional responsibility for the dead. Yet, more than just an institutional responsibility, the suggestion is that this is also a jurisdictional responsibility to care for the dead. Remembering office as a dynamic set of relations of duty, responsibility and conduct,[182] the office of coroner carries with it a responsibility to the dead; the creation and conduct of lawful relations with the dead. This is a jurisdictional relationship. Despite the often low-level bureaucratic placing of a coroner, whether as a lower court judge, a magistrate or a quasi-judicial role in a tribunal, it is important to remember the inheritance of the office of coroner and the very particular responsibility this office carries in relation to the dead. For the office of coroner has a jurisdictional responsibility to care for the dead and it is because of this relationship that the office of coroner carries responsibilities that, at times, might seem over and above its relatively minor placing in common law judicial hierarchies. This responsibility, whether framed as an inherent jurisdiction or placed, as it is here, as a responsibility of office, is important in deciphering the relation between a Christchurch Coroner and the body of Rodney Marks while it rested at the south pole.

Coronial assumptions

Turning to the question of 'why this coroner', in what is clearly a rather unusual set of circumstances surrounding the death of Rodney Marks, one of the more striking features is the elongated passage of time and geographical space between the death of Rodney Marks and the final burial. As outlined earlier in this chapter, Marks died at the south pole on 12 May 2000 and his body was temporarily buried at the south pole on 3 July 2000, disinterred in November 2000 and flown to McMurdo Station, Antarctica, and then Christchurch, New Zealand, before being flown to Victoria, Australia and finally buried, again, in late 2000. This is approximately six months and several thousands of kilometres between the time and place of death and final burial. What was the role of the coroner in these movements of the body of Rodney Marks? Again, why *this* coroner?

Although the *Coroners Act 1988* (NZ) has since been repealed (replaced by the *Coroners Act 2006* (NZ)), the coronial inquest into the death of Rodney Marks was

---

182 See Chapter 1, 1.2.

conducted under the *Coroners Act 1988* (NZ) due to the operation of transitional provisions.[183] In 2000 section 16(a) of the *Coroners Act 1988* (NZ) was the relevant provision that established the jurisdiction of coroners to hold inquests and required that a coroner 'shall not hold an inquest' unless the 'body of the person concerned is *in* New Zealand'. When he died, the body of Marks was certainly not in mainland New Zealand although it remains possible that the site of death was within the Ross Dependency, New Zealand's territorial claim in Antarctica. Obviously, from the moment the plane landed in Christchurch in November 2000 and the body of Rodney Marks was unambiguously 'in' New Zealand, the Christchurch Coroner had grounds to assume jurisdiction and hold an inquest.[184] Yet, the significant point is that the Christchurch Coroner clearly assumed jurisdiction *prior to* this event and started exercising jurisdiction at some point *prior to* the arrival of the body of Rodney Marks in Christchurch.

How was jurisdiction assumed? There are three possible ways in which s 16(a) of the *Coroners Act 1988* (NZ) may have authorised the Coroner's earlier assumption of jurisdiction. The first relates to the movement of the body of Rodney Marks to McMurdo Station, the second relates to the burial at the south pole and the third relates to the plane. However, while helpful to briefly consider these three scenarios, neither independently nor collectively do these sufficiently explain the coroner's early assumption of jurisdiction.

First, en route to Christchurch, the plane carrying the body of Rodney Marks landed at McMurdo Station, an American research station based in New Zealand's Ross Dependency in Antarctica. While clearly the body was in the Ross Dependency during this stopover, did this prior landing satisfy the requirement of s 16(a) that the body be 'in' New Zealand? It is possible that New Zealand common law moves in relation to the Ross Dependency in a manner akin to the jurisdictional re-mapping of Anglo-Australian common law into the AAT and if so, the body would have been 'in' New Zealand. Yet, not only were the movements of Anglo-Australian common law in relation to this dead unsuccessful, suggesting that New Zealand common law may similarly struggle, but in addition there is a different texture to the nature of the non-land of the Ross Dependency that may make it even more difficult for New Zealand common law to attach to territory. For unlike other territorial claims to Antarctica that claim land covered by ice, Ross Dependency is a territorial claim to a 'huge mass of ice'.[185] Located on the Ross Ice Shelf, the largest ice shelf in the world, the assertion of the Ross Dependency directly challenges the relation between territory, land and law.[186] Even more so than with the geological distinction between Australia (land) and

---

183 *Coroners Act 2009* (NZ) ss 143, 144, and items 4(1)(a)–(b) of Schedule 3. Despite major legislative reform between the 1988 and 2009 Acts, in respect of the matters addressed in this chapter, the provisions in the former and current legislation are substantially equivalent. See, e.g., *Coroners Act 1988* (NZ) s 16; cf: *Coroners Act 2006* (NZ) s 59.
184 *Coroners Act 1988* (NZ) s 16.
185 Sahurie, *The International Law of Antarctica*, above, n 8, 17.
186 Ibid, 17–19.

the AAT (ice on top of land), there is an earthly distinction between Christchurch, New Zealand (land), and McMurdo Station, Ross Dependency (ice on top of water). Although both places are, arguably at least, in New Zealand, there is a very different texture between the nature of land, the nature of sovereignty and territory and therefore the place of New Zealand common law in these two places. Coupled with the 1979 statement that New Zealand citizens on the Air New Zealand crash at Mount Erebus in the Ross Dependency were 'outside their home territory' (i.e. outside New Zealand), the territorial basis of New Zealand common law in the Ross Dependency is highly tentative.[187] Although certainly arguable, it is far from clear whether s 16(a) was satisfied by the landing of the plane at McMurdo Station. At best, it seems highly unlikely and in my view, it did not. In other words, this short stopover when a plane landed on ice did not satisfy the jurisdictional threshold required to inaugurate the Coroner's jurisdiction into this matter.

Second, it is possible that the body of Marks was at some point 'in' New Zealand territory at the south pole. With the precise relation between territorial claims and the location of Station buildings remaining unclear, especially given the movements in the ice that have occurred in the 14 years since this death, it is possible that at some point between death, burial and disinterment the body of Marks was in the Ross Dependency, perhaps when placed outside in the storage tunnels at the Station, during preparations for burial or, depending on its location, the burial site near the south pole. Assuming for the moment that this was so at some point, the problem of an ice shelf at McMurdo Station fades, although the problem of New Zealand's territorial practices, including its 1979 comments, still remain. More significantly, however, from the scant detail offered in the *Findings*, it seems clear that the place of death (i.e. the relation between the body and the south pole) was not the ground for assuming jurisdiction in this case.[188]

Third, the placing of the body of Marks on the plane that flew from the south pole to Christchurch via McMurdo may have triggered the Coroner's assumption of jurisdiction under s 16(a). According to international law, planes are governed by the laws of the state that own the plane.[189] If the plane that carried the body of Marks from the south pole to McMurdo and then to Christchurch was a New Zealand plane, all bodies on that plane would be governed by New Zealand law and potentially satisfy the requirement of being 'in' New Zealand. However, despite USA–New Zealand collaboration in Antarctica, the flight from the south pole to Christchurch that carried the body of Rodney Marks was in all likelihood

---

187 Ibid, 19.
188 *Findings*, above, n 1, 4–5.
189 See, generally, Gbenga Oduntan, *Sovereignty and Jurisdiction in the Airspace and the Outer Space: Legal Criteria for Spatial Delimitation* (Routledge, 2012). See also *Coroners Act 1988* (NZ) s 16(c)(i), which provides a coroner with jurisdiction where the death occurred 'on or from an aircraft or ship', offering an implicit reminder that New Zealand flights carry New Zealand common law and its attendant coronial jurisdiction.

not a New Zealand flight. In general, it seems, flights between Christchurch and the south pole are considered to be US flights, and it is reasonable to assume the plane that carried the body of Rodney Marks was an American plane with an American flight number carrying another form of (American) common law. In these circumstances, it is highly unlikely that the placing of the body of Marks on the plane would satisfy s 16(a) and authorise the Christchurch Coroner's early assumption of jurisdiction.

So, although s 16(a) was clearly satisfied with the landing of the plane in Christchurch, which placed the body of Marks unambiguously 'in' New Zealand, three potential prior applications of s 16(a) – at the south pole, McMurdo Station or on the plane – fail to convincingly explain the Christchurch Coroner's early assumption of jurisdiction. This is because the early assumption of jurisdiction by the Christchurch Coroner did not fall within s 16(a) and was not authorised by this legislation. Rather, the apparently early assumption of jurisdiction was a matter of office; a matter of coronial responsibility and jurisdictional care.

Coronial responsibility and jurisdictional care

From the moment the plane landed in Christchurch in November 2000, the Christchurch Coroner had jurisdiction. Significantly, the *Findings* and *Coronial File* clearly begin before this time. While a precise starting time is not identifiable, it is clearly after his death in May, yet sometime before the moment when the body of Marks arrived in Christchurch in November, and most likely seems to be sometime during the period when the body of Marks was buried at the south pole. In other words, it seems the Christchurch Coroner's jurisdiction began at some point during the interim between the death of Rodney Marks and his removal from his south pole grave. Although it is not possible to pinpoint precisely, from a close reading of the *Findings* and the *Coronial File*, the Coroner assumed jurisdiction at some point while the body of Marks was buried at the south pole. With its legislative grounds in s 16(a) seemingly lacking, there are a number of other possible reasons for this 'early' assumption of jurisdiction, including legal error, diplomacy and institutional or official responsibility. While error and diplomacy are certainly possible, I argue that it was through a jurisdictional responsibility to care for the dead that the Christchurch Coroner came to assume jurisdiction and conduct an inquest into the death of Rodney Marks.

The possibility that the Christchurch Coroner overstepped the limits of his jurisdiction cannot be ignored. As mentioned, s 16(a) of the *Coroner Act 1988* (NZ) certainly does not appear to provide any clear grounds for the assumption of jurisdiction prior to the body of Marks arriving in Christchurch. Did the Coroner erroneously assume jurisdiction prior to the arrival of the body of Marks in Christchurch and if so, was this error rectified by the arrival of the body and the proper authorization of jurisdiction in accordance with s 16(a)? On a strict interpretation of the legislative grounds, any action taken by the Coroner prior to the arrival of the body of Marks in Christchurch would fall outside of the parameters of s 16(a). While the early assumption of jurisdiction was arguably *ultra vires*, the assumption of jurisdiction passed without comment in the *Findings*, suggesting a firmer jurisdictional ground than erroneously overstepping coronial limits without comment. Beyond these legislative grounds, there are at least two other possible sources of authorisation: diplomatic authorisation or a broader responsibility of office that amounts to an inherent jurisdiction to care for the dead.

A further possible explanation of the early assumption of jurisdiction is diplomacy. As a matter of diplomacy and international friendship, did the USA and Australia through some form of diplomatic communication, grant, consent to or simply accept the Christchurch Coroner's early assumption of jurisdiction? Due to the silences in the *Findings* and the *Coronial File*, both in relation to jurisdiction generally and the specific silences resulting from restrictions of access to diplomatic communications, it is impossible to know what might have occurred as a matter of diplomacy and certainly tempting to interpret this simply as a story of bureaucratic and diplomatic administration. With the planes flying in one direction (i.e. Antarctica to New Zealand; New Zealand to Australia), the body was obviously going to arrive in Christchurch at some point, which would mean the Christchurch Coroner would be the first to assume jurisdiction, triggered by the presence of the dead on earthly ground. This was always going to be before the Victorian Coroner's jurisdiction could be triggered through the final stage of the repatriation; bringing the dead home. On this basis, it makes administrative and bureaucratic sense to accept, as a matter of institutional practicalities, the early assumption of jurisdiction by the Christchurch Coroner. Regardless of the content of diplomatic communications, whether this amounted to consent, acceptance or some form of a 'grant' of jurisdiction to the Christchurch Coroner, it is important to acknowledge that this could simply be a story of meaningless administration. However, if such an interpretation is adopted, something quite important is overlooked. What is overlooked is the techniques and practices of legal movement. For this is much more than simply a story of meaningless bureaucratic administration; this is a story of lawful movements.

More than merely administrative, the early assumption and exercise of a coronial jurisdiction by the Christchurch Coroner arose from the way Antarctic planes fly. Flight lines are neither jurisdictionally nor jurisprudentially meaningless. There is only one line of flight in and out of the south pole and that is a flight line that runs between the south pole and Christchurch via McMurdo Research Station. New Zealand has a long history of a close working relationship with the USA, which includes the sharing of resources and facilities and the direction of flight lines.[190] Due to a longstanding working relationship between New Zealand and the USA, including the basing of the United States Antarctic programme in Christchurch, the plane that removed the body of Rodney Marks from the south pole flew in a particular direction, with Christchurch being the ultimate (and only)

---

190 Sahurie, *The International Law of Antarctica*, above, n 8, 18.

destination. This meant the Christchurch Coroner assumed jurisdiction along anticipated flight lines.

More than mere haphazard administration, bureaucracy or diplomacy, this is a story of how a coronial jurisdiction moves into the polar South. At the beginning of this chapter, three engagements with the South were offered, including a methodological engagement of operating on a 'southerly register' in order to pay attention to the techniques and material practices of common law's movements.[191] It is on this southerly register that what might seem otherwise meaningless becomes meaningful. It is meaningful in that this redescription of the death, burial and reburial of Rodney Marks reveals some of the ways in which laws move in the polar South. *This is a movement of law along flight lines.* On this 'southerly' register, therefore, this is more than just a story of haphazard administration but a story of how law moves in relation to the dead.

A Christchurch Coroner assumed jurisdiction in relation to the death of Rodney Marks at the south pole because of the lines of flight and in doing so, instituted lawful relations with the dead in the polar South. This leads, finally, to the issue of responsibility. As mentioned earlier in this part, in a common law country, consistent with the medieval origins of the office, the coroner has jurisdictional responsibility to care for the dead. It was this responsibility that somehow enabled or authorised the establishment of lawful relations between the Coroner and the body of Rodney Marks, stretching from Christchurch to a burial site at the south pole along anticipated flight lines. Whether on the expectation or the anticipation of the body of Rodney Marks reaching New Zealand territory, the Coroner responded to the call of the dead and called for its removal to New Zealand and the sanctity of more earthly ground.[192] This was a movement of law between Christchurch and the south pole, establishing lawful relations between a Coroner and the dead. This is a jurisdictional movement along the flight lines between a burial site at the south pole and the office of Coroner in New Zealand.

For the relationship between the coroner and the dead is a lawful one. Through the coroner's jurisdictional responsibility to care for the dead the office of Coroner in Christchurch was able to move and stretch along flight lines in order to care for the dead, despite its long-distance and icy location. Rather than a jurisdictional void or a pragmatic response to a difficult legal and administrative situation, the significance of this relationship is that it was the conduct of office that authorised the movement of common law in the form of a coronial jurisdiction along the flight lines between Christchurch and the south pole. It was as a result of these movements that a Christchurch Coroner was able to communicate and establish lawful relations with this particular dead.

Recalling the burial party of Chapter 3, and remembering Antigone and her duty to care for Polynices, it was through technologies of jurisdiction that a

---

191 See Paul Carter, 'Public Space: Its Mythopoetic Foundations and the Limits of the Law' (2007) 16(2) *Griffith Law Review* 430, 439.
192 See Chapter 3, 3.4.

Christchurch Coroner communicated with the dead, responding to a call to care for the dead and calling in return, bringing the dead home.[193] This is jurisdiction as a technology of movement; movement as a technology of jurisdiction.[194] What authorised this movement beyond the earthly bounds of the unambiguous land of New Zealand to the more ambiguous icy land in Antarctica was the establishment of jurisdictional relations between the common law office of coroner and the dead of the polar South. It is through the establishment of lawful relations with the dead that the jurisdiction of the coroner was able to move in the polar South.

An important feature of the relation between the coroner and the dead that enabled the movement of a coronial jurisdiction is the common law technique of 'camping'.[195] It was through camping with the dead that common law in the form of a coronial jurisdiction was able to move along the flight lines between Christchurch and the south pole. Without the jurisdictional technology of camping with the dead, there would not have been any movement of common law in this instance. What enabled this movement was the coroner's responsibility to the dead. This was the coroner's responsibility of office to respond to the call of the dead and find a way to care for this dead. In this instance, it was the care of the Christchurch Coroner that moved the dead from the 'Ice' to a more earthly place in order to be buried, again. This was a movement of law along flight lines through the creation and conduct of lawful relations with the dead. It was through movements along flight lines that technologies of jurisdiction created and conducted lawful relations with the dead of the polar South. To this end, it was the office of coroner that moved a coronial jurisdiction in the polar South through the institution of lawful relations with the dead; coronial responsibility and jurisdictional care.

Instituting care

There are different methods of caring for the dead. While the office of coroner certainly took responsibility and care of the dead, this was not the only form of care. For although the coroner instituted lawful relations with the dead through jurisdictional movements along anticipated flight lines, there were limits to the coroner's method of care.

To this end, it is important to recognise that common law camps with the jurisdiction of the dead, and it does so both officially and somewhat less officially. In the case of Rodney Marks, a New Zealand Coroner conducted an inquest; there was no coronial engagement from any Australian coroner. Anglo-Australian common law, working without office, it seems, struggled to move and place in the polar South, which included a failure to bury the dead in Antarctica and a failure to care for the dead. Yet, for a New Zealand coronial jurisdiction, which

---

193 See Chapter 3, 3.4.
194 See Chapter 2, 2.2.
195 See Chapter 3, 3.4.

moved more readily in the polar South, there was also a struggle to bury the dead in Antarctica and also, in a sense, a failure to care for the dead. Through the office of coroner, however, and its jurisdictional call for the dead to come home, common law moves through a New Zealand coronial jurisdiction as it camps with the dead. Through the institution of office and more particularly, the office of coroner, therefore, common law camps with the jurisdiction of the dead, offering a method of care.

However, despite the efforts of the Christchurch Coroner, this official account of care is somewhat thin and necessarily incomplete. In the narrative and redescription of the death, burial and reburial of Rodney Marks, not only is the quality of this seemingly official form of care revealed as somewhat limited, but what is also revealed is a period of time where those taking up and holding office were unable to care, or perhaps incapable of caring for the dead. There was, however, a comparatively less official mode of caring for the dead. Through a careful and caring ceremony performed by friends and colleagues in their unofficial capacity, Rodney Marks was temporarily buried at the south pole. While unofficial, at least as far as that is possible, for it was certainly not without office, this burial ceremony instituted lawful relations in the polar South, albeit temporarily.

Institutionally, there is very little information in the *Findings* or the *Coronial File* about what occurred in the remaining months of the astral winter, except to note:

> His body was held during the astral winter, at south pole Station and in accordance with normal protocols evacuated by the American authorities through Christchurch, New Zealand, when this became logistically possible in November 2000.[196]

What these 'normal protocols' actually are, and how normal these protocols might actually be, especially where there is 'an investigative and jurisdictional void for deaths in Antarctica, in some circumstances',[197] is questionable. With the USA National Science Foundation ('NSF') responsible for the Station, subcontracting daily operations to Raytheon, some insight into these 'normal protocols' are revealed in a message from the NSF manager on 13 May 2000:

> There is no plan to fly to south pole to evacuate Rodney's remains. The extremely cold temperatures at south pole during the winter render it prohibitively dangerous and risks to flight crews too great to permit flights into the station. The body will be kept at south pole until the first flight of the 2000–2001 season, which traditionally takes place in late October or early November depending on temperature considerations.[198]

---

196 *Findings*, above, n 1.
197 Ibid, 3, 43.
198 Coughran, 'Rodney Marks', above, n 113.

How the body 'will be kept',[199] however, remains institutionally unexplained. Beyond a reference to 'normal protocols', the *Findings* and *Coronial File* effectively and efficiently brush over the intervening six months between the time of death in May and the official beginnings of the coronial inquest in November. Unable to care for the dead in this time and place, although not particularly surprising given the purpose and parameters of a contemporary coronial inquest, the *Findings* and *Coronial File* include no mention of a south pole burial. Yet, Marks was temporarily buried in Antarctica, and buried quite near to the south pole. Moving beyond the limitations of the *Findings* and *Coronial File*, scientific diary entries, including blogs and memorial websites, provide some insight.

Having died on 12 May 2000, Rodney Marks was buried on 3 July 2000. During the intervening eight weeks before burial, his body remained in storage in the tunnels. As one of Marks' colleagues, Dave Pernic, explained in a public message posted on the University of Chicago's CARA website, being the research institute coordinating Spirex, Marks' research project, and most probably Marks' employer:

> Yesterday, we had a funeral for our friend here. It seems like a long time since he died in order to have a funeral, I know. But here is what happened ... His death was a surprise, and the normal procedure is to store the body in the cold somewhere until it can be flown out. They put him on a sled and stashed him in an arch, kind of out of sight, as to not spook anyone that might work in there doing rounds and such. Some of us were thinking about a week later, that this was wholly unsatisfactory, and was not treating our friend with the proper respect, after all, he came here to study the sky, at least he could be put to rest under the aurora and stars. Let's build him a casket, and bury him out at the pole for the rest of the winter.[200]

Like Polynices, whose body was left in the open for carrion, the body of Marks was left lying on the ground,[201] although unlike Polynices, the body of Marks was 'stashed ... kind of out of sight'. In a different act of authority, the US authorities in the role of Creon, it seems, neither cared nor failed to care for this dead, but simply waited; suspending burial.

So, a funeral was arranged by his colleagues at the Station and attended by many, but not all, of those remaining at the Station. There does not seem to have been bureaucratic or administrative support for the burial from those responsible for the management of the US research station, including the NSF and Raytheon.

---

199 Ibid.
200 Dave Pernic, 'Rodney Marks (1968–2000)', in *Center for Astrophysical Research in Antarctica* (4 July 2000), http://astro.uchicago.edu/cara/marks/funeral.html.
201 Sophocles, 'Antigone' in Sophocles, *The Theban Plays: King Oedipus, Oedipus at Colonus, Antigone* (E.F. Watline trans, Penguin, 1947). See Chapter 4, 4.3.

Under difficult circumstances, friends of Rodney Marks slowly built a coffin in their spare time outside their usual, long working hours. With the south pole in complete darkness during the winter-over, Marks' colleagues went out in the dark in order to find wood and despite snow 'blowing over the lumber berm' found some rough oak planks, as well as the 'planer/joiner'.[202] Time was then spent preparing the wood from 'rough lumber to furniture quality.'[203] With a 'team of volunteers', a coffin was built:

> All oak with decorative trim all routed smooth, and an awesome grain and finish … copper rails with brass brackets, polished to a mirror finish, and a padded and upholstered interior. And a plaque inscribed to him with a brass inlay of the constellation Scorpio. It weighs, I estimate, around 250 lbs, and is quite a work of art. We are very proud of it. One neat aspect is that we scraped up a lot of parts from stuff that normally wouldn't be used for this purpose. … Plumbing pipe, and tablecloth, and bearing bronze, eggcrate bedding foam … we had limited stains and finishes, and we had to set up a wood shop, since the old one was dismantled because the station is in transition of rebuild. Our carpenter in charge of directing us has a broken wrist and arm and sprained left wrist. Lots of people helped … it took a month to build.[204]

With the challenge of scientists building a coffin at the Station with limited resources, limited time, difficult environment, extreme temperatures and apart from an injured carpenter, presumably limited carpentry skills, the initial estimation that it might take '10 days or so' to build was an underestimate, taking a month to complete. When finished, however, with such detailed care involved in building this coffin, it was quite appropriately described as a 'beautiful casket'.[205] Having scrounged materials, and volunteered time, it seems clear from this account that the desire to build a coffin was expressed and enacted by Marks' Station friends and colleagues, seemingly without institutional support from the Station's administrative managers based in the USA.

Having built a coffin, on Saturday 1 July 2000, a 'group had gone out … in −102F temps and dug a grave near the geographic pole. The location was a taxiway a few years back and was pretty hard digging.'[206] On Monday 3 July 2000, a funeral was arranged by Marks' friends and colleagues at the Station. The following day, Dave Pernic writes:

> Yesterday was the day of the big move. … We placed Rodney in the casket and carried him to dome entrance arch. There the casket was strapped onto

202 Pernic, 'Rodney Marks (1968–2000)', above, n 200.
203 Ibid.
204 Ibid.
205 Ibid.
206 Ibid.

a Nansen sled. The main doors were opened to expose the 15 ft drift wall that has accumulated. The tractor digs its way in monthly, and our walking path curves off to the left, following the contour of the drift up to the surface of the plateau. This was really a very surreal scene. The arch lights were off. It was very cold and dark, with lots of vapor and ice forming on peoples faces and masks. We are a motley crew dressed up our extreme weather gear, working together by flashlight ... there are nearly 50 of us ... and 25 or so gather ropes to pull and push our 450lb load ... our friend, up to the surface ... its a descent grade, but no problem for our cooperation. The snow wall, and the dark, the red and white flashlight beams, and the vapor and ice crystals made it into a surreal scene, it was beautiful. At the pole we placed him into the ice grave, with a great deal of cooperation and teamwork. Two people spoke. Simple and elegant, and definitely 'cool'. Rodney would think so. I feel very good about it. I am proud to have given him this respect. He was a good friend. I am proud that we all worked together to make this happen. I am proud that our community here made this happen. This place is harsh, but in its extremes there is also beauty. The aurora and incredible sky can be amazing. And now our friend is laid to rest, albeit temporarily, under that sky.[207]

Caring for the dead, in the darkness of an Antarctic winter, a coffin was crafted, a grave dug and a ceremony performed. Surrounded by friends, Rodney Marks was buried in the ice near the geographic south pole, 'albeit temporarily, under that sky'.[208] A plaque and Australian flag marked the burial site.[209]

To conclude, it is clear that there are different methods of caring for the dead. In this part, the office of coroner has been redescribed as central to the movements of a coronial jurisdiction in the polar South and the institution of lawful relations with the dead. Yet, with different offices come different forms and methods of care and while the office of coroner instituted lawful relations along flight lines, it was through the office of friendship that the responsibility to care for the dead in the polar South was taken up through the institution of burial. In other words, although the Coroner instituted lawful relations and cared for the dead by removing the dead from an icy grave and returning the dead home for reburial, this was not the only form of care. Others also took responsibility for this dead. Although not immediately or obviously placed as actions and activities of office, those who attended to his burial in the polar South did so through a duty and responsibility to care for the dead. This was also a duty and responsibility of office. While it is tempting to render this as mere friendship or a sense of moral duty, these acts and activities are the responsibilities of another office; the office of friend. Like Antigone, and her 'must' to bury the dead,[210] the friends and colleagues of

---

207 Ibid.
208 Ibid.
209 Cockrell, *A Mysterious Death at the South Pole*, above, n 139.
210 See Chapter 3, 3.4.

Rodney Marks refused to leave his body unburied, lying in storage. Remembering Condren's reminder of the difficulties in registering a non-institutional form of office,[211] such as the office of poet or in this case, the office of friendship, the above account of the first burial of Rodney Marks at the south pole is an account of duty, responsibility and office. Where others struggled to move and in different ways failed or struggled to care, including the failure of Anglo-Australian common law and, despite its efforts, also a New Zealand Coroner, those who took up and held the office of friend were able to take responsibility and care for this dead, instituting lawful relations in the polar South.

In Antarctica, different forms of law struggle to move and care for the dead in the polar South. Across this chapter, some of the ways in which different forms of law move in the polar South have been attended to through the redescription of the death, burial and reburial of Rodney Marks. By paying attention to technical forms and material practices and everyday action and activity of laws, across four parts, it has been noticed how different forms of law move and through these movements, establish or fail to establish lawful relations. By attending to the jurisdiction of the dead in the polar South, therefore, an illustration of how common law moves has been provided and how, by moving, different forms of law locate or fail to locate a lawful place in the polar South. It is these movements and these relations that contribute to the patterning and placing of the laws of the polar South.

---

211 Conal Condren, 'The *Persona* of the Philosopher and the Rhetorics of Office in Early Modern England', in Conal Condren, Stephen Gaukroger and Ian Hunter (eds.), *The Philosopher in Early Modern Europe: The Nature of a Contested Identity* (Cambridge University Press, 2006) 66. See, generally, Chapter 1, 1.2.

Part III
Returning jurisprudence

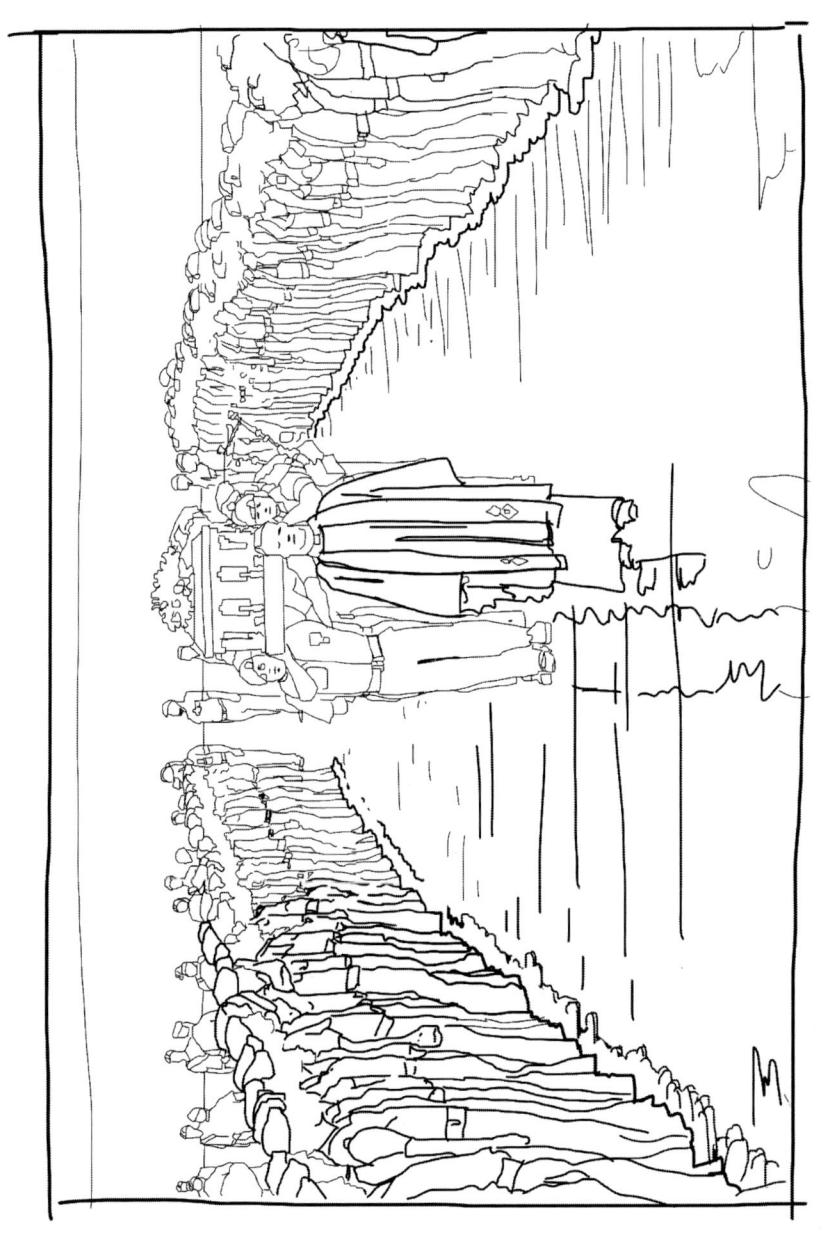

Figure PIII.1 Jenny Barr, *Untitled Ceremony* (2015)
Digital sketch

Chapter 5

Return

> They will protect their living,
> not their dead.[1]

In her 2006 inquiry into the circumstances surrounding the failure to properly repatriate the body of Private Jacob Kovco from Iraq to Australia, Brigadier Cosson reported that it was: '[U]nfortunate that no-one examined the body with sufficient care to notice a cardboard tag attached to the hand bearing the name Juso Sinanovic and his passport number.'[2] It was unfortunate, and it did lack care, as it led to the repatriation of what was referred to as the 'wrong' dead.[3] More than human error or administrative blunder, however, this troubled and troubling repatriation draws attention, yet again, to matters of movement, but also draws attention to jurisprudential questions of ethos and how such questions relate to the conduct of office. A turn to conduct, therefore, is the central gesture of this last chapter, and serves as the final gesture of this jurisprudence of movement.

Throughout this book, by working with both traditional and non-traditional legal materials, I have sought to offer a better understanding of the place of movement in the technical and material forms of common law practice. Having provided conceptual guidance in the first two chapters, the last two chapters demonstrated the work of a minor jurisprudence of movement. In doing so, across the course of the previous four chapters, this book has addressed the central question of 'how does common law move?', by directing attention to technologies of jurisdiction as expressed through the exemplar material practices of walking and burial. In short, there is now an understanding that common law moves with the footsteps of the subject, place-making in silence, which serves as part of the practice of lawful relations. Yet in Australia, the quality of lawful relations, whether

---

1 Australian Broadcasting Corporation, 'Losing Private Kovco' on *Australian Story* (12 February 2007), http://www.abc.net.au/austory/content/2007/s1846984.htm.
2 Elizabeth Cosson, 'Inquiry into Circumstances Surrounding the Failure to Repatriate the Body of Private Jacob Kovco to Australia on 25 April 2006' (Australian Department of Defence, June 2006) 2 (*Cosson Report*).
3 Ibid, 1.

relations with other forms of law or relations with the dead, remains less than ideal, especially the manner in which lawful relations continue to be conducted. Embracing this reoriented and realigned jurisprudential understanding of how common law moves, it now becomes possible to ask the question of how to move well. Until now, what has rested quietly throughout this book is the ethos of how to move well: a matter of conduct.

Although unobtrusive, questions of ethos and practices of character in action have not been entirely absent. For example, by tracking those who take up office, including the jurist, the coroner and the friend, throughout this book, I have asked those in both official and unofficial roles to pay attention to how they conduct themselves in office, and to ask how they might do this well. Yet the question of justness, that is, the quality of being just has often remained somewhat oblique. Of course, in a minor jurisprudence, selections were made and not all was revealed to the same extent. This does not mean, however, that these jurisprudential strands have passed unnoticed.

For example, consider the relation between movement and place. In earlier chapters, I raised the possibility that one of the potentially significant results of common law movement is the manner in which, at least through burial practices, such movements contribute to the humanisation of the earth, and also, perhaps, the becoming of a juridical earth. This possibility, however, has rested quietly and certainly has not been exhaustively explored, at least not overtly. Covertly, movements through the institution of burial have been noticed, and the question of the juridical earth softly percolated. In this regard, consider again the two previous chapters, one set in colonial New South Wales and the other in Antarctica, both of which took up the task of this minor jurisprudence, and both of which included two moments of humanisation. More specifically, in Chapter 3, where members of a burial party walked into the woods beyond to bury the dead, four bodies were left lying on the ground: those the burial party sought, and those the burial party later killed. Recall how the bodies of Hodgkinson and Wimbo had been left in the woods, 'naked covered by wood ... their Cloaths provisions and Arms and Blankets were taken from them'.[4] Recall too how the bodies of Lule Geo and Jemmy were buried in shallow graves then 'dug ... up and left the Bodies laying on the Ground'.[5] Twice unburied in Chapter 3, in Chapter 4, the dead were buried, twice. First at the south pole with careful ceremony, the body of Rodney Marks was moved and buried a second time in coastal Victoria. In this final chapter, there are also two burials.

In each of these examples, by linking movement to place through the institution of burial, the question of the juridical earth becomes a question of place-making and manifests as a jurisprudential challenge of lawful place. Never permanent,

4 Evidence of Jonas Archer in *R v Powell* [15–16 October 1799, Court of Criminal Judicature, Dore J A] Minutes of Proceedings, State Records Office of New South Wales, NRS 2700 [X905] 348 ('NRS 2700 [X905]').
5 Thomas Rickerby NRS 2700 [X905] 330; Prisoners' defence NRS 2700 [X905] 310-1.

always fractured yet constantly reproduced through the repetition of mundane material practices, again and again, 'lawful place' is a phrase I use to capture the critical potential of paying attention to the place of law, and the law of place, as well as attending to the ways in which we live with law in place.[6] As the discipline responsible for the *prudentia* of law (i.e. its practical wisdom or good conduct), the question of lawful place is a task that falls within the realm of jurisprudence. While further jurisprudential research is needed to properly link movement to place, and explore the possibilities of lawful place, when asked in Australia, as when asked in other settler colonial nations, the question of lawful place is also, and must always be, a question of how to live in place with multiple forms of law, in other words, a question of conduct. Therefore, taking seriously the challenge of living with law, and thinking more carefully about ways of living with a colonial form of law, and living that life well, requires noticing how common law's technical and material practices not only move, but are also place-related, and placed. Therefore, as part of the conduct of my office, that is, the office of jurisprudent, what is drawn out in this final chapter is the relation between movement, the institution of burial, humanisation and what it might mean to care for lawful place.

To this end, this final chapter is a reflective practice that draws out the importance of conduct. Closing with repatriation, it does so by creating a jurisprudential tale of both movement and return. However, before ending the book with one last allegorical vignette, I offer three final comments on what this book has revealed through its minor jurisprudence of movement. First, by taking seriously the question of office, this book showed the jurist how they might account for and take responsibility for some of the forms of common law practice as a matter of office. This involved paying attention to the material dynamic of movement and its relation to the practice of the care of the dead. This is certainly not an easy task, especially in the context of a colonial form of law such as Anglo-Australian common law that continues to struggle in the creation and conduct of lawful relations. But it is a necessary task of office and, for the responsible jurist, one that forms part of what it means to take up and hold office. Second, this book revealed how Anglo-Australian common law moves with a tendency to slide by, unnoticed, but through technologies of jurisdiction. With jurisdiction placed as a technology of movement, this book noticed different forms of movement, focusing on movements in relation to the dead. By paying attention to technical forms and material practices of movement, some of the ways in which common law moves in its relations and comes to be in place, or at least seems to come to be in place, were demonstrated. One of these ways is through the institution of burial. Third, and finally, with movement in place, this book illustrated that there are different offices with different tasks, privileges, duties, responsibilities and modes of conduct. With different forms of movement, including movements in relation to the dead, and different offices, this book illustrated that there are also different ways of caring

6 See Olivia Barr, 'A Jurisprudential Tale of a Road, an Office and a Triangle' (2015) 27(2) *Law and Literature* 199.

for the dead, which is an important activity of caring for place. By attending to the inheritance of office, and what it means to take up and hold office, different offices have been revealed as carrying distinct yet interlacing responsibilities to care for the dead. The reflection of this final chapter joins these diverse offices through their acts of caring for the dead.

Therefore, in this book, what has been offered to the jurist through the creation of a minor jurisprudence of movement is an attention to the conduct of office, techniques of movement and practices of caring for the dead. Having addressed the question of how does common law move, it is now possible to ask the question of how to move well. To this end, this book closes with a repatriation as a jurisprudential tale of how to care for the dead, conduct lawful relations with the dead, and the need to conduct those relations well. Paying attention to the material movements of two dead, ceremonial practices and the technical movements of Anglo-Australian common law, this chapter offers one final jurisprudential redescription; one that attends to the difficulties of returning the dead as part of a struggle not only to care for the dead, but also to conduct lawful relations with the dead, and to conduct those relations well. As a practice in jurisprudence that returns the question of movement to the technical and material forms of common law practice, a reminder is offered that it is for the jurist to attend to the conduct of office, including moving the dead with care.

Caring for the dead

On 21 April 2006 at 6:52 pm, an Australian soldier, Private Jacob Kovco, died in a United States-run hospital in the Green Zone in Baghdad, Iraq.[7] It was later determined by both military inquiry and coronial inquest that he had accidentally shot himself in the head.[8] Private Kovco was the first Australian soldier to die while deployed in Iraq. It had been many years since Australia had repatriated a military dead. It was four days before Anzac Day. A national day of remembrance observed on 25 April each year to commemorate Gallipoli, today Anzac Day is 'the day on which we remember Australians who served and died in all wars,

---

7 As this death was widely reported, this chapter draws generally on institutional reports, media releases, newspaper articles and a book written by the Australian journalist Dan Box that amalgamates much of the disparate information, and cites specific references only. See, especially, Cosson, *Cosson Report*, above, n 2; State Coroner Victoria, 'Identification of Deceased Person by Way of Circumstances, Coroner's Order, Case No 1524/06, 1 May 2006', in Cosson, *Cosson Report*, above, n 2, Annex O; Warren Cook, Michael Charles and James Patrick O'Sullivan, 'Report of the Board of Inquiry into the Death of 8229393 Private Jacob Kovco at the Secdet Accommodation in the Australian Embassy Compound Baghdad on 21 April 2006' (redacted version, 27 October 2006); Australian Department of Defence, 'Implementation Plan for Board of Inquiry (BOI) Recommendations: Death of Pte Jacob Kovco' (undated); Dan Box, *Carry Me Home: The Life and Death of Private Jake Kovco* (Allen &Unwin, 2008).
8 Cosson, *Cosson Report*, above, n 2; State Coroner Victoria, 'Identification of Deceased Person by Way of Circumstances, Coroner's Order, Case No 1524/06, 1 May 2006', in Cosson, *Cosson Report*, above, n 2, Annex O.

conflicts and peacekeeping operations. The spirit of Anzac, with its human qualities of courage, mateship and sacrifice, continues to have meaning and relevance for our sense of national identity.'[9] With a desire to return the dead home for Anzac Day, ignoring forensic concerns, within hours, the body of Kovco was moved by Blackhawk helicopter to the US military morgue at Baghdad airport. Accompanied by Kovco's platoon leader, a sergeant codenamed in the later coronial hearing as 'Soldier 2' was appointed as escort,[10] paperwork completed, recording name, military number, injuries and remaining medical equipment. Two thin cardboard tags, marked 'Kovco', were attached to the toe, as well as the zipper of the bodybag.

While remaining at the Baghdad airport morgue for a day and a half, decisions were being made. Various travel routes were considered and discarded, with bearer party and 'Soldier 2' to escort. In a brief 3am meeting, the duties of escort were discussed, absent details. A written duty statement followed, with little detail, including no explicit requirement to identify the dead. Although a series of military documents governed the repatriation process, they were inconsistent and

---

9 Australian War Memorial, 'Anzac Day: Saturday 25 April 2015', in *Australian War Memorial*, https://www.awm.gov.au/commemoration/anzac-day/. The term 'Anzac' is derived from the acronym 'ANZAC' – the telegraphic code for 'Australian and New Zealand Army Corps' – and has come to be indelibly associated with the landing of Australian and New Zealand soldiers at the Gallipoli peninsula along the Turkish coastline on 25 April 1915. See, e.g., Graham Seal, 'ANZAC: The Sacred in the Secular' (2007) 31(91) *Journal of Australian Studies* 135, 136. While the Anzac forces were actually defeated by the Ottoman Turkish defenders after an eight-month campaign, Seal points to a 'a significant gap' between the rhetoric and public commemoration of Anzac Day itself, describing the extract referring to the 'spirit of Anzac', quoted in the preceding text, deriving from a programme for the 2006 National Anzac Day ceremony at the Australian War Memorial as 'characteristic' of this apparent dissonance; Seal, at 137. For a critique on the militarisation of Anzac Day, see Marilyn Lake and Henry Reynolds, *What's Wrong with Anzac? The Militarisation of Australian History* (New South, 2010). Significantly, 25 April 2015 marked the 100th anniversary of the Anzac landings at Gallipoli. To coincide with this, the Australian government launched the Anzac Day Centenary campaign, comprising a series of commemorative events, educational strategies, and an historical research grants programme, from 2014 and beyond: Australian Government, 'Launch of the New Anzac Portal Website' on *100 Years of Anzac: The Spirit Lives 2014–2018* (3 December 2014), http://www.anzaccentenary.gov.au/. As part of this programme, the Australian War Memorial in Canberra – Australia's capital city – will host the Dawn Service and National Anzac Day Ceremony. Canberra, as the temporal and spatial site where commemorative events marking national days such as Anzac Day intersect with the inclusionary/exclusionary politics of what it means to be Australian therefore becomes an especially powerful site of myth making: see Chris Beer, 'Spectacle, Urban Governance and the Politics of Nationhood: Canberra and the Production of Anzac Day Commemorations and Australia Day Live' (2009) 27(1) *Urban Policy and Research* 59. For an exposition of Anzac Day narratives and how the relationship between myth and place is central to the personal/public experience of past mythic events, see Robyn Mayes 'Origins of the Anzac Dawn Ceremony: Spontaneity and Nationhood' (2009) 33(1) *Journal of Australian Studies* 51.
10 AAP, 'Kovco body escort "exhausted"', Special Broadcasting Service (online), 24 February 2015, http://www.sbs.com.au/news/article/2006/07/25/kovco-body-escort-exhausted.

generally unknown to those making decisions.[11] With more experience repatriating their dead from Iraq, the US usually took eight days, and the British 14. It was four days before Anzac Day. Poignant.

Lacking planes, and lacking mortuary facilities, a decision was made to utilise the services of a private company, Kenyon International, which specialises in recovering the dead. To make these arrangements, a standing contract between Australia and Kenyon needed to be triggered by a second contract, detailing specific requirements such as the identification and processing of remains.[12] Instead, Kenyon was telephoned and simply asked to 'go to work'.[13] The plan was to use military transport from Baghdad to Kuwait City, Kuwait (the site of Australia's central base for its military operations in the Middle East) and from Kuwait, a civilian Emirates flight to Melbourne. Based in rural England, Kenyon subcontracted part of the work to the Gulf Agency Company ('GAC'), based in Kuwait. One week later, the Australian Defence Force sent Kenyon the contract. The single-page written work authorisation agreement was impressively brief: 'Fatality of PTE Jacob Bruce Kovco, fatal shooting 21 April 06. Reatriation [sic] of the remains of PTE Kovco back to Australia.'[14] One line. No detail. No requirement to identify or process remains. Just 'return'.

At the US airport morgue in Baghdad, on suggestion of the bearer party, the body of Kovco was identified by the escort before being placed in an aluminium transfer case packed with ice to delay decomposition. In what is known as a ramp ceremony, an honour guard of American, British and Australian soldiers stood on either side as the bearer party carried the transfer case onto a C130 Hercules plane. Carrying the body of Kovco, bearer party and escort, the Hercules landed several hours later in Kuwait. Flanked by US soldiers, another ramp ceremony was performed as the transfer case was taken to the US military morgue at the Kuwait airport. More paperwork was completed, and three further tags, including identification details and a registration number for that morgue were attached to the finger, zipper and handle of the transfer case.

Given the planned use of a civilian flight out of Kuwait, Kuwaiti domestic law required the body be processed at a civilian morgue.[15] Unbeknown to Kenyon, its subcontractor GAC, and all Australian defence and government personnel involved in the repatriation, there was an international trade agreement between Australia and Kuwait waiving this domestic requirement. However, on the understanding that it *was* a legal requirement, Kenyon via GAC moved the body of

---

11 Cosson, *Cosson Report*, above, n 2; Australian Defence Force, 'Mortuary Affairs Plans', in *Inquiry into Circumstances Surrounding the Failure to Repatriate the Body of Private Jacob Kovco to Australia on 26 April 2006: Executive Summary*, June 2006.
12 'Commonwealth and Kenyon International Standing Offer of 2003 provides ADF access to the services of Kenyon International for the repatriation of deceased ADF personnel', in Cosson, *Cosson Report*, above, n 2, 1.
13 Box, *Carry Me Home*, above, n 7, 114.
14 Ibid.
15 Ibid.

Kovco from the US morgue at Kuwait airport 15 kilometres north by civilian ambulance to the Al Sabah civilian morgue within Kuwait City. The bearer party followed in a minibus. At the Al Sabah morgue, as the transfer case was too large, the bodybag was removed from its coffin and placed directly in one of the 22 refrigerator units. In Arabic, a handwritten label was marked with Kovco's name and nationality and placed on the door of the unit. Familiar with the layout and atmosphere of US military morgues, and concerned with the different environment of this civilian morgue in a country where the dead are normally buried as soon as possible in accordance with Islamic law (and hence, little need for a morgue), one of the bearer party observed it was just 'not military'.[16]

As the days were rapidly passing, it was now apparent to all that the body of Kovco would not be home for Anzac Day on 25 April 2006, yet urgency remained. On the morning of Anzac Day, the escort code-named Soldier 2, embassy consul (having just cancelled Kovco's passport) and military representatives from Australia's Kuwaiti base (Joint Operation Command for Australia's presence in the Middle East) went to seal the coffin. At Al Sabah morgue, a number of coffins were already open, some containing bodies. A black bodybag, seemingly too big, was forcibly stuffed into the aluminium transfer case. Two men – escort and consul – watched as it was unzipped. Having never met Kovco, the consul noticed the lack of military tags and a moustache that did not match Kovco's passport photo. The escort, exhausted, having already seen the body in death, and having already identified on several occasions, looked again. Neither had the responsibility of identification, both thought it was the other's duty. Both nodded. Both said yes. Bodybag zipped, lid closed, steel bands soldered, red wax stamped with the embassy seal, and on the lid, the escort wrote 'Kovco: Dest Melbourne Australia.'[17]

Taken by civilian ambulance to Kuwait airport, the escort continued; the bearer party did not. Waiting outside the airport fence, the bearer party watched. Through the airport windows, wearing civilian clothes in preparation for the non-military flight, the escort watched the loading of the aluminium transfer case onto the plane. No ramp ceremony here. Departing Kuwait, changing planes in Dubai before refuelling in Singapore, the civilian Emirates flight was destined to arrive in Melbourne in the early hours of 27 April 2006, two days after Anzac Day.

During the flight, it became apparent that the body of Kovco was not on the plane.

In Kuwait, GAC received a phone call from a US company, KBR, a subsidiary of Halliburton, the US multinational corporation that is also one of the largest oil companies in the world. The phone call concerned Juso Sinanovic, who had worked as a carpenter for KBR, building US military accommodation at their Balad airbase, north of Baghdad, Iraq. On an unknown date, several days prior, Sinanovic had been playing table tennis in Iraq when he collapsed. He died

16 Ibid, 137.
17 Ibid, 147.

from a brain haemorrhage. At some unknown point, as part of KBR's repatriation process to take his body home to Djurdjevik in northern Bosnia, the body of Sinanovic was moved from Balad, Iraq to Kuwait City, Kuwait. On Anzac Day, the same day the Australian embassy sealed a body, the body of Sinanovic was in the Al Sabah morgue, waiting to be sealed by the embassy of Bosnia and Herzegovina. Yet as KBR told GAC, the body of their worker, Juso Sinanovic, was now missing from Al Sabah morgue and the body of Kovco was still there. Had the wrong body been sent home?

The realisation of the 'wrong body' unfolded quickly. In Kuwait, the Australian consul and a military representative attended Al Sabah morgue to identify the body that remained. Clearly a different body from the one sealed as Kovco: different medical equipment, no facial hair, severe facial disfiguration. Due to the head injuries resulting from Kovco's fatal gunshot wound, the passport photo of Kovco was of little use. A family doctor in Australia was called to describe the impact of a gunshot wound to the head. It matched. The US morgue in Baghdad was called for a description of Kovco in death: a match. Kovco's death certificate contained an anatomical diagram of medical equipment: again, a match. Morgue staff pulled a loose cardboard tag out from the bottom of the bodybag, unattached with the eyelet torn, marked with a series of numbers and the name 'Jacob Kovco'. For conclusive proof, photos of Kovco in death were requested. When received, nearly 24 hours after the misidentification, Kovco was identified as a body remaining in Al Sabah morgue in Kuwait City, and not on a plane soon to arrive in Melbourne.

News travelled: bearer party in Baghdad; Australian Minister for Defence Brendan Nelson at Canberra airport about to fly to the small regional city of Sale in Gippsland, Victoria, to take Kovco's family to Melbourne to meet the plane supposedly carrying the body of Kovco. Having flown from Canberra to Sale with the knowledge of the 'wrong body' before breaking the news to the family in person, Nelson impulsively offered to take everyone on his government jet to the Middle East to find the 'right' body. Kovco's wife, Shelley Kovco, had no passport, it was nearly midnight, and her two small children were exhausted. Refusing the extravagant offer, the family flew to Melbourne as planned. Inside the Melbourne international airport terminal, the family waited with Kovco's 3RAR platoon, chosen as bearer party to carry the coffin from the plane. Yet when Emirates flight EK404 landed, the bearer party did not bear: there was no ramp ceremony. Except for the escort accompanying the body, all knew the body was not that of Kovco. Stepping off the plane to no ceremony, the escort Soldier 2 was told he had brought the wrong body home and sent back to Iraq the next day.

Removed from the Emirates flight EK404, the transfer case containing the not-yet-confirmed body of Juso Sinanovic was taken to the Victorian Institute of Forensic Medicine in Southbank in central Melbourne. Waiting, it was not opened for a further six days. Meanwhile, intense efforts were being made to bring Kovco home. New travel arrangements and new paperwork were needed. Continuing to use Kenyon for the repatriation, the Australian military's weekly

A330 sustainment flight that flew between Sydney and Kuwait was requisitioned, which led to a change in flight destination from Melbourne, where the already-arrived Emirates flight had landed, to Sydney, where the sustainment flight was due to arrive.

At the Al Sabah morgue, with the previous transfer case now in Melbourne with another body, the body of Kovco was placed in a locally made wooden coffin from Al Sabah, sealed by the embassy, draped in an Australian flag and moved by civilian ambulance to the US airport morgue where it had been four days prior. Staff at the US morgue at Kuwait airport offered to replace the wooden coffin with a military coffin, which the new escort accepted. The embassy seals were broken, body taken from the wooden coffin and placed in a heavy silver casket, polished handles, Australian flag tucked neatly under the lid. Appropriate.

At Baghdad airport, with a new escort but no bearer party, American soldiers provided a ramp ceremony. Departing Kuwait, the requisitioned sustainment flight landed in Sydney, where Kovco's 3RAR unit performed another ramp ceremony, as illustrated by Jenny Barr in her artwork opening this final chapter.[18] In the rain, lined in columns, wearing black armbands, the soldiers marched on the spot before coming to rest. Carrying the silver casket across the tarmac, led by an army chaplain, a solitary piper followed. Placed in the terminal, members of Kovco's family, including his wife, children and mother, approached.

In Sydney, from the airport, the casket was taken by hearse to the Glebe Institute of Forensic Medicine in central Sydney. A problem: according to the paperwork, it was not the same coffin that had been sealed at Al Sabah morgue. Panic, before successful identification. Not having told anyone the coffins had been changed in Kuwait from a wooden coffin to a silver casket, the new escort quickly explained. The following day was a Sunday morning, and in preparation for a post mortem, medical equipment was removed, and also an identification tag attached to the right wrist, and a piece of string, absent its tag, from the left big toe. The next day, the body of Kovco was flown from Sydney to the Sale RAAF base in Gippsland, Victoria and driven to a funeral parlour in the small town of Maffra (population 4149), where family visited and the casket sealed, again. The next day, a funeral service was held in Briagolong (population 937) then at Sale cemetery, with simultaneous memorial services in Sydney, Solomon Islands and Baghdad. Graveside, in Sale, military roulettes flew past, a 14-man rifle squad fired three volleys and a solitary bugler played the last post.

In Melbourne, at the Victorian Institute of Forensic Medicine, six days after having arrived, the transfer case marked 'Kovco' was finally opened. Attached to the zipper of the bodybag was the fragment of a tag. In the transfer case, the rest of the tag was labelled with the name, Juso Sinanovic, a passport number and a 15-digit alphanumeric code that matched the paperwork the Victorian Coroner had waited on before opening the coffin. A second matching tag was on

---

18 Jenny Barr, Untitled Ceremony (2015) (Figure PIII.1).

the right wrist. Sinanovic was formally identified.[19] On the same day the body of Kovco was returned to Gippsland, the day before Kovco's funeral, the Victorian Coroner released the body of Sinanovic to begin (again) the long return home.

In Bosnia, the family of Sinanovic waited, only receiving updates from Sinanovic's former employer, KBR. Waiting, the Sinanovic family received no communication from Australia, except for an envelope from the Australian embassy in Kuwait containing copies of newspaper articles about the death of an Australian soldier, written in English, untranslated. Nothing more: no information, no estimation of arrival or route, no details, no explanation, no apology. Nothing.

On an unknown date via an unknown route, the body of Sinanovic travelled back to Kuwait in the same too-small transfer case; the lid still marked 'Kovco, Dest Melbourne.' At Al Sabah morgue, Sinanovic was again identified. From Kuwait, the body of Sinanovic finally arrived in Bosnia at Sarajevo, taken north to Djurdjevic and buried the following day, 12 May 2006 – 11 days since release from the Victorian coroner; 17 days since wrongly forced into Kovco's smaller transfer case, and even longer since Sinanovic had died. For a dead who was meant to be buried before sunset according to the law governing his body, this was more than simply a long journey home.

Moving well?

In suspicion of the speed and the strikingly intense brevity with which this troubled and troubling repatriation is rendered mere error, whether human error or administrative blunder, a jurisprudential method of slowness reveals not only that the speed of classification renders the potentially meaningful as meaningless, but that in doing so, what is lost – or at least what is at risk of being lost – is, quite simply, the law story. For this troubled repatriation is more than simply a tale of accident, error and incompetency by government institutions wandering in the mired illogic of bureaucratic structures; it is a practice in a minor jurisprudence of movement.

By attending to the role of ceremony, jurisdictional technologies of movement and the conduct of office as part of the lawful responsibility to care for the dead, this book concludes by raising the question of 'how to move well' as a matter of jurisprudential concern. While moving the dead with care is a jurisdictional responsibility of the office of coroner, in this case arising through common law movements along flight lines, as a practice in jurisprudence or a jurisprudence of practice, a reminder is offered that it is not only the coroner that has responsibilities to care for the dead. For it is also a task for the jurist. This is in the sense that it is for the jurist to attend to the technical forms and material practices of common law as part of the conduct of office, including moving the dead with care.

---

19 State Coroner Victoria, 'Identification of Deceased Person by Way of Circumstances, Coroner's Order, Case No 1524/06, 1 May 2006', in Cosson, *Cosson Report*, above, n 2, Annex O.

In this troubled repatriation, who was responsible for the care of the dead? An Australian soldier from country Victoria died in Iraq and a NSW Coroner conducted an inquest. A Bosnian carpenter died in Iraq and a Victorian Coroner released the body without inquiry or inquest after holding it for 11 days. Obviously, when both planes landed, two different coronial jurisdictions were triggered. But, as addressed in Chapter 4 in the context of who governed the dead in Antarctica, who had jurisdiction prior to the planes landing, and how? Generally, a coronial jurisdiction in Australia is triggered by territorial attachment (bodies, cause of death, prior residence etc.).[20] For Kovco, with a prior residence in both states – personal home in country Victoria, military base in New South Wales – and despite a tenuous argument that the cause of death was deployment from his workplace, that is, the military base, there was no clear attachment to NSW. Yet, when the flight destination changed from Melbourne, Victoria, to Sydney, NSW, after the first failed attempt to return Kovco home, there was a jurisdictional dispute, or perhaps less dramatically, a telephone conversation between two state coroners. With the Victorian Coroner previously assuming jurisdiction, successful after a telephone conversation, the NSW Coroner claimed jurisdiction the day the flight route was changed, exercising it immediately. Even noting an eight-hour difference in time zones, when the NSW Coroner assumed jurisdiction, the body of Kovco was not in Australia, but remained in Kuwait.

Like the decision of the Christchurch Coroner in New Zealand to take jurisdictional responsibility for the body of Rodney Marks while it remained in Antarctica, there is more to this jurisdictional decision than mere convenience, error or practicality. For such an interpretation not only renders this early assumption of jurisdiction effectively meaningless, but also fails to notice a coroner establish lawful relations and take responsibility for the dead. As explored in Chapter 4, in the common law tradition, it is the medieval office of coroner, as inherited through its contemporary form, which has jurisdictional responsibility to care for the dead. This is a jurisdiction that formerly required the coroner to travel to the dead, but over time, the direction of movement has changed: the dead now come to the coroner. What this means is that despite its relatively low-level judicial status, the office of coroner inherits a set of duties and responsibilities from its medieval office that includes the care of the dead.

Here, through this responsibility to care for the dead, a jurisdictional relation was established between the office of coroner in NSW and this particular dead in Kuwait, even before the dead had arrived on territory. Inheriting from a medieval office, there was a call from the coroner – a jurisdictional call – for the dead to come home. Establishing relations through this call, there was a jurisdictional movement along the anticipated flight lines from Sydney to Kuwait. This was a jurisdictional call that moved a coronial jurisdiction, moved common law, bringing a NSW coroner into lawful relations with this military dead located so far north, waiting in another hemisphere.

20 See Chapter 4.3.

But who cared for Sinanovic? Clearly, the Victorian Coroner did not demand expedited paperwork let alone communicate with the family, provide a fitting coffin or assist in a proper return. This suggests a different relation between the coroner and this dead, the one not being called home. If a coroner can call the dead home, can a coroner also send the dead home? Or was the task of the coroner to guard the dead, awaiting the call of an uncommon other? This raises the question of repatriation as a responsibility to return and restore, especially having taken this dead without care. Yet, it is not just the coroner that cares for the dead. A number of offices are responsible for caring for the dead, including the office of coroner, office of friend, office of soldier – as both bearer and escort – and also, of course, the office of jurist. While caring for the dead in different ways, some with more attention to the conduct of office and forms of care than others, these offices are joined through their responsibilities to care for the dead.

Consider ceremony as one of the ways in which different offices take up their responsibility to care for the dead. Ceremony is evident in the many stages of bringing Kovco home. At ramp ceremonies on different tarmacs, the body of Kovco was carried on and off planes, flanked by various combinations of national armies, attendant in perfect alignment, uniformed with precision, performing respect. Covered with an Australian flag, the transfer case and the later silver casket were carried by a military bearer party in the company of an escort. Sermons delivered, bugler's lament, the last post played. Blackhawk helicopter, civilian ambulance, requisitioned military plane, government jet, black hearse flanked by police sirens in a travelcade on a wet morning through central Sydney, stately vehicles in a funeral procession in country Victoria. Ceremonies of burial conducted simultaneously in both hemispheres. In the very small rural town of Briagolong, although it was not a state funeral, the Australian Prime Minister, Minister of Defence and Chief of the Defence Force attended, as did many others, overflowing the capacity of the weatherboard Briagolong Mechanics Institute, established 1874. Airforce fly-bys, ritual gunshots graveside: a military burial. Memorial plaques at Holsworthy and the war memorial in Canberra.

Yet, in contrast, Sinanovic did not receive ceremonial care. Forcibly stuffed into a transfer case too small, unknowingly removed from a civilian morgue in Kuwait and loaded onto a plane, watched through an airport window and airport fence by another's bearers. On arrival in Melbourne, knowingly, a bearer party stood, unbearing. From tarmac to morgue, awaiting paperwork, six days pass, identified, returned to the too-small-coffin, still marked with the name and destination of another. Returned to where Sinanovic was taken, not to where Sinanovic needed to be returned. Silence; so very little known. Absent time, absent knowledge, absent communication, absent care. There was so little ceremony, and so little care, in returning this dead home.

To repatriate is to care for the dead, and therefore to conduct lawful relations with the dead, and the need to conduct those relations well. Tellingly, the Australian Minister for Defence at the time of this troubled repatriation, Brendan Nelson, offered: 'The problem occurs for us is when we are in the hands of other organisations in other countries, and so I'll leave it at that.'[21] No. The problem occurs when those in office fail to take responsibility for the care of the dead as part of the conduct of office. As quoted in the opening of this final chapter, Jacob Kovco's mother, Judy Kovco, offered her judgment: 'They will protect their living, not their dead.'[22]

Directed to the army, and their struggle to properly perform their duties of care, the words of Judy Kovco resonate for the responsible jurist: reminding the jurist that although other offices may also have responsibilities of care, it is for the jurist to take up and hold office and care for the dead; caring for place. So, while the authority of the Australian state as practised through the conduct of Nelson's office sought to place responsibility elsewhere, with a private company, a civilian morgue, the challenges of traversing another's territorial jurisdiction etc., this troubled and troubling repatriation is more than just a story of administrative and human error: it is a lawful story of responsibility and care.

Repatriation is both a return to land and a return to law. Yet, for the responsible jurist, taking up and holding office, and attending to common law practice, repatriation is also a return of movement, as well as a return to lawful place. In this minor jurisprudence of movement that noticed how common law moves into place, and the importance of caring for the dead as part of those movements, this book concludes with the reminder that it is for the jurist to move the dead with care as part of the conduct of office. This is the jurisprudential question of how to move well; this is the return of movement to jurisprudence, and of the dead to lawful relations.

21 Box, *Carry Me Home*, above, n 7, 166.
22 Australian Broadcasting Corporation, 'Losing Private Kovco', above, n 1.

Index

Notes: National laws and court cases are Australian unless otherwise stated.
Page numbers in *italic* refer to illustrations. n = footnote.

Aboriginal law: jurisdiction 123–4; relationship with common law 21, 28, 37–8, 40–1, 42–3, 93–4, 124; as *sui generis* 37–8
Aboriginal sovereignty 43–4; non-justiciability 44, 83–4, 85–6, 93–4
Aborigines: accompanying settlers into woods 136–7, 144; clashes with settlers 113, 119, 119n38, 120–4; inadmissibility as court witnesses 118–19; killings of 116–20, 119n38, 126–8, 225; legal status 118–19, 118–19n33; places appropriate to dealing with 138–40; settlers' attitudes to 86n66, 112; settlers' first contacts with 111–13; sexual relations with settlers 41–3; *see also* Aboriginal law; Aboriginal sovereignty
aeroplanes, jurisdiction on 211–12
Agamben, Giorgio 54
Al Sabah morgue, Kuwait City 229–31, 232–3
al-Tal, Abdullah 13
Alÿs, Francis 13–17, *14*, *16*, 20, 70
Amundsen, Roald 168–9
Amundsen-Scott South Pole Station 162, 174, 180–7, *181*, *182*, *183*, *184*; communication with outside world 189; geographical situation 191–2; location relative to Pole 184–5; location relative to territorial boundaries 186–7, 198–9; medical equipment 192; movement 185–7
Antarctic Treaty 1959 172–4, 175, 183, 195, 202
Antarctic Treaty Act 1960 (Cth) 202

Antarctica 6, 29–30, 62, *160–1*, 162–220, 225; ambiguous nature of land 167, 196–7; burials 178–9, 197; common law in 162–3, 164, 171–2, 198, 201–6; diaries 170; history 166–72; ice shifts 177–9; as 'jurisdictional void' 162, 172, 176, 207; landmark discoveries 168–9; legal relocation of individuals 202–3; maps *173*, 174, 186; movements in 164, 165–87; mythologising 166–7; nomenclature 166, 168n25; range/conflicts of laws 163–4, 171–5, 176–7, 179–80, 194–5, 202–3, 220; Specially Managed Areas (ASMAs) 186–7; territorial divisions/claims 172–7, *173*, 199–201; tourism 170–2, 171n41
Antarctica (Environmental Protection: Liability Annex) Amendment Bill 2009 (NZ) 167n22
anthropology, legal 38
Anzacs/Anzac Day 227–9, 228n9
Aquinas, Thomas, St 68n5
Archer, Jonas 122–3, 125, 142, 144, 152–3
Archer, Mary 127
Aristotle 7n16, 42, 53–4, 67–71, 83, 167
Arthurs, Philip, Governor 42
Atkins, Richard, Judge-Advocate 117n26
Australia: basis of legal system 85–6, 87–8; British claims to 111, 112–13, 114–15; colonisation 86n63; forms of law 37–8; legal inheritance 1–2; state borders 39n17; *see also* Australian Antarctic Territory; common law; New South Wales

Australian Antarctic Territory (AAT) 163, *173*, 176, 177; applicability of law to Australian citizens 202, 204; geographical extent 172–4, 199; legal system 199–201, 202–3; non-Australian citizens in 202

Australian Antarctic Territory Act 1954 (Cth) 200

Australian Capital Territory (ACT): AAT 're-mapped' onto 199; case law 86–7

Australian Courts Act 1829 (UK) 118–19n33

authorisation, relationship with jurisdiction 25, 80, 82

authority: colonial exercise of 115; to make law 53; problems of representation 85–6; relationship with jurisdiction 25, 82

Baghdad *see* Iraq
Barr, Jenny, *Untitled Ceremony* 223
Baudelaire, Charles 7, 7n20
Bauman, Zygmunt 45
'beating the bounds,' custom of 74–6, 74n27; legal significance 75, 76–7; relationship with common law 75–7
Bellingshausen, Fabian Gottlieb von 167–8
Benjamin, Walter 7, 7n20
Berlin Wall 17–20
'beyond': location of 139–40; significance/etymology 134
Biomed 181, 193; territorial location 198–9, 203–4
Black, Christine 8, 8n24
Blackstone, William E. 1, 4–5, 6, 76, 98, 115, 134, 145, 175
Blomley, Nicholas 8, 8n22, 23–4, 89–90
Bowers, Henry, Lt 178
Boyce, Mike 195–6
Braithwaite, Robert 137–8, 139, 140, 153n173
Bransfield, Edward 167–8
British Empire 108; expansion 110; travel writing 170
Browne, David, Constable 128
building, as example of *kinesis* 70
'bumping' 84
burial 6, 28–30, 95–103, 224–36; diversity of rituals 151–2; duty of 150–2, 154–7; humanisation of the earth 95, 100–1, 204; institution of 65–6; jurisdiction over 29–30; materiality of 101; practices 3, 4; repeated 165; significance for common law 95–6, 101–3; in unconsecrated ground 97; *see also* burial party; Marks, Rodney

burial party (Hawkesbury, 1799) 28–9, 61–2, 108, 124–5, 130, 133–8, 140–1, 142–53, 215, 225; composition 135, 141, 142–6; motivations 150–1, 152–4; orders to kill 124–5, 140–1; walking practices 133–4, 134–5, 142, 146–9, 156–7, 157–9

Burne, John 139
Butler, William 116–18, 125, 126, 127, 128, 130, 143, 152
Byrd, Richard E., Admiral 168n26, 179

Caenegem, Raoul van 33–4, 52–3
'camping' 29, 77, 157–8; with the dead 149–50, 153, 158–9, 215
Canada: case law 37–8n12; indigenous laws 37
Carter, Paul 13n34, 18n42, 21, 42, 67n2, 71n19, 84n59
Certeau, Michel de 8, 8n21
Charley (Aborigine) 121–2, 135, 138–40
Christchurch Coroner's Court, inquest on Rodney Marks 29–30, 162, 188–9, 198–9, 215–17, 219–20; assumption of jurisdiction 210–12, 234; findings 188n89, 190, 193, 194–5, 216–17; legislative provisions governing 209–10; overstepping of jurisdiction 212–13; reasons for choice of court 207, 209–14
Cicero, M. Tullius 58
Clark, Gordon 89n72
Clark, Thomas A. 1, 12–13
Coe v Commonwealth 44, 44n44, 83n57, 86n63
Coke, Edward 97n98
Collins, David, Judge-Advocate 117n26
colonialism 19–20, 86n66; legacy 1–3; political context 110; role of common law 116, 226
colonists, walking practices 5
common law: in Antarctica 162–3, 164, 171–2, 198, 201–6; 'carried' by subjects 4–5, 76, 110, 134, 145; dominant position 85–6, 87–8, 93–4, 200–1; flaws/lacunae 29, 73, 80, 85–6, 103, 205, 226; introduction into Australia 40; isolation 73; as itinerant justice 72–4, 77–8, 79; (limits on) jurisdiction 132,

134–5, 137–8, 141–2, 157; material practices of 21–2, 27–8, 109, 133–4, 146–8; mechanics 2–3; method of description 62–3; movements of 27, 28–9, 75–8, 88–9, 94–5, 130–1, 132, 146–9, 156–7, 164–5, 197–8, 204–5, 210–11, 226; origins 88; place-making activities 3, 4; place of 65, 73, 80, 85–6, 87, 88–9, 93–4, 102–3, 139–40; places beyond reach of 135–7, 147–9; relations with the dead 101–3, 109, 149–52, 156–9, 164–5, 204–5; relationship with movement 3, 4–5, 12–13, 27, 36, 65, 78–9, 84–5, 102–3; relationship with other forms of law 34, 87–8, 200–1; responsibility for current situation 2; retrospectivity 131–2; superficiality 146–7; techniques of 227; traditions of 1–2, 4, 46–7, 48, 73; *see also* jurisdiction; jurist(s); *stare decisis* principle
Condren, Conal 50–1, 220
conduct 165
Connolly J 86–7
Cook, James, Captain 86n63, 111–15, 135, 167–8; mandate 111–12
Cooper, Ben, 'The Ceremonial South Pole' 183, *183*
Cormack, Bradin 26
coroner, office of 29–30, 53, 164, 206–9, 216; assumption/conflicts of jurisdiction 209–14, 234–5; etymology 207–8; history 207–9; mandate 208; medieval duties 208–9; responsibilities to the dead 208–9, 214–15, 219–20, 235–6
Coroners Act 1988 (NZ) 188, 209–10, 212–13, 212n189
Coroners Act 2006 (NZ) 209–10
Cosson, Brigadier 224
Cotterell, Roger 55
critic, office of 58–9, 91
critical dilemma *see* jurist(s)
critical legal geography 23–4, 88–9, 94–5
critique: distinguished from jurisprudence 59–60; legal 26, 58–9; limits of 26
Cunningham, Phillip 145

David, T.W. Edgeworth 168
Davis, John 168
Dawes, William 41–3
Dayan, Moshe 13, 16
the dead 44–8; accoutrements 97; call of 155–6, 157, 214–15; care of 46, 47–8, 53, 66, 102, 204–6, 215–17, 219–20, 226–7, 234–6; ceremony, role of 235; and common law tradition 46–7, 48; desacralisation 97; failure in care of 152; jurisdiction of 156–7, 215–16; as legal persons 96–7; military 224, 227–36; movements in relation to *see* movement(s), jurisdictional; mythopoetic relationship with 47–8; as property 97–8; relations with the living 156–7; relationship of common law with 28, 45–8, 95–7, 98–9, 101–3; repatriation 30, 224, 227–36 (*see also* Marks, Rodney); responsibilities to 53, 102, 149–57, 208–9, 214–15, 234–6
Delaney, David 24, 26, 91
Deleuze, Gilles 150, 158
Delgamuukw v British Columbia (Canada, 1997) 37–8n14
delving, meanings/etymology of 99
Derrida, Jacques 8n27, 54
desacralisation 97
Descartes, René 99
description, minutely detailed nature 62–3
diaries, keeping of 170
Dick, Philip K. 177–8
discovery, doctrine of 40–1, 43, 44, 110–11, 112
Doodeward v Spence (1908) 97–8
Dore, Richard, Judge-Advocate 116–17, 117n26, 129
Dorsett, Shaunnagh 26, 55, 81–2
duanamis 68–9, 68–9n8, 70

earth: humanisation 95, 100–1, 204; juridification 101–2
Elder, Catriona 86n66
Empire, movements of 78, 108; *see also* British Empire
energeia 68–9, 68–9n8, 70
entelechia 68–9
Erebus, Mt 168n26
Evans, Teddy, Lt 178

Family Law Act 1975 (Cth) 39–40
Farrell, Peter, Cpl 121–2, 138–9
feminist theory 55n82, 166–7n14
flag, planting of 111
flight lines 29–30
Ford, Lisa 117n25, 143n143
forms of law: in Antarctica 163–4; multiple 37–8, 87–8

Freebody, Simon 116–18, 123, 125, 127, 128, 130, 142, 152
friend, office of 53–4, 206, 219–20
Fuchs, Sir Vivian 179–80
Fuller, William 125, 136, 142
Fulton, Hamish 10n30

Gaita, Raimond 55
Gallipoli, battle of 227–8, 228n9
geography, law and 89–90; *see also* critical legal geography
Gladwell, Shaun, *Apologies* 1–6 *107*
Goodall, William 120–1, 120n47, 130
Goodrich, Peter 26, 55, 60n93, 65, 77, 77n40
grave-robbing 97
Green Line 13–17, *14, 16*
Gross, Charles 207
Guattari, Félix 150, 158

Hades (mythical location) 155–6
Haldar, Piyel 26
Harrison, Robert Pogue 100–1, 102, 152
Harvey, David 23, 23n57, 92n85
Hawkesbury, NSW 115–16, 119; placement of farms 137–8
Heaney, Seamus 51n63, 76n37
Heidegger, Martin 70n16, 83n56
Herodotus 167
High Court of Australia 39; circuits 77; decisions 43–4, 83–4, 97–8
Hillary, Sir Edmund 179
Hobart, Lord 118, 118n31
Hobby, Thomas, Lt 120–1, 124–5, 135, 138, 139, 140–1, 141n136, 143, 144–5, 153–4, 157
Hodgkinson, Thomas 122–6, 135, 136, 143–4, 144n143, 150–1, 152–4, 225
Hui Te Rangiora 167
Hunnisett, R.F. 207–8
Hunt, Alan 57–8n89
Hunter, John, Governor 117, 117n29
Huntington, Richard 152

ice, movements of 177
inheritance 46–7
Iraq, Australian deaths in 227–8
Ireland, English relations with 144–5
Israel, borders of 13–17
itinerant justice, common law as 72–4

Jervis Bay Territory, AAT 're-mapped' onto 199, 201
jurisdiction 211–12; on aeroplanes 211–12; in Antarctica 162, 172, 176, 194–5, 198–203; of the dead 156–7; defined 25, 79–80; etymology 25; as first question of law 24–5, 79–80, 82; as idiom 25; linked to movement 26–7, 81–2, 95, 233–4; overruled by sovereignty 85–6; 're-mapping' 199–200, 202–3; relocation of individuals 202–3; studies 25–6; subjects of 129–30; technologies of 24, 28, 65, 81–5, 95, 175, 214–15, 233–4; *see also* jurisdictional care; jurisdictional thinking; jurisprudence; movement(s), jurisdictional
jurisdictional care 212–15
jurisdictional thinking 80
jurisprudence 6, 22, 30; distinguished from critique 59–60; of jurisdiction 26–7; major 60–1; minor 27, 28, 36, 58–61, 63–4, 91–2, 162–3
jurist(s): common *vs.* civil law 52–3; critical dilemma 58–9; descriptive method 62–3; distingushed from critic 58–9, 91; distinguished from subject 54–5; jurisprudential action 36; office of 27–8, 48–57, 59, 226; range of roles 35, 52–3; responsibilities 34–5, 36, 48, 49, 66, 79, 102, 103, 109, 226; as scholar 52

Kafka, Franz 18n42
Kendall, Henry 113–14
Kennedy, David 89n72
Kenyon International 229–30
Kercher, Bruce 116–17n25
kinesis 68–9; walking as example of 69–70
King, Philip, Governor 118, 118n31
King, travels of 77
King's two bodies, doctrine of 46
Klee, Paul 13n34
Kohlhoff and Kohlhoff 18n44
Kovco, Jacob, Pte 227–33, 235–6; conflict of jurisdiction 234; funeral/memorial services 232, 235; mistaken identification 224, 230–1; transport of body to Australia 227–30, 232
Kovco, Judy 236
Kuwait 229–33; legal requirements concerning the dead 229–30

land art 10n30
lawful place, maintenance of 75, 225–6
lawful relations 35–6, 37–48; creation/
   conduct of 28, 55–6, 84, 87–8, 113,
   164, 206, 224–5; with the dead 29,
   150, 156–7, 208–9, 219–20; defined 35;
   problems of 2–3, 28, 33, 48, 73
lawfulness 47–8
law(s): failure to meet well 37, 43–4;
   responsibility towards 35; as social fact
   23–4; *see also* common law; forms of law;
   legal meetings
Lefebvre, Henri 22–3, 80, 92–3, 94–5
legal meetings 20, 39–44
Legge, George 42n33
Leibing, Peter 18
lines 8–17; grounds for caution regarding
   27; *see also* flight lines
Little America Station (Antarctica)
   179
Long, Richard 8–12, 10n30, 20, 70; *Dusty
   Boots Line* 10–12, *11*; *A Line Made By
   Walking* 8–10, *9*, 12; *Sea Level Waterline*
   10–12, *12*; *Walking a Line in Peru* 10–12,
   11

Mabo v Queensland (1992) 43, 44, 112*n10*
MacFarlane, Brian 8
Maitland, Frederic 73, 207
Malouf, David 51n63
Maori, sea voyages 167
Marks, Rodney 162, 164, 165, 168n25,
   180, 187–99, 203–20, 225, 234;
   biographical background 190–1;
   burial in Antarctica 193, 196, 197–8,
   204–5, 217, 218–19; cause of death 190,
   190–1n107, 192, 194–5; circumstances
   of death 189–90, 197; coffin 218;
   commemoration 195–6; coronorial
   investigation *see* Christchurch Coroner's
   Court; disinterment and relocation
   193–4, 196, 215, 225; health in last
   weeks 192; incompleteness of records
   187, 188–9, 193, 194; jurisdiction over
   death 198–9, 203–4, 206–7, 209–12;
   place of death 192–3, 197, 198–9,
   203–4; reburial in Australia 196, 198,
   204, 225; storage of body (pre-burial)
   193, 217–18
Marle, Karin van 57–8n89, 57–8n91
marriage, law of 39–40
Massey, Doreen 93

Massumi, Brian 8, 8n23, 72n22
Mawson, Douglas 168, 170
McKellar, Neil, Lt 141n136
McVeigh, Shaun 25–6, 55, 81–2
meeting(s) 20–1; place of 20–1; *see also* legal
   meetings
Memmi, Albert 20
Metcalf, Peter 153
Metcalfe, James 116–18, 125, 126, 127,
   130, 136, 142, 143
Minkkinen, Panu 60n93
Minow, Martha 26
Montaigne, Michel de 46n47, 54
Moore, Marianne, 'A Grave' 196–7
motion *see* movement
movement(s): Aristotelian definitions
   67–71; importance of 6, 22, 65–6, 67,
   84, 95–6, 109; jurisdictional 78, 79–85;
   moving well 79, 233–6; practices of
   74–8; range of forms 65, 66–7, 78–9;
   unsettling nature 67; *see also* common
   law; walking
Murray River 39n17
Mussawir, Edward 26
mythopoesis 47–8, 135, 137

native title, recognition of 43, 44
Nelson, Brendan 235–6
New South Wales 28–9, 40–3, 78, 108,
   225; conflicts of jurisdiction 234–5;
   diversity of laws 137–8; establishment
   of colony 40, 110–11, 115; imposition
   of common law 40, 116; Irish separatist
   movement 145–6; meeting of laws
   40–1; movements within 109, 110–11,
   115, 116, 159; sites of punishment
   138–40; Supreme Court case law 41–2;
   territorial expansion 115–16, 115n19; *see
   also* New South Wales Court of Criminal
   Judicature
New South Wales Act 1823 (UK)
   118–19n33
New South Wales Court of Criminal
   Judicature: case law 116–32; jurisdiction
   129–31; location 129; rules of evidence
   118–19
New South Wales v Commonwealth (1975)
   85n61, 86n63
New Zealand: Antarctic territory 172–4,
   176, 177, 210–11; common law in
   210–11; domestic legislation 167n22; *see
   also* Christchurch Coroner's Court

NSF (National Science Federation) 196, 216–17

Oates, Lawrence, Captain 178
office 48–52, 226; of critic 58–9; defined 50; diversity of duties 54; institutional framework 51–2; nature of responsibilities 55; of poet 51–2; political 51; significance to legal process 56–7, 59; *see also* coroner; friend; jurist

Palmer, Nathaniel 167–8
paradiastole 36, 61, 63
Patyegerang 41–3
Pearson, John 127, 143
Peripatetics 7, 7nn16–17
Pernic, Dave 195–6, 217, 218–19
Phelps, Joseph 139
Philippopoulos-Mihalopoulos, Andreas 24, 35, 36
Phillip, Arthur, Governor 115
place, relationship with movement 4, 78, 225–7; *see also* common law, place of; lawful place; movement(s), place of
pluralism, legal 21, 38
poet laureate, office of 51–2, 51n63
postcolonialism 1–3, 21
Powell, Edward, Constable 116–18, 124, 126, 127–8, 130, 143, 153n173; *see also R v Powell*
precedent, doctrine of 34n4
Prescott, Victor 174–5
propertty, transfer of 46–7
prudentia 2, 226
Pythagoras 167, 167n17

R v Ballard (1829) 41–2
R v Bonjon (1841) 41–2
R v Buzzacott (2004) 85
R v Minor (1992) 37–8n14
R v Murrell (1836) 41–2, 42n33
R v Powell (1799) 62, 116–17n25, 116–32; giving of evidence 118–19, 124–6, 127–8, 130, 135–8; jurisdiction over 123–4, 129–31; pardoning of accused 118, 128n98; reserving of judgment 117, 117n28, 128; verdict 117–18, 128
ramp ceremonies 229, 230, 232, 235
Ramsay, Isabella 122–3, 126, 143
Raytheon 193, 194, 216–17
redescription, practices of 36, 61–4, 197–8; benefits 63–4; materials 61–2

repatriation, of the dead 30, 224, 227–36
repetition 123, 148–9
retrospectivity 131–2, 131n102
Rickerby, Thomas, Chief Constable 127, 153
Romanticism 7n19
Ross, David 68
Ross Dependency 172–4, 176, 193, 210–11
Rousseau, Jean-Jacques 7, 7n18
Rush, Peter 25, 82
Ryan, Michael 26

Sale, Victoria 231, 232
Samaras, Connie: *Buried Fifties Station, V.A.L.I.S. 161*; *Dome and Tunnels, V.A.L.I.S. 160*, 177–8
Sanburn, Thomas 127–8, 153
Sarat, Austin 26
Schlusche, Gunter 18n44
Schneider, Darryn 196
Schopenhauer, Arthur 45, 45–6n49
Schumann, Konrad 18
Scott, Robert F., Captain 168–9, 170, 178, 179–80
Shackleton, Ernest 168, 170
Sidley, Mt 168n26
Sinanovic, Juso 224, 230–3, 234; faulire of care for 235–6
slowness: method of 57–8, 61, 63–4, 79, 91–2
Smithson, Robert 10n30
Sophocles, *Antigone* 149, 154–7, 154n178, 214–15, 217, 219–20
South Pole(s) 163, *182, 183, 184*; ceremonies 184–5, *185*; expeditions to 168–9, 178–9; multiplicity of 182–3, 182n80, 185; shifts 184–5, 187; sign marking *169*, 169n29, *184*; solar/atmospheric conditions 188n94
sovereignty 1–2, 37, 80; in Antarctic territories 175–6; distinguished from jurisdiction 25; dominance of legal systems 85–7; proclamations of 111; relationship with common law 85–6; sources of 46; stages in acquisition of 111, 114–15; *see also* Aboriginal sovereignty
space 22–3; abstract 22–3, 92–4; defined 92–3; production of 75, 93–4; relationship with law 23–4, 88–95; social 93, 94; *see also* abstract space;

social space; spatial turn; time and space
spatial turn 22–3, 92–3
Stanner, William Edward 87n68
stare decisis principle 34, 34n4, 62
Stone, Julius 55
Sutherland, Forby 113–14

technology: etymology 82–3; *see also* jurisdiction, technologies of
terra nullius, doctrine of 41
terrain 20–1
territory 80; distinguished from jurisdiction 25
Teufelsberg, Berlin 19–20
Thompson, Bishop 127
Thrift, Nigel 92–3
time and space 94–5
Timms, William 116–18, 125, 126, 127, 128, 130, 152
Tollund Man 76n37
Torres Strait Islands 114
tourism, in Antarctica 170–2; statistics 171n41
Triggs, Gillian 174–5

uninhabited land: application of settlers' laws in 4–5, 76, 110, 134n103; Australia treated as 112–13, 114–15; claims to sovereignty over 111

United States, mapping of Antarctica 174
United States Antarctic Programme 189, 193, 194, 214

Valverde, Mariana 26
Vattel, Emmerich de 115
Vico, Giambattista 4, 95, 99–101, 102, 137, 152, 165
Victoria, coroner's court 234–5
Virilio, Paul 57

walking: Aristotelian commentary 69–70; juridical 146–9; as legal practice 4–5, 76–7, 109, 133–4, 146; modes of 6–7, 109; practices 3–4; 'well' 109; *see also* 'beating the bounds'
Waterhouse, Henry, Captain 117
Weizmann, Eyal 15–16, 17
White, David 126, 127
White, Major 122–4, 126, 136, 144
Wilson, Edward 178
Wimbo, John 122–6, 135, 136, 143–4, 144n144, 150–1, 152–4, 225
woods: otherness/mythic nature 135–7; requirements for venturing into 135–7, 141–2
Wordsworth, William 7

Yellowgowy (Aborigine) 122, 136